BROOKLANDS BOOKS

VOLVO 1800
Gold Portfolio
1960-1973

Compiled by
R.M. Clarke

ISBN 1 85520 1305

Booklands Books Ltd.
PO Box 146, Cobham, KT11 1LG
Surrey, England

Printed in Hong Kong

BROOKLANDS BOOKS

BROOKLANDS ROAD TEST SERIES

AC Ace & Aceca 1953-1983
Alfa Romeo Alfasud 1972-1984
Alfa Romeo Alfetta Coupes GT. GTV. GTV6 1974-1987
Alfa Romeo Giulia Berlinas 1962-1976
Alfa Romeo Giulia Coupes Gold Portfolio 1963-1976
Alfa Romeo Giulia Coupes 1963-1976
Alfa Romeo Giulietta Gold Portfolio 1954-1965
Alfa Romeo Spider Gold Portfolio 1966-1991
Alfa Romeo Spider 1966-1990
Allard Gold Portfolio 1937-1959
Alvis Gold Portfolio 1919-1967
American Motors Muscle Cars 1966-1970
Armstrong Siddeley Gold Portfolio 1945-1960
Aston Martin Gold Portfolio 1972-1985
Austin Seven 1922-1982
Austin A30 & A35 1951-1962
Austin Healey 100 & 100/6 Gold Portfolio 1952-1959
Austin Healey 3000 Gold Portfolio 1959-1967
Austin Healey Sprite 1958-1971
Avanti 1962-1990
BMW Six Cylinder Coupes 1969-1975
BMW 1600 Col. 1 1966-1981
BMW 2002 1968-1976
Buick Automobiles 1947-1960
Buick Muscle Cars 1965-1970
Buick Riviera 1963-1978
Cadillac Automobiles 1949-1959
Cadillac Automobiles 1960-1969
Cadillac Eldorado 1967-1978
High Performance Capris Gold Portfolio 1969-1987
Chevrolet Camaro SS & Z28 1966-1973
Chevrolet Camaro & Z-28 1973-1981
High Performance Camaros 1982-1988
Camaro Muscle Cars 1966-1972
Chevrolet 1955-1957
Chevrolet Corvair 1959-1969
Chevrolet Impala & SS 1958-1971
Chevrolet Muscle Cars 1966-1971
Chevelle and SS 1964-1972
Chevy Blazer 1969-1981
Chevy EL Camino & SS 1959-1987
Chevy II Nova & SS 1962-1973
Chrysler 300 Gold Portfolio 1955-1970
Citroen Traction Avant Gold Portfolio 1934-1957
Citroen DS & ID 1955-1975
Citroen SM 1970-1975
Citroen 2CV 1949-1988
Shelby Cobra Gold Portfolio 1962-1969
Cobras and Cobra Replicas Gold Portfolio 1962-1989
Cobras & Replicas 1962-1983
Chevrolet Corvette Gold Portfolio 1953 1962
Corvette Stingray Gold Portfolio 1963-1967
Chevrolet Corvettee Gold Portfolio 1968-1977
High Performance Corvettes 1983-1989
Daimler SP250 Sport & V-8250 Saloon Gold Portfolio 1959-1969
Datsun 240Z 1970-1973
Datsun 280Z & ZX 1975-1983
De Tomaso Collection No.1 1962-1981
Dodge Charger 1966-1974
Dodge Muscle Cars 1967-1970
Excalibur Collection No.1 1952-1981
Facel Vega 1954-1964
Ferrari Cars 1946-1956
Ferrari Dino 1965-1974
Ferrari Dino 308 1974-1979
Ferrari 308 & Mondial 1980-1984
Ferrari Collection No.1 1960-1970
Fiat-Bertone X1/9 1973-1988
Fiat Pininfarina 124 + 2000 Spider 1968-1985
Ford Automobiles 1949-1959
Ford Bronco 1966-1977
Ford Bronco 1978-1988
Ford Consul. Zephyr Zodiac MkI & II 1950-1962
Ford Cortina 1600E & GT 1967-1970
Ford Fairlane 1955-1970
Ford Falcon 1960-1970
Ford GT40 Gold Portfolio 1964-1987
Ford RS Escorts 1968-1980
Ford Zephyr Zodiac Executive MkIII & MkIV 1962-1971
High Performance Capris Gold Portfolio 1969-1987
High Performance Escorts Mk1 1968-1974
High Performance Escorts Mk II 1975-1980
High Performance Escorts 1980-1985
High Performance Escorts 1985-1990
High Performance Fiestas 1979-1991
High Performance Mustangs 1982-1988
Holden 1948-1962
Honda CRX 1983-1987
Hudson & Railton 1936-1940
Jaguar and SS Gold Portfolio 1931-1951
Jaguar XK120 XK140 XK150 Gold Portfolio 1948-1960
Jaguar MkVII VIII IX X 420 Gold Portfolio 1950-1970
Jaguar Cars 1961-1964
Jaguar Mk2 1959-1969
Jaguar E-Type Gold Portfolio 1961-1971
Jaguar E-Type 1966-1971
Jaguar E-Type V-12 1971-1975
Jaguar XJ12 XJ5.3 V12 Glold Portfolio 1972-1990
Jaguar XJ6 Series II 1973-1979
Jaguar XJ6 Series III 1979-1986
Jaguar XJS Gold Portfolio 1975-1990
Jeep CJ5 & CJ6 1960-1976
Jeep CJ5 & CJ7 1976-1986
Jensen Cars 1946-1967
Jensen Cars 1967-1979
Jensen Interceptor Gold Portfolio 1966-1986
Jensen Healey 1972-1976
Lamborghini Cars 1964-1970
Lamborghini Countach Col No.1 1971-1982
Lamborghini Countach & Urraco 1974-1980
Lamborghini Countach & Jalpa 1980-1985
Lancia Stratos 1972-1985
Land Rover Series I 1948-1958
Land Rover Series II & IIa 1958-1971
Land Rover Series III 1971-1985
Land Rover 90 & 110 1983-1989
Lincoln Gold Portfolio 1949-1960
Lincoln Continental 1961-1969
Lincoln Continental 1969-1976
Lotus and Caterham Seven Gold Portfolio 1957-1989
Lotus Cortina Gold Portfolio 1963-1970
Lotus Elan Gold Portfolio 1962-1974
Lotus Elan Collection No.2 1963-1972
Lotus Elite 1957-1964
Lotus Elite & Eclat 1974-1982
Lotus Turbo Esprit 1980-1986
Lotus Europa Gold Portfolio 1966-1975
Marcos Cars 1960-1988
Maserati 1965-1970
Maserati 1970-1975
Mazda RX-7 Collection No.1 1978-1981
Mercedes 190 & 300SL 1954-1963
Mercedes 230/250/280SL 1963-1971
Mercedes Benz SLs & SLCs Gold Portfolio 1971-1989
Mercedes Benz Cars 1949-1954
Mercedes Benz Cars 1954-1957
Mercedes Benz Cars 1957-1961
Mercedes Benz Competion Cars 1950-1957
Mercury Muscle Cars 1966-1971
Metropolitan 1954-1962
MG TC 1945-1949
MG TD 1949-1953
MG TF 1953-1955
MG Cars 1959-1962
MGA & Twin Cam Gold Portfolio 1955-1962
MGB MGC & V8 Gold Portfolio 1962-1980
MGB Roadsters 1962-1980
MGB GT 1965-1980
MG Midget 1961-1980
Mini Cooper Gold Portfolio 1961-1971
Mini Moke 1964-1989
Mini Muscle Cars 1961-1979
Mopar Muscle Cars 1964-1967
Morgan Three-Wheeler Gold Portfolio 1910-1952
Morgan Cars 1960-1970
Morgan Cars Gold Portfolio 1968-1989
Morris Minor Collection No.1
Mustang Muscle Cars 1967-1971
Oldsmobile Automobiles 1955-1963
Old's Cutlass & 4-4-2 1964-1972
Oldsmobile Muscle Cars 1964-1971
Oldsmobile Toronado 1966-1978
Opel GT 1968-1973
Packard Gold Portfolio 1946-1958
Pantera Gold Portfolio 1970-1989
Panther Gold Portfolio 1972-1990
Plymouth Barracuda 1964-1974
Plymouth Muscle Cars 1966-1971
Pontiac Tempest & GTO 1961-1965
Pontiac Firebird and Trans-Am 1973-1981
High Performance Firebirds 1982-1988
Pontiac Fiero 1984-1988
Pontiac Muscle Cars 1966-1972
Porsche 356 1952-1965
Porsche Cars in the 60's
Porsche Cars 1960-1964
Porsche Cars 1964-1968
Porsche Cars 1968-1972
Porsche Cars 1972-1975
Porsche Turbo Collection No.1 1975-1980
Porsche 911 1965-1969
Porsche 911 1970-1972
Porsche 911 1973-1977
Porsche 911 Carrera 1973-1977
Porsche 911 Turbo 1975-1984
Porsche 911 SC 1978-1983
Porsche 914 Gold Portfolio 1969-1976
Porsche 914 Collection No.1 1969-1983
Porsche 924 Gold Portfolio 1975-1988
Porsche 928 1977-1989
Porsche 944 1981-1985
Range Rover Gold Portfolio 1970-1988
Reliant Scimitar 1964-1986
Riley 11/2 & 21/2 Litre Gold Portfolio 1945-1955
Rolls Royce Silver Cloud 1955-1965
Rolls Royce Silver Shadow 1965-1981
Rover P4 1949-1959
Rover P4 1955-1964
Rover 3 & 3.5 Litre Gold Portfolio 1958-1973
Rover 2000 + 2200 1963-1977
Rover 3500 1968-1977
Rover 3500 & Vitesse 1976-1986
Saab Sonett Collection No.1 1966-1974
Saab Turbo 1976-1983
Shelby Mustang Muscle Cars 1965-1970
Stubebaker Gold Portfolio 1947-1966
Stubebaker Hawks & Larks 1956-1963
Sunbeam Tiger & Alpine Gold Portfolio 1959-1967
Thunderbird 1955-1957
Thunderbird 1958-1963
Thunderbird 1964-1976
Toyota Land Cruiser 1956-1984
Toyota MR2 1984-1988
Triumph 2000. 2.5. 2500 1963-1977
Triumph GT6 1966-1974
Triumph Spitfire Gold Portfolio 1962-1980
Triumph Stag 1970-1980
Triumph Stag Collection No.1 1970-1984
Triumph TR2 & TR3 1952-60
Triumph TR4-TR5-TR250 1961-1968
Triumph TR6 Gold Portfolio 1969-1976
Triumph TR7 & TR8 1975-1982
Triumph Herald 1959-1971
Triumph Vitesse 1962-1971
TVR Gold Portfolio 1959-1990
Valiant 1960-1962
VW Beetle Collection No.1 1970-1982
VW Golf GTi 1976-1986
VW Karmann Ghia 1955-1982
VW Kubelwagen 1940-1975
VW Scirocco 1974-1981
VW Bus. Camper. Van 1954-1967
VW Bus. Camper. Van 1968-1979
VW Bus. Camper. Van 1979-1989
Volvo 120 1956-1970
Volvo 1800 Gold Portfolio 1960-1973

BROOKLANDS ROAD & TRACK SERIES

Road & Track on Alfa Romeo 1949-1963
Road & Track on Alfa Romeo 1964-1970
Road & Track on Alfa Romeo 1971-1976
Road & Track on Alfa Romeo 1977-1989
Road & Track on Aston Martin 1962-1990
Road & Track on Auburn Cord and Duesenburg 1952-1984
Road & Track on Audi & Auto Union 1952-1980
Road & Track on Audi 1980-1986
Road & Track on Austin Healey 1953-1970
Road & Track on BMW Cars 1966-1974
Road & Track on BMW Cars 1975-1978
Road & Track on BMW Cars 1979-1983
Road & Track on Cobra, Shelby & GT40 1962-1983
Road & Track on Corvette 1953-1967
Road & Track on Corvette 1968-1982
Road & Track on Corvette 1982-1986
Road & Track on Corvette 1986-1990
Road & Track on Datsun Z 1970-1983
Road & Track on Ferrari 1950-1968
Road & Track on Ferrari 1968-1974
Road & Track on Ferrari 1975-1981
Road & Track on Ferrari 1981-1984
Road & Track on Ferrari 1984-1988
Road & Track on Fiat Sports Cars 1968-1987
Road & Track on Jaguar 1950-1960
Road & Track on Jaguar 1961-1968
Road & Track on Jaguar 1968-1974
Road & Track on Jaguar 1974-1982
Road & Track on Jaguar 1983-1989
Road & Track on Lamborghini 1964-1985
Road & Track on Lotus 1972-1981
Road & Track on Maserati 1952-1974
Road & Track on Maserati 1975-1983
Road & Track on Mazda RX7 1978-1986
Road & Track on Mazda RX7 & MX5 Miata 1986-1991
Road & Track on Mercedes 1952-1962
Road & Track on Mercedes 1963-1970
Road & Track on Mercedes 1971-1979
Road & Track on Mercedes 1980-1987
Road & Track on MG Sports Cars 1949-1961
Road & Track on MG Sprots Cars 1962-1980
Road & Track on Mustang 1964-1977
Road & Track on Nissan 300-ZX & Turbo 1984-1989
Road & Track on Peugeot 1955-1986
Road & Track on Pontiac 1960-1983
Road & Track on Porsche 1961-1967
Road & Track on Porsche 1968-1971
Road & Track on Porsche 1972-1975
Road & Track on Porsche 1975-1978
Road & Track on Porsche 1979-1982
Road & Track on Porsche 1982-1985
Road & Track on Porsche 1985-1988
Road & Track on Rolls Royce & B'ley 1950-1965
Road & Track on Rolls Royce & B'ley 1966-1984
Road & Track on Saab 1955-1985
Road & Track on Toyota Sports & GT Cars 1966-1984
Road & Track on Triumph Sports Cars 1953-1967
Road & Track on Triumph Sports Cars 1967-1974
Road & Track on Triumph Sports Cars 1974-1982
Road & Track on Volkswagen 1951-1968
Road & Track on Volkswagen 1968-1978
Road & Track on Volkswagen 1978-1985
Road & Track on Volvo 1957-1974
Road & Track on Volvo 1975-1985
Road & Track - Henry Manney at Large and Abroad

BROOKLANDS CAR AND DRIVER SERIES

Car and Driver on BMW 1955-1977
Car and Driver on BMW 1977-1985
Car and Driver on Cobra, Shelby & Ford GT 40 1963-1984
Car and Driver on Corvette 1956-1967
Car and Driver on Corvette 1968-1977
Car and Driver on Corvette 1978-1982
Car and Driver on Corvette 1983-1988
Car and Driver on Datsun Z 1600 & 2000 1966-1984
Car and Driver on Ferrari 1955-1962
Car and Driver on Ferrari 1963-1975
Car and Driver on Ferrari 1976-1983
Car and Driver on Mopar 1956-1967
Car and Driver on Mopar 1968-1975
Car and Driver on Mustang 1964-1972
Car and Driver on Pontiac 1961-1975
Car and Driver on Porsche 1955-1962
Car and Driver on Porsche 1963-1970
Car and Driver on Porsche 1970-1976
Car and Driver on Porsche 1977-1981
Car and Driver on Porsche 1982-1986
Car and Driver on Saab 1956-1985
Car and Driver on Volvo 1955-1986

BROOKLANDS PRACTICAL CLASSICS SERIES

PC on Austin A40 Restoration
PC on Land Rover Restoration
PC on Metalworking in Restoration
PC on Midget/Sprite Restoration
PC on Mini Cooper Restoration
PC on MGB Restoration
PC on Morris Minor Restoration
PC on Sunbeam Rapier Restoration
PC on Triumph Herald/Vitesse
PC on Triumph Spitfire Restoration
PC on VW Beetle Restoration
PC on 1930s Car Restoration

BROOKLANDS HOT ROD 'MUSCLECAR & HI-PO ENGINE SERIES

Chevy 265 & 283
Chevy 302 & 327
Chevy 348 & 409
Chevy 350 & 400
Chevy 396 & 427
Chevy 454 thru 512
Chrysler Hemi
Chrysler 273, 318, 340 & 360
Chrysler 361, 383, 400, 413, 426, 440
Ford 289, 302, Boss 302 & 351W
Ford 351C & Boss 351
Ford Big Block

BROOKLANDS MILITARY VEHICLES SERIES

Allied Mil. Vehicles No.1 1942-1945
Allied Mil. Vehicles No.2 1941-1946
Dodge Mil. Vehicles Col. 1 1940-1945
Military Jeeps 1941-1945
Off Road Jeeps 1944-1971
Hail to the Jeep
US Military Vehicles 1941-1945
US Army Military Vehicles WW2-TM9-2800

BROOKLANDS HOT ROD RESTORATION SERIES

Auto Restoration Tips & Techniques
Basic Bodywork Tips & Techniques
Basic Painting Tips & Techniques
Camaro Restoration Tips & Techniques
Chevrolet High Performance Tips & Techniques
Chevy-GMC Pickup Repair
Custom Painting Tips & Techniques
Engine Swapping Tips & Techniques
Ford Pickup Repair
How to Build a Street Rod
Mustang Restoration Tips & Techniques
Performance Tuning - Chevrolets of the '60s
Performance Tuning - Ford of the '60s
Performance Tuning - Mopars of the '60s
Performance Tuning - Pontiacs of the '60s

CONTENTS

BROOKLANDS BOOKS

ACKNOWLEDGEMENTS

It is ten years now since we published our first Brooklands Book on the Volvo 1800 range. The fact that we were obliged to reprint this when stocks ran out in the mid-1980s, is ample demonstration of the popularity of these fine cars and led us to think of a much-expanded volume third time around.

So here it is . . In this Gold Portfolio you will find not only most of the important stories contained in our original Volvo 1800 book, but also 109 additional pages of road tests and other material which appeared in the automotive press during the 1800's production life.

We offer our sincere thanks to the publishers of Australian Motor Sports, Autocar, Autosport, Canada Track and Traffic, Car and Driver, Car South Africa, Car and Car Conversions, Cars Illustrated, Classic and Sportscar, Hot Rod, Modern Motor, Motor, Motor Life, Motor Manual, Motor Sport, Motor Trend, Popular Imported Cars, Practical Classics, Road & Track, Road Test, Sporting Motorist, Sports Car Graphic, Sports Car World, Wheels, World Car Guide and Your Car for allowing us to include their copyright stories. Our thanks go also to motoring writer James Taylor who kindly penned the following introduction.

R.M. Clarke

Attractive styling is not one of the features generally associated with Volvo cars, but the 1800 range undoubtedly had it. Allied to the traditional Volvo strengths of durability and strength, it resulted in a car which stood out among the Swedish manufacturer's products and which is deservedly seen as a "classic" today.

It was not surprising that the 1800 looked different from other Volvos, for the company sought outside help with its styling. The Italian stylist Frus was the first to be consulted, but in the end the shape chosen for production was not Italian but the work of Swedish yacht designer Pelle Pettersen.

The new car was introduced in 1961, perhaps an unfortunate date as it was initially rather overshadowed in the glamour stakes by another 1961 introduction, the Jaguar E-type. The fact that the Volvo cost about the same as an E-type outside Sweden cannot have helped sales, either. But the 1800 had its own strengths, not the least of which was its rally-proved B18 1.8-litre engine. This ran through until 1968, when the larger but equally rugged B20 2-litre was substituted, initially with carburettors and 105bhp but, from 1969, with Bosch electronic fuel injection and 135bhp.

For the first two years, 1800 bodies were built in Britain by Jensen, but increased manufacturing capacity at Volvo's Gothenberg plant allowed production to be transferred to Sweden in 1963. The model, initially marketed as a P1800, was then renamed the P1800S. Six years later, the introduction of fuel injection turned it into a P1800E. Lastly, in 1971, Volvo's Chief Designer Jan Wilsgard redesigned the bodyshell to make a three-door sporting estate, the 1800ES, which gave welcome increases in both rear headroom and luggage space. Production of the 1800 range ceased in 1973.

Looking through the articles reproduced here, it is sometimes hard to understand why fewer than 50,000 Volvo 1800s were made. They were, undoubtedly, very good cars. Fortunately for enthusiasts, their robust construction has ensured that a large number still survives to be enjoyed today.

James Taylor

![VOLVO P-1800](image showing the Volvo P-1800 coupe in a forest setting)

VOLVO P-1800

New Swedish GT coupe will be produced in England

FEW NEW CAR ANNOUNCEMENTS have aroused as much excitement as Volvo's P-1800 coupe. It appears that they have the formula—smart design and proven components—to crack a segment of the auto market which will give them both prestige and profit.

The P-1800, designed in Italy by Frua, bears a strong resemblance to some of the beautiful custom coupes which were installed on Ferrari chassis during the mid-'50s. Wheelbase, 96½ inches, is shorter than their sedan, and unit construction has been used to insure typically solid Volvo construction. Although the factory claims that the engine is of completely new design, it appears to be a bored-out, slightly hotted-up version of the sturdy sedan powerplant. The four-cylinder in-line displaces 108½ cubic inches (1780cc) and develops 100 bhp at 5500 rpm. An all-synchro four-speed gearbox, optional overdrive, braking system that incorporates 10⅞-inch discs at front and drums at rear, independent front suspension and live rear axle suspended with coils complete the mechanical components. Interiors are lavishly appointed. Individual bucket seats appear to be carefully designed while the dash panel and steering wheel could have come right out of Detroit.

No real word yet on how the car handles but there is every reason to believe that it should handle as well or better than the already good handling PV-544 sedan—making the coupe a first-rate Gran Turismo machine.

Production will start in September but not at the home plant in Sweden. Pressed Steel Ltd. in England will produce the bodies and assemble the cars. According to the factory, existing facilities in Sweden are running to capacity, necessitating the move. By January of next year production is expected to be about 100 cars a week. If price is kept between $3000-4000, we believe there will be a ready market.

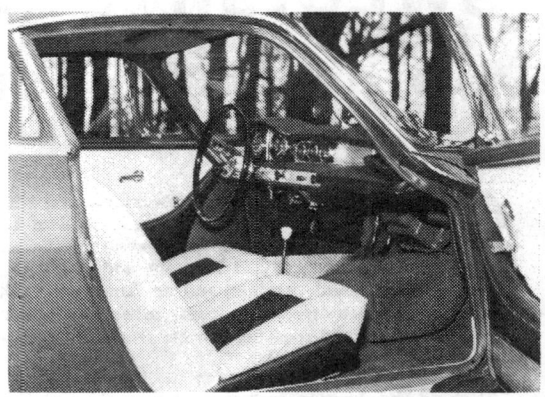

Interiors are set up for sportscar minded even though steering wheel and instruments are on the flamboyant side. The seating appears good.

Cleanly executed fin, lack of extra chrome, and Italian styling make the P-1800 one of the most attractive medium-priced coupes we have seen.

SWEDISH BRED : BRITISH BUILT

VOLVO P.1800 SPORTS COUPÉ IN PRODUCTION IN BRITAIN

CARS are gradually losing their national character, but surely no other essay into internationalism is so complex as that of Volvo in the production of their new P.1800 coupé. With a body styled in Italy and made in England, a Swedish engine and gearbox, and an American back axle; with miscellaneous components from other European countries brought in for good measure, no car could better qualify for the description, international.

Behind the decision to manufacture the Volvo P.1800 outside Sweden was the inescapable fact that the demand for Volvo cars was fast outpacing the rate at which people could be found or trained to build them. In the United Kingdom, on the other hand, there existed the know-how and a small pool of suitable labour to build this type of car; moreover at least 50 per cent of the components were British made, so considerable savings in shipping cost would be made if production were transferred here. Thus the monocoque shell of the P.1800 is being produced by the Pressed Steel Company in Scotland, and several less bulky mechanical units are shipped from Sweden.

Because of their experience in this kind of work, Jensen of West Bromwich have been entrusted with the assembly of the P.1800, and an extension of the Kelvin Way factory contains the production line. Already 400 cars have been built, and production at the rate of 150 a day is planned. Volvo have set up an office in West Bromwich, and there is a staff of Swedish inspectors at the works to make sure that the job is done in accordance with Volvo precepts.

The P.1800 is a new model in its own right, and although some parts of the Volvo saloon are common to it, the intention, which has been successfully realized, has been to produce a true grand tourer—fast, comfortable, with refinement of handling to go with its high performance and comfortable appointments for the driver and passenger.

To propel this new model at speeds in excess of 100 m.p.h., a completely new 1,780 c.c. five-main-bearing engine was evolved, producing 100 b.h.p. (gross). A Girling front disc and rear drum brake layout was adopted to provide stopping power, and for the first time the convenience of a de Normanville overdrive is offered on a Swedish car.

Construction of a Frua-styled body follows the conventional practice. For example, the passenger envelope has as its base a heavily ribbed floor with boxed-in sills. A vestigial chassis, consisting of enclosed top-hat section members, extends forward to carry the engine and radiator. To these members also is

Only the large carburettors and the twin branched inlet manifolds give a clue to the possibilities of the 1,780 c.c. engine. The creditable figure of 100 b.h.p. (gross) at 5,500 r.p.m. is developed

In achieving a long, low line, passenger comfort has in no way been sacrificed. Unitary construction helps to maintain a low floor and great attention has been paid to internal appointments

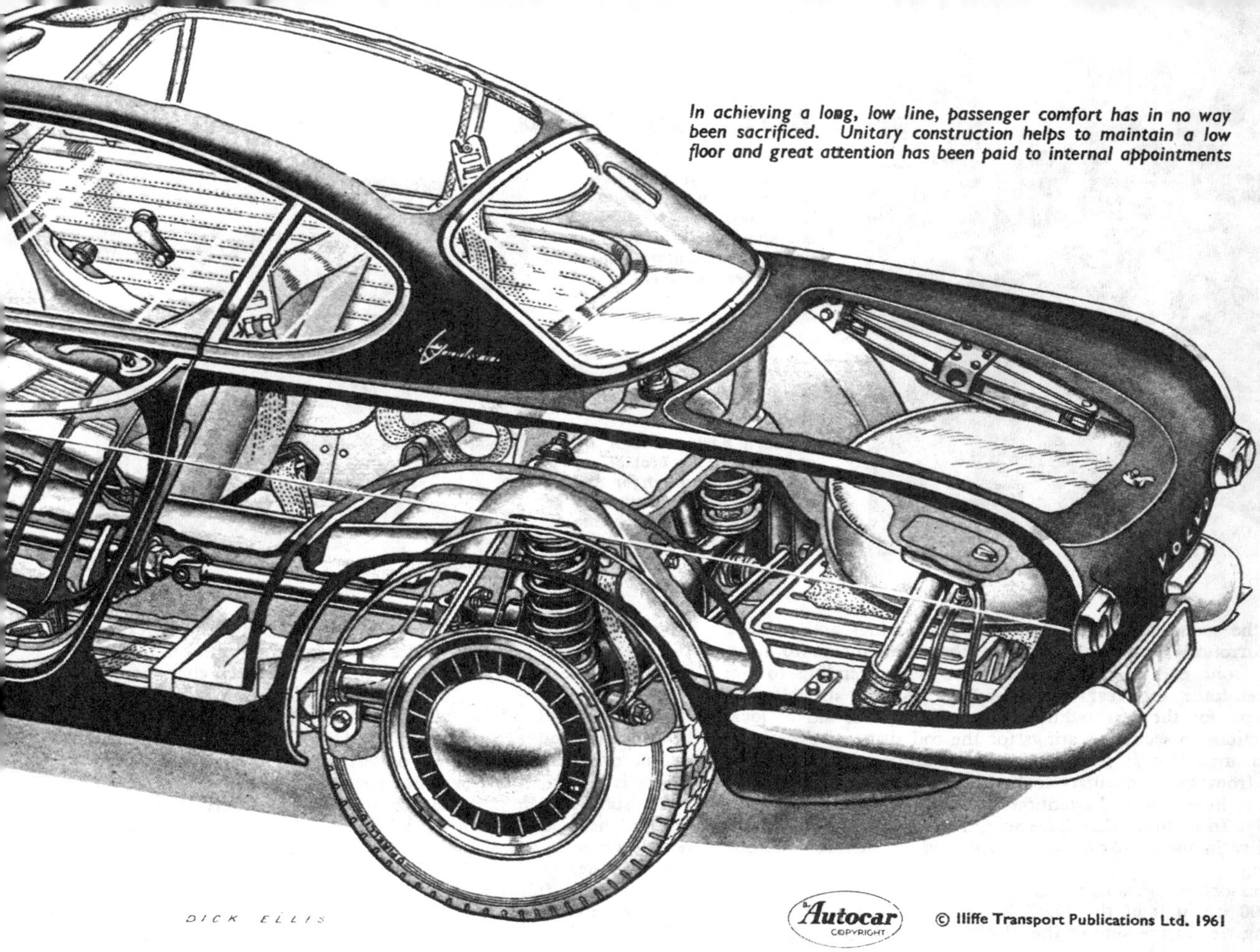

DICK ELLIS

In an attempt to avoid a design which would date quickly, restrained lines were favoured. Frua's solution for a fin termination is neat and elegant ▼

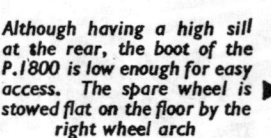

Instrument layout is stylish and practical. In front of the driver are tachometer and speedometer with water and oil temperature gauges between them

Although having a high sill at the rear, the boot of the P.1800 is low enough for easy access. The spare wheel is stowed flat on the floor by the right wheel arch ▶

bolted the suspension assembly. The front wings and radiator grille surround also attach to these chassis members to form a rigid front end. Similar top-hat sections extending to the back, reinforce the rear wheel arches, provide strengthened anchorages for the rear radius arms and, with the aid of local modifications to section, seatings for the coil suspension springs.

Volvo are adept at producing large quantities of power and torque from quite ordinary-looking engines; the secret, they believe, is in exceptional attention to design detail and in careful assembly. In addition they have sought to achieve the maximum of rigidity in the crankcase and block, and to provide generous breathing.

On cursory inspection, the engine appears to differ little from the 1,600 c.c. unit of the 122S, but closer examination reveals stiffening ribs at the side of the block. Internally the crankcase is made more rigid by the transverse webs supporting the additional main bearings. The overall length of the block casting has been increased to accommodate a crankshaft made longer by the inclusion of the two extra main bearings. These bearings are 2·60in. in diameter and 1·52in. wide; the diameter of the big end journals is 2·13in. and the width 1·26in.

The connecting rods are of H section, with the split line at right angles, and the gudgeon pins, of fully floating type, are retained by circlips in the pistons. The solid-skirt pistons have steel, cast-in expansion control struts, two compression rings (the upper one chromium plated) and one oil control ring. Perhaps the only unusual feature in this small mass-produced engine is the geared drive for the camshaft.

Made of cast iron, the cylinder head has modified bath-tub combustion chambers, the edges of the chambers having a pent-roof configuration. The inlet valves are 40mm (1·57in.) in

diameter, and the exhaust, 35mm (1·77in.). The compression ratio is 9·5 to 1. Separate inlet and exhaust ports are a feature of this engine as they are of the smaller one, and the arrangement is the same—the two HS6 S.U. 1¾in. carburettors feeding through forked, cast aluminium manifolds. The three-branch cast-iron exhaust manifold has a double pipe for the middle cylinders and separate outlets for numbers one and four. There is no provision for a hot spot.

On such a high performance small engine there is a possibility of heat build-up in the lubricant; to counter this a simple heat exchanger, consisting of a loop of tube surrounded by coolant water is used. The cleanliness of the lubricating oil is ensured by a full-flow Wix Porosite oil cleaner with quickly replaceable element.

Needle roller bearings are used on the layshaft and first motion shaft pilot bearing of the Volvo-made all synchromesh gearbox, which is otherwise identical with that of the 122S unit. It may be recalled that this has helical gears running in a cast-iron casing. Peculiar to the P.1800 model is the long remote control extension, cast in aluminium, to bring the gear lever well back into the driving compartment. An 8·5in. dry plate clutch with hydraulic operation, is employed.

A divided propeller shaft takes the drive to the Spicer rear axle, which is a conventional, semi-floating hypoid unit with a pressed steel casing and heavily ribbed cast nosepiece.

Volvo suspension has always attracted favourable comment so the makers have seen no reason to depart from their normal layout in the P.1800. Indeed, the coil spring and radius arm rear suspension of the 122S is transplanted almost intact to the new model, only the spring rates and damper settings being altered to suit the changed conditions. Likewise, the unequal

---

SPECIFICATION

ENGINE

No. of cylinders	4 in line
Bore and stroke	84·14 x 80mm (3·31 x 3·15in.)
Displacement	1,780 c.c. (108·6 cu. in.)
Valve position	Overhead in line, pushrods and rockers
Compression ratio	9·5 to 1
Max. b.h.p. (gross)	100 at 5,500 r.p.m.
Max. b.m.e.p.	150 p.s.i. at 4,000 r.p.m.
Max. torque	108 lb. ft. at 4,000 r.p.m.
Carburettors	Two S.U. 1¾in.
Fuel pump	Delco diaphragm
Tank capacity	10 Imp. gallons (45 litres)
Sump capacity	6·5 pints (3·75 litres)
Oil filter	Full flow
Cooling System	Water cooled with engine pump and four-bladed fan
Battery	12 volt, 58 ampère hour

TRANSMISSION

Clutch	Single dry plate, 8·5in. dia., hydraulic operation
Gearbox	Four-speed; synchromesh on all forward ratios; central floor change. Optional extra, Laycock overdrive
Overall gear ratios	Top 4·1; 3rd 5·58; 2nd 8·15; 1st 12·82; reverse 13·3 to 1. With overdrive: O/D top 3·45; top 4·56; 3rd 6·2; 2nd 9·1; 1st 14·3; reverse 14·8 to 1.
Final drive	Hypoid; ratio 4·1 to 1. With overdrive, 4·56 to 1.

CHASSIS

Brakes	Girling disc front, drum rear, servo assisted.
Disc dia.	10·875in.
Drum dia., shoe width	9 x 2in.
Suspension: front	Independent, wishbone and coil springs.
rear	Coil springs, live axle, radius rods and Panhard rod.
Dampers	Telescopic, double-acting hydraulic
Wheels	Pressed steel, 4·5in. wide rim
Tyre size	5·90—15in.
Steering	Cam and roller
Steering wheel	16in., two-spoke
Turns, lock to lock	3·2

DIMENSIONS (Manufacturer's figures)

Wheelbase	8ft 0·5in. (245cm)
Track	4ft 3·75in. (131·5cm) front and rear
Overall length	14ft 5·25in. (440cm)
Overall width	5ft 7in. (170cm)
Overall height	4ft 3in. (130cm)
Ground clearance	6in. (15·5cm)
Turning circle	31ft (9·45m)
Kerb weight	2,490lb, 22 cwt (1,130 kg)

PERFORMANCE DATA

Top gear m.p.h. at 1,000 r.p.m.	17·4; with O/D, 21·0
Torque lb. ft. per cu. in. engine capacity	0·994
Brake surface area swept by linings	F, 232 sq. in.; R, 113 sq. in.
Weight distribution	F, 52·5 per cent; R, 47·5 per cent

Before long, P.1800s may be seen on the roads all over the world. This view of the car, taken when we tried it in Sweden, emphasizes the high waist and the absence of straight lines or pointed features

length front suspension wishbones are common to the saloon, but a small modification to the vertical pillars has been necessary to accommodate the different offset of the disc brakes. Again spring rates and damper settings are changed, and in addition, the front anti-roll bar is of larger diameter to increase the front roll stiffness.

A cam and roller steering box is used, with a ratio giving 3·25 turns from lock to lock. Considered in relation to the 31ft turning circle, this is quite high gearing.

Much pre-production road testing was carried out in Southern Germany and at the M.I.R.A. testing establishment, with the aim of combining good handling with a comfortable ride. The best results were apparently obtained with tyres of radial ply type and the Pirelli Cintura has been adopted as standard on all cars, being the only tyre of this kind currently available.

Internally the car is comprehensively and quite luxuriously appointed. Although sold as a two-seater, there are additional seats for small children in the back; these and the main, bucket seats, are trimmed in imitation leather. Pile carpet covers the floor, and the door panels are trimmed in a synthetic material to match the seats. Long armrests, incorporating door pockets and pulls, run the full length of the doors, sweeping up the forward ends to provide a " gate " for the interior door handle. Unusual are the curved side window glasses which will wind completely down into the doors; and there are lockable quarter vents.

The facia panel has a good, non-reflective covering to its upper surface and the main instruments are hooded to prevent glare on the screen. Both trip speedometer and revolution counter are standard equipment. Keen drivers will appreciate a number of sensible fittings such as an oil temperature gauge—

a very useful instrument when long-distance, high-speed motoring is in mind—two-speed screen wipers, a separate lever-switch for the loud tone of the horn and, of course, Volvo seat belts.

The relatively small, 16in., steering wheel is styled with a rather heavy Nordic elegance but is at a good angle for tireless driving; a rubber rest is provided for the driver's clutch foot. A " proper " handbrake lever is placed at the right of the driving seat on right-hand-drive cars and to the left on the left-hand-drive cars, and the short remote-control gear lever is conveniently positioned in relation to the rim of the steering wheel.

Climatic extremes are catered for, as befits a truly international motor car. Separate controls for cold air are provided for both driver and passenger, and there are grouped central controls for the powerful heater and defroster.

For the time being the P.1800 coupé will only be available in three colours—red, white or grey—with upholstery in the standard red, white and black in each case. In a luxury car this restriction may seem something of an anomaly, but it does permit the quality of the finish to be controlled more accurately. This would not be so easy with a wide range of colours—and paint quality is something of a fixation with Volvo.

It is a compliment to the British industry that Volvo, who have carefully built up an enviable reputation for quality and attention to detail, should entrust the production of what is their luxury model to British hands. Moreover more than 50 per cent of the components are of British manufacture. There remains the task of producing enough of these desirable motor-cars in right-hand as well as left-hand-drive form for the British motorist to be able to join those of America and Sweden in sampling the benefits of this international experiment.

Driving the VOLVO P-1800

by Douglas Armstrong

Journalist Armstrong followed the P-1800 from England, where it was assembled, to Sweden, where this road test took place.

Rear styling of the Volvo sport coupe is clean and uncluttered. Trunk room, while not huge, is ample to store luggage for two.

Robust four-cylinder engine sports five main bearings, twin S.U.'s, puts out 100 hp from 108.5 cubic inches.

Volvo sport coupe's blend of British excellence, Swedish engineering turns out a fleet, sturdy, attractive package

ALTHOUGH IT'S CLASSED as a Swedish car, the Volvo P-1800 sports coupe is in fact assembled in England, with more than 50 percent British components. The rest are Swedish, German and American. To top off its international flavor, the tires are British-made Italian Pirellis.

The reason for this far-flung assembly process is because Sweden has a peculiar labor situation. There's a shortage of workers: the country's eight-million population is practically fully employed. Also, their present factories just don't have room for expansion. The Volvo Group is building a large new plant a few miles out of Gothenburg, but it will be 1963 before this is in operation. In the meantime, Volvo has decided to go ahead with "foreign production."

At present, the Pressed Steel Co. of Linwood, England, makes the P-1800 bodywork, and this is delivered to the Jensen Motor Co., Ltd., for assembly (Jensen has been building its own line of sports cars for several years, and will continue to do so).

To give an idea of the mixed bag involved in gathering this car, the engine, gearbox and suspension are Swedish-built Volvo. The rear axle is American Spicer, the ignition and some of the lighting equipment is German Bosch, and the rest is British. The P-1800's eye-catching exterior was styled by Frua of Italy, but was redesigned from the production viewpoint by Pressed Steel — although it looks exactly the same.

After following the Volvo across the North Sea from my home base in England to our rendezvous in Sweden, I was able to try the car on auto-routes, country byways and those fantastic dirt roads which abound in Scandinavia. Make no mistake, this is a quality sports car with room for two, plus two children or one not-so-comfortable adult (the latter sitting transversely) in the back. The car looks bigger than its 1.8 liters suggest, and it certainly goes a lot faster. Its performance, though, is a trifle misleading because this is such a refined four-cylinder car that it's always traveling faster and accelerating more strongly than its acoustics indicate.

On the auto-route (roughly equivalent to Germany's autobahns and Italy's autostradas), I found the Volvo would cruise at 100 mph effortlessly and with a remarkably low noise level. In fact, this overdrive-equipped model (an optional extra) would run near its maximum 106-107 mph with no signs of distress or even shortness of breath. Acceleration was noteworthy for a 2500-pound, four-cylinder car. Zero to 60 took 12.5 seconds, and again the whole maneuver was so fussless that nothing seemed out of the ordinary.

The reason for all this is the splendidly robust engine and its five-bearing crankshaft. It runs as quietly as a sewing machine even though it has pushrod overhead valves, a compression ratio of 9.5:1, and twin British S.U. carburetors with only "pancake" air filters. There was no ping on 97-octane Swedish fuel, and neither did it run-on or show any sort of fussy temperament. Volvo worked 30 months on the P-1800 engine, progressing from five-bearing experimental versions of the 1.6-liter units to enlarged 1.8-liter engines, and finally to the full-sized, 1.8-liter, five-bearing setup.

The basic thinking was to produce a new engine which would give a great deal of power for its capacity, yet lose nothing of the marque's reputation for smoothness, flexibility and longevity. An incidental problem was to achieve all this without increasing the weight, and although the use of a light alloy block and head was discussed, the idea was abandoned in the interest of maximum rigidity. In the end, Volvo finished the P-1800 engine with a weight bonus (over the 1.6-liter unit) of only five pounds by casting the timing gear case, flywheel housing, oil pump, water pump, etc., in light metals. The cast-iron block, crankcase and head add up to tremendous stiffness, and this, coupled with the five-bearing crank in a comparatively short engine, makes an exceptional package.

Other attributes include fully machined combustion chambers (for power and ping-free running), *hardened* big-end and main bearing journals for long life, water-cooled (and heated) oil radiator, and a water pump which supplies coolant to the hottest parts of the cylinders, thus ensuring smooth running and maximum efficiency at all times.

More than a million kilometers were covered in the experimental engine test program; 40 power units were built, each costing about $6000. How's that for making sure?

Handling the new car was a splendid experience. It has a really first-class driving position and the slightly dished steering wheel with polished, light alloy spokes is set close to the facia. The separate front seats are trimmed in high-quality, washable plastic and are adjustable for fore-and-aft movement and for rake. It's easy to put almost any length or shape driver into a proper driving stance.

Volvo's P-1800 has Girling discs on the front wheels, drum brakes on the rear — and they do their job impressively. Pedal pressure is light, yet the car will slow from *any* speed with no grab or trace of fade, even after repeated 100-mph stops.

The Swedes are highly safety conscious (more than 60 percent of the nation's cars have safety belts), and this is borne out in the interior design of the P-1800. In addition to an effective (and standard) three-point shoulder harness *and* lap belt arrangement, the dash is foam-rubber padded, the switches and control knobs are recessed, and the dashboard shape and height are such that

even in the event of a collision it would be almost impossible for passenger or driver to catch or crush his legs. Disc brakes, too, are a step forward in road safety, and all indications point to the Volvo 122-S model being so equipped before long.

The P-1800 handled to a hair, even with the typically deep-ditched dirt roads one finds in Sweden. Pirelli's braced-tread "Cintura" tires are great aids to surefooted cornering, but the stiffness of the casing walls presents a problem for slow running. Normally, with high-speed shock absorber settings, a hard ride at slow speeds is inevitable. But the P-1800 designers, in conjunction with the shock absorber manufacturers, have done a wonderful job on valves and settings. The car gives a very comfortable ride at slow speeds, yet is completely stable at high velocities.

Headroom is a bit restricted in the coupe body, but the suspension is so good that a tall man rarely hits the roof. The road view is superb, and the gearbox pushes quickly and slickly through all four speeds (this is all-synchro, of course). On overdrive, a tiny tumbler switch near the driver's right hand engages the extra gear. Even in direct high, the Volvo will run up to 95 mph.

Fuel consumption with the o.d. model is claimed at 36-37 mpg at a sustained 50 mph, but in day-to-day, fast motoring it would be nearer 20-25 mpg.

With its unusual tail fins, high waistline and low build, the P-1800 is an eyeful. But having been two years getting off the drawing boards, it has a rather dated front-end design — to these eyes at any rate. It is a fast, robust, well engineered car that looks expensive but isn't. U.S. price is to be near $3800 p.o.e. Anyone who buys one can count on it still giving faultless performance and reliability five years hence. ●

Plush interior includes padded dash and well grouped instruments. Hefty doors close with a sound that characterizes car.

HIGH WAIST LINE, MILD TAIL FINS INDICATE THAT P-1800 WAS AWHILE GETTING OFF DRAWING BOARD — YET STYLING IS UNIQUE.

VOLVO P-1800

Long-Awaited Sports Coupe From Sweden

The Car

Swedish designed, Italian styled, British built, the P-1800 is Aktiebolaget Volvo's caviar addition to its bread-and-butter line of utility-first cars and trucks.

Orthodox in design, the P-1800 uses proven mechanical components from existing Volvo cars — thus cutting costs and adding reliability — with exception of the all-new B 18 B engine. Designed for high-speed running and representing 20,000 man-hours of development, this ultra-sturdy 4-cylinder unit carries light alloy pistons and other parts, a five-main-bearing crankshaft, twin 1¾-in. S.U. carburetors and a rev-limit redlined at 6,000 rpm.

Suspension is by coil springs all around, with the rear axle located by special support arm and a track bar in connection with coil springs and shock absorbers.

Production is planned at 150 per week.

Styling

Frua of Italy has created looks that couldn't be bettered for conveying the P-1800's Swedish-modern character. Timeless simplicity will keep this car handsome years from now. Upward-curving chrome trim on sides is distinctive but somehow fights the P-1800's otherwise straightforward appearance. Three colours: red, white and grey are listed.

Body-building has been sublet to Pressed Steel Co. Ltd. of England and assembling is being done by Jensen, but traditional Volvo standards are maintained. Despite its carriage-trade intentions the P-1800 isn't fussy or frilly; it's neat and functional. Workmanship follows suit. Bumpers, a good case in point, are not only integrated with the car's styling but actually serve their protective purpose well. Doors clunk and controls click on and off; the ash tray (big enough to hold more than butts) slides easily out and back; panels fit snugly. One sour note: the wheel covers seem a little tinny.

Interior

Follows current GT coupe practice of two seats with room in back on small bench for occasional passengers, dogs or small parcels. Trimmed in bright vinyl with carpeted floor and such appreciated touches as padded sun visors and under-dash storage compartments for driver or passenger use — with map lights for rallying or rummaging.

Instrument panel is sporting in flavour with large speedometer (incorporating odometer and trip mileage recorder), tach, water and oil temperature gauges, oil pressure gauge, fuel gauge and clock. Deluxe touches as standard equipment include cigarette lighter and twin horns. Visibility par excellence and large dash-mounted mirror refuses to vibrate at speed.

A stubby shift lever is mounted on the transmission tunnel and in combination with the drilled-spoke steering wheel and snug, firm seating position sets the driver up well for comfortable motoring. Seats adjust fore and aft to suit any length of driver and there is more leg-room than a car this low usually delivers, though headroom in our test car was minimal. We understand seats on future models are to be lowered two inches to overcome head-bumping.

Driving

Key-started ignition brings the 4-cylinder, 100-hp engine alive quickly but noise is barely perceptible. Accelerator pedal requires firm pressure. With a rear axle ratio of 4.56:1 and overdrive, the all-synchro M-40 gearbox (same as used on other Volvo models except for forward gears being carried in needle bearings) is undiluted pleasure to use and pushes the P-1800 through its well-spaced paces flawlessly. Electrically operated (Laycock de Normanville) overdrive is flicked on via a dash-mounted toggle switch and a small blue light beams when it's in operation. Steering seems to become progressively lighter with higher speeds but is tight and accurate in any range. Standard Pirelli Cinturato tires assist the P-1800's road-holding which, with its low centre of gravity and hefty anti-roll bar is absolutely the best we have yet encountered in a car of this type. Suspension is not independent at the rear but this car doesn't miss it; rough roads and twisty driving can be undertaken with as much verve as the driver has nerve to use. Noise is unobtrusive at cruising speeds.

Servo-assisted disc brakes in front with V-type drums at rear must be used hard and often to be fully appreciated. They are virtually fade-free and allow leaving the anchors to the last split second during vigorous driving. Special shields in front ward off water's effects. Pressure is medium, making it hard to induce sudden crash-stops unless you want to.

Rough riding reminded us that whatever Volvo builds stays built; the P-1800 is no exception and a tribute to its construction is the fact that passengers are considerably more shook-up over bad surfaces than the car is. A few slight squeaks could be detected somewhere in the interior panelling but that was it. This should be a winning rally car, if only because the navigator is unlikely to become carsick.

Economy

Average consumption (premium fuel) over combined city and highway driving was 32 mpg with overdrive. Cruising at 60-70 mph steadily in o/d could appreciably hike this figure, while 30 mpg with the nonoverdrive model is easily attained.

Storage space

Aside from passenger-compartment space for trifles there is a wide, deep trunk capable of carrying luggage for two on an extended trip with little crowding. The spare tire (covered) rests on the trunk floor in the right lower corner, rather marring the rectangular layout. In spite of this, the P-1800 still has more room behind than almost any GT-type coupe and as much as some compacts.

Heater and Ventilation

Sweden has few palm trees, and the P-1800 has been realistically planned for a variety of climates. Thus the heater is big and efficient and there are fresh air intakes on each side of the passenger compartment, beneath the dash.

Options

Considering the items listed as standard equipment on the P-1800, options are superfluous except for a radio (mounted on the instrument panel), and such goodies as a power-operated radio antenna. Overdrive is a worthwhile extra for long-range cruising. The standard-equipment list includes: servo-assisted disc brakes in front; oil cooler; electric windshield washer; Pirelli Cinturato tires; electric clock; cigarette lighter; shoulder safety belts; double horns; overdrive warning light, anti-theft coil device and Abarth exhaust.

Last word

At $6,000 this car would be a bargain. At $3,995 we feel it's a steal and Volvo will be hard-pressed to fill the orders. Carefully advertised as a sports coupe and not a sports car, the P-1800 has as much to offer as most sports cars we have encountered plus a degree of creature comfort and sheer liveability unmatched by anything near its price class. With Volvo's reputation for ruggedness, reliability and low maintenance behind it, it can't lose.

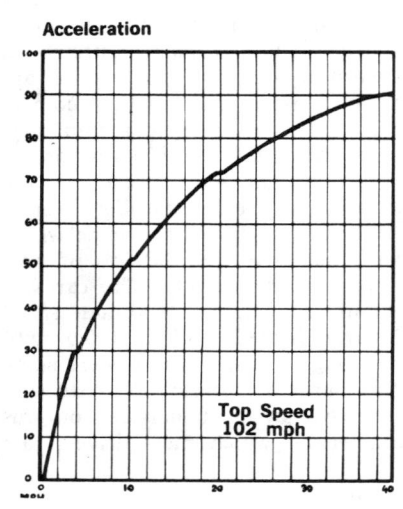

Acceleration

Top Speed 102 mph

Data & Specifications - **Volvo P-1800 Sports Coupe**

ENGINE: 4 cylinder in-line, water cooled. Bore & Stroke: 3.312" x 3.15". Capacity: 1.78 liters (108.6 cu. in.). Output: **100 b.h.p. (S.A.E.) at 5,500 rpm.** Torque: 108 lbs./ft. at 4,000 rpm. Compression ratio: 9.5 to 1.

SUSPENSION: Front, independent, coil springs, wishbones, anti-sway bar; Rear, solid axle, coil spring, trailing radius arms and Panhard rod.

TRANSMISSION: 4-speed, all-syncromesh with overdrive optional.

DIMENSIONS: Wheelbase - - 96.5 in. Length - - 173 in. Ground Clearance - - 6.3in Test Weight; 2655 lbs.

TURNS LOCK-TO-LOCK: 3 2/3. **TURNING CIRCLE:** 31 ft.

PRICE: $3,995.00 (Toronto).

IT is fully twelve months since the Volvo P1800 was announced yet this exciting grand touring car is still very scarce on the roads of Europe. Volvo themselves did not have the facilities to build the beautifully designed Frua body, and after approaching most of the leading European coachbuilders the British firm of Pressed Steel was awarded the contract to produce the bodies, while Jensen Motors were to build the cars. The arrangement is not so strange as at first appears, for all Volvos incorporated a high percentage of British parts and so far as the P1800 is concerned it is doubtful if much more than the engine alone comes from the Swedish factory.

The reason for the tardy appearance of the P1800 on the roads is that the firm's policy was to allocate the first few months' production to the Swedish market so that the factory could examine and rectify the teething problems that are bound to exist with a new model.

During a recent visit to the Volvo factory near Gothenburg in Sweden we were given opportunity to drive a P1800 for a few hours. The car tested was one of the prototypes and had already been subject to much use. The immediate impression on seeing and sitting in the sports Volvo is one of robustness. The roominess is unusual considering the low overall height of the car and even the tallest of passengers can find no complaint on the grounds of leg room although overhead the clearance would be minimal. The occasional seats for two passengers at the rear are scarcely luxurious, but two adults would have sufficient room to be at ease for journeys of reasonable length. The front seats were extremely com-

A drive in the P 1800

The prototype car differed in some small respects from the latest production models

fortable, a quality derived from both the soft padding and the excellent shape. Clearly marked instruments and controls are well laid out, while the stylish and attractive steering wheel is inclined to dominate the car's interior. The remote control gear lever is on top of the transmission hump and while the movement is long by sports car standards, it does not necessitate groping or stretching. Excellent is the only word to describe the interior appointments as a whole. Much use is made of light colours in the trim and the overall design is very contemporary.

During the first part of the test the P1800 was driven along an autoroute, so we soon had some measure of the car's high speed performance. When the high kerb weight of over 22 cwt is remembered the 1.78 litre engine which produces 100 hp (S.A.E.) makes a splendid job of propelling the biggish car along very quickly. The car was given plenty of opportunity to achieve maximum speed and we found this to be an indicated 170 kph (105·6 mph) which did not take very long to reach. There were some long fast curves on this particular stretch of road and there was just a slight tendency to understeer on this type of corner, a characteristic which most drivers rate as desirable.

A little later we tried the car on secondary roads with a great variety of surfaces with slow and fast corners. Here the greatest virtue of the Volvo became apparent:

Instrument panel

Front seating

its steering is so positive and direct, the car going exactly where it is pointed. The steering is suitably high-geared yet is surprisingly light. It is no trouble to negotiate a series of tight bends quickly with such handling. Even over the unsealed and sometimes rough surfaces often encountered the steering and handling characteristics were never at fault.

The ride is soft enough to cope with uneven surfaces without causing the passengers discomfort yet firm enough to ensure that during hard cornering there is little body roll. Braking equipment includes Girling disc brakes at the front, ensuring that the stopping power measures up well to the P1800's performance.

The test was all too short, for the Volvo was indeed a pleasure to drive and we look forward to a longer association with a P1800. The body proved as functional as it is attractive, of good aerodynamic shape while allowing plenty of passenger and luggage space. The boot has much more capacity than one usually expects in this type of vehicle and by itself would accommodate the luggage of two people without using the generous space inside the car. Altogether the P1800 appears to be a car well worth waiting for, for it has an unusual combination of speed, good handling, roominess, and a robustness of construction which should ensure a lengthy and reliable ownership.

Small rear seats

Beneath the bonnet

Luggage accommodation

ROAD TEST/26-61 VOLVO P-1800

Solid Design plus Solid Construction equal Solid Comfort

THERE ARE SOME CARS that, while utterly delightful, give one the feeling that they should never be taken more than a hundred miles or so from home base. There are others, equally delightful, that make one feel that they could be driven around the world with little more in the way of service than replenishing the fuel tank and an occasional change of oil.

Sitting firmly on top of this latter category is *Aktiebolaget* Volvo's long awaited confection, the P-1800 GT coupe. The accompanying pictures and past verbiage by others suffices to convey the impression that the P-1800 is without doubt one of the most attractive automobiles on the road or anywhere else, for that matter. What isn't and hasn't been conveyed is that beneath that delectable frosting is a mechanism of almost awesome solidity, giving a feeling of strength on the order of something built by the Moseler Safe people. This in itself is a change from all too many GT coupes but it isn't by any means all. With this solidity comes a degree of passenger and driver comfort on the road, at virtually any speed over any reasonable surface, that is almost beyond belief.

An incident during the course of the test will suffice to illustrate this point. Not trusting our own first impressions we invited a secretary, a knowledgeable girl, along for a ride. Little was said for awhile except for a few cogent comments regarding interior appointments and a remark or two concerning the unexpected stillness inside the car underway. Then the young lady whipped out a dictation book and began to record our remarks, calmly and neatly setting down precise rows of shorthand, with never a bobble. At that time we were moving at 75 mph over a not-too-smooth and gently twisting piece of secondary highway.

Said the girl in pleased surprise: "It's as easy as writing in an airplane!"

What is all the more surprising is that this comfort is accompanied by handling of an impeccable order — conventionally suspended, solid rear axle machinery just isn't supposed to have both comfort *and* superior road holding. The new Volvo sticks to the road like paint under virtually any conditions. It can be gotten out of shape but it takes a lot of doing. While the car is, thanks to its somewhat forward weight bias, a basically understeering car, it will go into an oversteer condition under certain circumstances. Hard throttle application on a tight corner in second gear, for instance, will provoke it but the same degree of throttle in a fast bend in top gear will only increase the understeer. This imparts a feeling of immense stability and only becomes hazardous in application when one is impossibly far over one's head for highway conditions. The provoked oversteer is very handy on mountain road switchbacks where one can liter-

Dash and instrument panel of the new P-1800 is practical without being stark. All instruments can be read at a glance and controls are little more than finger reach from wheel.

Provided as standard equipment are lap belts and shoulder harnesses with metal-to-metal fastenings. When properly adjusted belts give full protection without hampering driver.

Deep side sections make roof line seem lower than it really is. Streamlining is good and little wind blast comes through windows. Despite low silhouette ground clearance is ample.

Rounding a tight downhill turn (right and opposite page) car is seen to lean but the tilt is barely noticeable inside by either driver or passenger. Stability and bite are amazing.

PHOTOS: PAT BROLLIER

ally boot the car around, cutting corner time in half.

On the course at Riverside, where experiments could be made that might have been foolhardy on the open road, other pleasant handling traits came out. First it was found that the adhesion of the car was of such an order that all of the Esses, including hazardous, tightening Turn 4, could be taken in Fourth-direct in the neighborhood of 80 mph. At no time was it necessary to drop into second gear for any corner, not even the tightest. In each and every case the natural slight understeer (with tires filled to 32 psi, front and rear) could be over-ridden with the result that the exit line from any corner was just about anything the driver wanted it to be, either outside or inside. Thanks to the fantastic braking (which one staff member felt to be "the best, bar none" that he had seen on any production car), coupled with the adhesion provided by the Pirelli Cinturatos, the comparatively heavy car could be driven flat out into any corner with braking left to that last impossible moment when it would appear that only the suspension of one or more natural laws would save the situation.

An interesting thing about the car is that all these attributes take a day or more to sink in. The first impression one gets, after pushing through the usual horde of bystanders and climbing in, is the one of solidity mentioned earlier. The

VOLVO P-1800

next impression is that of heaviness both in terms of weight and in terms of handling. True it is that the Volvo is no lightweight, tipping the beam at around 2700 pounds with two people aboard, but that figure can hardly be considered excessive when the weights of most production sports cars are considered. Most roadsters run about 200 pounds less, with convertibles and coupes running almost the same. The feeling of weight apparently comes from the roominess and the general beefy contour rather than sheer poundage. There is a definite heaviness in the steering at speeds up to around 10 to 15 mph, which thereupon lessens progressively until about 40 mph at which point the car can literally be tossed around with near Sprite-like abandon. A good part of this low-speed steering weightiness is due to a fairly high caster angle and consequent strong return coupled with the very wide section, very gummy Cinturatos which help give the car its fantastic side-bite. These tires put as much rubber on the road as those designed for cars of considerably greater size and power. The size was not arbitrarily arrived at either, but came as a result of exhaustive tests of virtually every tire available on a worldwide basis. Soft and sticky though they appear, these flat-tread Cinturatos have a tremendously high wear factor under normal highway and street conditions; a similar set on one Ferrari, whose owner we know well, having lasted for a full two years of fairly constant use.

Another aspect that leads to the feeling of heaviness in the P-1800 is its unwillingness to make like a dragster from a standing start. There is no jump forward on initial clutch application in low gear but rather a slow but steady, almost truck-like push ahead that increases with progressive rapidity until it comes time to engage second gear. It seems as though the car will never overhaul the traffic that may have gotten the jump at the go-off but, almost as though by magic, everybody else seems to be diminishing rapidly in the rear-view mirror. This progressive, almost imperceptible build-up of speed must be watched for if entanglements with the law are to be avoided, especially on the freeways and expressways. One moment it seems as though the car will never get to 60 and the next moment the accurate speedometer says the car is doing 80 and still climbing. It is an almost eerie feeling since there is no accompanying push in the back and, with the windows closed, no rush of air or rising exhaust note to tell the driver what is happening. This silent rushing carries with it one great blessing in that the car can be cruised indefinitely at 80 mph or more in complete comfort and a conversation carried on among the occupants with no tendency toward that sports car malady known as "trip-end laryngitis" caused by shouting over an assortment of engine, wind and exhaust noises.

The unwillingness to "climb out of the hole" at the start is an effect brought about by the most controversial component of the new Volvo, the B-18B engine. The controversy arises from the fact that while the other Volvo cars, particularly the 544 Sport, might be considered almost overpowered for economy vehicles, the P-1800 is equipped with an engine of only 1780 cc, or 180 cc more than the bread-and-butter cars. Power developed is a mere fifteen horsepower more than that put out by the sedan engine. The other side of the coin is that while the sedan engines are bored out and hopped up units that started life as 1500 cc plants, the B-18B engine used in the P-1800 is a completely new over-designed unit now at the beginning of its development. The key word here is "overdesign." It had its beginning in the very neat and compact 3560 cc Volvo V-8 truck engine and is in fact exactly one half of that unit in size. Being ever-practical, the men of Volvo can use much of the tooling and basic equipment from the truck engine for use in the B-18B,

VEHICLE	Volvo	MODEL	P-1800
PRICE (as tested)	$3940 POE N. Y.	OPTIONS	Overdrive, radio

ENGINE:

Type:	4 cylinder in-line, water cooled
Head:	Cast iron, 8-port
Valves:	OHV inclined, pushrod
Max. bhp	100 @ 5500 rpm
Max. Torque	108 lbs. ft. @ 4000 rpm
Bore	3.313 in. 84.2 mm.
Stroke	3.15 in. 80 mm.
Displacement	108.6 cu. in. 1780 cc.
Compression Ratio	9.5 to 1
Induction System:	4-port, 2 SU Auc 996R
Exhaust System:	Single, cast iron manifold
Electrical System:	12V. Bosch single distributor

CLUTCH: Single disc, dry
Diameter: N.A.
Actuation: Hydraulic

TRANSMISSION: 4-speed, overdrive in 4th, full synchro

Ratios:	
1st	3.13 to 1
2nd	1.99 to 1
3rd	1.36 to 1
4th	1.00 to 1
4th O.D.	0.76 to 1

DIFFERENTIAL:
Ratio: 4.56 to 1. (w/OD)
Drive Axles (type): Enclosed, semi-floating

STEERING:
Turns Lock to Lock: 3.6
Turn Circle: 31 ft.

BRAKES: Combination; disc front, drums rear
Drum and Disc Diameter F-10.8, R-9.0 in.
Swept Area 350 sq. in.

CHASSIS:

Frame:	Integral
Body:	Steel unitized
Front Suspension:	Unequal arm, coils, tube shock
Rear Suspension:	Live, trailing arm, Panhard rod, coils, tube shocks
Tire Size & Type:	1.65 x 15 P Cinturato

WEIGHTS AND MEASURES:

Wheelbase:	96.5 in.	Ground Clearance	6 in.
Front Track:	51.7 in.	Curb Weight	2444 lbs.
Rear Track:	51.7 in.	Test Weight	2709 lbs.
Overall Height	51 in.	Crankcase	3.5 qts.
Overall Width	61 in.	Cooling System	N.A. qts.
Overall Length	173 in.	Gas Tank	12 gals.

PERFORMANCE:

0-30	3.2 sec.	0-70	16.0 sec.
0-40	6.2 sec.	0-80	21.2 sec.
0-50	9.0 sec.	0-90	27.5 sec.
0-60	12.1 sec.	0-100	39.9 sec.

Standing ¼ mile 21.0 sec. @ 78 mph
Top Speed (av. two-way run) 105 mph standard — 110 mph overdrive

Speed Error		30	40	50	60	70	80	90
Actual		30	41	51	60	70	79	89

Recommended Shift Points:

Fuel Consumption:	1st 28 mph
	2nd 46 mph
Test 24 mpg	3rd 70 mph
Average 28 mpg	RPM Red-line 6000 rpm

Speed Ranges in gears:

1st	0 to 31 mph	3rd	20 to 74 mph
2nd	10 to 52 mph	4th	26 (OD 38) to 105 mph

Brake Test: 80 Average % G, over 5 stops.
No fade encountered.

REFERENCE FACTORS:

Bhp. per Cubic Inch	0.926
Lbs. per bhp.	24.4
Piston Speed @ Peak rpm	2888 ft./min.
Sq. In. Swept Brake Area per Lb.	0.143

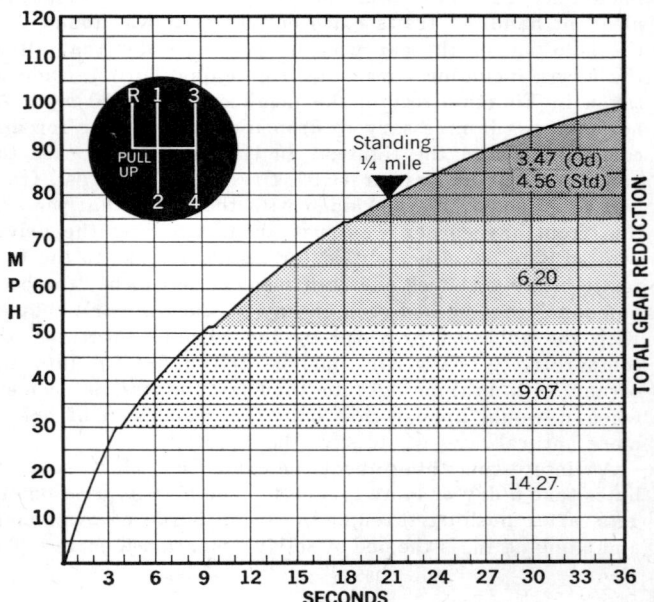

including such things as pistons, rods, and accessory equipment, and thus produce an entirely new engine at considerably less cost and no sacrifice in quality. While the competition minded enthusiast or the seeker after power might prefer a full two liters — which the car really needs — the engine as it comes is entirely equal to the task set for it.

No effort was overlooked in making this engine as close to being foolproof and unbreakable as possible. Almost outrageously oversquare and carrying its crank in five main bearings, the engine would be hard to destroy, even deliberately, especially in light of a cam that is anything but violent and which signs off almost completely at the redline. The crank is carried well up in the block, above the lower mating surface of the crankcase, and the cylinder bores are widely separated. Considering the beefy rod journals and the space between the bore centers it is easy to see which way development can go. It is entirely possible to increase the stroke as much as a quarter of an inch and, given an overbore of a standard 0.060 of an inch, come up with an engine that is still nearly square.

It would also be close to two liters, 2.016 to round it off. If this gives mechanically minded prospective owners any ideas, so be it. An increase in displacement would also allow — in fact call for — somewhat more generous cam timing but it would be wise to go easy here since the car needs that bottom end torque to get underway. Be that as it may, for those who like to leave things as the factory built them, the engine as it comes will do the job nicely if one is content to allow more prosaic equipment to get the jump at stoplights and intersections and then overhaul them with contemptuous ease at some point not too far

distant down the pike. The almost ridiculously high average speed one can maintain with this car over any sort of road more than makes up for any momentary discomfiture at standing starts. Too, if one learns that the throttle is not to be jammed to the floor on rapid takeoffs but rather eased through its travel there won't be many cars that will move off more rapidly.

As mentioned earlier many of the finer points of the car take a while to worm their way into one's consciousness. The P-1800 is not a car that one fits on in a trip around the block. Those who are tall, for instance, will at first feel as though the top is about to rub a bald spot at the peak of the pate while the very short will feel that they are being shoved into the padded sun visors. However, the seats adjust for rake as well as for distance from the controls and short types can rake the seat back in such a way that they are comfortably removed from the wheel with the pedals still in reach. Tall folk can rack the seat far enough back to avoid contact with the sloping top by a good two inches or so. So tightly is rebound controlled by the suspension that there is never any danger of getting tossed upward so that the two-inch clearance between skull and roof is more than sufficient.

Another aspect that takes a bit of sinking in is the fact that this is a roomy automobile. There is more leg room than one can reasonably use. Shoulder room is plentiful and there is no need to stuff one's elbow over the window sill. In fact this practice is discouraged by the height of the sill and by the placement of the windwing support which is a bit too far back for comfortable arm hanging. Too, a sharp edge on the lower window stripping makes for discomfort when pressed against a bare elbow. This discourage-

ment is all to the good since it is all but impossible to haul a hung-out arm back into the car in an emergency situation and in any case this is one of those cars in which a two-handed ten-and-two o'clock grip on the wheel is the most comfortable position in which to drive. Room is not limited to passenger space either. The occasional seat in back and the relatively large trunk allow the lugging of more baggage and equipment than most sports car purists would consider decent. Two jumbo sized suitcases will fit into the trunk alone and more cases will go behind the seats. Small stuff can be stowed in a luggage shelf behind the occasional seats and on the rear window shelf if need be. In short, anyone who can't get two weeks' worth of clothing and gear for two people into this car should be travelling by train or boat or both.

Virtually everything about the P-1800 is geared for travel, and fast travel at that. Once underway there is little need for stopping or slowing for anything but those pauses required for servicing car and occupants with the necessities of continued life. Fatigue is not one of those things that enter into the picture since this is a vehicle in which one can put 600 or more miles into a day and end up with none of that shoulder ache, voicelessness nor feeling of strain associated with long cross country hauls in lesser machinery. In short, the P-1800 is a Grand Touring car in every sense of the word, and into the bargain a prestige vehicle at what in these days of the half-buck dollar can be considered a bread-and-butter price. It is also one of a scant half dozen cars we have tested over the years that we really hated to return. In fact we hated the man for asking for it. As Tech Editor Titus put it: "This is a *car!*" —*John Christy*

Above, left, seats are adjustable for rake by small knurled knob. Sweeping arm rests on doors are fine for passenger but a bit low for driver. Hardware is well-placed and easily operated. Fresh air is ducted through vent, above right, either through heater or directly to the foot wells. Trunk, at left, is wide and deep and will hold two large suitcases in spite of spare. Tools stow in neat recesses at each side. Further stowage space can be found in the occasional seats and parcel shelf inside the car, as seen at right.

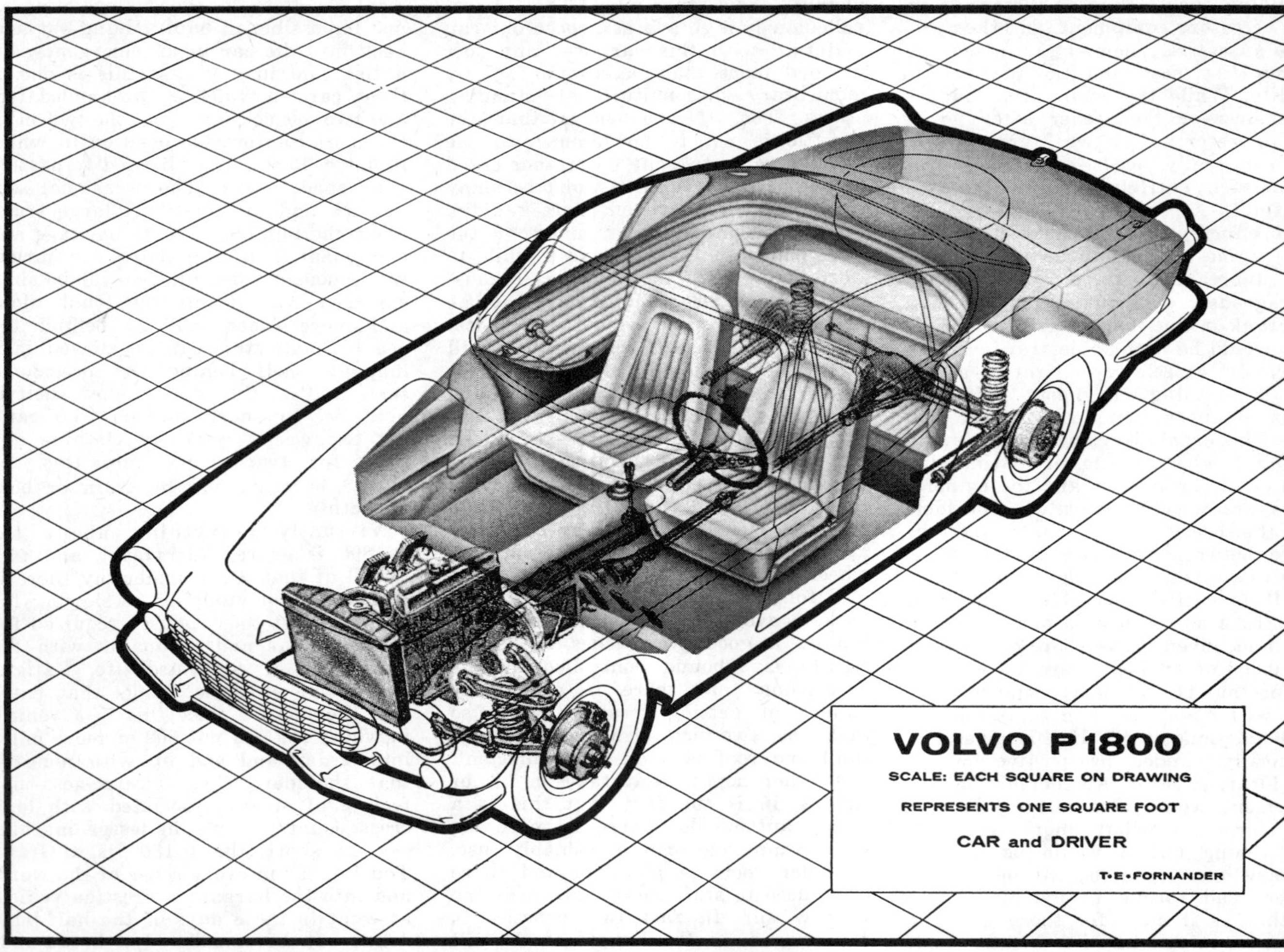

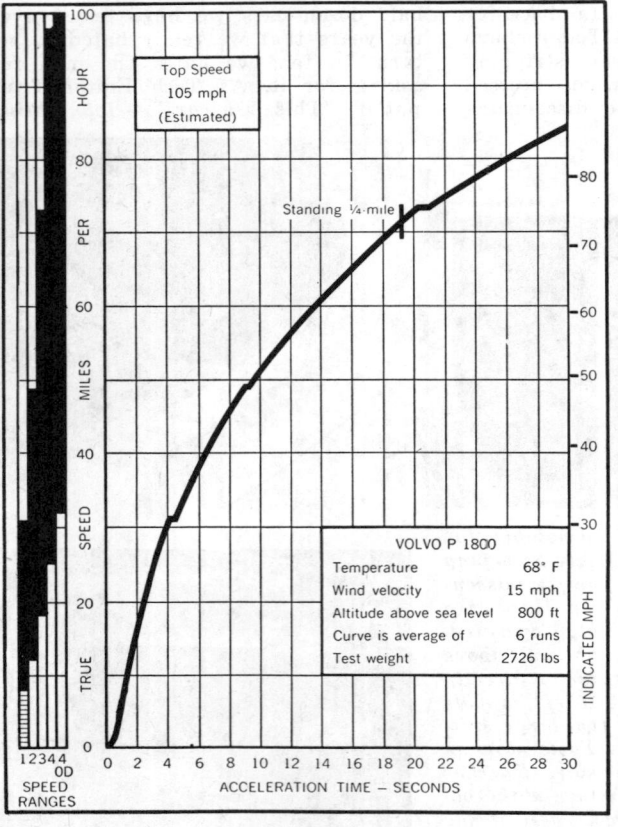

VOLVO P 1800
SCALE: EACH SQUARE ON DRAWING
REPRESENTS ONE SQUARE FOOT
CAR and DRIVER
T·E·FORNANDER

Top Speed
105 mph
(Estimated)
Standing ¼-mile
VOLVO P 1800
Temperature 68° F
Wind velocity 15 mph
Altitude above sea level 800 ft
Curve is average of 6 runs
Test weight 2726 lbs
TRUE SPEED MILES PER HOUR
INDICATED MPH
ACCELERATION TIME – SECONDS
1 2 3 4 4 OD
SPEED RANGES
0 2 4 6 8 10 12 14 16 18 20 22 24 26 28 30
0 20 40 60 80 100
30 40 50 60 70 80

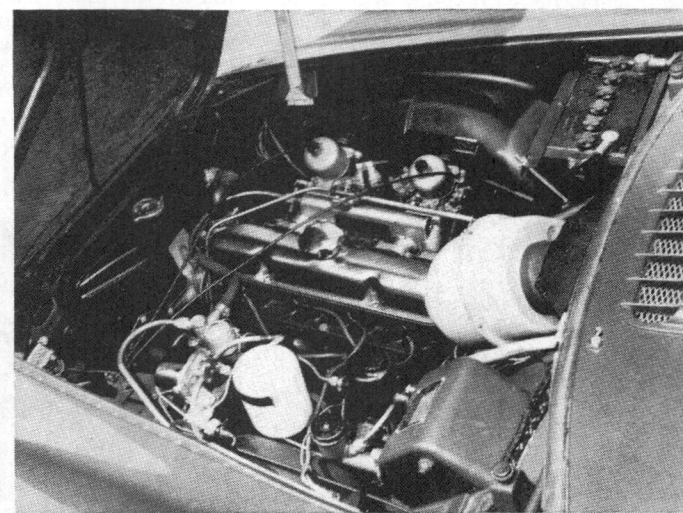

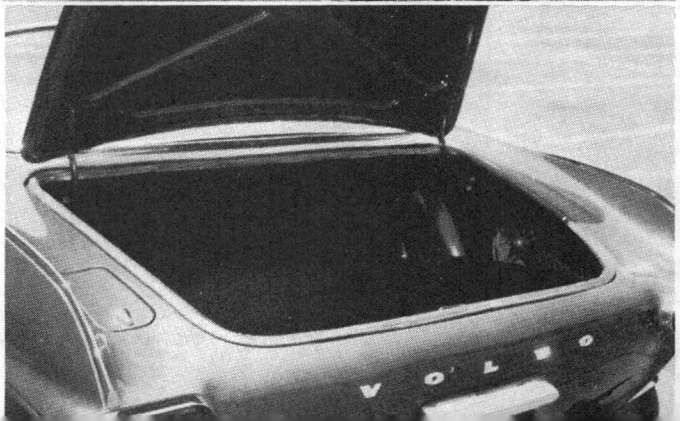

Road Research Report: VOLVO P 1800

► The hundreds of long-suffering enthusiasts who wrote checks for $3800 for the new Volvo P 1800 when it was introduced at New York's International Auto Show in April, 1960 are at last beginning to receive their cars. After putting the sleek coupe through its paces we feel their wait was well worthwhile. For the rest, who decided to hold off until the cars were actually available, we offer our condolences — they're missing out on some really fine driving and they too may find they'll have a bit of a wait before production gets up a full head of steam.

Just as the Jaguar XKE was acclaimed the star of the 1961 show, the P 1800 won that distinction in 1960. Still, when the Volvo was "reintroduced" earlier this year public interest was unabated although the element of surprise was, of course, dulled.

RARE AND DESIRABLE TYPE

Until the P 1800 came along, attractive 2/4 seater coupes capable of over 100 mph were scarce unless the buyer was able to pay $4000 and up (usually very "up"). However, it represents a type of automobile that is extremely attractive to enthusiasts and even though American manufacturers have already begun to cater to this market and though the P 1800 has gotten off to a slow on-sale start, it has merit in is own right that should augur well for financial success. At this point it would appear that the main problem facing A.B. Volvo is getting enough cars to the United States to appease anxious purchasers. The company's sales in the U.S. have been firm. Even without the highly desirable P 1800, its January, 1960 sales here were enough to move it from tenth to sixth position in the then-generally-lagging imported car sales race. Future plans call for expanding and solidifying the dealer network for even greater market penetration.

The lines of the coupe are unusual and distinctive without being grotesque; they are well within the confines of the "G.T. image." The outward appearance of the car expresses in smooth, flowing lines the smooth, flowing performance of the machine. It doesn't look like a racing car, it doesn't go like one and it wasn't intended to do either. Volvo had in mind the construction of a solid road car, one which would cruise quietly,

capably and safely at speeds in the 80-mph range. As such it's a resounding (though quiet) success. Its wind-cheating shape is such that the most noise at 80, for example, comes from the four-bladed fan. Wind noise is surprisingly low and exhaust noise, though louder than the prototype we tested in Sweden (see SCI, February, 1961) is almost disappointingly muffled. A further inducement to fast touring is the lack of breezes even with the side windows and vents wide open and the high-silled doors and rattle-free unit body give occupants a feeling of being nestled inside a transportation capsule.

SMOOTH PERFORMER

The 108.6-cubic-inch engine has an unbreakable feel all the way up to its 6000 rpm red-line, but feels happiest between 3000 and 4500 rpm. A particularly stiff accelerator return spring may give the first-time driver the impression that the throttle has to be floored for anything to happen. However, the rapid rise of the tach and speedometer needles show this is not true. Volvo says the minimum usable rpm is about 1500. We'll go along with that; although it's possible to go lower in a gear, the engine is definitely starting to lug. The nylon-bushed linkage is progressive in its action and assures parallel action of the two SU carbs.

The engine in our car was adjusted a bit low and idled lumpily in New York traffic on the city's hottest day of the year, but the water temperature stayed below 212° and the oil remained cool. The oil circuit plumbing is such that the lubricant is cooled by water from the radiator and throughout all our testing remained well below the danger point. Underway, oil pressure when hot was about 50 pounds; idling it registered the specified 5 to 10 pounds. Less than a quart of oil was used in all our driving, which included more than 500 miles in all sorts of conditions, having started when the engine had less than 500 miles on it. We were fortunate with the weather; it ran from temperatures in the 90s through crisp cool evenings and into soggy, wet, cold nights. The engine always started promptly, warmed up quickly and registered very reasonable fuel consumption even under the toughest and fastest driving situations.

Access to the engine is excellent. The forward-hinging

hood lifts high and the distributor, oil filter and spark plugs are readily at hand. The battery mounted on the firewall may be subject to some heat, but it's easy to service. The brake and clutch master cylinders are easy to check or fill and all of the electrical controls are protected from dust and water yet are easy to service.

OTHER POWER POSSIBILITIES

So spacious is the room under the hood that we couldn't help wondering whether one of Buick's aluminum V8s wouldn't fit. Width is limiting and there would have to be some alteration to the firewall, but perhaps the pioneering struggle would be worthwhile to get an extra 55 bhp, compared to the standard 100 bhp engine. This tail-twisting, we feel, would make the P 1800 really perk. It would provide a power lift many drivers would welcome but wouldn't turn the car into a rolling nightmare. Perhaps we may have a story on such an engine swap before too long.

For those who believe in working with what's at hand, the B18B engine used in the car should offer ample tuning scope. Its massive five-bearing crankshaft should be up to any power boosts that might be envisioned and the block and head are meaty enough to permit boring out for greater displacement and milling for more compression.

All of these comments are not to suggest that the stock engine is inadequate; it's just that we're sure readers will wonder what the possibilities are and we want to suggest two. Unfortunately we do not yet have full details on hopping up the B18B or carrying out an engine swap; when we do we'll pass them on.

TRANSMISSION IS PRECISE

The four-speed, all-synchromesh transmission deals quickly and effectively with any road situation whether it be dropping back into first for quick acceleration just as the light turns green or flipping the dash-mounted switch into overdrive for breezing down the freeways. The ratios are well-suited to the engine and the weight of the car and the lever movement is crisp. The feel was less than the "knife-through-butter" we remember from the four-speed PV544s, but this may be due to the extra linkage (see photo) or to the fact that the unit was not yet fully broken in. Nevertheless we had no complaint about its operation. The shift lever features a spring loading which enables fast "straight-line" shifts to be made from second to third and third to fourth, but which requires slight side pressure in engaging first and second. A lock-out prevents accidental engagement of reverse when shifting to first; the lever must first be lifted, then moved left, then forward. It's not too easy but it's positive. The engagement of overdrive is instantaneous with the flipping of the switch. There is no need to back off on the accelerator although the actual shift will be quicker if you do. Shifting back into fourth requires simultaneous pressure on the accelerator and the toggle-flipping ritual to prevent a lurch.

The hydraulically-operated clutch has a pleasant action, having neither long travel nor stiff action. It didn't slip under fast starts and no grabbing was ex-

perienced. The vacuum-assisted brakes (disc in the front and drum in the rear) gave ample stopping power. The amount of retardation was always directly proportional to the amount of pressure exerted on the pedal. The only objection about the pedal layout was that the accelerator is located nearer the firewall than either the brake or clutch and heel-and-toeing was pretty much out of the question. The accelerator pedal is of the organ type and it looked as if it would be possible either to substitute a hanging pedal or relocate the existing unit. The relation of the pedals to the steering wheel is good, allowing quick footwork without banging your knees on the wheel. The wheel itself is moderately dished and of a handy, small diameter. While it's non-adjustable, the seat positioning range should satisfy most drivers.

SOUND AND FEEL OF MOTION

In our test car, which was one of the first production types in the country, we heard some clunking noises from the rear end. Occurring when accelerating and backing off at low speeds, they seemed to be caused by a built-in slackness of either the universals or the

rear axle mounting. Some rear-axle hop was also experienced, although it was slight. We were informed prior to going to press with this Road Research Report that some minor changes have been made, which include new shock absorbers, rubber mountings on the rear axle and added sound insulation between the rear occasional seat and the trunk. It's quite likely these slight changes will silence, in cars currently being delivered, the sounds which we interpreted to be natural but somewhat distracting.

Pirelli Cinturato tires are standard equipment, following an exhaustive test by Volvo of all available types. Capable of sustained speeds in excess of the car's maximum, they are of the latest type, having squared-tread shoulders. They have a tenacious bite on all surfaces, wet or dry, right up to the limit of the car's capabilities. Cornering noise, which gets louder as you near the limit, is not excessive even when the side thrusts are of massive proportions. Roll is unapparent within the car. The ride is comfortable without becoming soggy. The combination of tires CONTINUED ON PAGE 25

The yellow and blue of the Swedish flag are used in the stylized V. The side windows have a slight curvature, and the back ones are fixed shut.

The wedge-shaped P1800 looks best when it's in fast-motion although the interesting body has a lot of eye-pleasing detail for close scrutiny.

Both the shoulder harnesses clip to the central forged bracket. More comfort from the harness could be achieved with a higher swivel point.

Volvo's own rugged four-speed, all-synchromesh transmission is used. A remote shift linkage and Laycock de Normanville overdrive are added.

The P 1800's broad, low hood permits excellent visibility, but the rear-view mirror blocks the right front fender a bit because of the low seat.

One of the two very neat interior lights, it's operated by lifting the diffusing lens. There is also a door-operated switch and a manual override switch which the driver can use. The pierced headliner helps to reduce interior noise to a low level.

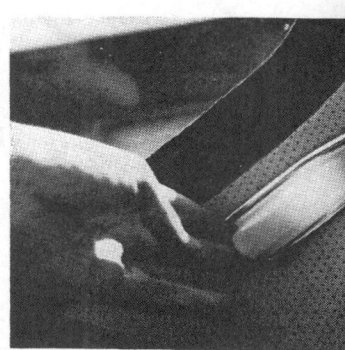

Volvo designed its own oil cooler for the P 1800, similar to deeper ones on its marine engines. It bolts to the right side of the engine, behind the spin-on filter. Water circulating through it speeds warm-up and helps keep the engine temperatures stable under way.

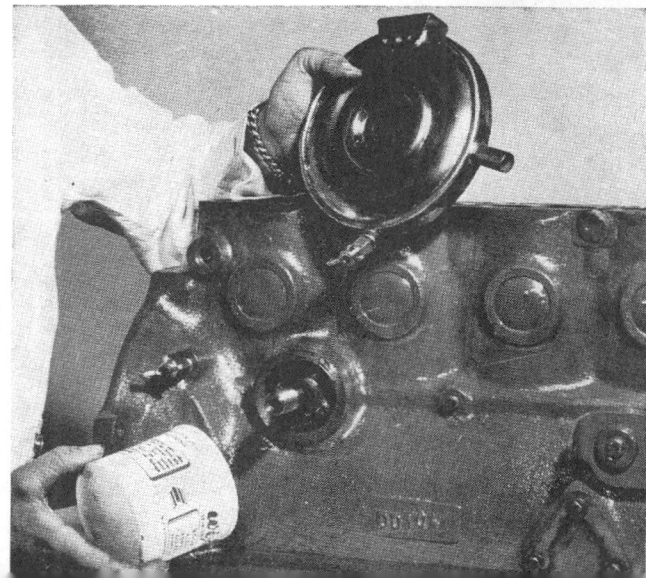

Road Research Report:
VOLVO P1800

Importer:

Volvo Distributing Inc.
452 Hudson Terrace
Englewood Cliffs, N. J.

Number of U. S. dealers: 400
Planned annual production: 6000 (late-1960 estimate)
Value of spare parts in U. S.: Not available from the manufacturer

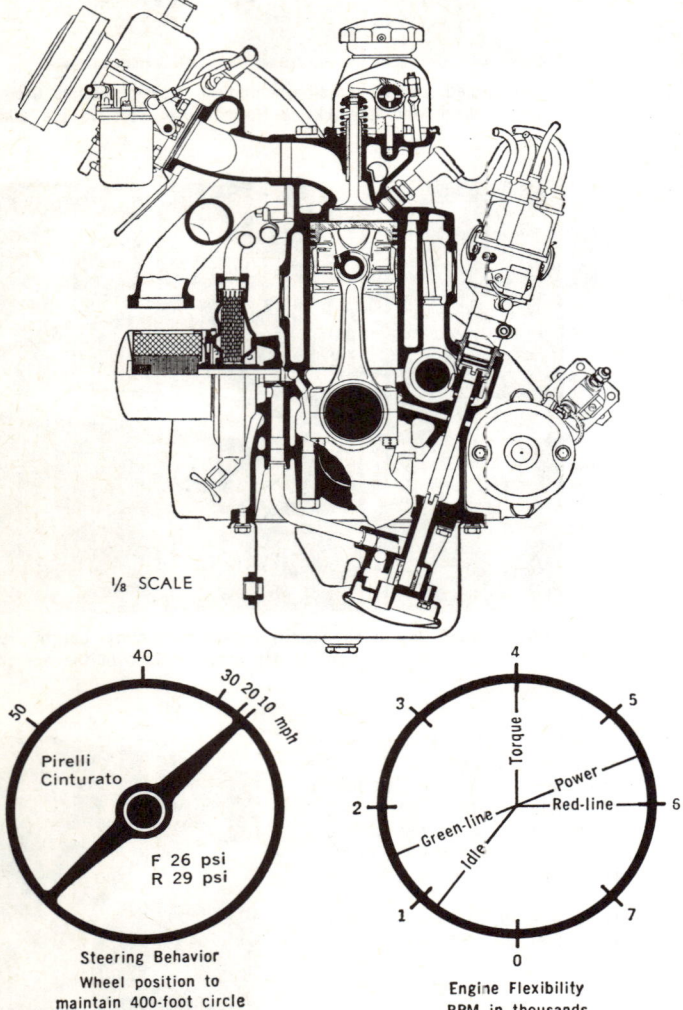

1/8 SCALE

Pirelli
Cinturato

F 26 psi
R 29 psi

Steering Behavior
Wheel position to
maintain 400-foot circle
at speeds indicated.

Engine Flexibility
RPM in thousands

PRICES:

Basic price	$3795 at East Coast Ports of Entry
Options fitted:	
Overdrive	$145
Total price as tested	$3940

OPERATING SCHEDULE:

Fuel recommended	Premium
Mileage	18-28 mpg
Range on 12-gallon tank	215-335 miles
Oil recommended	SAE 10W-30
Crankcase capacity	3½ quarts
Change at intervals of	3000 miles
Number of grease fittings	8 (4 on certain production groups)
Lubrication interval	3000 miles
Most frequent maintenance: Lubricate distributor and hand brake pull rod	—6000 miles

ENGINE:

Displacement	108.6 cu in, 1780 cc
Dimensions	Four cyl, 3.31 in bore, 3.15 in stroke
Valve gear	pushrods, vertical overhead valves in line
Compression ratio	9.5 to one
Power (SAE)	100 bhp @ 5500 rpm
Torque	108 lb-ft @ 4000 rpm
Usable range of engine speeds	1500-6000 rpm
Corrected piston speed @ 5500 rpm	2950 fpm

CHASSIS:

Wheelbase	96.5 in
Tread	51.7 in
Length	173 in
Ground clearance	6.3 in
Suspension: F, ind., coil spring, wishbones, anti-roll bar; R, rigid axle, coil spring, trailing radius arms and Panhard rod.	
Turns, lock to lock	3 2/3
Turning circle diameter between curbs	31 ft.
Tire and rim size	165 x 380 (5.90 x 15), 4½J x 15
Pressures recommended	F 26, R 29 psi
Brakes: type, swept area	F 10 7/8 in disc, R 9 in drum; 350 sq in
Curb weight (full tank)	2444 lbs
Percentage on driving wheels	46%

DRIVE TRAIN:

Gear	Synchro?	Ratio	Step	Overall	Mph per 1000 rpm
Rev	No	3.25	—	14.80	— 5.1
1st	Yes	3.13		14.25	5.2
			57%		
2nd	Yes	1.99		9.08	8.2
			46%		
3rd	Yes	1.36		6.20	12.1
			36%		
4th	Yes	1.00		4.56	16.4
			32%		
4th OD	Auto	0.76		3.45	21.7

Final Drive Ratios: 4.1 to one standard; 4.56 with overdrive.

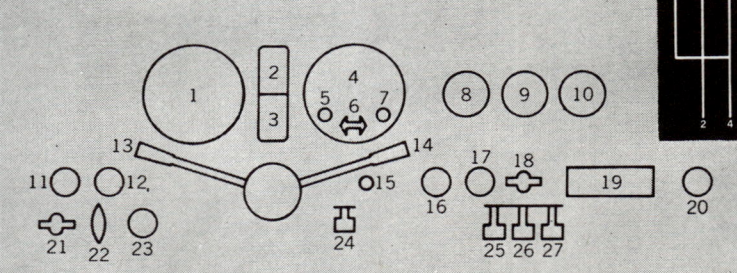

1 Tachometer
2 Water temperature
3 Oil temperature
4 Speedometer
5 Generator light
6 Turn signal light
7 High beam light
8 Fuel gauge
9 Oil pressure
10 Clock
11 Windshield wiper (pull) and washer (turn)
12 Headlight switch
13 Turn signal lever and headlight flasher
14 Highway horn lever
15 Overdrive indicator light
16 Ignition/starter switch
17 Heater fan switch
18 Overdrive switch
19 Ashtray
20 Cigarette lighter
21 Interior lighting switch
22 Choke
23 Fresh air vent
24 Odometer reset
25 Heater air
26 Defroster air
27 Temperature control

ROAD RESEARCH REPORT: VOLVO P 1800

CONTINUED FROM PAGE 22

and suspension gives the driver a distinct feeling of being able to cope with almost any situation. The power is there too, if it is used properly, but don't plan on trying broadsides or breaking the rear end loose. The P 1800 has definite understeer in all corners from "just rolling" types through those on the ragged edge, and the rear end stays put. In a sweeper, once the front end breaks loose — although, admittedly, this happens at very high speeds, much higher than anyone should ever encounter on the highway — it doesn't seem to matter where the front wheels are pointed. Attempting high speed in very tight corners, rather than finding the rear end breaking away, the inside tire will lift and, of course, spin. With no power reaching the wheel still in contact with the pavement, the car slows down. Throughout the rest of the cornering spectrum, the P 1800 is a pure delight.

The steering, which has a slightly heavy feel at parking speeds, becomes light and precise as speed increases and the self-centering action promotes driver ease. The P 1800 is a very easy car to drive; the panoramic vision and the four-square feeling of the wheels enable the drive to place it accurately in a corner. Feathering the throttle slightly brings it through swiftly, surely and controllably. It's a fast way to travel and the overdrive keeps revs respectively low. While top speed is about 105 mph, the car's not meant for all-out velocity but is right at home at any speed below the century mark and will stay there for hours.

EXCELLENT CONSTRUCTION

One tester commented the P 1800 is "the best car the Jensen brothers ever made." Admittedly partial toward German automobiles, he said it was "too bad" the German firm of Karmann did not undertake body fabrication for the new coupes. More objective minds prevailed and it was agreed there was little — very little — to criticize about the way the P 1800 was built. The few things that were noticed should be corrected under quality control or, perhaps, changed production specifications. We found two small spots on the edge of the molding where the chrome was thin. The rest was flawless and the paint was among the best we've seen, completely free from orange peel or thin spots, just an even bright red. Body panels were ripple-free and the fit was perfect. Even in the engine compartment the welds were neat and clean and paint over primer covered all the visible (and, we are assured, invisible) metal. Underneath it all, heavy undercoating helps blanket road noises.

The hood was undercoated with fiberglass, covered by a smooth plastic sheeting. Rubber matting helped deaden trunk noises, but it could have been and apparently has been made better. The trunk-mounted spare has a plastic cover to keep luggage clean. Drain tubes are built into the trunk rim and the cowl vent, but we found that some rain leaked in through both areas. In addition, there was slight leakage around the leading edge of the driver's door.

The interior workmanship was as good as any contemporary car. Some testers felt the plastic cloth seats could have been finished a little neater and some felt a firmer lateral edge would have been desirable. The wear surfaces on the front floor are rubber-covered for cleaning ease and durability, but attractive carpeting is used on the drive-shaft tunnel and rear seat floor. There is no glove compartment, though two deep wells on the cowl will hold several pairs of gloves plus lots of other small items.

DETAILED DIAL DEPARTMENT

The instrument panel is quite attractive, but caused some comments. There was not 100 percent approval of the styling of the dial faces. To some they appeared to have what has unfortunately come to be known as an American look (Studebaker Hawk excepted). They are lavishly styled but not altogether functional for split-second reading. They have deep shields, but still shine on the sharply raked windshield at night. Fortunately they are still sufficiently legible when the rheostat switch is dimmed. They are not fully marked, chrome bumps serving instead of figures for some numbers. The oil pressure gauge in the center of the dashboard is difficult to read. The thermometer-like water temperature gauge, though mounted right in front of the driver is hard to read at night since its blue indicator doesn't show up. The oil temp unit below it is fine with its yellow indicator.

There were other things that didn't quite sit right with us, although we might stress that we did like the car very much and these comments are as much personal opinion as much as they are, perhaps, caviling. These included the placement of the wiper switch next to the headlight switch. Once in the drizzling dusk we were plunged into darkness when we pressed the wrong knob. It was interesting, though, to find that the wipers are Autolite units made in the United States. They worked well with a thorough sweep and the washer operated by turning the knob to the right. It was a German SWF washer with a small centrifugal pump that shot a steady stream.

The overdrive toggle was not particularly convenient to the steering wheel rim. If we were asked to redesign the dashboard layout, here's what we'd do: locate the overdrive toggle in the position of the heater switch, then the heater switch could go next to the wiper switch while the light switch could go to the right of the overdrive. The overdrive control could also be mounted on the steering column in place of the loud-horn lever. We weren't able to discern a significant difference in volume between this and the regular button.

SPACIOUS SURROUNDINGS

Items on the plus side were numerous but they seemed so natural they are easy to overlook. There was more than enough legroom for both driver and passenger, although Reutter-type reclining seats might be a nice option. The solid foot rest for the driver's left leg is a welcome addition and the shift lever falls easily to hand. The ash tray is big and handy and the standard-equipment shoulder harness/seat belt is a worthwhile addition, although the top fixing point might have been a bit higher, as on the sedans, to minimize the chances of the wearer slipping out of it.

A large opening behind the rear seat, resembling the one on the Corvair Monza, will take several small parcels. The front seats are adjustable over a limited range for rake and the jump seats in the rear will accommodate two children. An adult will fit there transversely but headroom is lacking. The heater and defroster should handle their tasks ably, based on the brief use we gave them. Ventilation is good, although some heat radiates from the transmission.

UNITED NATIONS OF COMPONENTS

With the P 1800, Volvo continues its policy of "hands across the sea" when it comes to buying components. In addition to the fact that the prototype was built in Italy and that present cars are put together by Jensen Motors in Scotland, using a shell made by Pressed Steel, Ltd., there are numerous other non-Swedish components. We mentioned that Italian Pirelli Cinturato tires are standard. All the instruments are English, by Smiths. The battery is from Lucas who also provides most of the electrical circuitry. The carburetors are by SU, the overdrive by Laycock de Normanville and the brakes by Girling. The steering gear is German, made by ZF, the windshield washer is by SWF, while the ignition and spark plugs are Bosch. The fuel pump and air cleaners are apparently American (or made in England under license) AC units while the wiper motor is Autolite. Volvo's own (and very fine) transmission, rear end and of course engine are used. About the only other item immediately recognizable as being Swedish is the shoulder harness and seat belt.

This buying from everywhere doesn't indicate a scatterbrained purchasing agent, but reflects sharp corporate policy designed and practiced to give Volvo and its customers the best components for the job at the lowest unit cost. The English business magazine, THE ECONOMIST, commented, "Being one of Volvo's 700 or so suppliers does not buy a ticket to la dolce vita; it is a painful, humiliating, shocking, disciplinary but, in the end, no doubt healthy experience." Actually Volvo has little choice but to buy its parts abroad, the proprietary industry in Sweden being next to nonexistent. Yet since it has a free field in which to roam, it can be ruthless in demanding quality and competitive prices.

PRICE IS RIGHT TOO

Proof of the success of this policy is the fact that when the P 1800 was first revealed, the price was proposed to be "under $3800." Now that it's actually possible to buy one, that's the price you pay. Can you think of many other cars that have actually come in at their projected prices, with all normally "optional" equipment?

From our perspective the P 1800 seems to have all the makings of a winner. From its attractive egg-crate grille to its kicked-up rear fenders, it looks trim and fast, promising — and delivering — performance. Its first-time drivers will be confident and at ease and advanced types won't be disappointed. In a nutshell, it's yare. At its listed price, it has no real competition; it's low enough to lure buyers of both less expensive machines and ones that cost more. And if they ever make a roadster — wow! —C/D

Slightly finny tailend adds to the attractive lines of Volvo. Aerodynamic shape is very good.

VOLVO'S HOT-BLOODED

Handsome, superbly equipped and loaded for go, Volvo's P1800 is just the machine for the person who wants sports car performance with luxury car comfort.

By PETER HALL

SWEDEN, as far as most Australians are concerned, conjures up thoughts of tall, shapely, silver-blondes, a bitterly cold climate and the highest suicide rate in the world.

But really, as keen readers of this magazine will know, there is a lot more to Sweden than these not necessarily co-related snippets of information which pop up from time to time in the daily press.

This part of Scandinavia, for example, is one of the most car-conscious areas in the world and a country which is among the best-equipped as far as the average motorist is concerned with suberb roads, tough laws, high average speeds and a frighteningly high road toll.

During the past few months, Australians have become increasingly aware, too, that Sweden is a very formidable producer of motor vehicles, making considerably more cars per year than Australia.

Unusual styling of the P1800 gives it a very high waistline but overall effect is very pleasing to the eye.

Dashboard is very well instrumented. Note dished steering wheel and stubby gearchange lever.

P1800

When Regent Motors in Melbourne and Antill Motors in Sydney took over the Volvo agencies late in 1961, quite a few enthusiasts took a second look at Sweden. For the Volvo is the best known and biggest selling car made in Scandinavia.

The 122S sedan was the first model to arrive in this country and the limited initial shipment was snapped up by keen buyers despite its solid price and the fact that it was being replaced overseas by a modified version. Superb finish and workmanship and first class performance found enough people willing to shell out with nearly £1800.

Sometime in 1962, Sweden will toss out an even more exciting challenge to an even more fastidious corner of Australia's car market.

The low, glamorous P1800 sports coupe will be with us, and it is sure to attract much admiration and a buyer or two, despite a price tag that (unfixed at the time of writing) will probably nudge the £2700 mark.

When the P1800 was released late 1960 in Europe, it was built only as a left hand drive vehicle. But with commendable consideration for motoring writers in many parts of the world, the Volvo company took great pains to make its new glamorous, top-of-the-line car available to as many road testers as possible.

One of the early production models was registered in Sweden and handed out to European motoring writers for comprehensive road tests. Then it was sent to Britain for the same treatment.

Then, despite the obviously high cost of such a move and the comparatively low volume of sales the company, even in its wildest dreams, could hope to get in this country, it was shipped all the way to Australia for its agents to study and such as I to test.

It was only here for a few short weeks but during that time and despite the disadvantages flowing from the fact of it being a left-hand drive model, I was able to give it a thorough two-day test.

When it passed into my hands, it had done more

There is nothing very unusual about the Volvo's engine. It has twin carburettors, pushrod overhead valves.

than 14,000 miles, including a very hard, but short stint in Sydney and countless "feel-the-acceleration" demonstration drives by starry eyed salesmen for equally starry-eyed potential customers.

Since most of the 14,000 miles had been flat-out testing and the car had received very little servicing in between tests, it was not surprising that it seemed to have lost a little tune.

Even so, it returned a performance that would turn most other cars on Australian roads green with envy.

Fastest speed in overdrive top was 102.3 mph. I have little doubt that with a good tuneup, the P1800 would have gone very close to nudging the 110 mph top speed claimed by the factory. At that speed in overdrive, the engine would have been revving at considerably less than 5000 rpm — a sure indication that the Volvo was built to last, not merely to perform.

There was several signs of its built-in durability. There was nothing fussy or skimped about the solid 1780-cc four-cylinder engine with its oversquare

VOLVO'S HOT-BLOODED P1800

dimensions, big SU carburettors and honest 100 bhp developed at the moderately low point of 5500 rpm.

Everything about the car itself was solid, in the tradition of the more sedate Volvo sedans — and if there is one feature that stands out about them, it is their massive solidity.

Creature comforts had not been overlooked, either. All the accepted conveniences of modern motoring were there, including many that are usually specified as "optional extras."

The heating and demisting system was one of the best in the business, the windscreen wipers were two-speed electric —and they wiped clean the major portion of the broad windscreen — and other equipment included powerful windscreen washers, cigarette lighter and there were built in safety belts, which were elaborate lap and shoulder belts combined, with three attachments each.

The leather covered, thickly padded bucket seats were superbly comfortable and fully adjustable for rake and distance from the dash. Accommodation in the back was actually luxurious, but space was limited for any but one tiny adult or two reasonably patient children.

The floors were covered in thick carpet and thick, handsome safety padding lines the dashboard and window sills, the twin sun visors were also heavily padded.

The gear change lever was mounted high on the transmission tunnel, slightly forward of and a few inches away from the steering wheel rim. The box itself was one of the coupe's greatest delights.

Synchromesh was provided on all four gears and the movement itself was quite positive. In sports car fashion, the change was on the heavy side, but it did not take long to get the unaccustomed right arm muscles working in tune with the lever. The synchro itself was one of the best I've tried — the most dundering idiot of all would be hard pressed to

Volvo passengers lack nothing, the seats recline and there is a highly efficient heater. Diagonal safety harness is standard.

clash this Volvo's gears. And it seemed equally at home when you got tired of stabbing away with your right foot, and swapped cogs without benefit of clutch.

The electric overdrive, operating on top gear only, was controlled by a long, slender lever jutting from the lower dash panel. It was within easy finger reach of the steering wheel rim, and worked instantaneously. There seemed to be some transmission growl in the test car when overdrive was operating, probably due to the fantastically hard life the car had led.

Handling was everything one would expect from the car's low and agile appearance.

Coil sprung all round with a live axle at the back, the Volvo rode with a pleasant feeling of soft luxury on most surfaces at moderate speed. Not too soft, but gentle enough to please the well-heeled buyer who is more concerned with its individuality and what it does to his ego and popularity than with its ability to behave like a thoroughbred.

But thoroughbred it is. On corners it heels over only slightly, and all wheels stay firmly on the ground at the most exhilarating speeds. The Volvo will oversteer, but only slightly when pushed to its limit. Then, only the direct cam and roller steering comes into its own and the car flicks back onto course without the trace of a blush.

The steering wheel itself is a neat, very Swedish affair with two white aluminium spokes, holed like a gigantic meccano strip, and thick black rim.

Behind the top half of the wheel is a clear, simple but very attractive instrument panel which contains just about every dial and control you could want.

The main dials, in front of the driver and effectively binnacled to prevent windscreen glare are a rev counter calibrated to 7000 rpm and a speedometer of equal diameter. On the test vehicle, the speedo was unfortunately marked in kilometres, 200 of them. Re-calibrating the dial for mph, checking its accuracy and re-calibrating again . . . and so on, until we could get absolutely accurate reading for acceleration runs was one of the most laborious jobs connected with a road test I have ever done.

Potential Australian buyers will be pleased to know that the models on sale here will not only be fitted with right hand drive, but will also have more familiar speedometers.

Between the two big dials were two vertical gauges with thermometer-type readings of water and oil temperatures. In addition, there were three small dials spread neatly across the dashboard containing fuel gauge, oil pressure gauge and ammeter. A trip meter was fitted to the speedo, of course, as well as the customary total mileage meter.

To compensate for the complete lack of a glove box and the lack of space for a parcel's tray, a deep and practical oddments' box was fitted under the dash on each side of the front compartment. Map pockets were also fitted in the doors.

For all its performance, the Volvo coupe was much more a fast and comfortable touring car than a true sports sedan. Not that the handling was not in sports' class . . . it was.

But the designers clearly had as much eye on the comfort of its potential owners, as they did on his heart beat when he sank his foot into the floor.

That is clear from the Volvo's comparatively high weight for its size and by the opulence of its fittings and finish.

It is at is very best on fast highway cruises, when any speed between 50 and 100 mph is its happy cruising gait, where its nearly impeccable handling and first class brakes (power boosted discs at front, drums at rear) are meant to be used.

Its clean, low lines should win a lot of admirers, as should the practical way the relatively small (by world standards) Volvo company have gone about producing its graceful masterpiece.

Volvo builds the engine and gearbox, gets Germany to provide the electricals, America the back axle, Italy the tyres and Britain the body and assembly work — at the Jensen car factory.

The result is an international coupe of great strength and beauty and first class performance.   #

wheels ROAD TEST

TECHNICAL DETAILS
OF THE
VOLVO P1800

P.1800

PERFORMANCE

TOP SPEED:

Two-way average	102 mph
Fastest one-way	102.3 mph

ACCELERATION:

(test limit 6000 rpm)
Through gears:

0 to 30	4.5 sec
0 to 40	5.8 sec
0 to 50	8.55 sec
0 to 60	12.4 sec
0 to 70	16.5 sec

MAXIMUM SPEED IN GEARS:

I	30 mph
II	50 mph
III	75 mph
IV	100 mph

BRAKING:

No fade after 10 stops.

FUEL CONSUMPTION:

156 miles, including testing	25.2 mpg

PRICE:

Not available.

WEIGHT:

kerb	22 cwt

TEST CAR FROM:

Regent Motors, Sturt St, South Melbourne.

SPECIFICATIONS

ENGINE:

Cylinders	four-cylinder, water cooled.
Valves	pushrod, overhead.
Capacity	1780 cc.
Bore and stroke	84.14 by 80 mm.
Compression ratio	9.5 to 1.
Carburettors	twin SU.
Developed bhp	100 at 5500 rpm.

CHASSIS:

Wheelbase	8 ft 0½ in.
Track, front and rear	4 ft 3¾ in

SUSPENSION:

Front	independent by coil springs.
Rear	coil springs, solid axle.
Shock absorbers	telescopic.

BRAKES:

Type	disc front, drum rear

STEERING:

lock	31ft 2in

TRANSMISSION:

Type	four speed, synchro on all forward speeds, overdrive on top.

GEAR RATIOS:

I	3.13 to 1
II	1.99 to 1
III	1.36 to 1
IV	1.00 to 1
Overdrive	0.76 to 1
Rear axle	4.56 to 1

GENERAL:

Overall length	14 ft 8¼ in
Width	5 ft 7 in

Motor

MAKE: *Volvo.* **TYPE:** *P 1800 Coupé (with overdrive).*
MAKERS: *AB Volvo, Göteborg, Sweden.*
CONCESSIONNAIRES: *Volvo Concessionaires Ltd., 28 Albemarle Street, London, W.1.*

ROAD TEST • No. 29/62

DATA

CONDITIONS: *Weather : Warm and dry with 5 m.p.h. breeze. (Temperature 63°-66° F., Barometer 29.65 in. Hg.) Surface : Dry concrete and tarred macadam. Fuel : Super-premium grade pump petrol (approx. 101 Octane Rating by Research Method).*

INSTRUMENTS
Speedometer at 30 m.p.h.	3% fast
Speedometer at 60 m.p.h.	4% fast
Speedometer at 90 m.p.h.	6% fast
Distance Recorder	accurate

WEIGHT
Kerb weight (unladen, but with oil, coolant and fuel for approximately 50 miles)	21¾ cwt.
Front/rear distribution of kerb weight	55/45
Weight laden as tested	25½ cwt.

MAXIMUM SPEEDS (in overdrive)
Flying Mile
Mean of six opposite runs	105.5 m.p.h.
Best one-way time equals	107.1 m.p.h.

"Maximile" Speed. (Timed quarter mile after one mile accelerating from rest.)
Mean of opposite runs	97.6 m.p.h.
Best one-way time equals	98.9 m.p.h.

Speed in gears (at 6,000 r.p.m.)
Max. speed in 4th gear	93 m.p.h.
Max. speed in 3rd gear	68 m.p.h.
Max. speed in 2nd gear	47 m.p.h.
Max. speed in 1st gear	29 m.p.h.

FUEL CONSUMPTION
(Overdrive top gear)
38.0 m.p.g.	at constant 30 m.p.h. on level
38.0 m.p.g.	at constant 40 m.p.h. on level
37.0 m.p.g.	at constant 50 m.p.h. on level
36.0 m.p.g.	at constant 60 m.p.h. on level
34.0 m.p.g.	at constant 70 m.p.h. on level
30.5 m.p.g.	at constant 80 m.p.h. on level
26.0 m.p.g.	at constant 90 m.p.h. on level
21.5 m.p.g.	at constant 100 m.p.h. on level

(Direct 4th gear)
34.0 m.p.g.	at constant 30 m.p.h. on level
34.5 m.p.g.	at constant 40 m.p.h. on level
34.5 m.p.g.	at constant 50 m.p.h. on level

Overall Fuel Consumption for 1,688 miles, 69.7 gallons, equals 24.2 m.p.g. (11.7 litres/100 km.)

Touring Fuel Consumption (m.p.g. at steady speed midway between 30 m.p.h. and maximum, less 5% allowance for acceleration) 32.8 m.p.g.
Fuel tank capacity (maker's figure) .. 10 gallons

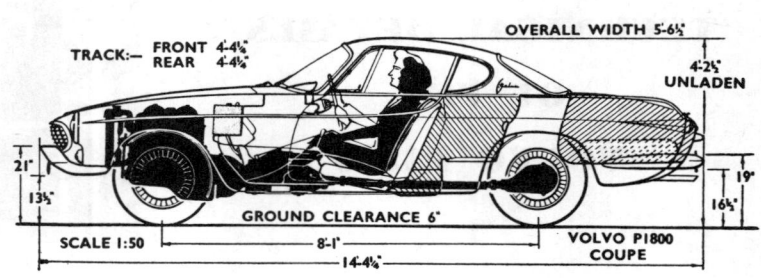

BRAKES from 30 m.p.h.
1.00 g retardation (equivalent to 30 ft. stopping distance) with 90 lb. pedal pressure.
0.97 g retardation (equivalent to 31 ft. stopping distance) with 75 lb. pedal pressure.
0.77 g retardation (equivalent to 39 ft. stopping distance) with 50 lb. pedal pressure.
0.38 g retardation (equivalent to 79 ft. stopping distance) with 25 lb. pedal pressure.

HILL CLIMBING at sustained steady speeds
Max. gradient on overdrive top gear ..	1 in 12.4	(Tapley 180 lb./ton)
Max. gradient on direct 4th gear ..	1 in 8.1	(Tapley 275 lb./ton)
Max. gradient on 3rd gear	1 in 5.8	(Tapley 380 lb./ton)
Max. gradient on 2nd gear	1 in 4.1	(Tapley 535 lb./ton)

ACCELERATION TIMES from standstill
0-30 m.p.h.	4.3 sec.
0-40 m.p.h.	7.0 sec.
0-50 m.p.h.	10.1 sec.
0-60 m.p.h.	13.8 sec.
0-70 m.p.h.	18.6 sec.
0-80 m.p.h.	24.8 sec.
0-90 m.p.h.	34.5 sec.
0-100 m.p.h.	53.2 sec.
Standing quarter mile	19.2 sec.

ACCELERATION TIMES on upper ratios
	Overdrive Top gear	Direct 4th gear	3rd gear
10-30 m.p.h.	—	8.3 sec.	6.1 sec.
20-40 m.p.h.	12.0 sec.	8.4 sec.	6.0 sec.
30-50 m.p.h.	12.4 sec.	8.3 sec.	6.0 sec.
40-60 m.p.h.	14.1 sec.	9.0 sec.	6.8 sec.
50-70 m.p.h.	15.4 sec.	10.2 sec.	—
60-80 m.p.h.	15.8 sec.	11.5 sec.	—
70-90 m.p.h.	19.8 sec.	15.9 sec.	—
80-100 m.p.h.	31.4 sec.	—	—

STEERING
Turning circle between kerbs :
Left	30 ft.
Right	31¼ ft.
Turns of steering wheel from lock to lock	3¼

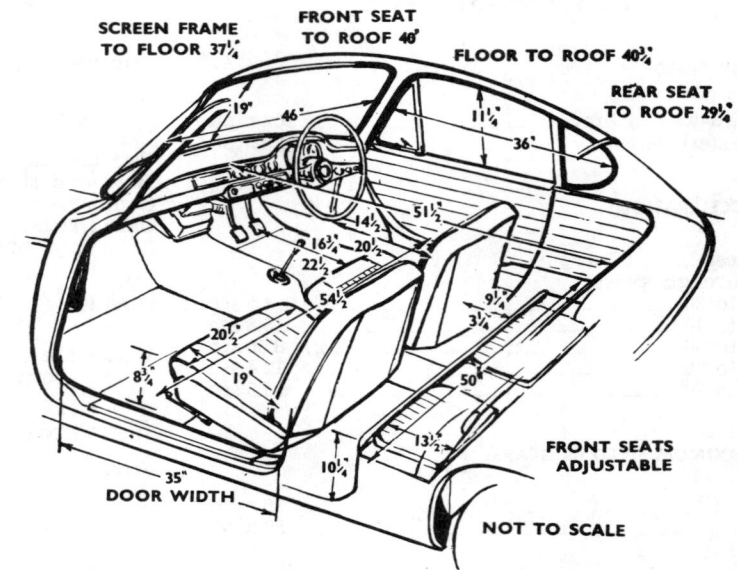

Specification

Engine
Cylinders	4
Bore	84.14 mm.
Stroke	80 mm.
Cubic capacity	1,780 c.c.
Piston area	34.4 sq. in.
Valves	o.h.v. (pushrods)
Compression ratio	9.5/1
Carburetter .. Two S.U. inclined type HS6
Fuel pump	AC mechanical
Ignition timing control	Centrifugal
Oil filter .. Full-flow (combined with oil-water heat exchanger)
Maximum power (gross)	100 b.h.p.
at	5,500 r.p.m.
Piston speed at maximum b.h.p.	2,885 ft./min.

Transmission
Clutch .. .. Borg & Beck 8½ in. s.d.p.
Top gear (s/m) .. ↓4.56 (Overdrive, 3.46)
3rd gear (s/m)	6.20
2nd gear (s/m)	9.07
1st gear (s/m)	14.26
Reverse	14.80
Overdrive Laycock-de Normanville, 0.76 ratio

Propeller shaft	Divided open
Final drive	9/41 Hypoid bevel
Top gear m.p.h. at 1,000 r.p.m.	15.5
	(Overdrive, 20.4)
Top gear m.p.h. at 1,000 ft./min. piston speed	29.6 (Overdrive, 39.0)

Chassis
Brakes .. Girling hydraulic, disc front and drum rear, with vacuum servo
Brake dimensions Front discs 10.86 in. dia., rear drums 9 in. dia. × 2 in. wide
Friction areas 94 sq. in. of lining area working on 345 sq. in. rubbed area of discs and drums
Suspension
Front Independent by coil springs, wishbones and anti-roll torsion bar
Rear Rigid axle located by pairs of trailing radius arms and Panhard rod, with coil springs
Shock absorbers Delco freon-filled telescopic
Steering gear ZF-built Gemmer cam and roller
Tyres .. Pirelli Cintura braced-tread, 165-15

VOLVO P1800 with overdrive

A 2/4-seater of Swedish design, built in Britain

SWEDEN is a spacious, thinly-populated country where the summer can be very hot and winters are cold, roads are often fast but sometimes rough, and the standard of living is very high. The Swedish-designed Volvo P1800 should be a magnificently appropriate car for its native land, where comfortable and effortless fast cruising over good or not-very-good surfaces matters more than vivid acceleration. A great many people outside Sweden will also be attracted by this sturdy and comfortable 1.8-litre fixed-head coupe, which can exceed 105 m.p.h. yet is capable of a touring fuel consumption better than 30 m.p.g.

Ancient and modern

STRIKINGLY individual in appearance and very distinctively Swedish, the P1800 coupé gives an unexpectedly old-fashioned impression when one first sits in the driving seat. It has a raked steering column ending in an almost vertical wheel, high body sides, a high scuttle and bonnet line, a windscreen raked back so that the padded sun visors are close to the driver's forehead, and rather limited headroom. If most of these features recall the sports saloons of 25 years ago, they are combined with a modern facia, slim windscreen pillars which do not obstruct vision, inbuilt safety harness, generous elbow room, a fresh air heating system, and all-synchromesh gearing. Tastes vary, but at least one member of our staff described this car's blend of old and new characteristics as "superb".

Primarily a two-seater, this car can carry one or two extra people for short distances on removable cushions in what will more frequently be treated as an interior luggage compartment. Legroom in the back can be made tolerable without the driver having to sit very much further forward than he would otherwise choose, but the stooping position enforced by limited headroom will discourage an adult from travelling very far in the back seat; one person sitting sideways is no better off in this respect than two facing forwards. Apart from the space inside the car, there is quite a lot of lockable accommodation for luggage in the boot, although the need to lower cases into it from above, and the

presence of a covered spare wheel flat on the luggage floor are minor disadvantages of the chosen layout.

With a screw adjustment for backrest rake, the driving seat is very comfortable and its range of movement suffices for tall people. Inclined runners raise the seat as it is adjusted forwards, and vice versa. Some passengers complain that the backrest is not curved to resist cornering forces, but presumably the designers consider that their safety harness (with three-point anchorage) should always be worn, and adjusted tightly enough to minimize this criticism.

Big doors make this as easy to enter as any low-built car. The facia does not provide any parcel shelf or glove box, but two deep compartments best described as pockets are set on the scuttle sides, and a parcel space behind the centre of the rear "seat" can be reached from the front seats. The hinged ventilation panels on

In Brief

Price (including overdrive as tested) £1,335 plus purchase tax £501 12s. 9d. equals £1,836 12s. 9d.	
Capacity	1,780 c.c.
Unladen kerb weight	21¾ cwt.
Acceleration:	
20-40 m.p.h. in direct 4th gear	8.4 sec.
0-50 m.p.h. through gears	10.1 sec.
Maximum direct 4th gear gradient.. ..	1 in 8.1
Maximum speed	105.5 m.p.h.
"Maximile" speed	97.6 m.p.h.
Touring fuel consumption	32.8 m.p.g.
Gearing: 15.5 m.p.h. in 4th gear at 1,000 r.p.m. (overdrive 20.4 m.p.h.).	

The Volvo looks low and rakish, with high sills which do not suit short drivers. Curved stiffening ribs in the panelling have been turned to decorative effect.

Right: The spare wheel takes up luggage space in the well-shaped boot. Cases must be lowered from above.

Below: The four-cylinder engine has five main bearings, push-rod overhead valves and twin S.U. carburetters. It is easy to get at and the bonnet is padded for quietness.

the front windows were exceptionally stiff to open; cold-air intakes on each side of the body can be used to combat a certain amount of engine warmth which is noticed in summer, and the interior heater is readily controllable. Amongst a very full set of instruments (including an r.p.m. indicator and an oil thermo-meter) the clock, fuel gauge and oil pressure gauge are decorative rather than legible. The controls are well laid out, easy to reach, and well distinguished. The overdrive switch is close to the steering wheel rim, the direction indicator switch is arranged to flash the headlamps when squeezed towards the wheel, and a matching control arm on the opposite side of the wheel serves as an alternative to the conventional horn button which is also fitted.

Go and stop

VOLVO performance has sometimes been referred to as a triumph of power over weight, and this model is in character with its roomier, slower predecessors. The engine is an orthodox 1.8-litre "four" with in-line overhead valves operated by push-rods and rockers, but with two S.U. carburetters and a five-bearing crankshaft it is astonishingly smooth and fussless at its 6,000 r.p.m. speed limit. A timed maximum of just over 105 m.p.h. shows that a catalogue claim to 100 b.h.p. (gross) is by no means an exaggeration.

Volvo believe, however, that their niche in the world's motor industry is as builders of exceptionally rugged, durable cars, and this 1.8-litre two-seater weighs 21¾ cwt. In the company of ordinary saloon cars it shows brisk performance, but for a Grand Tourer which can be cruised at 90 m.p.h. its acceleration (rest to 50 m.p.h. in 10.1 sec. and to 90 m.p.h. in 34.5 sec.) is not spectacular. It is, in fact, a car for the long, fast journeys that are commonplace in Sweden, rather than for accelerating through

VOLVO P1800

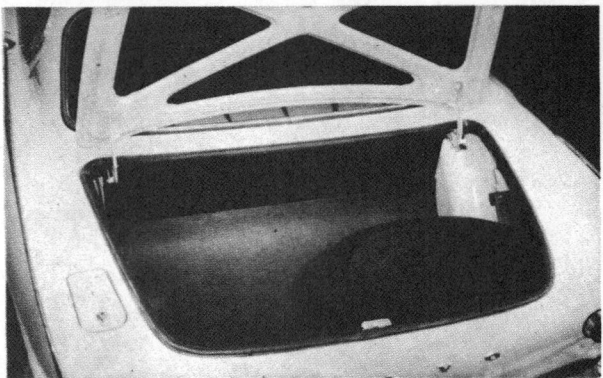

every slight gap which may occur amidst the suburban traffic of congested England.

Good performance depends upon right use of the gears, and this car's transmission delights hard drivers. The engine is docile, and using 100-octane petrol to overcome some low-speed pinking we were easily able to record quite reasonable top gear acceleration times from only 10 m.p.h., but it is better to let the engine rev. Upward changes at 3,500 r.p.m. give quiet and lively progress around town, whilst 5,500 r.p.m. (the suggested limit for regular use, with 500 r.p.m. in reserve for special occasions) is effortless on the open road. Whereas at very low speeds the synchromesh (provided on all four gears) can be somewhat obstructive, in faster driving the sturdy central gear lever can be slammed from notch to notch without ever a hint of protest. The spring loading of the lever towards the right-hand side of its gate is unnecessarily strong and some engine vibration is felt through the lever. The gears are quiet, and the clutch positive but not fierce.

Cars delivered in Britain are all equipped with the Laycock-de Normanville overdrive and an appropriate rear axle ratio; 5,500 r.p.m. gives about 82 m.p.h. in the direct 4th gear, and overdrive acts as a fairly high but regularly usable top ratio in which 105 m.p.h. represents about 5,300 r.p.m.

Stopping power in ample measure to suit the performance comes from servo-assisted Girling brakes with discs at the front and drums at the rear. A very light touch on the pedal brings the servo into action, promptly and even fiercely, so that in contrast with some disc-braked cars this model can be checked instantly from town speeds as well as having ample energy-dissipating capacity available for the fast driver. The pull-up handbrake, located to the driver's right, works on the rear drums and can hold the car on a 1 in 3½ slope which also represents the limit of 1st gear re-starting ability; should it be necessary to back up a steep hill, the clutch must be used gently or rear axle judder will occur.

Guiding and riding

SETTING out to produce a car midway in character between a sports two-seater and a family saloon, the Volvo engineers have boldly attempted to combine the handling characteristics of one with the riding qualities of the other; they have attained quite a high standard of success in blending what are sometimes thought to be incompatible characteristics. The weight which restricts acceleration is justified by the impression of complete structural rigidity which this car gives in rough road conditions, as well as by the total absence of tinny, high-frequency noise.

By sports car standards the P1800 is softly sprung. Its four coil springs are well enough damped for sharp bumps to be more evident at low speeds than during fast driving, but really bad surfaces are no worry and motorway travel is very comfortable. There is a certain amount of body roll during quite gentle cornering, so that one does not take sharp turns around town in the "flat" manner of stiffly-sprung traditional sports cars, but this initial angle of roll does not increase much further during harder driving.

In dry weather the Volvo's road holding inspired the utmost confidence, and it seemed possible to corner exceptionally fast with enough but not too much steering feel, and just enough understeer for "on rails" stability not to turn into sluggishness

of response. This seemed equally true on sharp corners and on more open high-speed curves. Showery weather revealed less happy characteristics, rather marked understeer on a wet surface being extremely easily reversed by any use of power, which readily induced wheelspin; an expert might play off these conflicting characteristics to make the P1800 do just what he wanted, but a less expert driver attempting to hurry on a slippery road was apt to become untidy. The rather garish discs which conceal bolt-on steel wheels can have an indirectly bad effect on handling, since they make it difficult to couple an inflator to the tyre valves at any time, and can even creep around to make the valves inaccessible, inviting neglect of tyre pressure adjustment.

Perhaps because of a relatively high roll axis, the P1800 seems very sensitive to changes in road camber, rocking noticeably as it rides down some sorts of secondary road and the steering also responding to camber variations. Most drivers gradually ceased to take much notice of these initially-conspicuous effects, finding that if it was driven with a light touch on the steering wheel the Volvo went accurately where the driver wished. Not particularly high geared, the steering gear (German-made but American in design) feels mechanically precise, and gives turning circles of conveniently small diameter; for parking the steering becomes rather heavy.

More of a marathon runner than a sprinter, the Volvo P1800 is a unique car which seems certain to make a lot of friends. The comfort which it combines with controllable 105-m.p.h. performance, "occasional four" seating within a reasonably compact body, and the parent factory's reputation for building strong, durable cars add up to truly "grand touring" characteristics. Since this Swedish car is assembled in England, using a Scottish body shell and a fair proportion of English and Welsh parts, Britain can justifiably be pleased about its excellence.

Above: **The comfortable front seats have ample fore and aft (and rake) adjustment though the rear seat is strictly "occasional." The unusual door handle/lock protrudes from a built-in arm rest on the door. Excellent seat belts are a standard fitting.**

Impressive looking instruments are more decorative than functional—especially the three smaller ones (fuel, oil pressure and clock). The minor controls are practical, being within finger-tip reach of the vertical steering wheel.

Coachwork and Equipment

Starting handle	None
Battery mounting	Behind engine
Jack	Lazy-tongs type
Jacking points	Four recesses under body sides
Standard tool kit:	Jack, wheel nut spanner, box spanner with tommy bar, adjustable spanner, pliers, screwdriver, Phillips screwdriver.
Exterior lights:	2 headlamps, 2 sidelamps/flashers, 2 stop/tail lamps, 2 rear number plate lamps.
Number of electrical fuses	Three
Direction indicators:	Self-cancelling flashers (combined with stop lights at rear).
Windscreen wipers:	Two-speed twin-blade electrical, self-parking.
Windscreen washers	Electric pump
Sun visors	Two
Instruments:	Speedometer with total and decimal trip distance recorders, r.p.m. indicator, clock, fuel contents gauge, oil pressure gauge, coolant thermometer, oil thermometer.
Warning lights:	Dynamo charge, oil pressure, headlamp main beam, direction indicators, overdrive engaged.
Locks:	
With ignition key ...	Ignition/starter switch
With other key ...	Luggage locker and doors
Glove lockers	2 compartments on sides of scuttle
Map pockets	None
Parcel shelves	Compartment behind rear seat
Ashtrays	One on facia
Cigar lighters	One on facia
Interior lights:	Map reading light under facia, and two lamps in rear quarters with courtesy switches on doors.
Interior heater	Fresh air type, with screen de-misters
Car radio	Extra (Motorola)
Extras available	None special to this car
Upholstery material	Leather
Floor covering	Pile carpet with rubber insets
Exterior colours standardized	Three
Alternative body styles	None

Maintenance

Sump...	6.8 pints S.A.E. 20 or 10W/30 multigrade
Gearbox	3.3 pints, S.A.E. 30 (on cars without overdrive, S.A.E. 80 gear oil)
Rear axle	2.3 pints, S.A.E. 80 hypoid oil
Steering gear lubricant ...	S.A.E. 80 hypoid oil
Cooling system capacity	15 pints (4 drain taps)
Chassis lubrication ...	By grease gun every 3,000 miles to 8 points
Ignition timing ...	18° b.t.d.c. at 1,500 r.p.m.
Contact breaker gap	0.018 in.
Sparking plug type ...	Bosch W.225 T.1
Sparking plug gap	0.030 in.
Valve timing:	
	Inlet opens 32° before t.d.c. and closes 72° after b.d.c.
	Exhaust opens 70° before b.d.c. and closes 32° after t.d.c.
Tappet clearances (hot or cold):	
Inlet and exhaust	0.020 in.
Front wheel toe-in	0 to $\frac{1}{32}$ in.
Camber angle	0° to +$\frac{1}{2}$°
Castor angle	0° to +1°
Steering swivel pin inclination	8°
Tyre pressures:	
Front	26 lb.
Rear	29 lb.
Brake fluid	to S.A.E. Spec. 70.R.3
Battery	12 volt, 57 amp. hr.

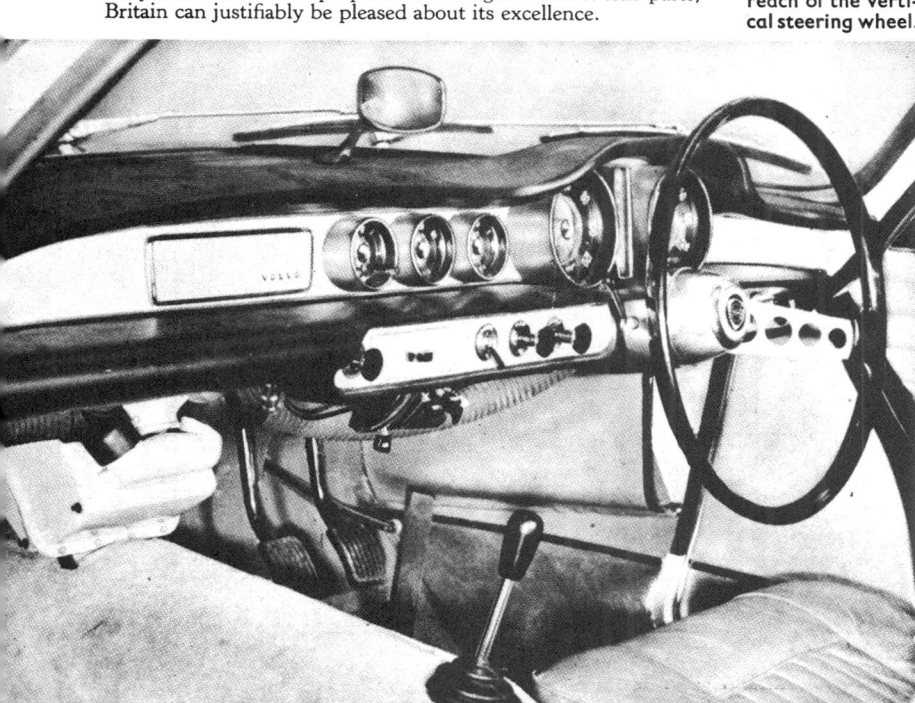

Make · VOLVO   Type · P1800

Manufacturer : AB Volvo, Göteborg, Sweden
Concessionaires : Volvo Concessionaires, Ltd., 28 Albemarle Street, London, W.1.

Test Conditions
Weather ... Dry and sunny with 7-20 m.p.h. wind
Temperature .... 56 deg. F. (13 deg. C.)
Barometer .... 29·9in. Hg.
Dry tarmac and concrete surfaces.

Weight
Kerb weight (with oil, water and half-full fuel tank)
           22 cwt (2,464lb–1,118 kg)
Front-rear distribution, per cent F, 54·2; R, 45·8
Laden as tested ...... 25 cwt (2,800lb–1,270kg)

Turning Circles
Between kerbs .... L, 32ft 4in.; R, 33ft. 5in.
Between walls ...... L, 34ft 5in.; R, 35ft. 6in.
Turns of steering wheel lock to lock .... 3·25

Performance Data
Overdrive top gear m.p.h. per 1,000 r.p.m. ... 21·0
Top gear m.p.h. per 1,000 r.p.m. .... 15·0
Mean piston speed at max. power ... 2,887 ft/min.
Engine revs. at mean max. speed ...... 4,880 r.p.m.
B.h.p. per ton laden 72

FUEL AND OIL CONSUMPTION

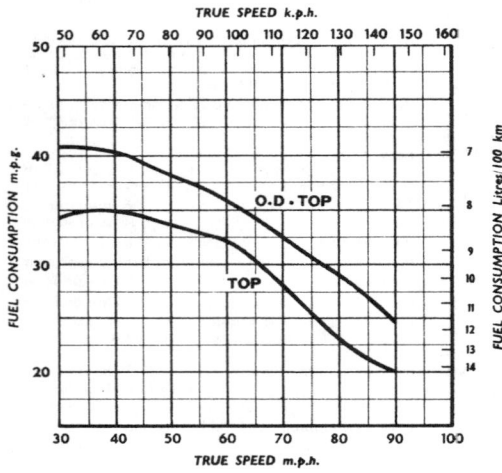

FUEL .... Premium Grade
                    (97 octane RM)
Test Distance .... 1,245 miles
Overall Consumption .... 24·9 m.p.g.
              (11·35 litres/100 km)
Normal Range .... 24–32 m.p.g.
           (11·77-8·83 litres/100 km)
OIL: SAE 30 ... Consumption: 10,000 m.p.g.

HILL CLIMBING AT STEADY SPEEDS

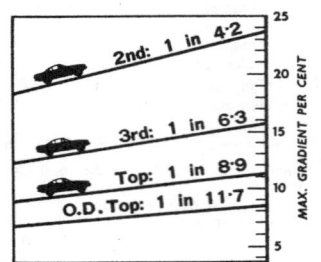

2nd: 1 in 4·2
3rd: 1 in 6·3
Top: 1 in 8·9
O.D. Top: 1 in 11·7

GEAR	O.D.			
PULL	Top	Top	3rd	2nd
(lb per ton)	190	250	350	520
Speed Range				
(m.p.h.)	54–60	48–53	35–45	28–35

MAXIMUM SPEEDS AND ACCELERATION (mean) TIMES

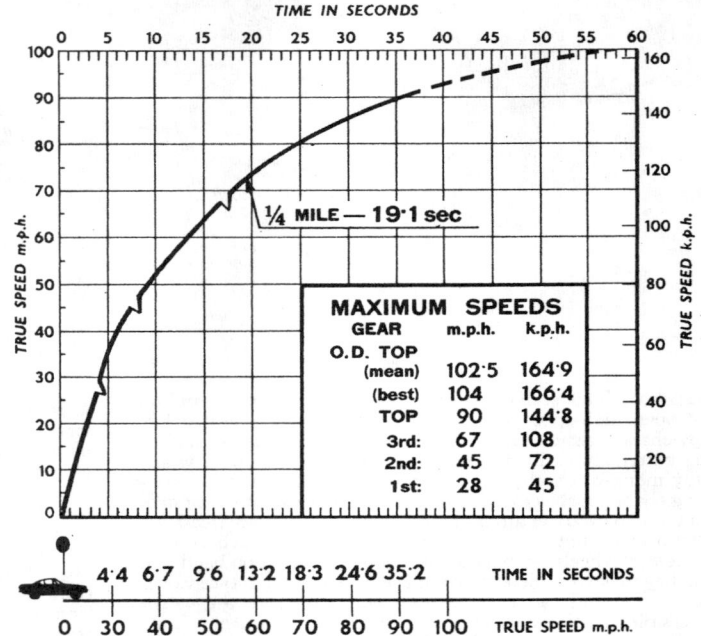

TIME IN SECONDS

¼ MILE — 19·1 sec

MAXIMUM SPEEDS		
GEAR	m.p.h.	k.p.h.
O.D. TOP		
(mean)	102·5	164·9
(best)	104	166·4
TOP	90	144·8
3rd:	67	108
2nd:	45	72
1st:	28	45

									TIME IN SECONDS
	4·4	6·7	9·6	13·2	18·3	24·6	35·2		
0	30	40	50	60	70	80	90	100	TRUE SPEED m.p.h.
	30	41	51	62	73	83·5	95	105	CAR SPEEDOMETER

Speed range and time in seconds

m.p.h.	O.D. Top	Top	3rd	2nd	1st
10—30	—	8·6	6·2	4·5	—
20—40	—	8·4	5·8	4·1	—
30—50	—	8·3	6·1	—	—
40—60	—	8·3	6·7	—	—
50—70	14·8	9·3	—	—	—
60—80	15·2	11·4	—	—	—
70—90	19·6	16·2	—	—	—

BRAKES	Pedal load	Retardation	Equiv. distance
(*from 30 m.p.h.*	25lb	0·35g	86ft
in neutral)	50lb	0·65g	47ft
	75lb	0·90g	33·6ft
	Hand brake	0·33g	92ft

CLUTCH   Pedal load and travel   45lb and 5·5in.

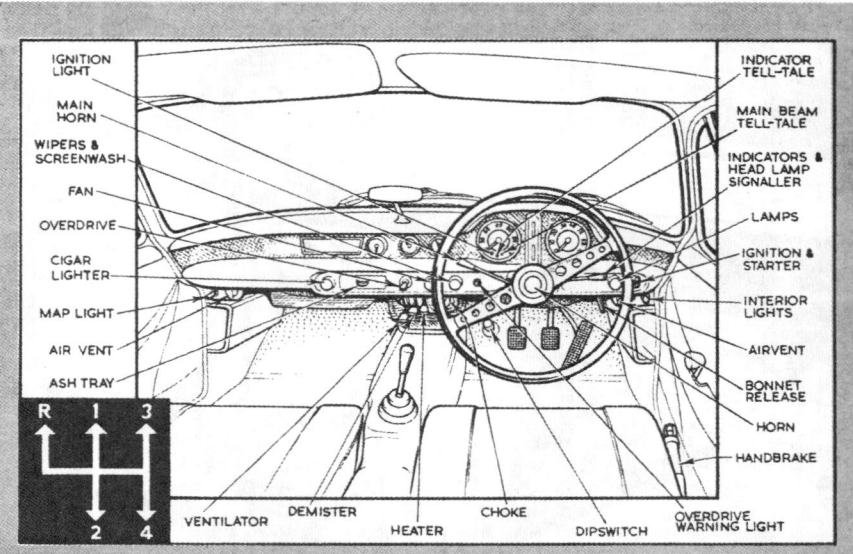

IGNITION LIGHT
MAIN HORN
WIPERS & SCREENWASH
FAN
OVERDRIVE
CIGAR LIGHTER
MAP LIGHT
AIR VENT
ASH TRAY

INDICATOR TELL-TALE
MAIN BEAM TELL-TALE
INDICATORS & HEAD LAMP SIGNALLER
LAMPS
IGNITION & STARTER
INTERIOR LIGHTS
AIRVENT
BONNET RELEASE
HORN
HANDBRAKE

R 1 3
2 4

VENTILATOR   DEMISTER   CHOKE   OVERDRIVE WARNING LIGHT
HEATER   DIPSWITCH

Autocar, 20 July 1962

Volvo P.1800 1,780 c.c.

PRICES				
Fixed-head Coupé...	...	...	...	£1,335
Purchase Tax	...	...	...	£501 12s 9d
		Total (in G.B.)		£1,836 12s 9d

BASED to a large extent on the design of their successful saloon cars, the P.1800 marks Volvo's first essay into the more expensive, luxury market. Right-hand-drive versions have been available only since last March, because previously the company had been concentrating its efforts on transatlantic sales, a fact which has obviously influenced several detail features of this car.

Most of the knowledgeable will be aware already that this car, although of Swedish ancestry, is assembled and finished in the United Kingdom. The bodies are made by Pressed Steel in Scotland, and Jensen in Birmingham, well-known both as coachbuilders and car makers in their own right, assemble the complete car using major mechanical components from Gothenburg. This Anglo-Swedish effort seems a happy compromise and certainly the large proportion of British components incorporated shows a great saving in duty for the British buyer.

Neither a sports car nor, if one is to be a purist, a true Grand Tourer, the P.1800 could well be described as a two-, occasional four-seater saloon with sporting instincts. Rear seat accommodation is mainly restricted by roof height. The high quality fixed-head coupé body allows plentiful room for luggage, and provides comfort far beyond normal sports car refinement. On the other hand, its road behaviour is better than that normally encountered in a saloon. As an in-betweener it suits many people's needs very well and is the type of car which is oddly rare in world markets.

The power unit, which in derated form appears in what is now known as the 122 saloon, is a four-cylinder pushrod engine of 1,780 c.c., which develops 90 b.h.p. (net) at 5,500 r.p.m. As our earlier road tests have shown, the standard saloons are no sluggards; nor, naturally, is the more sporting coupé. The performance of the P.1800 is slightly handicapped by weight, since it turns the scales at 22 cwt, 0·6 cwt more than the four-door, four-seater saloon.

Compared with the 122 saloon, tested last May, the more powerful P.1800 proves slower up to 40 m.p.h. but after that pulls away to reach 90 m.p.h. in 12sec less time. A standing quarter-mile can be covered in 19·1sec and this coupé is certainly a genuine 100 m.p.h. plus motorcar.

For the four-cylinder power unit, the five-bearing crankshaft engine is adequately smooth in the middle speed range; there is a slight lumpiness at tickover speed, and at higher r.p.m. a throaty but not unpleasant intake roar which is very reminiscent, though not so loud, of the 1,582 c.c. Volvo engine. Even on the chilliest of recent summer mornings, the engine started and ran instantly without need for any choke. It started equally well when hot. The engine is very flexible and one can trickle along quite slowly in either top or overdrive top; for best performance, more-than-usual use of the gearbox must be made.

The handbook recommends an engine speed limit of 6,000 r.p.m., at which the maximum speeds in the four forward gears (all having excellent synchromesh) are 28, 45,

67 and 90 m.p.h. These limits are well spaced but some of the road test staff considered the car to be slightly under-geared. However, the 4·56 to 1 rear axle ratio enables full advantage to be taken of the freely revving power unit, and gives improved acceleration. Overdrive is fitted as standard to the cars sold in this country, although in other markets this component is an option and a 4·1 to 1 axle ratio is the normal fitting. As can be seen from the gap between the maximum speeds achieved in top gear and overdrive, this unit, in fact, is doing duty as a fifth gear.

The short lever of the remote control gear-change has a pleasant action which allows positive and smooth changes. There is a rather strong spring loading towards the upper two ratios and one is initially inclined to select top inadvertently instead of second when coming out of bottom gear. Selection of reverse gear requires an upward lift and a forward and away movement; women, and others with slender wrists, might find it difficult to engage without a struggle. It is obviously much easier with a left-hand-drive version or in the saloon models because of an easier angle of movement. Smooth in its action and tireless under extreme test conditions, the clutch was entirely adequate.

A compression ratio of 9·5 to 1 is used in this engine. It was something of a surprise, therefore, to discover that it operated satisfactorily on premium grades of fuel; only if the engine was allowed to slog at slow speeds could pinking be induced.

Petrol Consumption

Consumption varied considerably with the manner of driving and the conditions encountered. The overall figure for the test was 24·9 m.p.g. and this is below that which the majority of users will return. Numerous fuel checks were taken: keeping mainly in top and overdrive, but not exceeding 60 m.p.h. on a main road, 29·5 m.p.g. was recorded. On the same road, with more frequent use of the gears and performance, this figure fell to 25·8 m.p.g. About 26-27 m.p.g. was the normal consumption for city driving in heavy traffic. On a motorway, cruising round the 90 m.p.h. mark gave a consumption of 23·5 m.p.g.; if the speed were dropped by 10 m.p.h., a consumption improvement of 5-7 m.p.g. was noted.

Girling disc brakes at the front and drums at the rear are used on the P.1800, and a Girling vacuum servo unit is fitted as standard equipment. On the test car the servo was not adjusted correctly and there was a slight lag before it acted. Until one became accustomed to this peculiarity it was difficult not to overbrake. A maximum retardation of 0·9 g was achieved at a pedal loading of 75lb—any greater pressure resulted in the rear wheels locking. The brakes give immense confidence, for they can be used, with minimum effort, hard and frequently to stop from any speed. Mounted between the door and the seat, the handbrake lever is of sufficient proportions for applying considerable leverage. The designer has thoughtfully put a guard round the release button, so that it cannot be accidentally knocked and let off when the driver is climbing in or out. The handbrake held the car on a 1-in-3 test hill, and from this incline the car moved off easily.

Few have ever complained about the roadholding of the Volvo saloons, so it is not surprising to find that the manufacturers have retained, with only detail modifications, a similar suspension layout for their more sporting coupé. In their advertisements Volvo seem to have struck the almost ideal description of their suspension—" soft, yet, at the same time, firm." Ride comfort is certainly the equal of, and perhaps better than, most other cars in this class, and the suspension coped adequately with the various special test surfaces tackled.

There is a certain amount of roll when this car is cornered fast, and it can be cornered very fast indeed. Even a series of twists taken at a speed high enough to foil cars of more sporting pretensions do not disturb the equilibrium of the P.1800. The steering characteristics are almost neutral, with just a faint trace of understeer, which provides a pleasant touch of stability under all conditions.

Light and accurate when the car is moving, the steering needs perhaps too much effort for slow speed manœuvring.

Below: This photograph shows well the compact layout of all the driving controls. The large lever below the handbrake is for the seat fore-and-aft adjustment. Above: When not in use the safety harness can be clipped up out of the way. A good ledge prevents objects sliding off the luggage shelf and the occasional seat cushions can be removed to leave deepish wells

Although the test car had covered some 5,000 miles, there still seemed to be some friction in the steering, which was most obvious through the absence of self-centring action just to either side of the dead-ahead position. On rough roads a certain amount of movement is transmitted to the steering wheel and it seems best, under these conditions, to let the wheel run lightly through the hands and allow the car to pick its own path. At slow speeds, cracks or joints in the road can be felt through the steering wheel and these deflect the car slightly; it seems possible that this may be attributable to the square-shouldered Pirelli Cintura tyres (of British manufacture) which are standard on the P.1800. Apart from this, the tyres are quiet, free from squeal and possess a most tenacious grip on the road.

On the test car the decorative wheel discs were inclined to revolve relative to the wheels and hide the tyre valves. Even when these discs were correctly positioned it was not easy to reach the valves.

Although added weight means loss in performance, this is compensated for by the fact that the body is well built, rattle-free and gives an impression of considerable strength and longevity. Astonishingly, it did not rain during the time the car was on test, but after an immersion at one of the automatic car washes the interior was found to be bone dry. Considerable quantities of sound-deadening material are used and there is a pleasant absence of road and mechanical noise, with the exception of a pronounced whine from the back axle of the test car.

Volvo were one of the pioneers of safety harness and all their cars are fitted as standard with their own combined

36

At present the P1800 is offered in red, white or dark grey finish. The thin, pressed wheel trims are a standard fitting

Volvo P.1800 . . .

diagonal and lap-strap type which has a sensible one-hand securing clasp. In the P.1800 the absence of rear doors allows the shoulder strap to be anchored at a better angle than in the majority of cars and the harness is thus even more comfortable than in the saloon models.

One criticism made by antagonists of seat belts is that one cannot always reach all the driving controls when strapped down. No such complaint can be levelled at the Volvo P.1800 for everything required when on the move

Although moderately crowded, there is plenty of room in the engine compartment for easy access to all items requiring any routine attention. Note the sound deadening material in the bonnet lid

is within easy reach. There is the short gear lever on the central transmission tunnel and the handbrake immediately down to the right of the seat. On the steering column to the right hand side is the trafficator switch and head-lamp flasher lever and to the left one that operates the loud horn, the softer horn having a button in the hub of the steering wheel. The headlamps are adequate for normal night use, and the dip switch is on the floor.

On the facia, to the right of the steering wheel, are the ignition-cum-starter switch and the side and headlamp control incorporating the facia lighting rheostat. To the left there are switches for the excellent two-speed wipers and windscreen washers, two-speed ventilation fan and overdrive. A slightly longer lever on the overdrive switch, or interchanging it with the one for the fan, would make it much easier to flick on and off without taking one's hand from the steering wheel. All these switches are of the pull-push type, except that for the overdrive.

Powerful Heater

Beneath the facia are other controls; in the centre there is the choke and those for air-demist and heat. On the extreme right and left are those for individual control of fresh air vents located above the occupants' legs. As might be expected from a car of Scandinavian origin, the heater and demister are extremely powerful. To obtain a good supply of fresh air, one of the windows needed to be open slightly. It is a pity that the manufacturer has not chosen to make the little rear windows of extractor type, with over-centre catches. If the main side windows are opened when travelling fast, the ears of the occupants are subjected to unpleasant reverberations.

Instrumentation is complete, but unfortunately the designer has succumbed to fitting rather gimmicky dials instead of straightforward and legible faces. Immediately in front of the driver are a large revolution counter and speedometer, with oil and water thermometers set between them. The mileage recorder mounted in the face of the speedometer is almost entirely obscured by the hub of the needle. To the left there are a petrol gauge, oil pressure gauge and a clock. None of these instruments is easy to read by daylight and night makes it somewhat more difficult. The petrol gauge is so scaled that one needs to look very carefully even to get a general indication and this, coupled with a 10-gallon fuel tank, means that a normal

safe driving range is just over 200 miles. There are all the usual warning lights, as well as one to indicate that overdrive is in operation.

Visibility is only moderately good, and to the front a view of the left wing is obscured by the facia-mounted driving mirror. The waistline of the body is rather high, so that most people found they were sitting a little too low in relation to it. On the other hand, the roofline is also low, so that their heads were too close to it. Someone with long legs and a shortish body seems to fit the P.1800 best.

Getting in or out of this car is naturally not so easy as with a normal saloon.

The seats are comfortable but provide limited lateral support, especially for the shoulders. The squabs are adjustable through a narrow angle, and seat trim is in leather. The floor is covered with carpet and with rubber matting where the occupants' feet lie. Over the rest of the interior the trim is of various types of synthetic material, which are of pleasing appearance except for that used to cover the cushions of the rear occasional seats, which has a peculiarly unpleasant and coarse texture. The facia and sun vizors are well padded.

There is a fair amount of room behind the front seats and it is possible to carry four adults in the car over short distances. When not used for passengers, this part provides very useful extra luggage accommodation. There are two rear parcel shelves, and small items can be stowed in little buckets on the sidewalls forward of the doors.

Large by two-seater coupé standards the boot is partly occupied by the spare wheel. To the left is the lockable fuel filler cap

The rear boot is quite capacious and has a self-supporting lid. It is necessary to move the spare wheel to take out the jack. A small kit of good-quality tools is provided.

This car is out of the ordinary in being completely free from any vice. While it is difficult to pick on any one outstanding virtue, the formula seems ideal and even at £1,850, the coupé is very well equipped. Volvo may very well have difficulty in meeting the demand.

Specification

ENGINE
Cylinders	4 in line
Bore	84·1mm (3·31in.)
Stroke	80·0mm (3·15in.)
Displacement	1,780 c.c. (108·5 cu. in.)
Valve gear	Overhead, pushrods and rockers
Compression ratio	9·5 to 1
Carburettor	Twin S.U. HS6
Fuel pump	AC mechanical
Oil filter	Full flow
Max. power	90 b.h.p. (net) at 5,500 r.p.m.
Max. torque	108 lb. ft. at 4,000 r.p.m.

TRANSMISSION
Clutch	Borg and Beck, single dry plate, 8·5in. dia.
Gearbox	Four-speed, all synchromesh
Overall ratios	O.D. Top 3.5, Top 4.56, 3rd 6·2, 2nd 9·1, 1st 14·3, reverse 13·34
Final drive	Hypoid bevel 4·56 to 1

CHASSIS
Construction	Integral with steel body

SUSPENSION
Front	Independent with coil springs and wishbones. Delco telescopic dampers. Anti-roll bar
Rear	Rigid axle; coil springs, radius arm, Panhard rod, Delco telescopic dampers
Steering	ZF cam and roller Wheel dia., 16in.

BRAKES
Type	Girling hydraulic; discs front, drums rear, with Girling vacuum servo
Dimensions	F, 10·9in. dia. R, 9·0in. dia., 2in. wide shoes
Swept area	F, 226 sq. in.; R, 113 sq. in. Total: 339 sq. in. (271 sq. in. per ton laden)

WHEELS
Type	Pressed steel, 5 studs, 4·5in. wide rim
Tyres	165—15in. Pirelli Cintura

EQUIPMENT
Battery	12-volt 57-amp. hr.
Headlamps	45-40 watt
Reversing lamp	None
Electric fuses	3
Screen wipers	2, two-speed, self-parking
Screen washer	Standard, Bosch electric
Interior heater	Standard, fresh air, two-speed fan
Safety belts	Standard, 3 point diagonal and lap
Interior trim	Leather and plastic
Floor covering	Carpet and rubber mats
Starting handle	No provision
Jack	Scissor type
Jacking points	Four points under body sills
Other bodies	None

MAINTENANCE
Fuel tank	10 Imp. gallons (no reserve)
Cooling system	15 pints (including heater)
Engine sump	6·8 pints SAE 20. Change oil every 3,000 miles; change filter element every 16,000 miles
Gearbox and over-drive	3·3 pints SAE 80. Change oil every 12,500 miles
Final drive	2·3 pints SAE 80. Change oil every 12,500 miles
Grease	8 points every 3,000 miles
Tyre pressures	F, 26; R, 28 p.s.i. (normal driving) F, 30; R, 32 p.s.i. (fast driving and fully laden)

Scale: 0·3in to 1ft.

Cushions uncompressed.

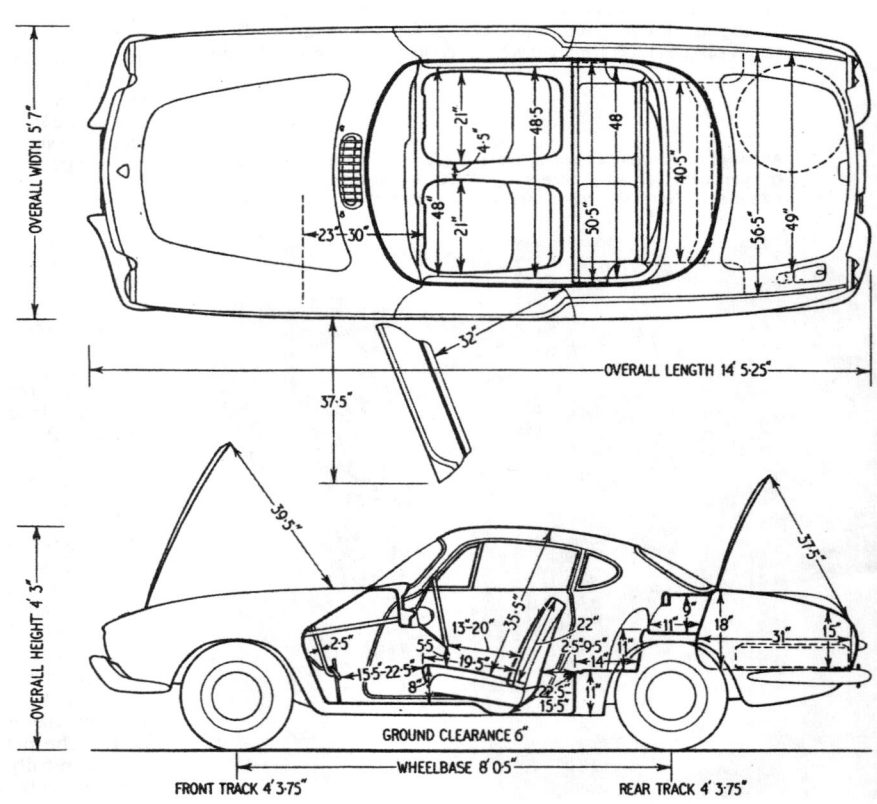

ANGLO-SWEDISH MILE-EATER

ABOVE. *Low-built and with an individualistic appearance the Volvo P1800 Coupé offers high performance with low fuel consumption. The bodywork was styled by Ghia, and the external wing mirrors are not standard equipment.*

The Volvo P1800 is an unusual car in several ways. It is certainly the first combined Anglo-Swedish car manufacturing project, it combines high performance with relatively low fuel running costs, and it has an almost unique appearance. As far as the last-mentioned attribute is concerned the P1800 arouses much controversial conversation amongst the car-minded. Many think the styling to be the last word in modernity—others are of the opinion that the shape is dated. Whatever else it may be, the P1800 is

VOLVO P1800 COUPÉ

a different shape, its high waistline and tailfins making it the subject of sidelong glances from motorists and pedestrians alike.

Although it is a modern car in essence it contains a great deal of the best type of vintage car in its driving make-up. The springing is firm, the four-cylinder engine lusty, and the gearing (particularly in overdrive) high—the last feature resulting in the most "long-legged" motoring.

The already-mentioned high waistline undoubtedly contributes to below-average all-round visibility, the low seating position, relatively small glass area (by modern standards) and thick windscreen pillars making 100 per cent vision difficult, particularly in wet weather. Driving the P1800 on a dark, rainy night is not a great deal of fun, but on a bright day it is exhilerating in the extreme.

The five-bearing four-cylinder engine is modestly dimensioned at 1.8-litres, yet the maximum is better than 100 m.p.h.; the overdrive cruising speed is an effortless 85–90, and more than 90 m.p.h. is obtainable in the direct top gear. Over a more-than-600 miles test the Volvo coupé averaged slightly more than 24 m.p.g. on premium spirit, and at touring speeds it would easily average 28 m.p.g. with intermittent use of the overdrive. The four-speed gearbox has effective synchromesh on all forward ratios with an optional electrically-engaged Laycock de Normanville overdrive on top gear only. The gear ratios are particularly well-chosen, maxima of 77 in third, and 94 in direct top gear being possible without signs of stress from the 100 b.h.p. engine. The short floor gear-lever is ideally placed, but the actual lever movement must be assessed as heavy in these modern times, although it must be said that it would be difficult with a lever of such shortness and convenience to increase operational leverage at all.

Due to the neatness and completeness of the steering column lighting and horn controls, AB Volvo set themselves a problem with the siting of the overdrive switch. This is located roughly in the centre of the lower facia, and is anything but easy to find, in amongst the other switches, without removing one's eyes from the road. The obvious solution

Volvo P1800 overdrive Coupé provides "long-legged" motoring with more than 100 m.p.h. from 1.8 litres. Robust yet simple construction combined with bold appearance. Relatively low fuel consumption, even at high speeds.

The high waistline, sharply-raked large rear window, and unusual tailfins are evident in this view. Unladen height is 4 ft. 4½ in. Ground clearance, in spite of the low build is a generous six inches.

Instrumentation is lavish, and the well-finished steering wheel has lever controls mounted underneath to control horns, headlight flashing, and turn indicators. The overdrive switch is in the centre of the facia in the disengaged position.

The four-cylinder, five bearing engine has two large S.U. carburetters with "pancake" air filters. Compression ratio is 9.5 : 1 but the unit was happy on premium fuel throughout the test. The brake servo unit can be seen furthest from camera.

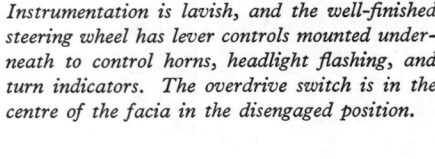

RIGHT. *Jacketed spare wheel sits horizontally in boot but leaves space for a reasonable amount of luggage. There is more space behind seats. Fuel tank holds ten gallons.*

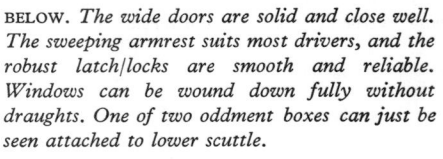

BELOW. *The wide doors are solid and close well. The sweeping armrest suits most drivers, and the robust latch/locks are smooth and reliable. Windows can be wound down fully without draughts. One of two oddment boxes can just be seen attached to lower scuttle.*

Doors were large and contributed to easy entry. The separate seats were more comfortable than their depth suggests, and had squabs which were finger-adjustable for rake. Powerful right hand-brake has ratchet guard.

SPECIFICATION

PERFORMANCE

0-30 m.p.h. ... 4.0 sec. 0-70 m.p.h. ... 18 sec. (1st,
0-40 m.p.h. ... 7.0 sec. 2nd & 3rd gear)
0-50 m.p.h. ... 9.0 sec. 0-80 m.p.h. ... 21.5 sec. (1st,
0-60 m.p.h. ... 13.6 sec. 2nd, 3rd & top gear)
30-50 m.p.h. (dir. top) 8 sec.
40-60 m.p.h. (dir. top) 8.5 sec.
Maximum speeds: Second, 52 m.p.h.; Third, 77 m.p.h.;
Direct top, 94 m.p.h.; Overdrive, 106 m.p.h.
Mileage at completion of test: 10,500.

ENGINE

Volvo P1800 four-cylinder in-line water-cooled. Cast iron
cylinder head. Overhead valves (pushrod). Bore: 84.14 mm.
Stroke: 80 mm. Cubic capacity: 1,780 c.c. Compression
ratio: 9.5 : 1. Power-output: 100 b.h.p. (SAE) at 5,500
r.p.m. Maximum torque: 108 lb. ft. at 4,000 r.p.m. Twin
1¾ in. HS6 horizontal SU carburetters. 12-volt lighting
and starting. AC mechanical fuel pump.

TRANSMISSION

Four-speed all-synchromesh unit with central floor lever,
Optional Laycock de Normanville overdrive fitted on test
car. Ratios: First, 14.3. Second, 9.08. Third, 6.20. Top,
4.56 : 1. Overdrive ratio (overall) 0.756 : 1. Reverse:
3.25 : 1. Rear wheel drive through hypoid bevel live axle.
Ratio: 4.56 : 1 with overdrive.

SUSPENSION

Independent front by double wishbones and coil springs
with telescopic dampers and torsional anti-roll bar. Rear
suspension by live axle, coil springs, telescopic dampers,
radius arms and Panhard Rod. Steering by cam and roller
box, 3¼ turns from lock-to-lock.

BRAKES

Girling, servo-assisted. Front, 10⅞ self-adjusting discs.
Rear, 9 in. leading and trailing shoe drums. Pressed steel
bolt-on wheels with embellishers.

BRAKING FIGURES

Using Bowmonk Dynometer. From 30 m.p.h.: 90 per cent
= 33.5 ft.

DIMENSIONS

Wheelbase: 8 ft. 0½ in. Track: front and rear, 4 ft. 3¾ in.
Length: 14 ft. 5⅜ in. Width: 5 ft. 7 in. Ground clearance:
6 in. Kerb weight: 22¼ cwt. Fuel capacity: 10 gallons (Imp.).
Average fuel consumption (mostly country and main-road
driving) 24.24 m.p.g. (Premium fuel). Tyres: Pirelli 165 ×
15. Braced tread with tubes.

WATER PRESSURE TEST

Slight leakage from area of scuttle air-intake in heavy rain,
and under pressure test.

BOOT CAPACITY

13 cubic feet (with spare wheel removed).

PRICE IN U.K.

As tested with overdrive: £1,836 12s. 9d. including Purchase
Tax. Price includes heater. Basic price: £1,335.

---

foot test driver however failed to make contact with the headlining over 600 miles of all sorts of driving over all sorts of surfaces —in spite of the firmness of the suspension.

The low seating position, coupled with the high waistline makes the P1800 incredibly draughtfree. It is possible to drive slow or fast with the driver's or passenger's (or both) in the fully wound-down position with only a gentle current of ventilating air circulating around the interior. This is a highly desirable feature, for it means that the car can be driven as an "open model" if the weather is at all clement. The quarter ventilating windows are sensitive wind deflectors and if cooling air is required in large quantities they will quickly provide it.

The "fast" rear window is at a very steep angle and the rear sill-mounted mirror provided little vision, accented by the fact that it was tinted to avoid dazzle. The test car had been fitted with Walpres wing-mirrors and these effected a great improvement, but were of little use in the rain.

Everything about the Volvo suggests rigidity and solid build. The big doors shut well; the high-compression engine (9.5 : 1) idles as though the crankshaft really *is* held in five main bearings, and the car feels indestructible. The pedal controls work with silky smoothness—the clutch being as sweet as a limousine in spite of having high torque to contend with, not to mention racing changes and acceleration tests!

The brakes were extremely powerful and showed no signs of fade during the test, but the demonstration car had to be treated very gently in traffic or at low speeds, for the moment the pads touched the discs they would grab, particularly in wet weather. It became necessary to apply the brakes with a thistledown foot to get the initial pad/disc contact before extra pressure could be applied, and could have been due to movement in the calliper assembly.

Although the Volvo coupé looks and is a

sports car it is surprisingly flexible and will potter sweetly away from rest at low revs. with early gear-changes being made into direct top gear. For two driving the transmission is extremely well-suited, for the direct top is geared at about 18 m.p.h. per 1,000 r.p.m., and so much or the normal driving can be done without recourse to the indirects. It is also well-suited to road conditions for the overdrive is a "supplementary" gear (although it does result in the ultimate maximum speed) to reduce engine revs., fuss, fuel consumption, and wear, rather than as part of a five-speed gearbox. Once on the open road the P1800 can be driven virtually on the overdrive switch, there being well over 90 m.p.h. in direct top, and more than 105 in overdrive. If the engine revs. (6,000 were always readily obtained) are taken well up in direct top, a hundred miles per hour in overdrive can be achieved on most reasonable straights. The overdrive gearing provides 21 m.p.h. per 1,000 r.p.m., so at 100 m.p.h. the engine is turning at less than 5,000 r.p.m.

The Volvo's handling is fully in keeping with its type. It corners "flat" even at high speed, and its cornering capabilities are great. Front suspension is conventional independent by double wishbones and coil springs, and the rear suspension is by ordinary live axle and coil springs. Secret of the steering and suspension effectiveness is the very definite location of all components. The front suspension has a robust torsional anti-roll bar, and the rear axle is located by radius arms and a Panhard Rod. With location and stresses so carefully worked out the Volvo "goes where its pointed" with near-neutral handling characteristics, the ultimate being slight oversteer when pressed to the limit.

As already mentioned the ride is firm, the springs and dampers making for stability at high speeds but demanding smooth roads for the best "feel". On second-class roads with irregularities and corrugations in surface

CONTINUED ON PAGE 58

---

would have been to mount the switch on the gear-lever itself, or to use one of the new Laycock "twist switches" which are incorporated in the lever knob. The gear-lever is always easy to locate and what more sensible place for a gear switch?

In spite of the low-mounted separate seats the Volvo designers have managed to achieve a high standard of comfort, although slightly more "roll" for thigh support would improve the cushions, but this would of course decrease kneeroom under the handsome two-spoke steering wheel. The seats slide back with a generous amount of adjustment, the legroom being ample for tall drivers, but anyone more than 6 ft. 1 in. would find that headroom was sadly lacking. The near-six-

Roger Moore who plays the part of Simon Templar (the "Saint") in the current Associated Television series adapted from the famous Leslie Charteris novels, uses a Volvo P1800 throughout.

A Pleasing Anglo-Swedish Sports Coupé—
THE VOLVO P·1800

IN GOOD SHAPE.—The low build and sleek lines of the well-appointed and comfortable Volvo P1800 give it the appearance of faster, more expensive G.T. coupés.

VOLVO cars from Sweden are very conscientiously made and accurately assembled, as readers of MOTOR SPORT's account of a visit to the Göteberg plant (June, 1960) will know. That they go extremely well and possess desirable features of design and equipment has also been made clear in our road-test reports of the 122S and 122S/B18 saloon models.

More recently the long-awaited P1800 sports coupé has been subjected to a 1,000-mile road-test. This is a particularly interesting car, for at the kerb-side it rivals the best Italian G.T. cars for eyeable good looks, being long, low and of wind-defeating form, yet it is really a durable, refined cross between out-and-out *sportswagen* and Grand Touring car, with the additional item of interest that the body is a product of Pressed Steel in Scotland, the P1800 being assembled by Jensen in West Bromwich, using such British components as certain Lucas lamps and electrical equipment, Smiths instruments and Girling brakes.

In appearance the P1800, as I have said, is exciting, although rather less chromium embellishment along the body sides and tail-fins would be an improvement. The Ferrari-like front grille and shapely roof-line enhance the general ensemble but the wheel discs rather give the impression of "model" wire wheels.

Open one of the two well-hung, nicely-shutting doors and it is possible to enter easily into an interior that is tastefully and luxuriously appointed. A tall but not unduly wide transmission tunnel divides the separate leather-upholstered front seats, which are adjustable by means of long base levers. The squab angles are adjustable if a nut at the base of each fold-forward squab is turned. There are soft seats of generous size, which remain comfortable on a long day's motoring even though they are not specifically formed to support the occupants against cornering stresses.

Behind these seats are the occasional seats, in the form of two cushions that lift out of their retaining wells. Presumably the idea is to offer greater depth of luggage but I prefer a flat-shelf, such, for example, as Porsche contrive by folding down the squabs of the occasional seats. In any case, the sharply sloping roof of the Volvo P1800 prevents any but the smaller species of children enjoying travel in these seats unless the Volvo owner is prepared to drive the heads of his "occasional" passengers into their shoulders. One person sitting centrally may endure the experience better, especially if the front seats, in which leg-room is particularly generous, are set well forward. But generally it is better to regard this as a 2-seater car.

Behind the occasional cushions is an arched shelf for parcels stowage but if suitcases are carried on the rear seats such stowage is rendered inaccessible. Another poor aspect of the car is ventilation. The front doors contain big glasses that wind down with 3¾rd turns of the substantial winders, and quarter-lights that lock with a pip and recess into their rubbers, so that they become very stiff to open. But the back quarter-lights are fixed, so a

flow of draught-free air through the body is difficult to achieve. There is a scuttle intake with small toggle controls under the scuttle but this does not provide any great volume of cold air, and then only to the feet.

The doors have ornate horizontal quadrant-type interior handles that make opening them easy; pushing these knobs forward locks the doors but as the action works if the doors are closed subsequently it would not be surprising to come upon a Volvo owner locked out of his beautiful P1800. The windows are framed only as far back as the quarter-lights; they have good sealing rubbers.

The interior of the body is upholstered in plastic material matching the red leather seats and black facia trim. The doors have curious "pulls" in the form of curved shelves that would scarcely hold a cigarette packet. These have a drain hole, so presumably Pressed Steel are aware that rain is going to seep past the quarter-lights when these are shut and run in when they are

CONTROL LAYOUT of the Volvo P1800 includes hooded speedometer and tachometer before the driver, with vertical thermometers between and two-tiered instrument and control panels. Note the remote gear-lever and drilled spokes of the steering wheel.

This view of the Volvo coupé shows how the tail-fins continue the plated embellishments that run along the sides of the body.

THE VOLVO P1800 COUPE

Engine : Four cylinders, 84 × 80 mm. (1,780 c.c.). Push-rod-operated overhead valves. 9.5-to-1 compression-ratio 100 b.h.p. (net) at 5,500 r.p.m.

Gear ratios : 1st, 14.3 to 1; 2nd, 9.1 to 1; 3rd, 6.2 to 1; top, 4.56 to 1; overdrive top, 3.5 to 1.

Tyres : 165–15 Pirelli Cintura on bolt-on steel disc wheels.

Weight : Not weighed (maker's figure : 22 cwt. (kerb weight)).

Steering ratio : Just over 3 turns, lock-to-lock.

Fuel capacity : 10 gallons. (Range approximately 249 miles.)

Wheelbase : 8 ft. 0½ in.

Track : 4 ft. 3¾ in.

Dimensions : 14 ft. 5¼ in. × 5 ft. 7 in. × 4 ft. 3 in. (high).

Price : £1,335 (£1,836 12s. 9d. inclusive of purchase tax and import duty).

Makers : AB Volvo, Göteberg, Sweden.

Concessionaires : Volvo Concessionaires Ltd., 28, Albemarle Street, London, W.1.

open, as no gutters are provided! In any case, the purpose of these " pulls," which could so easily have constituted pockets or arm-rests, is obscure.

The instrumentation is in keeping with the demeanour of this Volvo coupé. The well padded facias are on two planes, the top one recessed further forward than the lower one. The lower carries two panels, of which the central one contains the overdrive-switch (found only on Home Market cars) flanked on its left by a cigarette-lighter and drawer-type ash-tray; on its right by knobs controlling a quiet 2-speed heater fan, and the 2-speed wipers-cum-washers, with, in addition, a rather unnecessary mauve warning-light to show when overdrive is in use.

The r.h. panel has on it pull-out lamps knob (foot dipper) and Assa ignition-key-cum-starter control.

The top panel has provision for a radio on the left and three Smiths dials, of rather ugly protruding type, covering clock, fuel gauge and oil pressure. Hooded before the driver are the Smiths speedometer and tachometer with a vertical thermometer unit, like a child's barometer, between them. The thermometer records water temperature with a vertical yellow ribbon in the upper scale (marked at 90, 160, 212 and 230° F.) and oil temperature with a blue ribbon in the lower scale (marked at 140, 212, 265 and 280° F.). The speedometer incorporates trip and total with decimal mileometer, warning lights, labelled with symbols, for generator and (sensibly subdued) main-beams. The dial is rather casually calibrated every 20 m.p.h. to 120 m.p.h. The tachometer again, is crudely marked in steps of ten, to 7,000 r.p.m., with a red warning between the 5,500 and 7,000-r.p.m. points. The dials are neat, with white figures on a black background and all, with most of the knobs, are neatly marked as to purpose. The knobs, as I have found on other Volvos, are apt to unscrew, but a far more serious short-coming was failure of the screen-washers to function. The petrol gauge is marked E, ½, F but the " E "

The performance of the Volvo P1800 is somewhat restricted by use of a similar engine to the B18 unit used in the 122S saloon, but raised compression-ratio increases the output from 90 to 100 b.h.p.

is set away from the faint pip indicating empty, which can thus be mistaken for the ¼-full mark, causing one driver to run out of petrol in one of August's severe rain-storms.

Up under the scuttle, somewhat inaccessibly placed, are the aforesaid toggles for the fresh-air intake, flanked on the left by a lever-switch for a map-light and on the right by a matching switch for the interior lamps in the back of the body, with a setting for courtesy action. Under the centre of the facia are three neat, labelled levers controlling demisting, ventilation and heating, these being flanked by a zero-setter for the trip odometer and a toggle controlling the mixture enricher for the twin S.U. HS6 carburetters.

There are no door pockets or cubby-hole but rigid map carriers are provided on both sides of the scuttle and there is a wide but only slightly lipped rear shelf for more bulky objects. The roof is low, so that the soft swivelling anti-dazzle vizors come close to the driver's head. The pedals, of which the accelerator is of treadle type, are of generous size and well placed. An oval rear-view mirror provides an excellent view but, mounted centrally on the screen sill, completely obscures the near-side front wing, which would otherwise just be visible to drivers of moderate height. The test car had streamlined Walpress external mirrors.

The rear boot has a self-supporting, lockable lid, which, however, can be blown down by a gust of wind. The boot is reasonably capacious and adequate if this Volvo is regarded as normally a 2-seater with luggage space behind the front seats. The spare wheel, in a cover, lies on the floor, however.

The exterior of the P1800 is characterised by substantial if flimsily mounted bumpers, upswept at the front, and twin, unplated tail-pipes. The fuel filler consists of a locked flap on the near-side rear panel. This did not seal properly, and a strong smell of petrol invaded the car as the level fell towards empty. Apart from a coloured Volvo motif on the rear quarters and the name Volvo in separate letters below the boot-lid, together, of course, with the Volvo badge, there is no indication to curious strangers, of which I encountered many, that this is the P1800 version of this well-made Swedish motor car.

Push-button exterior door handles are used and all the lamps are Lucas, except for Robo headlamps, which give excellent illumination.

The bonnet opens from the trailing edge to reveal the 1,780-c.c. 5-bearing, twin-carburetter engine with polished valve cover.

CONTINUED ON PAGE 58

VOLVO P-1800 S

Now it's all Swedish...

TO REGULAR READERS a test of the Volvo P-1800 S might seem just a bit redundant, but when we saw the proof of an advertisement that said: "Remember the $10,000 car for $3,995? Well, we've improved it!" we were intrigued. We spent two weeks and a 1000-mile trip with the first one we could get our hands on. As might be expected it was a very pleasant two weeks and an interesting trip.

We can say right now that owners of the earlier series built in England need have no fear of obsolescence. The improvements in the P-1800 S are there all right, but they aren't exactly obtrusive and some would be better called "changes" rather than improvements. The biggest improvement doesn't even make itself felt until the car is totally and thoroughly broken in. The "S" engine has the high performance C or 707 cam but the effect isn't felt until about 5000 miles have been covered. In the case of our test car we started out with a little over 4000 miles on the clock and it wasn't until almost the end of the trip that we felt the improvement at the top end brought about by the cam. Prior to this point the car felt like just about any P-1800 built during the last couple of years, a little quicker than some and a little slower than others. It had the same seeming reluctance to get off the line and the same quietly deceptive rush forward once rolling. After the 5000 mile point was passed however this rush increased noticeably, especially above 4000 rpm.

Taken overall, from the outside, there are only two clues to the fact that this is the Swedish-built rather than the British-assembled car. One is a small medallion on the rear deck that tells you it is an 1800-S. The other is the presence of amber rather than white turn signals at the front. On the inside the clues are found in the seat-belt hardware and its attachments, unperforated upholstery and trim, and the use of leather rather than plastic for the seats. Also some of the metalized plastic kick panels are gone. Otherwise all else is the same in the living space. Like its predecessors it is eminently livable for long spells on the road. Once the location of the various controls are learned there are no awkward moves required of the driver.

It is hard to see how the handling of any P-1800 could be improved, other than changes made for racing, which will make the car a bit less livable and the manufacturer has avoided this in the S series. The ride is a combination of firmness and softness that is joy to experience. There is none of that sporty car harshness

ROAD TEST 28/63

SPORTS CAR GRAPHIC

Far left — P-1800 S, like earlier versions makes fade-proof straight line stops although rear wheels will lock on panic stops. Above, left and below, major identification points are medallion on the rear deck, amber turn signals and unattractive hubcaps.

PHOTOS: BOB D'OLIVO

VOLVO P-1800 S

Interior, right, of the P-1800 S coupe is little changed from the English versions except for leather on the seats and unperforated trim. Controls, gauges, etc., are unchanged. Below, the engine is outwardly the same but is equipped with hotter cam and has been bumped to 10 to 1 compression. It can be pushed hard almost from the beginning and is nearly unbreakable.

but full control of wheel movement is maintained at all times. The car can be accelerated over incredibly bumpy washboard surfaces that would have lesser machinery skittering like a go-kart on marbles. Part of our test trip took us through Nevada desert roads and over some mountain detours that were little more than cart tracks, and this solid road holding plus the high ground clearance were much appreciated. This is one Grand Touring car that can be taken almost anywhere with no fear of leaving little bits and pieces of muffler, crankcase and other components littering the landscape.

On smooth surfaces the road holding approaches the uncanny for a fairly heavy, hypoid axle car. The absolute control built into the suspension, coupled with the Pirelli Cinturato tires, creates a situation where one can belt the car around turns, especially fast ones, at a rate that is almost frightening. One feels that this is one of those cars that sticks up to the point where one is impossibly over one's head before it lets everything go all at once. It doesn't really, but it does give that feeling until one has lived with the car for quite a spell. We can only think of one other car, a piece of highly desirable and expensive Italian property, that has this effect.

Braking on the P-1800 S is absolutely smooth and straight with virtually no fade in the hardest application. On some panic stops the rear drum brakes might tend to lock, but it happens seldom. The brakes are vacuum assisted but the assistance seems almost redundant after trying one on which the assist had been removed. It does come in handy in traffic situations where there is a lot of stopping and starting, since a toe-touch triggers the assist to give just that little bit of stopping necessary without the need to ride the brake pedal.

With all this performance economy is still the long suit of any Volvo and the P-1800 in particular. In flat-out performance tests the car gave 23 miles per gallon, and 26 around town. Cruising on the highway gives even greater range per gallon, 30 mph being usual and 32 mpg has been noted not only on the pocketbook but is very convenient on trips as well. It's nice to know that one can start out on the 500-odd mile trip from Reno to Los Angeles and only have to stop for fuel once along the way.

Getting back to the engine in the S-series car, readers may notice that our shift points were pegged at 6000 rpm. Actually, the book says you can go to 6500, which will add about 10 miles per hour to each shift point. However, after our experience on the dynamometer with the project car, in which we discovered that power fell off radically just below 6000 with the 707 cam, we felt that the over-run to 6500 would be useless. Up to a little over 60 mph the car was quicker using the lower shift point. Over the quarter-mile it was not so quick by about two seconds, but reached a higher top speed than when the 6500 rpm point was used. This was probably due to the fact that gearing is so spaced that using the 6000 rpm point in shifting up place the revs at just above the point of peak torque. Using the higher figure placed the revs in the next higher at the point where torque was beginning to fall off rapidly with resultantly less forward urge.

All things considered the new Swedish series P-1800 is still the same combination of tank and sports car that give one the distinct impression that it could be driven around the world, never mind the condition of the road, in complete comfort and with little more bother than keeping it in fuel and rubber. You can buy a faster car and you can buy a more expensive car, but it is hard to see how for the investment involved you can buy a better one.

ROAD TEST 28/63

SPORTS CAR GRAPHIC

VOLVO P-1800 S

PRICE (as tested) .... $4225. POE, L.A.
OPTIONS .... Overdrive

ENGINE:

Type	4-cylinder, in-line, water-cooled, 5-main crank
Head	Removable, cast-iron
Valves	OHV, pushrod/rocker actuated
Max. bhp.	108 @ 5,800 rpm
Max. Torque	110 lbs. ft. @ 4,000 rpm
Bore	3.313 in. 84.2 mm.
Stroke	3.15 in. 80 mm.
Displacement	109 cu. in. 1780 cc.
Compression Ratio	10.0 to 1
Induction System	2 SU carburetors
Exhaust System	Cast headers to single exhaust
Electrical System	12v distributor ign.

CLUTCH:
Single disc, dry
Diameter .... N.A. in.
Actuation .... hydraulic

DIFFERENTIAL:
Hypoid, live
Ratio .... 4.56 to 1
Drive Axles (type) ...... enclosed, semi floating

TRANSMISSION:
4-speed, full-synchro with overdrive on 4th
Ratios: 1st .... 3.13 to 1
2nd .... 1.99 to 1
3rd .... 1.36 to 1
4th .... 1.0 to 1
O.D. .... 0.76 to 1

STEERING:
Sector type (cam & roller)
Turns Lock to Lock 3.6
Turn Circle .... 31 ft.

BRAKES:
Disc front, drum rear — power assisted
Diameters 10.8 in. front; 9.0 in. rear
Swept Area .... 350 sq. in.

CHASSIS:

Frame	Integral
Body	Steel, unitized
Front Suspension	Unequal arm, coil springs, tube shocks
Rear Suspension	Live, trailing stabilizer arms, panhard rod, coil springs, tube shock
Tire Size & Type	165 x 15 Cinturatos

WEIGHTS AND MEASURES:

Wheelbase	96.5 in.	Ground Clearance	6 in.
Front Track	51.75 in.	Curb Weight	2330 lbs.
Rear Track	51.75 in.	Test Weight	2684 lbs.
Overall Height	51 in.	Crankcase	3.8 qts.
Overall Width	61 in.	Cooling System	n.a.
Overall Length	173.25 in.	Gas Tank	12 gals.

PERFORMANCE:

0-30	3.5 sec.	0-70	14.2 sec.
0-40	5.7 sec.	0-80	18.0 sec.
0-50	8.2 sec.	0-90	22.7 sec.
0-60	11.0 sec.	0-100	29.0 sec.
Standing ¼ mile			20.8 sec. @ 86 mph
Top Speed (av. two-way run)			110 mph

Speed Error	30	40	50	60	70	80	90
Actual	30	40	50	59	69	79	89

Fuel Consumption: Test .... 23 mpg Average .... 26 mpg
Recommended Shift Points: Max. 2nd .... 44 mph
Max. 1st. .... 24 mph Max. 3rd .... 64 mph
RPM Red-line .... 6000 rpm
Speed Ranges in gears:
1st .... 0 to 24 mph 3rd .... 16 to 64 mph
2nd .... 5 to 44 mph 4th .... 21 to 95 mph
Brake Test: 71.5 Average % G, over 10 stops. No fade encountered on stop.

REFERENCE FACTORS:

Bhp. per Cubic Inch	0.99
Lbs. per bhp	21.5
Piston Speed @ Peak rpm	3045 ft./min.
Sq. In. Swept Brake area per Lb.	0.149

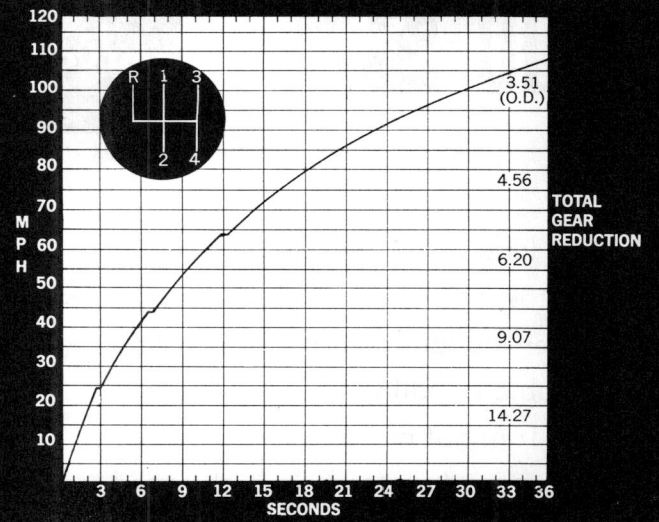

TOTAL GEAR REDUCTION

3.51 (O.D.)
4.56
6.20
9.07
14.27

SECONDS

Smooth and sleek, the Volvo 1800 S must
be many men's ideal of luxury motoring.

VOLVO 1800 S

Driving long distances can be fun if you choose the right car. Volvo's 1800 S combines lounge-room comfort with predictable handling and a 108 bhp engine. It might not be a fire-breathing sports car but for effortless high speed cruising it's hard to beat.

TRYING to find the right category for the Volvo 1800 S is not easy. Even the maker's glossy catalogue doesn't pin it down, preferring to cover a broad field with catch-phrases such as "fast and elegant", "spacious, comfortable and well equipped" and "well built, agile city car".

So what is it, sports car, touring car, sophisticated coupe? It is all of these in part, plus a dash or two of other ingredients.

It defies hard-and-fast classification, and this, probably, is one of its main charms.

There are few basic differences between the 1800 S and the P 1800 that preceded it. Aesthetically, the 1964 version is more pleasing, even though the exterior changes amount to little more than ditching the soup-plate hubcaps and their background of phony "spokes" and substituting smaller coverings with centre emblem.

Under the bonnet the four-cylinder oversquare 1780 cc engine has had more life breathed into it through a higher lift camshaft, boosted compression ratio and altered timing.

Power is now 108 bhp at 5800 rpm, as against 100 bhp at 5500 rpm; there is a modest increase in torque, but weight has been lifted by 25lb. to roughly 22½ cwt.

The twin SU-fed engine now requires a headier brew for satisfactory running — compression is 10.0 to 1—as pump super causes pinking, running on and similar digestive upsets.

The grille resembles the early 1950 Ferrari design and conveys a slightly misleading impression of brute power.

Interior is sumptuously furnished to make long distance touring as comfortable as possible

Undoubtedly the P 1800 was a comfortable car with excellent seating. The S version is even more so, and has a couple of shaped individual seats unequalled on any other car with sporting pretensions available in this country.

The backs are contoured to support the driver and his passenger from neck to hips, and the cushion puffs up into a roll that keeps leg fatigue away. The leanest of us all wouldn't chafe on a Melbourne-Sydney trip with this comfort.

Do you like the styling?

To complete the ecstasy, the seats are adjustable for rake and reach. At the back there is a padded perch for youngsters, extra luggage, or a trainee contortionist.

Looks are a matter of taste, and the Volvo has the type of styling that provokes beer-flattening arguments. The front strongly resembles the mid-'fifties Ferrari, while the finny rear is definitely early-'sixties Detroit.

It is the rump that causes all the rumpus and I don't want to buy into the discussion. But if pressed for an opinion, I'd come out on the side of the anti-fin brigade.

Where there can be no argument is in the lay-out and completeness of the cockpit. From the neat slotted wheel to the stubby gear lever and heel-and-toe pedals, a lot of thought has gone into making the Volvo a car for the aficionado.

VOLVO 1800 S

ENGINE: Four cylinders, overhead valves, 1780 cc, 108 bhp at 5800 rpm; Torque, 110 lb./ft. at 4000 rpm; Bore, 84.14 mm; Stroke, 80 mm; Compression Ratio, 10 to 1.

TRANSMISSION: Four-speed, all-synchro-mesh, with overdrive on top gear.

GEAR RATIOS: First, 3.13 to 1; second, 1.99; third, 1.36; top, 1 to 1; overdrive, 0.756 to 1.

SUSPENSION: Front, independent by coil springs and stabiliser; Rear, coil springs, live axle. Telescopic dampers all round.

STEERING: Cam and roller, 3¼ turns lock to lock. Turning circle, 31ft.

BRAKES: Servo-assisted discs at the front, drums rear.

WHEELS: Ventilated disc type.

TYRES: 165 x 15in. Pirellis.

BODY TYPE: Integral, two doors.

DIMENSIONS: Wheelbase, 96½ins.; track (front and rear), 51¾ins.; overall length, 173¼ins.; width, 67ins.; height, 50½ins.

SPEEDS IN GEARS (at 6000 rpm): First, 30 mph; second, 48; third, 69; top, 93; o/d top, 107.4

ACCELERATION: 0-30 mph, 3.9 secs.; 0-40, 6.4; 0-50, 8.6; 0-60, 12.8; 0-70, 14.7; 0-80, 20.5; 0-90, 27.2; 0-100, 39.8. Standing quarter-mile, 18.7 secs.

FUEL FIGURE: 27.5 mpg over 433 miles.

PRICE: £2693.

Test car from Regent Motors, Sturt St., South Melbourne.

VOLVO 1800 S

Fascia panel houses all the instruments a driver needs — and what's more, he can see them all.

The design of the Volvo 1800 S is good for an argument wherever enthusiasts gather. Do you like fins?

Every major control is only a handspan away and the instruments cover all functions — engine speed, oil pressure and temperature, water temperature, and petrol level. Warning lights are used for generator charge, headlamp full beam, and also as a reminder that overdrive is in operation.

This is fine and as it should be on a car with a performance better than 100 mph, but it appears that the stylists had the last word. Consequently the dials are easy on the eye, but not easy for the eye.

Instead of being plain black figures on white—or white on black—a blue background has been injected, which, coupled with chrome surrounds and dished faces, makes snap readings almost impossible. Reflections have a wonderful time.

Atoning for this—in part—are the big flat-headed switches for the two-speed wipers with electric screenwash, the heater fan, fresh air intakes and lights.

Safety is cared for with padded dash, thick sun visors and standard equipment three-point seat belts.

The Volvo looks sporty—from the front at least—but the ride it gives tends more towards a well-bred sedan's. Front springing is by coils, with coils and live axle at the back.

Suspension is soft but satisfactory

Although soft by MG TC standards, there is no slop or squashiness to take the edge off good manners. This goer from Gothenburg can be hustled through tight bends with bags of vigor and just a touch of body roll.

It absorbs bumps and humps, and the big Pirelli-clad 15in. wheels are real pothole fillers. Servo-assistance is used on the disc-drum braking, and although it's no fairy in terms of weight, there is no fade to blemish the Volvo's character.

Noise level is low up to the 90 mph point, where mechanical hustle sets in. The shape is such a good wind-cheater that the windows can be left open without stirring up a willy-willy in the ashtray.

The engine carries a five-bearing crank and oil cooler and is happy to run up to 6500 rpm without cremating itself. It has an unbreakable feel, a happy disposition on the right fuel and sound engineering.

The all-synchromesh gearbox swaps cogs smartly and

Big solid bumper bars might add some weight but they will save the owner from other drivers who park by feel.

with minimum effort at the gear lever, and must be classed as a "tunes to be played on" variety. The electric overdrive cannot be taken so lightheartedly. Changing from fourth to "fifth" produces a small amount in the transmission, but going back into direct drive sends a shudder down the car's spine. To overcome this, a quick flick on the clutch smooths out matters and stops the transmission from self-strangulation.

On the test car there was excess vibration in the gearbox around 100 mph, which rose to Mach One proportions at the car's maximum of 107 mph. And, of all things, the body responded with its own sonic effect which the eardrums didn't appreciate.

The wear-reducing qualities of the overdrive can be gauged this way: At 60 mph in top the engine spins at 3900 rpm. At the same speed in overdrive this is slashed to 2900 rpm. And 80 mph in o/d causes less effort— 3800 rpm—than a mile a minute in fourth.

As I said at the beginning, putting a tag on this shapely Swede is well nigh impossible. It is sporty without being harsh, quick but no jack-rabbit in acceleration, comfortable in a way that entices 60-year-old buyers and courteous in its manners without being a fop.

As a quiet, speedy, relaxing personal machine it comes very close to the non-sporting concept of grand touring.

VOLVO 1800S

THE Swedish Volvos have a reputation for being rugged, conventional, essentially practical cars which are in all cases extremely well thought out. This is a description which is certainly true of the 122 and 121 saloon models, both of which have already been tested by *Cars Illustrated*, and one which is in turn completely accurate when related to the 1800S, the latest version of the two-seater coupe which, a few years ago, marked Volvo's entry into the high-performance bracket.

Like all Volvos, this feeling of strength and purpose makes itself apparent at first sight of the car. Its lines are graceful, vigorous and, with a high waist and shallow window areas, slightly old-fashioned in appearance. The big doors shut with a pleasantly solid feeling; raising the bonnet reveals extensive bracing and sound insulation, while the overall appearance is distinctive. Naturally, such stout construction, while inferring long life and an ability to deal easily with rough conditions, is provided at the expense, to some extent, of the performance, and that of the Volvo 1800S is that of a fast touring car rather than that of a true sports car. Nevertheless, few motorists would quibble at a machine of under 2 litres which offers a maximum speed of well over 100 m.p.h., with an ability to

reach 60 m.p.h. from a standstill in less than 12 seconds. The mastery of the Volvo, however, is in its untiring ability to cover long distances at high speed, than in its vivid acceleration: this it does in full measure, and there can be few more comfortable cars in which to enjoy high-speed touring with a moderate fuel consumption.

The power unit is the well-known Volvo 4-cylinder engine, in 1·8 litre form, with cylinder dimensions of 84·14 mm. × 80 mm. (1,780 c.c.). As fitted to the 1800S, there are twin S.U. carburettors; overhead valves are operated by push-rods, and the crankshaft runs in five main bearings. Modified exhaust and inlet systems result in the development of slightly more power than the present model's predecessor, the P1800, and the maximum output is 108 b.h.p. at 5,800 r.p.m., with 110 lb./ft. torque at 4,000 r.p.m. An oil cooler is fitted as standard equipment.

Smoothness and flexibility are outstanding attributes of this engine, and indeed at times one can scarcely believe that there are in fact only four cylinders. There is nothing harsh or temperamental about the unit, and it develops its power steadily through a usefully wide range. Hot or cold, the test car was always easy to start, and the engine pulled well from cold, with a commendably short warm-up period: in the warm weather of the test the choke was seldom necessary for "cold" starts. An excellent top gear performance is a feature of the car, and speeds as low as 20 m.p.h. can be used in direct top gear without fuss or snatch from the transmission. At the other end of the scale, prolonged cruising at around 100 m.p.h. in the overdrive ratio optionally fitted to top gear resulted in no significant increase in water temperature, nor drop in oil pressure.

A single dry-plate clutch mates the engine to a four-speed and reverse gearbox, with synchromesh on all four forward ratios and, on the test car, the optional overdrive which operates on top gear alone. The clutch is light to use, and grips firmly and progressively, with sufficient bite to allow some wheelspin on fast take-offs. The transmission is silent in operation and the gear-lever, a short rigid control mounted on the floor, is light and has a short travel, permitting extremely fast gear changes at high r.p.m. At lower speeds the synchromesh which is powerful and effective, occasionally impedes the change of ratio, and imparts a notchy feel to the lever. The switch controlling the overdrive is mounted on the dashboard, and rapid selection of third gear occasionally caused the knuckles to foul and operate the switch inadvertently. The gear ratios are well-spaced, and with a maximum speed of only just under 80 m.p.h. third gear is particularly useful for overtaking.

The suspension, independent, with wishbones and coil springs at the front, and with a rigid rear axle sprung on coil springs and located by radius arms and a panhard rod, emphasises the fact that the Volvo is a "grand touring" car, in the widest sense of the phrase, rather than a sports machine. By sporting standards the ride is soft, a feature which is particularly noticeable at low speeds on rough surfaces. At faster gaits, however, the suspension seems to "toughen up", and even at over 100 m.p.h. there is relatively little body movement. Fast corners produced only small amounts of body roll, and on rough surfaces wheel movement is well controlled by telescopic shock absorbers. The car's steering is curiously susceptible to road camber, and needs a surprising amount of correction on steeply-cambered surfaces. For comfortable, fast touring, however, it is hard to think of a more satisfactory compromise, and the Volvo's suspension endows it with extremely likeable handling qualities, aided by pleasantly-direct, light steering which enables the car to be placed accurately. On dry roads all four wheels remain on their chosen path until the limit of the car's high cornering power is reached, with detectable understeer on fast bends. In the wet, this understeer becomes rather more pronounced, but can be readily overcome by judicious application of power, by which means the tail can be "prodded" round evenly and progressively. Directional stability is good, and the body is little affected by gusty side-winds. Excellent stopping power is provided by splash-protected disc brakes at the front and large-diameter drums at the rear, with vacuum servo assistance. Pedal pressure is light, and repeated applications from high speed produced no indication of fade or uneven pulling, despite the fact that the task of stopping this fairly heavy car gives them a good deal of hard work.

The interior of the car is laid out almost ideally for transporting two people over long distances in comfort and with convenience. In fact, the seating arrangements provide for the occasional transport of four people, and during the test four adults were in fact carried on a journey of some eighty miles, in hot weather, without discomfort other than restricted headroom in the rear. The rear seats are rather more generously provided with padding than is usually found in similar circumstances, and the cushions are supported on hammocks of rubber straps. The front seats, with adjustable back-rests and a generous range of fore and aft adjustment, are extremely

comfortable, and provide adequate lateral support as well as being well-upholstered. With the Volvo's rather high scuttle and waist lines, the driving position is rather low in the car for optimum visibility, and this is further impaired by the standard scuttle-mounting of the rear-view mirror. Most owners would probably re-locate this fitting, possibly suspending it from the top screen-rail. In other respects, however, the Volvo's driving position is good: the adjustment of the seat cushion and squab combines with a well-angled steering wheel and sensibly laid-out controls to provide an arrangement which is comfortable and efficient. Pedals are well-arranged for heel and toe operation, and the instrumentation is adequately full. A matching speedometer and rev-counter, the former incorporating trip and total mileage recorders, as well as warning lights for ignition and headlamp main beams, are set immediately in front of the driver with, between them, water and engine oil temperature gauges. A fuel contents gauge (its dial occasionally obscured by the steering wheel rim), oil pressure gauge and a clock are located in the centre of the facia, while along the lower edge of the dashboard are switches controlling the two-speed screen wipers and washers, lighting, ventilation and heating, overdrive and the ignition/starter switch. Two stalks protruding from the steering column operate flashing direction indicators, headlamp flashers and a loud-tone horn: this latter control is handily-placed and, on fast journeys on crowded roads, much appreciated. Instrument needles are well-damped and easily read.

In terms of performance the Volvo must be judged on fast touring standards, although it shows up far from badly when compared with similar machines more directly intended as sporting vehicles. A mean maximum speed of 108·7 m.p.h., together with the optional overdrive on top gear which provides 100 m.p.h. at just over 4,000 r.p.m., gives a cruising speed which, at somewhere in the upper nineties, is well within the car's compass. In actual fact, the 1800S can be cruised extensively at three-figure speeds without any sign of distress, lubricant and coolant temperature and pressure gauges continuing to show encouraging readings. The gear ratios are well-spaced, and third provides a maximum speed of 78 m.p.h., while the suitability of the other ratios is indicated by acceleration figures from rest to 60 m.p.h. in 11·9 seconds, and from rest to 80 m.p.h. in 20·9 seconds. During our performance test we recorded an unusually fast time for the standing-start quarter-mile, a searching judge of the car's acceleration, with a mean time of 17·9 seconds—the best one-way time recorded was 17·5 seconds, both worthy of much faster cars.

The Volvo is an unusually non-tiring car to drive fast for long distances: its rugged strength, and a complete absence of rattles or draughts, combines with a lusty character which makes the car seem to enter into the spirit of things. There is generous luggage space, and for long-distance fast touring the car would be difficult to improve. Despite the car's weight of over 22 cwt., with driver and fuel aboard, it remains economical even when the performance is fully used. Our overall consumption figure for the test mileage was exactly 24 m.p.g., and this could be improved, under less vigorous driving, to 28 m.p.g.

Cars on Test

VOLVO 1800S

Engine: Four cylinder; 84.14 mm.×80 mm. (1,780 c.c.); pushrod-operated overhead valves; compression ratio 10.0 to 1; twin S.U. carburettors; 108 b.h.p. at 5,800 r.p.m.
Transmission: Single dry-plate clutch; four-speed and reverse gearbox with synchromesh on all four forward gears and central remote-control gearlever; overdrive on top gear only.
Suspension: Front, independent, with wishbones, coil springs and anti-roll bar; rear, rigid axle with torque tube and coil springs. Telescopic dampers front and rear. Tyres: 165×15.
Brakes: Front, 11 ins. discs; rear, 9 ins. drums.
Dimensions: Overall length, 14 ft. 5¼ ins. overall width, 5 ft. 7 ins; overall height, 4 ft. 2¾ ins; turning circle, 30 ft; dry weight 23.5 cwt.

PERFORMANCE

	m.p.h.			secs.
MAXIMUM SPEED	—109.1	ACCELERATION	0–30 —	3.9
(Mean of 2 ways)	—108.7		0–40 —	6.1
			0–50 —	8.6
SPEEDS IN GEARS First —	33.0		0–60 —	11.9
			0–70 —	15.8
Second —	50.0		0–80 —	20.9
			0–90 —	26.8
Third —	78.0		0–100 —	41.0
Direct Top —	106.0	Standing quarter-mile	—	17.9

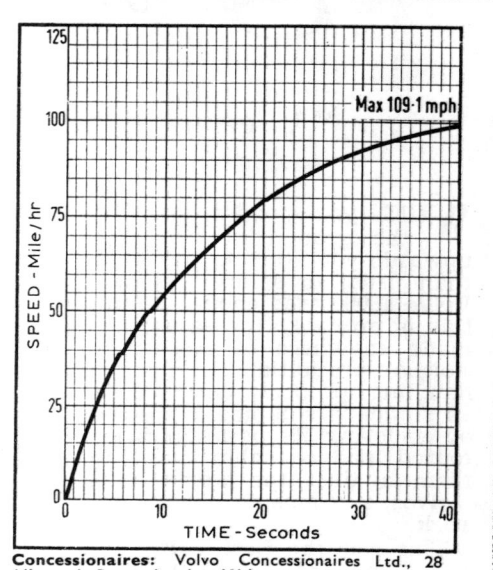

Concessionaires: Volvo Concessionaires Ltd., 28 Albemarle Street, London, W.1.
Price: £1,651 2s. 11d. including purchase tax.

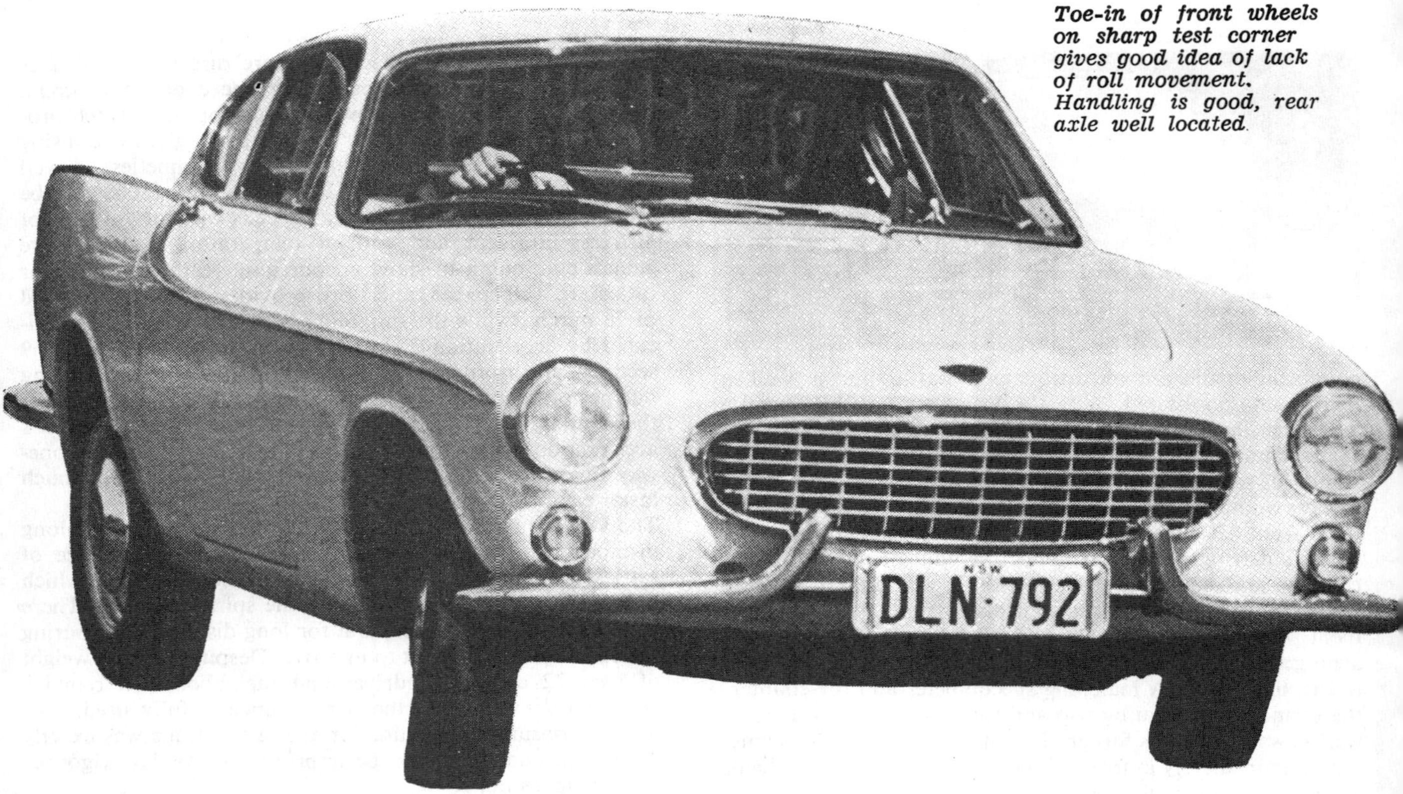

BILL TUCKEY DRIVES . . .

THE SWIFT SWEDE

SPORTS CAR WORLD · ROAD TEST

"A cosmopolitan hot-blood with refinements"

WHEN you spend a deal of your time covering the ground at velocities of 100 mph and upwards you start to pay a little more attention than usual to safety. Ten minutes of this in a Volvo 1800S was enough to impress upon us that this is probably the safest high-performance car made anywhere in the world. Apart from the normal precautions of good brakes, predictable handling, properly designed facia and seat belts as standard equipment, the Volvo has the effect of enclosing its passengers in a high-silled, contoured, padded cabin that successfully insulates them against the world outside. And, like all Volvos, it seems to have been hewn out of solid rock.

This was the first Volvo to come our way for test, thanks mainly to the increasing energies of Sydney distributor, British and Continental. Its predecessor, the P1800, was the hit of the 1960 New York Auto Show, and quite a few of these found their way to Australia. The 1800S was introduced in Sweden late last year, and while identical to the first car in matters of body, most running gear and equipment, it was uprated in power and torque.

Volvo's enormous reputation for building solid, precision-made cars is legendary. What is less well known is that the 1800S is one of the most "international" of all cars made. Because Sweden has little indigenous component manufacturing, pieces of the Volvo originally came from all over the world to Britain, where the car was finally assembled by Jensen. Now assembly is in Sweden. The tyres are Italian Pirelli Cinturato, the instruments by Smiths England, much electrical wiring by Lucas, brakes from Girling, steering gear the German ZF, overdrive by Laycock de Normanville (British),

Some idea of high sill height can be gained from this picture. Standard seat belts buckle to central latch. Seats can be adjusted for height.

Driver's view: Clock (far left) is hard to read, lettering a little too colorful. Overdrive switch at left is too far away for quick use.

Volvo's unusual styling has excellent airflow habits, but doesn't please everybody. Small badge is only clue to "MkII" model.

carburettors are SU, ignition and spark plugs by German Bosch, while the air cleaners and fuel pump are of American design. Volvo is known to wave the big stick over all its suppliers, on the principle that since it buys on a world-wide market it can expect the highest quality at the lowest cost. From the look of the 1800S, that is exactly what it gets.

The paint, finish, trim quality and panel fit on the Volvo are among the best we have seen. Everything fits beautifully, with no spot welds or rough undersides anywhere. The doors open and shut like those on a bank vault, and the spare wheel even has its own plastic cover — lined on the inside, no less. It is not hard to see £2843 worth of workmanship in this car.

Body styling remains controversial. It is most unusual, but highly efficient from the point of view of airflow. Its most unusual feature is the "fin" treatment of the rear end and the small vertical section of the cabin in comparison to the depth of the flanks. The relatively small window area is also in sharp contrast to the big glass zones used by most Italian stylists in comparable cars, but they are indigenous to the rest of the

body styling. Most of the staff thought it was a beautiful car.

It gets its excellent performance less from astronomical rpm than from a high torque figure and a notably low final drive ratio matched to an overdrive that is less of an overdrive than a true fifth gear. The results of the low final drive show up in the first three indirects and relatively good-average quarter-mile acceleration, but torque peak at 4000 rpm and maximum power at 5800 chime in with the airflow characteristics and low frontal area to provide staggeringly high cruising and top speeds.

The excellent four-cylinder engine is the same dimensionally as the 1780 cc oversquare unit which powers the Volvo B18 121, 122S and Volvo 544. However, it develops its 108 bhp at 5800 rpm, compared with 90 bhp at 5000 rpm for the 122S and 75 bhp at 4500 rpm for the other two models. It also runs on 10 to 1, where the previous P1800 was on 9.5 to 1 compression and the others are on

Rear seat squab can be dropped for load area, and cushion can also be removed. Note hook for seat belts, lamp glass in side panel.

8.5. Notable for excellent breathing, it feeds through two SU carburettors covered by paper element air cleaners that allow the unmistakable SU sucking to be heard clearly under hard acceleration. The crankshaft is carried in five main bearings (should we say, naturally?) and valve timing is not that frantic.

The Smiths tachometer is red-segmented from 6000 to 7000 rpm. We set 6500 as the sensible maximum in each gear, but used a limit of 6300 during normal running and in all performance tests except the standing quarter-mile, when we used 6500. However, the car will spin comfortably to 7000 rpm with no noticeable objection. Fourth (top) gear pulls strongly right up to almost 100 mph, but we found it best to switch in overdrive long before that.

Overdrive could be switched in without using the clutch, but at high speed switching it back to fourth would momentarily lock the wheels. We did this once to find the reaction and then promptly reverted to a habit of flicking the clutch out whenever engaging or disengaging the indirect cruising gear. After some practice the staff became sensationally good at this; they were synchronising their movements so that the sequence of shut-down into a slowish corner was a series of rapid hand and foot movements—dab, flick, back to fourth, steady, then snap the short lever into third. This, with the aid of the magnificent braking, could all be performed in less time than it takes to read it.

Habits like these make the 1800S a most appealing car to drive. Every single function works properly and well, but — and more importantly — each has been integrated into the whole so well that all the driver's actions become automatic and precise, in the knowledge that any movement he makes will naturally have the right result. This is the secret of its utter safety at high speeds; we had one wild moment when what Romsey Quints would call a triffid U-turned his

SPECIFICATIONS

CHASSIS AND BODY DIMENSIONS:

Wheelbase	8 ft 0½ in
Track, front	4 ft 3¾ in
Track, rear	4 ft 3¾ in
Ground clearance	6.5 in
Turning circle	31 ft 6 in
Turns, lock to lock	3⅞
Overall length	14 ft 5 in
Overall width	5 ft 7 in
Overall height	4 ft 2½ in

GENERAL INFORMATION:

Steering type	cam and roller
Brake type	disc front, drum rear
Swept area	350 sq in
Suspension, front	coils, wishbones, anti-roll bar
Suspension, rear	coils, trailing radius arms, Panhard rod
Shock absorbers	telescopic
Tyre size	5.90 x 15
Weight (kerb)	2444 lbs
Fuel tank capacity	12 gals
Approx. cruising range	300 miles

6A Customline in our path when we were touching 105 mph. What should have been a phenomenal avoidance converted itself into a gentle sidestep with no drama involved at all.

The Volvo understeers constantly right throughout the range, but to only a slight degree. Nevertheless, it is very hard to shake loose at the rear and even in ultra-fast sweepers one felt that the front would break adhesion first. Any sideways motoring that you can bring about is just-about self-correcting, so that you can take tight corners at quite high velocities with the trick of putting on too much lock in the entry and allowing the car to widen the radius consistently.

The gearbox is excellent, as one would expect, seeing that Volvo make it, and the clutch has very good feel and action. The brake pedal is not quite as sensitive and progressive as it could be, but near-1g stops producing shrieking deceleration in clouds of blue smoke from the Pirellis.

Our drivers were not entirely happy with the steering at first. It is fairly heavy at parking speeds, but lightens as the car starts moving, and is fine around 60 mph. Above that, it at first seemed to lose too much feel and became too sensitive, so that one was putting on a little too much lock and taking off a little too much each time. However, we checked tyre pressures and found the front ones way out of plumb. After this the steering was much, much better, although still slightly lacking in exact precision at very high speed.

There is almost no wind noise, right up to the ton, where most cars, even high-performance ones, seem to batter their way through a solid wall of air, with eddies roaring around the cockpit. Not so for the Volvo. It just slips through quietly and silently. Also, road noise is particularly low. Another major feature of the styling is that no wind rushes in through the driver's window, no matter what the speed.

Sports cars, as a general rule, and this is a real sports car, make no mistake about it, do not take kindly to bad roads. They get fits of the trembles, scuttle dance, door jitters, fender flap, and several other alarming symptoms. Often, things fall off. The strong Swede is nothing like

Spare wheel has its own tailored plastic cover, and although lying flat on floor it still leaves surprising amount of luggage room. Suitcases store flat.

this at all. It will stride across potholed bitumen without changing pace or altering line. The coil-sprung rear end is tied down firmly with trailing radius arms and a stiff Panhard rod. There is some axle tramp under hard standing-start acceleration, although we felt this could be due more to the adhesion of the Cinturatos exaggerating the torque reaction in the differential, but no sign of wheel hop over changing surfaces. Tyre noise, is however, pronounced in hard turns, but this is merely a warning of increasing understeer. Roll movement is very limited.

The 1800S demands — and deserves — fuel rated at 100 octane or a few points better. We tried it on the popular blend of 1-in-3 methyl benzine mix, which approximates 98 in number in the octane rating system, but on this we could develop some pinking at mid-point in the throttle range. However, fuel consumption is very commendable, so the pinch on the pocket will not be too severe.

Passers-by and other motorists still look at the Volvo 1800, which is a fair compliment to its unusual styling, because it has been in Australia for almost three years now.

(Continued on page 59)

ENGINE:

Cylinders	four
Bore and stroke	73.07 mm x 70.01 mm
Cubic capacity	1780 cc
Compression ratio	10 to 1
Fuel requirement	100 octane
Valves	pushrod, overhead
Maximum power	108 bhp at 5800 rpm
Maximum torque	110 lbs/ft at 4000 rpm

TRANSMISSION:

Overall ratios:

First (synchro)	14.25
Second (synchro)	9.08
Third (synchro)	6.20
Fourth (synchro)	4.56
Fourth (overdrive)	3.45
Final drive	4.56 to 1
Mph per 100 rpm in top in OD	21.7 mph

PERFORMANCE

All figures checked to 0.5 percent by Smiths electric tachometer.

Top Speed Average	107.1 mph
Fastest Run	112.5 mph

Maximum, first (6500 rpm limit)		35	mph
Maximum, second (6500 rpm limit)		50	mph
Maximum, third (6500 rpm limit)		79	mph
Maximum, fourth (direct) (6500 rpm limit)		98	mph
Standing quarter mile average		18.4	secs
Fastest run		18.2	secs
0-30 mph		3.7	secs
0-40 mph		6.2	secs
0-50 mph		8.6	secs
0-60 mph		12.4	secs
0-70 mph		19.0	secs
0-80 mph		NA	
0-90 mph		NA	
0-100 mph		NA	
0-110 mph		NA	
0-60-0 mph		15.7	secs

	Top	Third
40-60 mph	7.7 secs	6.1 secs
50-70 mph	7.9 secs	7.0 secs
60-80 mph	8.3 secs	6.5 secs
70-90 mph	9.9 secs	— secs
80-100 mph	NA secs	— secs
90-110 mph	NA secs	— secs
100-120 mph	NA secs	— secs
Fuel consumption, cruising		32-34 mpg
Fuel consumption, overall		27 mpg

CONTINUED FROM PAGE 41

the firm suspension tends to transmit itself through the steering, a certain amount of "yaw" being prevalent. Control is never in doubt, but it does necessitate work with the steering wheel. The steering wheel is slightly dished and of large diameter with handsome perforated stainless steel spokes. It would seem reasonable to assume that a high percentage of potential P1800 buyers would be men who like to drive fast, and who would appreciate a "long-arm" driving position. The Volvo just falls short of this requirement, and although a non-dished wheel would improve the situation such a modification would involve a major facia redesign, or there would be little finger clearance.

The under-steering wheel controls are well worked out on the Volvo. On the right-hand side a neat lever controls the turn indicators with up-and-down click movement, and flashes the headlights with a very short pull towards the wheel rim. On the left-hand side a similar lever blows the Bosch-type horns no matter how it is touched. So whichever lever is pulled a warning is transmitted—first-class planning. There is another horn button in the steering wheel centre.

Instrumentation is lavish, but not very well planned. In front of the driver's eyes are the two large-dial instruments for m.p.h. (with season and trip odometers) and r.p.m. These are both easy to read during daylight, but the smaller instruments for fuel contents, oil pressure, and time are not nearly so easy. The Volvo P1800 really came into being due to the repeated requests from American dealers for a Volvo sports car—a state of affairs brought about by the enthusiasm for and the high reputation of the 1.6-litre saloon models. There is little doubt that the facia was styled to please the transatlantic eye. All instruments are countersunk within a deep plated rim, with short indicator needles, and jazzy chromium embellishment in the shape of large needle bosses and "crinkled" strips around the dials. It looks impressive but is not conducive to easy readability. The three smaller round-dialled instruments are difficult to take in at a glance, and the electric clock in particular is almost impossible to read unless the eyes are brought directly in front of it. To confuse the issue further the after-dark dash illumination provides good lighting of the numerals, but it is almost impossible to see the needles. The vertical "tube" thermometers for water and oil are set ideally between the rev.-counter and speedometer.

There is generous padding around the facia and the small switches for two-speed wipers, driving lights, and heater fan are reasonably well-placed. The leather seats and plastic door trims are well carried out, and the sloping armrest/doorpulls are some of the best we have tried. Heater and demister performance was good, and the extra air ventilators (controlled from each side by cables) would provide a welcome stream of cool air at foot level during warm autumn weather.

There was considerable space behind the seats for extra luggage, and also a most useful countersunk oddments tray of surprising depth. Two small seat cushions were countersunk into the rear compartment and although these looked uncomfortable at first glance, further examination revealed them to have cushions of great depth. It was possible to carry one adult transversely for short distances, but the steeply-raked roof precluded any sort of serious travel for full-size passengers. The rear compartment would undoubtedly accommodate two children in comparative luxury.

Much heavy rain was encountered during "CI's" test and although the stability of the car was excellent it had a persistent leak from the scuttle air-intake area which deposited a slow drip on the driver's ankle. The interior noise level was low, particularly when overdrive was engaged. The car would cruise at 85–90 at around 4,000 r.p.m. in a most gentlemanly manner, the engine emitting only a purr, but if a lower gear was selected for overtaking and the accelerator fully depressed, the familiar but subdued Volvo snarl was audible as the air rushed through the "pancake" air filters of the twin S.U. carburetters. Comparatively expensive, the Volvo P1800 nevertheless has a great deal of inbuilt glamour, first-class engineering, and is undoubtedly economic to operate, besides providing very high performance without any kind of complication. Its specification and capabilities make it equally suitable for the enthusiast, or for the man with a growing family who still likes individuality in his cars, and an ability to cover the ground on business journeys. The impression gained during the test was that the Volvo gave not only high performance from a relatively small engine, but that it would go on doing so for years.

D.A.

VOLVO P1800 ROAD TEST—CONTINUED FROM PAGE 43
Lucas battery, oil filler and dip-stick are accessible but the spare fuse and main fuse-box are tucked too snugly up under the bonnet sill. The wiring is a strange mixture of Bosch and Lucas, the harness being Lucas, the fuse-box Bosch, while the coil and distributor are Bosch. The bonnet is automatically retained in the open position but, irritatingly, the prop needs human aid before it will release. The bonnet-panel seats on a tubular bar but didn't follow the curve of the scuttle as snugly as one would have liked. Volvo safety-belts with good release mechanism are standard equipment.

Driving the Volvo P1800

The Volvo P1800 can claim to have an excellent driving position. The 2-spoke rigid 16-in. steering-wheel is well placed; its spokes have rather dramatic lightning holes. Two slender, slightly too short stalks control, on the right, direction-flashers and daylight full-beam headlamps flashing, on the left the horn. The latter stalk is slightly higher than its fellow and would be more instantaneously available if it were not. The horn note is a depressing growl, matched by that sounded by the steering-wheel hub, the advertised presence of loud and soft horn notes not being apparent.

The short, rigid gear-lever protruding from the transmission tunnel couldn't be better placed. But unless the clutch, which has a very long travel, is fully depressed, the gear-change is affected, and the lever also "hangs up," so that rapid change of ratio are rendered unpleasant. This is a pity, in view of the excellence of the lever and the silence of the indirect gears. The clutch is positive and not heavy but has, as has been said, too long a movement, so those without long legs are obliged to sit closer to the steering-wheel than they would wish in order to change gear cleanly. This apart, the change is acceptable and the synchromesh effective. There is unduly strong spring loading to the right, or high ratios, side of the gate and a heavy spring to be overcome before the lever can be lifted to engage reverse, beyond the 1st gear position.

The Volvo is not a light car and it rides in a "dead" manner. But it is very comfortable, even on bad roads, and roll when cornering ambitiously is consistent and by no means excessive. Only occasionally are you aware that there is a rigid back axle although it does add to the liveliness of the ride; it is sprung on coil-springs and located by radius arms and a Panhard rod. Front suspension is wishbones and coil-springs, with anti-roll bar. The steering, geared just over 3-turns lock-to-lock, with mild but useful return action, is positive and accurate. It transmits no kick-back but "rocks" a little from straight-ahead as the front wheels ride obstructions.

The cornering tendency is towards initial understeer but the throttle can be used to bring the tail out on wet roads and generally the P1800 takes corners very predictably, can be flung about without alarming consequences and normally has neutral cornering, the steering pleasantly light and smooth except at very low speeds.

The handbrake lever, with safety guard for the ratchet-button thumb, lies unobtrusively by the outside of the driver's seat cushion—out of the way, yet very conveniently to hand. The Girling 10.9-in. disc front and drum rear brakes are very powerful, progressive, light and in every way an asset to the car. They are vacuum-servo-assisted, with very slight lag in light applications. Girling make the best disc brakes and they work superbly in this Anglo-Swedish application. Neither under fast cornering nor heavy braking do the British Pirelli Cintura tyres emit any sounds of protest.

Because this handsome coupé is a comparatively heavy car relying on a push-rod o.h.v. 100-b.h.p. engine performance is not particularly noteworthy. In the gears speeds of 28, 45 and 67 m.p.h. are possible at 6,000 r.p.m., and a top-cog cruising speed of 70 m.p.h. is readily attainable, in fact in just over 18 sec. from letting-in the clutch. A rather longer straight road allows this to be extended to 80 m.p.h. but a considerable distance is required in which to attain the top speed, in overdrive, of 105 m.p.h. For some unapparent reason the Volvo feels to be going faster than, in fact, it is, at speeds around 50 m.p.h. The speedometer is not to blame, as it is only 1 m.p.h. fast at 50, two at 60 m.p.h. At 85 m.p.h. in overdrive the engine is lazing at under 4,000 r.p.m., the same crankshaft rate in top equalling 60 m.p.h. In fact, the lower gears are rather too low, and I should be interested to try the P1800 in its native country, where an axle ratio of 4.1 to 1, with or without overdrive, is used, instead of the 4.56-to-1 ratio of the test car. As it is, overdrive is flicked in and out frequently, because at times the normal top gear feels too low, at others overdrive is too high. Its switch is well placed, but if it and the heater fan knob were changed over it might be possible to flick it without taking the left hand from the steering-wheel.

The Volvo is a smooth-travelling, quiet car for long journeys, ideal for those who want a coupé smacking of a Ferrari and a top speed well clear of the ton if they are prepared to wait for it and can put up with a s.s. ¼-mile time in excess of 19 sec. There is a crisp but never obtrusive exhaust note.

I cannot help feeling ashamed, however, of faults in British workmanship which it is improbable the meticulous engineers at Goteberg would have permitted. Besides the inoperative screen-washers and water leaks (a little more rain appeared to get past the scuttle air-intake), during the test a throttle spring came adrift and the wipers "shorted" and blew a fuse. Examination of the wiring harness in the beastliness of the gales and rain on the eve of August Bank Holiday showed very ragged wiring behind the switch and a red-hot harness, which caused severe burns before the fault was cured. A car costing over £1,836 that had ran only some 7,000 miles should be immune from such faults.

The makers claim a 10-gallon fuel tank and this ran dry from brimful in 248.8 miles, suggesting 24.8 m.p.g. under traffic con-ditions. A check in similar conditions gave a figure of 24.2 m.p.g. and a long run into mid-Wales returned 26.9 m.p.g., an average of 25½ m.p.g., using 100-octane fuel in deference to the 9.5-to-1 compression-ratio. Premium fuel is, however, quite acceptable. After 1,039 miles most of the sump oil had been consumed and 4½ pints were required to restore the level. Oil temperature was normally 175° F., water temperature 160° F. The engine started promptly without choke and is a smooth, willing power unit. Oil pressure varies from about 30 to 75 lb./sq. in.

In conclusion, there should be a sizeable market for this Volvo coupé on looks alone and many people requiring primarily a 2-seater will not be able to resist it. Thinking in Common Market terms, it is an exceptionally attractive proposition at its basic price of £1,335.—W. B.

THE SWIFT SWEDE

(Continued from page 57)

The fins seem to be the most controversial point, although they are essential to complement the "straight-through" high waistline styling and are very handy when parking.

The rest of the rear end has just enough decoration, with the lockable fuel cap, horizontal lamp clusters, deliberately small boot latch and unobtrusive number plate lamp. The rear bumpers wrap around the flanks a considerable way. The "dart-shape" styling of the car means that the front end converges toward a point, and this is accentuated by a semi-oval, forward sloping grille and the way the bumpers sweep up at their inner ends to point to an invisible arrowhead. Head and parking lights are plain, and the only "effect" working on the body is the chromed rubbing strip which adds to the dart-shape effect.

When you first get into the Volvo you are surprised at how low you sit. Actually, the seats are not so low as the sills are high. The car virtually wraps itself around the passengers from the shoulderblades down. Inside you find two full-shaped slightly narrow bucket seats, very soft foam inner over Pirelli webbing, pleated horizontal for the backside and back areas and locating right up to the shoulders and in behind the knees, as a good seat should. Two sets of Volvo harness clip into a common lock, a steel hook in the centre of the tunnel, and while they are a fine idea as standard equipment we found that adjustment was too fiddly and we would have liked a higher mounting point for the rear end of the belts. Both hang on hooks when not in use, but a lot of three-pointer webbing gets tangled up with the doors.

The doors are shaped to incorporate arm-rests and finger grips that act as door pulls. The heavy door handle runs in a chromed slot in this ledge and the window winder above this is slightly too low-geared at 3½ turns and too far rearward for comfort. Quarter-vents have push-button locks, sun-visors are crushable foam-filled, and the headlining is grained. Haircord carpet, bound at the edges, covers all the floor and the transmission tunnel. The rear windows, small areas of non-opening glass, are surrounded inside with a grey rubber filleting that looks out of place in such elegant surroundings.

The rear squab clips down flat to reveal a carpeted load area, and the seat cushion also lifts out for more room. The rear seat is adequate for one adult sitting sideways, and two children under, say, four years of age.

There are lights in each rear roof panel, worked by lifting the diffusing glass, and as well as courtesy buttons on the doors there are master override switches under each side of the facia. The seats have long rearward adjustment, but do not recline; squab adjustment is made by a disc pivoted on the eccentric that gives progressive fine and coarse adjustments. A little crude for a Volvo, but it works fine. Most drivers get very comfortable behind the slightly dished, alloy-spoked wheel that is set hard against the facia (why do other manufacturers retain the anachronism of steering columns?).

We found a 6 ft driver could very nearly get straight-arm driving with his legs fully extended and still be able to reach the gearlever. Good design, this. If anything, the wheel is a fraction too high. The rear vision mirror is mounted above the facia, and is wide and steady.

The facia itself is a split-level job, carrying instruments in the top layer and controls in the second, lower strip. In front of him the driver has two large dials, giving him speedometer, with odometer and tenths trip meter, on the left, and tachometer at right. Between these is a vertical registering water temperature in yellow and oil temperature in blue, both by moving bands of color. Left of the main dials are three smaller dials reading, from left, clock — impossible to read from the driver's seat — oil pressure gauge, and fuel gauge.

This instrument layout is where the Volvo falls down. There is too much gimmickery. Surrounded in patterned aluminium alloy, the instruments use a floating white needle behind white lettering on the glass against a blue centre and a black surround. The tachometer is segmented first in red and white candy stripes and then in red. The odd numbers on the speedometer are marked by a small chromed hump. Add to this gauges registering in yellow and blue and a magenta warning light for the overdrive and the effect becomes overwhelming. Additionally in the test car the tachometer hand wavered far too much.

In the second layer we have, from left, lighter, a very loose and tacky ashtray, overdrive tumbler switch (down for off), two-speed heater fan, two-speed windscreen wipers, overdrive warning light, headlight switch and ignition switch. On the left of the wheel boss is the trafficator stalk, on the right the loud horn (the soft horn is in the boss, and is loud enough for anybody). Under the facia, in the centre, are sliding levers controlling choke and the heater-demister. These are lit by a thrown band of light at night, and clearly lighted. The heater is colossal; we never got it above one-fifth capacity on a cold spring night, and the "slow" spot for the fan would bring on heat exhaustion.

Most of our drivers said they would have liked the overdrive switch to be closer to the wheel rim, for they have to move a hand to flick it.

All in all, a marvellous motor car. Although it has a few minor detail deficiencies, the ultimate character and construction of this Swedish import is far superior to any other car we have driven in the last six months.   #

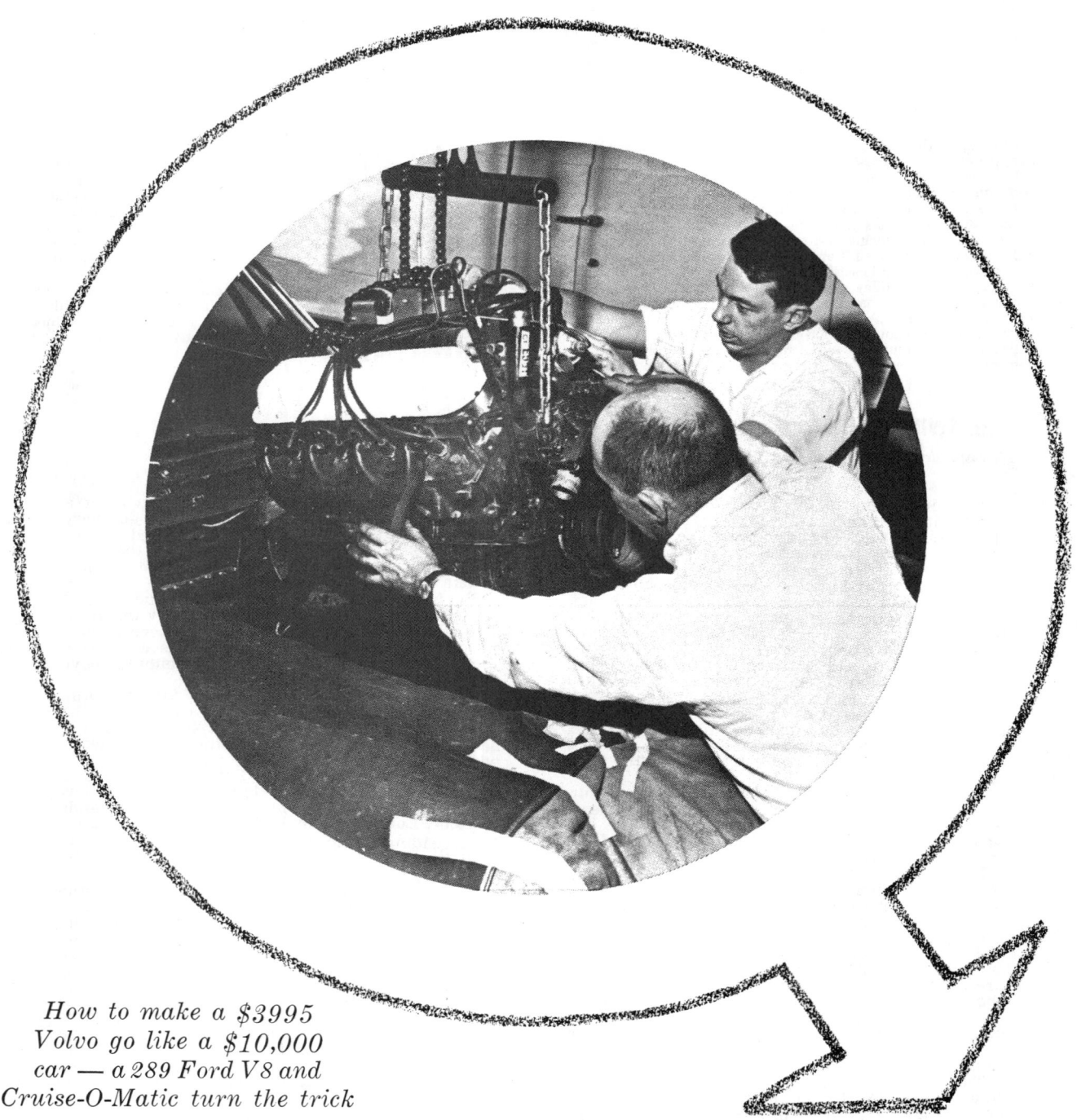

*How to make a $3995
Volvo go like a $10,000
car — a 289 Ford V8 and
Cruise-O-Matic turn the trick*

VOLVO *with*

by Stephen Wilder ■ About 18 months ago, the saucy importers of the Volvo P1800 sports coupe headlined an ad, "What's it like to own a $10,000 car? Find out for $3995." Illustrated were one each Aston Martin DB4, BMW 507, Facel Vega, Ferrari 2 + 2, Maserati 3500GT, Mercedes-Benz 300SL and, of course, the P1800. While in the copy it was allowed that all six were faster than the P1800, it was made clear that in the eyes of Volvo management "over 100 mph" was, to swipe a phrase from Rolls-Royce, sufficient. The rest of the ad was uncontroversial. It stated that for less than half the price, you get in a P1800 many of the features found in a Ferrari or Aston Martin. It was all quite forthright and honest. The P1800 does have clean styling, it is solidly built, and it does handle well — all of these, but it doesn't scald any cats in performance.

Well, you'd be amazed at the number of people who will spend ten grand to get in a car that has all those Volvo virtues and also goes *well* over 100 mph. They rarely drive that fast, but they sure like knowing they can—and who doesn't? So, for drivers who would like to get the speed potential at something less than $6005 extra, here is a Volvo P1800 powered by Ford. And one-upping all that high-priced iron is this tickler: the floor-mounted stick shifts a three-speed Cruise-O-Matic transmission!

In this engine swap, the goals were more power and smoothness with no loss in reliability, no deterioration in handling, and no reduction in the monolithic sturdiness of the Volvo's integral body-frame. Much-improved acceleration was a goal that was definitely not to be obtained at the sacrifice of any of the Volvo's many virtues, excepting fuel

photos by Don Hunter

RIGHT—The scene is set: crated 289 Ford V8 and the light Cruise-O-Matic trans beside it stand by while Volvo is prepared for operation. Entire power train came out (engine, trans and driveshaft) for replacement; rear axle for a ratio change, new hubs; plus new wheels, brake linings, shocks.

LEFT—After cutting the firewall, dummy engine is lowered into Volvo compartment, eliminating possibility of damaging the "real" one during lengthy cut-and-try period of fitting.

BELOW — Although the full-scale template engine fitted the engine compartment, it left no room for the radiator; if it was moved back a few inches, then oil pan (with pump inside) hit front crossmember. Solution: cut firewall, slide aft.

economy. If anything, it was hoped that with the increased power could come an improvement in handling. If that sounds like having your cake and eating it too, more's the credit to the man who figured how to do it and saw that it was done. Robert Cumberford is his name and industrial design is his occupation. He designed the conversion and had the work done at Holman & Moody in Charlotte, N.C., where he had been employed on their Indy car project.

Ford's 289 cubic inch V8 seemed an obvious choice but it raised two familiar questions. How do you fit 289 inches where 109 used to go? Would the rear axle stand up to the added strain?

This engine, which fits the full range of Ford Division cars but the T-bird, is relatively narrow but somewhat long. In the Volvo, its width was not much of a problem but its length certainly was, especially because of a conflict in oil-pump location. The Volvo's is at the rear, the front crossmember passing under the front of the engine, while the 289's is at the front (Ford crossmembers typically pass under the rear of the engines).

Since the crossmember was regarded as inviolate structure with absolutely no notching or modifying allowed, the oil pump situation meant that the engine had to be shifted either forward a little or rearward a lot. It could also have been raised but that would have meant a large bump in the hood and a higher center of gravity. Going forward meant cutting a hole in the radiator for the water pump or moving the radiator forward also but that would have meant shifting the hood hinges and getting into messy details trying to retain body contour and a reasonable hood-opening action. Either would have meant increasing the percentage of

V-V-VOOM!

weight on the front wheels, which at 54% in stock trim was already on the high side.

The answer was clearly to shove the engine to the rear far enough that the pan would clear the crossmember by a full inch (to allow for engine movement on the rubber mounts during hard bumps or abrupt changes of throttle setting). And this meant chopping a hole in the firewall big enough to drive a Honda through and then welding up a new firewall section to restore full frame rigidity.

Chopping up a firewall leads to images of driver and passenger sitting hunched over their knees, but the P1800's very wide foot wells provided an easy out. And since the new transmission was an automatic, the brake pedal could swing from where the clutch pedal had been, while the accelerator could be moved over to where the brake had

been. It worked out amazingly well. The foot well is 12 inches wide at the narrowest place and as far forward as before; a bit outboard from the steering column, but such lack of symmetry is found on several $10,000 cars, too.

Since the Cruise-O-Matic is wider though no higher than the Volvo four-speeder, the saber-saw operation on the firewall had to include an equally large section of the tunnel. The car, of course, was up on four tripod stands at the time and was not moved until new sheet metal was welded in. It was a long interval. First the engine and transmission were slid in from above and placed on wooden blocks and garage jacks while their final position was sorted out. Retaining ground clearance for the oil pan, placing the U-joint companion on the center-line of the original drive-

(Continued on following page)

VOLVO WITH V-V-VOOM! *continued*

ABOVE LEFT — Round cross-member under pan locates the engine mounts, a rectangular tube at extreme left bolts to trans, while center angle iron only braces the frame rails.

ABOVE RIGHT — It fits, but only if exhaust manifolds are taken off. Cutout in firewall was later widened to include part of brake/clutch cylinder mount, allow for manifold. Note where Volvo mounts were.

LEFT — A one-by-two rectangular tube welded across firewall adds strength after the surgery. The battery box was removed, shifted to the trunk.

BELOW LEFT — In solid, V8's non-stock items are H-M manifold, alternator, Carter carb (better clearance for yoke). Heater clears hood, and brake booster mounts in stock spot.

BELOW RIGHT — Now watch from the other point of view. At first, the Cruise-O-Matic barely protrudes into cockpit.

shaft, and getting the carburetor approximately level were the three criteria; fortunately, everything worked out.

Regular Galaxie engine mounts were used, bolting onto new brackets that were welded to the framelike box-sections that outline the bottom of the engine compartment. A 1¾-inch round tube connects the two new brackets, sweeping down under the shallow portion of the oil pan. Just behind the bell housing, a 1¼ x 1¼ angle, 25 inches long, is bolted in to brace the frame. A third such connection is the 1 x 2 rectangular tube that crosses behind the transmission, carrying a '56 Ford transmission mount on quarter-inch-thick, forward-facing, welded-on arms.

In cutting the firewall, the battery box got sliced up, so the battery moved to the trunk where it found a healthier environment and shifted many pounds usefully rearward. The heater-defroster unit came down from its high on the center-line position to fill the void left by the battery. A 1 x 2 rectangular tube was welded in across the top of the entire firewall cutout to provide a sturdy reinforcement where the new transmission tunnel was to intersect with

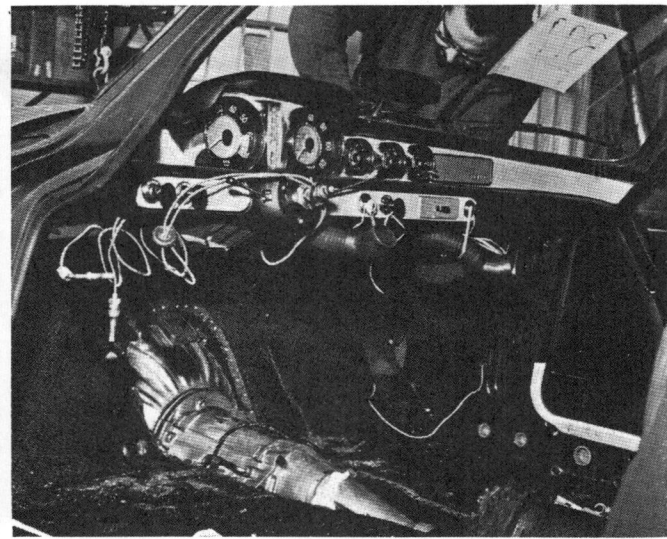

original firewall. As further reinforcement, once the installation was complete, a corrugated Ford Falcon yoke was bolted in, connecting the top of each wheel arch with top-center on the firewall. While this part may not have been absolutely necessary, the firewall is so important as a structural bulkhead that no changes could be afforded and no facilities were available to stress-analyze or static-test its modification. After a Carter carb, half of the Falcon Sprint's dual quad set-up, was substituted, the yoke cleared it, the master cylinder and the heater motor so it was simple, economical.

While the 289 is not as narrow as a four, it is quite narrow for a V8 of its displacement. The problems at the sides of the engine were therefore of the shoehorn type. The left exhaust manifold, which has to clear the steering column, is the left-side part from a Falcon Sprint which empties at the bottom. The right manifold is the left-side part of a Galaxie 289 and empties at the front because it is mounted upside-down. Asymmetry has its unexpected blessings.

ABOVE LEFT — So a bigger hole was made — and how! Location of stock pedals shows how slightly feet need be shifted left. Check narrowness of 289.

ABOVE RIGHT — Engine and trans were covered with formed, welded sheet-metal. A regular Cruise-O-Matic "stick-shift" and quadrant falls readily to hand. Volvo disc brakes are boosted but Ford pedal advertises same, is wider.

To the rear, the companion flange of the Cruise-O-Matic was so much farther to the rear than the Volvo's that it was decided to abandon the Volvo's two-piece driveshaft completely and install a shortened, one-piece Galaxie shaft. This is a stronger unit and avoids any chance of an odd, hard-to-find vibration.

It's a bit startling, but the entire rear axle on Swedish Volvos is U.S.-built, brakes and all. The axle is a Spicer series 27 unit, similar to those used by Studebaker, Willys and International Harvester, though with different hubs, spring perches, and shock mounts. For the time being, it remains stock but for a ratio change and the

installation of heavy-duty hubs and brake linings. While that may sound simple, a great deal of thought went into deciding not to change to the next larger series 44 axle. Axle assemblies are rated by output torque; that is, torque delivered to the rear wheels. Neglecting the small friction losses inherent in any gear train, output torque equals engine torque times the lowest transmission ratio (first or reverse) times the ring-and-pinion ratio. For a stock P1800, this 110 ft./lbs. times 3.25 (reverse) times 4.56 (or 4.10 without overdrive). It comes out to 1600 ft./lbs., and Spicer rates the 27 axle at 1800.

Although the rear axle and the final drive gears are often the Achilles heel of many an engine swap, there are several escape routes. One is to use an appropriately lower final drive ratio; another is to use a close-ratio transmission (or block off first gear as in the early Austin-Healeys). And if your car is light enough on the rear tires, they may break loose at considerably less than maximum torque to serve as a sort of protective slip joint in the drive

(Continued on page 71)

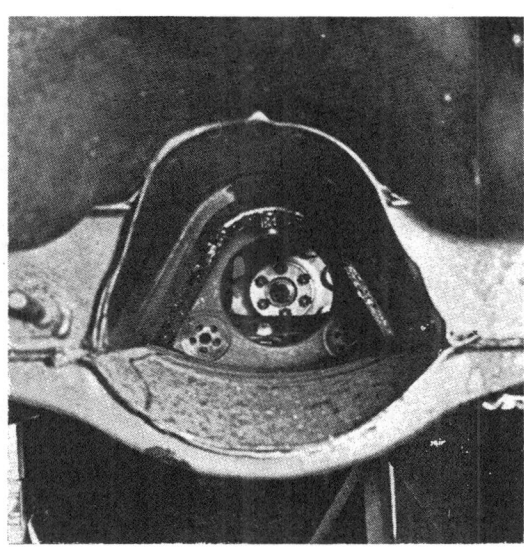

RIGHT — Rear axle's view of Ford V8 ensures engine alignment for center and height. Bulkhead for the steady-bearing at mid-point of Volvo two-piece driveshaft was later removed since one-piece shaft was employed.

FAR RIGHT—Shimming of new 3.07 ring and pinion in original Spicer series 27 axle assembly is checked. With original 4.56 ratio, acceleration would have been hampered by frequency of axle failure.

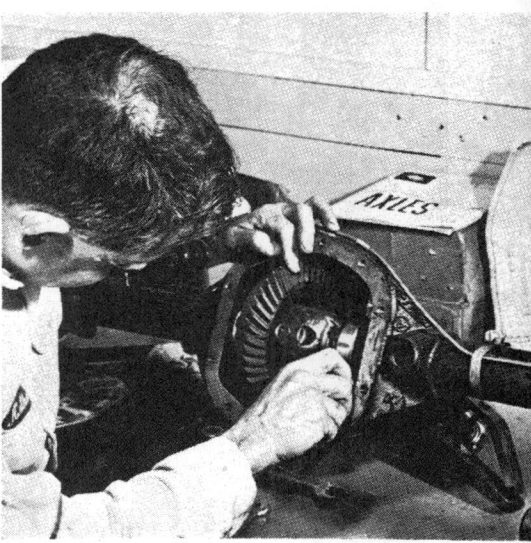

THE Volvo 1800S is an unusual car. Though it is a sporting fixed-head coupé, with an occasional rear seat, it is very solidly constructed and most luxuriously equipped, with no thought of weight saving. It is fairly costly, but by employing a four-cylinder engine the makers have kept down the fuel consumption to a figure which is acceptable on the Continent.

The engine is an orthodox five-bearing unit with pushrod-operated overhead valves, but it differs from typical modern practice in having a gear-driven camshaft. Twin SU carburetters are fitted. The Volvo gearbox was one of the first to have synchromesh on bottom gear (no, I haven't forgotten Alvis!), and it has a pleasantly short lever mounted on a remote control tunnel. The propeller shaft is divided, with a central steady bearing, and the hypoid axle is positively located both fore and aft and laterally, the suspension being by helical springs.

An orthodox wishbone front end also has helical springs and a torsional anti-roll bar, with cam and roller steering. The Girling brakes have discs in front and servo assistance. The Pirelli Cinturato tyres are fitted with inner tubes.

The body is of an attractive shape, though the low roof line entails the use of a rather shallow screen and windows. One seems to sit low down inside the car but the all-round view is nevertheless perfectly satisfactory. A delightful instrument panel carries such dials as oil pressure *and* temperature gauges, as well as the more usual one for water temperature. The upholstery and carpets are of the highest grade.

The big four-cylinder engine of the Volvo is quite flexible and will pull strongly at low speeds. It revs. very freely, running well past the 6,000 r.p.m. mark as a matter of course, but it gets pretty busy as the revs. rise. There is some vibration, which is usual with a four-cylinder unit of 1,800 c.c., but the overdrive permits fast cruising with the engine running below its busy speed. This gives the easy and effortless running that a big four can so well provide.

The gearchange is excellent and the gears are quiet, while the clutch grips well after a quick change. A very good feature is the use of direct connection by rods of the accelerator, without any flexible cable. Flexible cables usually give a sticky, jerky movement, and to eliminate this source of trouble is to guarantee a permanently smooth operation. The brakes are also sweet in action, though they are powerful when a panic stop is demanded.

Fairly wide spacing of the gears is not noticeable with this flexible engine. I went a little over the 6,000 r.p.m. mark to reach 50 m.p.h. in second gear and 70 m.p.h. in third, to the benefit of the acceleration graph. Curiously enough, the well-located rear axle hops

a bit during a rapid getaway, but it behaves very well on bumpy corners. It is possible to touch 97 m.p.h. on the direct top gear, but most people would prefer to use the overdrive above 80 m.p.h., in the interest of smoother and quieter running.

The steering is quite light to handle, in spite of the fairly substantial weight of the car. The handling characteristic is neutral, though the tail can be hung out on power. This is a car which never does anything unexpected, nor does it suddenly change its handling in the middle of a corner. The comfortable seats give good support but the scuttle and bonnet line are rather high for a short driver. There is some roll during fast cornering.

Giving plenty of space, the boot is partly occupied by the spare wheel, though this is enclosed in a cover. There is useful additional space on a shelf behind the folding rear seat back, but there is a shortage of storage room for odds and ends in the front compartment, there being no glove locker or map shelf. Laminated glass is standard, so a suddenly opaque screen need not be feared. Much of the detail work repays close study, the method of pulling down and securing the bonnet without slamming it being worthy of praise. The doors shut nicely but the rear quarter lights do not open. The controls of the heating system are sensibly arranged.

The 1800S is not really a sports car, but it will exceed 100 m.p.h. with something in hand. It would be a pleasant vehicle for long journeys, though it is also suitable for shopping as the large doors make entry and exit quite easy, in spite of the low roof line. Safety is very much to the fore, for Volvo was one of the first manufacturers to standardize safety belts. The car is also thoroughly safe in its handling, and the immensely strong and rigid steel structure would be a splendid protection.

The Volvo 1800S is a thoroughly well-made medium-sized car with many luxurious appointments. Its unusual appearance singles it out from the rows of ordinary saloons, and if it is rather costly for a four-cylinder machine it has an individuality that will appeal particularly to the fair sex. It has obviously been built to have a very long life and to stand up to the toughest conditions. It carries an honoured name which is respected all over the world.

SPECIFICATION AND PERFORMANCE DATA

Car Tested: Volvo 1800S fixed-head coupé, price £1,814 1s. 3d.

Engine: Four-cylinders 84.14 mm. × 80 mm. (1,780 c.c.). Pushrod-operated overhead valves. Compression ratio 10 to 1. 108 b.h.p. (gross) at 5,800 r.p.m. Twin SU carburetters. Bosch coil and distributor.

Transmission: Single dry plate clutch. Four-speed all-synchromesh gearbox with central remote control and Laycock-de Normanville overdrive, ratios 3.34 (overdrive), 4.56, 6.16, 9.07 and 14.27 to 1. Divided propeller shaft. Hypoid rear axle.

Chassis: Combined steel chassis and body. Independent front suspension with wishbones, helical springs and anti-roll bar. Cam and roller steering gear. Rear axle on two pairs of radius arms, Panhard rod and helical springs. Telescopic dampers all round. Servo-assisted hydraulic brakes with discs in front and drums at rear. Bolt-on pierced disc wheels, fitted 165-15 in. Pirelli Cinturato tyres.

Equipment: Twelve-volt lighting and starting. Speedometer. Rev. counter. Water and oil temperature gauges. Oil pressure and fuel gauges. Clock. Cigar lighter. Heating, demisting and ventilation system. Two-speed windscreen wipers and washers. Flashing direction indicators. Seat belts.

Dimensions: Wheelbase, 8 ft. 0½ in.; Track, 4 ft. 3¼ ins.; Overall length, 14 ft. 5¼ ins.; Width, 5 ft. 7 ins.; Weight, 1 ton 2 cwt.

Performance: Maximum speed, 104.6 m.p.h. (overdrive). Speeds in gears: direct top, 97 m.p.h.; third, 70 m.p.h.; second, 50 m.p.h.; first, 31 m.p.h. Standing quarter-mile, 18.6 secs. Acceleration: 0–30 m.p.h., 3.6 secs.; 0–50 m.p.h., 9 secs.; 0–60 m.p.h., 13 secs.; 0–80 m.p.h., 23.2 secs.

Fuel Consumption: 23 to 27 m.p.g.

ACCELERATION GRAPH

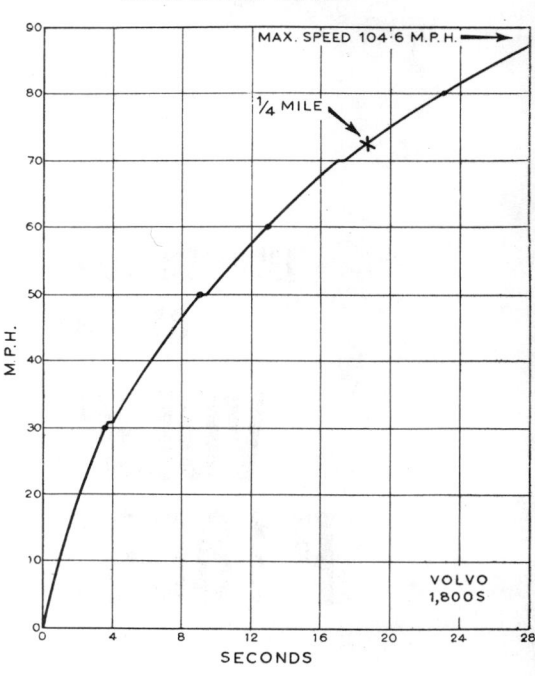

MAX. SPEED 104·6 M.P.H. →

¼ MILE

VOLVO 1,800S

M.P.H.

SECONDS

IMPRESSIONS OF THE VOLVO P1800S

PERHAPS one of the most unexpected new cars of recent years was that sporting model from Volvo, the P1800. All previous Volvos had been solid and very reliable saloons, which nevertheless achieved a remarkable record in the rougher rallies of the late 50s. The P1800 was announced almost as soon as one prototype car had been finished, in May 1959, but it was not until mid-1961 that this fascinating hybrid, with Pressed Steel body, Volvo mechanical parts and final assembly by Jensen at West Bromwich, appeared on the market.

Today, the body is still British-made but final assembly is in Sweden Volvos built at the Gothenburg factory are known as the P1800S (S being the clue). Since our last road test of the car in July 1962, there have been few changes; twin exhausts have increased maximum power to 115 b.h.p., and some of the controls have been re-positioned.

My first visit to Sweden—a quick trip into the depths of a severe Scandinavian winter with photographer Ron Easton to report on the Swedish International Rally—seemed to offer a perfect excuse for trying the latest car. We wanted to confirm that even a sporting car aimed principally at the American market could cope with the very-sub-zero temperatures which are so common over there.

A quick flight to Gothenburg by BEA Comet (tricky landing on an ice-covered runway) dropped us literally on the doorstep of the Volvo factory; our car was sitting in the airport car-park awaiting collection.

The Volvo makes no concessions to seating four; the upholstered shelf behind the seats is more useful for stowing cameras and delicate luggage. On the other hand, driver and passenger have a lot of room to make themselves comfortable. As I am one of the most difficult staff members to "fit" into any car, I was astounded to discover for the very first time that I didn't need the seat right back. Once that is set, further adjustments can be made. The angle of the back rest can be altered a little by twisting a knurled knob at the base of the squab, and the shaped lumbar

VOLVO P1800S ...

Graham Robson checks the pressures of the studded Goodyear Ultragrips

support in the squab is adjustable. To truss me in completely I pulled the (standard) Volvo seat belts nice and tight.

So here I am, tied into place. Can I reach all the controls? The handbrake hides between the seat and the door (with enough leverage to start hand-brake turns on the snow) and the stubby gear lever is alongside the wheel. New to me was the "any-direction" trigger-switch for the overdrive; fan it once and overdrive engages (with a red warning light to remind you), fan it again and it disengages. The only peculiarity is that overdrive, which works only on top gear, does not cut out automatically when one changes gear; next time one changes back into top the overdrive cuts in automatically.

Studded Grip

The snow-covered roads looked daunting until I remembered the part-studded Goodyear Ultragrip tyres fitted all round. There could have been barely 80 tiny tungsten-tipped studs in each of the wide, flat, winter treads, but the increased grip on ice (particularly under braking) made me positively exuberant after a bit of practice. Ron Easton is still saying that he will never come with me again. . . .

It's not a temperamental car at all; even on ice everything feels very stable, though the steering seemed heavy at times because of the coarse tyres. A bit of understeer at low speeds on ice could be countered by "bringing the tail round" under power. I soon learned not to brake in mid-corner on these studded tyres; front-end breakaway was almost certain on this car, as the servo felt rather "dead," with little feel to the pedal at light pressures.

While the majority of cars seemed to be using studs in the depths of the Swedish winter, we found all the main roads well ploughed. Snow-ploughs are in use round the clock, and plain tyres would be safe enough on the highways.

The Volvo stood outside every night in temperatures approaching 70 deg. F. of frost, but it still started first pull in the mornings with liberal use of the choke. The starter groaned a bit, and turned the engine slowly, but never let us down. Once warm, the engine pulled smoothly up to a useable 6,500 r.p.m. Occasionally I suspected carburettor icing when snapping open the throttle at low speeds, but this quickly cleared, and *could* have been just a minor fault in settings. We didn't take performance figures because of excessive drag from the studded tyres; nevertheless the P1800S could be cruised at an indicated 140 k.p.h. (87 m.p.h.) without strain.

With all this, and a lot of idling while parked (to keep the heater working) we still managed about 24 m.p.g. on 100 octane petrol.

I was grateful for a really efficient heater. Once the engine was warm, a positive gale of hot air was on tap, allowing us to drive in comfort without coats or gloves. Even so, the cold outside was so intense that condensation froze on the inside of the side windows.

Of course, the overall impression—as expected—was of a very solid, well-made product. The Volvo reputation for reliability, backed up by competition successes throughout the world, is hard to beat. When this is linked with sports car looks, handling and performance, the only drawback is the price: At £1,814 (in G.B.) it has to compete with Alfas and E-types; in Sweden, or in the U.S.A., it is a very different story. **Graham Robson** ∎

Vunderful Volvo

Barry Cooke tries stretching the long legs of Sweden's P1800S, and finds it very classy indeed. As it ought to be, at $5300 . . .

ONE thing about television. At least the kids are getting to know their cars.

There I was the other day driving the Volvo P1800S coupe past a very posh private school on Sydney's North Shore. One Billy Bunter type shouted, "There's the Saint!" and the entire school — which was at recess — turned and watched as the Volvo whispered past.

I'd have been something less than an ordinary human being not to derive pleasure at the sidelong glances which came the way of the Volvo while I had it.

It's that sort of car — sleek, unusual looking, and not sufficiently well known yet to arouse anything but interest, curiosity and envy in the average bystander.

I found it a car that takes time to learn. The controls don't encourage sloppy driving techniques, although once you get the hang of things it is really an easy and forgiving car to operate.

Consequently, I found the concentration it demanded to be well driven awakened in me much of the traditional pleasure of motoring, dulled by a long string of lesser cars.

Learning the Volvo is a problem which can't be solved in a hurry. The low seating position, combined with high waistline and low roofline, restricts visibility to such a degree that, for the first few hours of driving, you're not sure of the precise position of the car's extremities.

Learning to use the gears is another thing. There is very little movement between positions, either fore and aft or across the gate.

This proves to be a good thing if correct techniques are used — such as palming the lever backhand for a change from first to second or third to second. Do it any other way, and it's odds on that you'll find top, accompanied of course by some embarrassing coughing and spitting from the motor.

Once you realise that the Volvo is a car that demands correct driving techniques, it responds perfectly and does everything asked of it.

Styling

I've - said - it - before - and - I'll - say - it - again: styling likes and dislikes are very much a matter of taste.

The P1800 has the sort of looks that are universally impressive to the uninitiated: low, streamlined, rakish, functional — sexy, if you like.

Aerodynamically it is first-class, with that near-perfect wedge shape designed for good penetration.

Appearance of this model is only slightly changed from its predecessor.

Most obvious difference is the wheels, which are now distinctively slotted to improve brake cooling.

There are also rubber bumper overriders front and rear to improve protection. The bumpers themselves are more solidly constructed and firmly braced, so they should be some help in the event of a biff.

Slight changes to the grille give the P1800 a slightly smiling countenance, and the egg-crate insert of yore has been replaced by a metal mesh stamping.

Inside, seats are modified to improve comfort and support. They do both, although there is still room for improvement in the latter department.

Comfortwise, they have no peer, and even include an adjustable

68

TOP: *The classically sleek profile of the P1800S.* LEFT: *Front view shows essential simplicity of line.* ABOVE: *Rear doesn't quite reach the same standard, and vision isn't all it could be.* BELOW: *Those seats are very comfortable — but they could give more support.*

VUNDERFUL VOLVO

lumbar support that slides up and down inside the backrest.

Instrumentation is very comprehensive, includes a speedo, tacho, oil pressure gauge, oil temperature gauge, water temperature gauge, and fuel gauge. There is no ammeter, just a warning light marked "Gen."

There are simple button controls for two-speed wipers (with integrated washer), manual choke, lights, and a very efficient heater-demister unit.

The whole effect of the cockpit is spoiled to some extent by rather "stylistic" dash decor. The instruments are sparsely calibrated, and stand proud from the instrument panel in chunky chrome-plated surrounds.

However, in their favor is a very good lighting system that brought an envious comment from an overseas airline pilot friend. He wished the 707 layout was as well lit as the Volvo's.

Driving position is very good, and, thanks to infinite seat adjustment possibilities, should fit everyone. Foot pedals are well spaced, and big.

In addition to individual front seats, there is a small upholstered bench in the rear. Rakish angle of the rear roofline cuts down headroom severely here, but it is nonetheless a useful area for two small children.

Its usefulness is further enhanced by provisions which allow the seat to be folded flat and converted into a luggage compartment to supplement the boot.

The latter, incidentally, is quite a reasonable size, but spoiled by the spare wheel laid flat on the floor. If you're game to travel without a spare, it will take quite a good load.

Mechanicals

Volvo's power unit is a thoroughly refined ohv water-cooled four. Originally a 1.5-litre, it was enlarged to 1780c.c. for inclusion in the P1800 and 122 sedan series.

So massively strong is it that considerably more boring and stroking could be done without risk.

It is quite conventional in layout, using in the coupe a compression ratio of 11 to 1 and twin 1¾in. SU's. It develops 115 bhp at 6000 rpm and 112 ft./lb. of torque at 4000 rpm. That compression ratio makes the addition of a high-power additive like methyl benzine almost arbitrary.

If you're stuck, it will run on straight super, but not very quietly.

Most striking aspect of the motor is its almost indecent smoothness, which is superior to any other four I've ever driven. It will trickle down to 20 mph in top and accelerate away almost like a turbine. Very impressed, I was.

The generous proportions of the five-bearing crankshaft, which has a huge inbuilt safety margin, account for much of this.

Gearbox, as already mentioned, encourages correct usage. But it, too, is very smooth when mastered, the short lever with its contoured knob slicing through the gate like the proverbial hot knife.

Fully synchronised, the ratios are

well chosen, and have the added attraction of an electric overdrive on top gear. This overdrive, operated by a small wand on the steering column, has a ratio of 0.756 to 1, and is good for 21.2 mph per 1000 rpm.

Clutch is one of the sweetest I've ever used, is gradual in take-up, and reasonably light in operation.

Suspension is a conventional coil and wishbone set-up at the front. The rigid rear axle, however, is located by a complex system employing two longitudinal support arms and two longitudinal torque arms. Transverse location of the axle is taken care of by a track rod attached to the axle near the nearside coil spring and to the chassis just inside the offside wheelarch.

Very effective, too.

Big discs are fitted on the front, and they are heavily shrouded to protect them from dust and rubbish thrown up by the wheels. Rear drums complement the discs.

Swept area of the brakes is 339 sq. in. A brake servo unit is standard equipment, although its effect is so well controlled that it is virtually undetectable in use.

Pedal pressures are light, but not so light as to suggest servo assistance, and for that reason I like it.

On the Road

The P1800 is at its best on the open road, where its fairly soft ride and long overdrive legs make it ideal for really swift cruising.

Ninety mph can be maintained quite comfortably in overdrive, this being equivalent to about 4300 rpm.

At these speeds the springy, responsive cam-and-roller steering gives precise control, and the excellent

brakes are a considerable reassurance.

Ride is surprisingly soft, and there is also a considerable amount of body lean.

As is often the case, though, it's not really noticeable from inside the car, although on one or two occasions I partially slid from the seat.

Lateral location of passengers is greatly helped by the excellent three-point safety belts which are standard.

Vigorous cornering on loose surfaces is great fun, thanks to the absolute predictability of the Volvo's behavior. Under such circumstances all cars can be made to oversteer in the sense that the tail will hang out.

Not all, however, will respond with the rapidity and precision of the P1800.

On sealed surfaces we never once succeeded in getting the back end unstuck. An acceptable degree of understeer was evident in all the corners we tackled, no matter how fast.

Travelling fast over rough surfaces produced only subdued noise from the suspension, and at all times the car seemed to have all four feet well and truly planted on the ground.

Not until we came to our performance tests were we troubled by fierce wheelspin and back axle tramp — all this despite the track rod and torque rods.

We solved the problem (only partly the fault of the Volvo, for the bitumen of the strip was very hot and consequently sticky) by popping the clutch on about 2500 rpm.

The motor would die momentarily, then pick up and spin right out — well into the red zone above 6000 rpm unless we were very quick with the gear-change.

Turbine-smooth right through the

range, the motor is one of the most outstanding features in an altogether outstanding car.

But the other components — gearbox, clutch and brakes—have a brand of excellence seldom experienced these days. They operated smoothly and without complaint throughout the pretty merciless pounding.

The effectiveness of our methods of getting it off the line is amply demonstrated by the figures in the performance panel. They're very good.

Keeping all this performance potential company is a set of brakes which are altogether excellent. As mentioned, pedal pressures, despite servo assistance, aren't so light that the brakes are grabby.

They retain a surprising amount of "feel" and consequently can be used with great precision.

Noise is not obtrusive until the motor is revved hard, although I feel sure this series of the coupe is not as well insulated as earlier models.

With all the windows in place, wind noise is very subdued, a tacit comment on the car's excellent streamlining.

Returning to the city from our out-of-town test strip, we were able to stretch the Volvo's long legs on some of N.S.W.'s fastest rural roads.

The car demonstrated that it has all the ingredients necessary for hour after hour of effortless high-speed motoring. It remained balanced and poised throughout the journey, out-braking, out-accelerating, and out-handling every other car we came across.

It left an indelible impression on my mind, just as I'm sure it will do on anyone else who is lucky enough to drive it. ●

VOLVO WITH V-V-VOOM!

continued from page 63

train. But if this is the case, you must beware of popping the clutch on any surface that gives a better-than-usual bite such as little-used concrete.

In this case, the latter course was out because smoothness was as important as performance. A close-ratio transmission was out, Cruise-O-Matics having only one set of ratios (2.46—1.46—1.00) but there was a last resort thought available — to limit use to D-2, effectively blocking out first gear. But there is one more exit from this predicament. Firms like Spicer tend to be very conservative when rating their products, so that they can operate indefinitely at rated load. Peak torque in a passenger car comes only rarely and then only for a brief moment (brief but exhilarating). It didn't take long to check all the other uses of the 27 and find that it's used on the Studebaker with V8 and automatic and that ratios up to 3.73 are offered. The appropriate multiplication is 260 x 5.16 (at stall) x 3.73 = 5,000 ft./lbs. Stude axles were never faulted (although it's worth noting that station wagons, taxis, and police cars come with the larger 44 axle). So, pending an unexpected misfortune, this Volvo still has its original

axle fitted, of course, with a 3.07 ratio. If it should break, or if a limited-slip is called for, a 44 will be made up with Volvo spring perches and hubs.

Rounding off the modifications was the swapping of 15 x 5½ Ford wheels (part #C1AZ-1007A) for the 4½-inch wide originals, the installation of bronze racing pads in the front disc brakes and sintered iron linings in the rear drums, and the fitting of Koni shocks.

Before the car was finished — private customers come a belated second to the Ford Motor Company at Holman & Moody — Cumberford had moved to

New York to open his own design offices. Since picking up the car, certain changes have been made. To cure persistent overheating, even when it was driven gently, the hose connections on the radiator were changed to larger diameter Ford-size parts so that the water pump's high-velocity output would not be restricted. And a new Ford filler neck was also soldered on, sidestepping a fruitless search for a 14-pound cap that would fit the Volvo neck. At the same time, the transmission oil cooler was removed from behind the radiator and placed in the lower tank of the radiator, so that a fan shroud could

be fitted. All this subsequent work was done at Jocko's Speed Shop in Poughkeepsie, New York. Jocko also built an air duct to connect the cowl vent with the heater motor and installed Volvo sedan springs in place of the original rear coils to reduce the excessive bottoming brought about by rearward shift of the center of gravity.

Now that the work is done, Cumberford finds he has nearly doubled the horsepower (108 to 210), dropped from premium to regular in fuel requirements, and increased the weight on the driving wheels from 46 to 49½ per cent while adding a mere 60 pounds on the front wheels. Externally the only change is the larger-than-usual pair of exhaust pipes — until the car's in motion. As intended, the 3.07 axle sees to it that it cruises like a jet on final approach, 70 mph taking only 3000 rpm. The unexpected pleasure is the sterling acceleration, even from a standstill. The car hasn't been to the drags yet to get an official timing, but it has pulled a GTO without any difficulty, the better weight distribution more than balancing 100 extra inches. And the GTO owner was driving the Volvo — how's that for learning the hard way. ▪▪

SPORTS CAR WORLD · ROAD TEST

By BILL TUCKEY

VOLVO P1800 S:

SAUCY SWEDE

The Volvo Sports Coupe, perhaps more than any other car, has a certain charm that seems to radiate an unspoken request and pledge a silent oath: come hither, go further.

Driver's lounge — comfort, sheer comfort.

TELEVISION is a wonderful thing; the last time we drove a Volvo 1800 S hardly a soul turned his head. We spent a week with the new one — which looks identical — and started feeling like The Saint after two days. He drives one. And we don't blame him. This is probably the most durable, safest and best made sports car in the world, ideal for rugged dashes after elusive crooks.

Among hard core enthusiasts the name of Volvo is a legend in Australia. This, surprisingly, is not so much because of the sports car as the 122S sedan, an almost superhuman car which does everything one demands of it. The 1800 S has all the attributes of the sedan, but adds an aristocratic, almost feminine flair that is found only in good Scandinavian furniture or fine Danish earthenware. The Scandinavians build into

their furniture and their crockery dual personalities of masculine ruggedness and feminine grace — hard items to combine. The 1800 S has both.

It is true that the 1800 S looks little different from last year's car. But the grille has closer mesh and the small front bumperettes no longer curve upward into the grille. More significantly, the power has gone up from 108 bhp to 115 bhp by the use of a double exhaust system. The braking system also gets a new reduction valve to balance braking between front and rear, and nine lubrication points have been eliminated.

These are simply refinements to what was already a very refined car. The power lift does not make such a great difference to the performance figures, but it has had the effect of closing up the gearbox ratios slightly as well as making the

The engine — willing horses.

car a little more flexible in top gear. But what it does do most effectively is improve still further the car's natural good balance.

A Volvo has always been a quiet car; the 1800 S is astonishingly silent for a car that runs so hard. With all windows up you can whistle along at 90-plus in almost complete stillness. Despite radial ply tyres, road noise is very low and the excellent airflow characteristics of the dart-shaped body give it superb penetration through the air blanket. The windows slope inward at the top but when you roll them down at speed there is no sudden roar or wind rush into the cockpit — always a sure sign of good aerodynamics.

This road and wind quietness, however, emphasises the engine noise. The Volvo engine in its several forms is a very quiet unit, but in the 1800 S you can hear quite clearly the suck of the SUs under hard acceleration and some valve gear clatter at idle. The tyres themselves (Pirelli Cinturato on the test car) do not reflect into the body the normal radial ply thump.

Electric overdrive is fitted to top gear only, with the switch moved in this model from the dashboard to the right hand side of the wheel, and the car is geared so that overdrive top is a true fifth gear. You can run out of breath at just over 6000 in direct top at around 94 mph, and overdrive top comes on quite strongly above that. The selector lever seems omni-directional — just the slightest touch from any angle will operate it. It needs the clutch popped quickly just to ease it in and out. The gearing is additionally

The boot — adequate.

sensible in that when cruising hard in OD substantial retardation is available simply by slipping back into direct top. The good driver uses this to great advantage, barrelling along the road and using the OD switch up and down to slow him for corners and accelerate out of them.

The gearbox itself is superb — short movements through a remote lever, very quiet, and with powerful synchromesh. The spring-loading against first and second is a little too strong, and it is easy to drop back into top when doubling from third to second. Otherwise the transmission is faultless, even the rear axle, which has given seals trouble in past 1800 models.

The same can be said about the steering; apart from slight lost motion from dead ahead, the steering has a beautiful action. It is a little heavy at parking speeds, and lightens up a little too much over 75 mph, but directional control and accuracy in corners give the driver tremendous confidence. We did find some feedback through the steering under brakes and on lumpy surfaces, but not too much.

AB Volvo has gone to great pains with its spring and damper rates for this car. The result is a firm, well-controlled ride with enough wheel movement to soak up severe bumps but with little roll movement. The 1800 S rides very well for a sporting car, with only some chop from the rear axle on poor roads. It rides equally well on dirt. There is absolutely no scuttle or door shake, no body tremble, and very little wheel hop. The rear end is properly located, so that you can hammer this car through long fast bends studded with bumps without the car moving an inch off line. This is a more important factor in a sports car than most people realise. If the car leaps around with power on in a corner you might just as well pack up and go home. It MUST stay on the line you have selected for it with the amount of throttle you judge necessary for the corner.

If the Volvo does anything other than behave neutrally, it has a touch of understeer. There does seem to be a fraction too much weight toward the rear — possibly due to engine location — as we have the lightening steering condition we mentioned as well as a tendency for a front wheel to lift when a lot of lock is applied suddenly on an uneven surface. For the same reason the front tends to weave a little in long sweepers taken in overdrive; quite often we went back into direct top for enough power to keep the car tracking correctly.

But it is a very hard car to lose, despite the conditions. If you can get it out sideways, it can be slapped back into place with that accurate steering. In the wet, it is as safe as a Mini, not changing its handling characteristics at all, with almost as much adhesion as it has in the dry. It is a car which makes good drivers out of indifferent ones, and experts out of the above average.

This safety bit is the keynote of the car — of all Volvos. We said about the previous car that the high sills, all-round padding, and properly placed controls gave the feeling of being enclosed in a space capsule. You could walk away from most crashes (God forbid) in this car where another car might be rolled up in a ball.

Naturally, seat belts are standard equipment. Three pointers, they both lock with a massive latch onto a U-bolt on the transmission tunnel. Adjustment is fiddly, but covers a wide range.

Many changes were made to the seats in this model. The seats are actually orthopaedically designed with proper support in the small of the back and running up behind the knees and above the shoulders. Once in — you're in. There is an occasional seat behind the two buckets, but this is less for children than as an extra luggage carrier with the squab folded down (showing a carpet-lined back) and the straps provided used to tie down the luggage.

The floor has durable haircord carpet which extends to cover the biggish transmission tunnel. Upholstery is in leathercloth, with the centre panels of the seats vented and pleated for adhesion. However, the material tends to get slippery and sweaty in hot weather, particularly as the car is not very well ventilated for hot weather. There are elastic map pockets in each bulkhead.

The armrests in each big door are shaped as door pulls and curve along the whole width of the door, with the door handle set vertically in the armrest. The window winders are a little far back, and are awkward to use. The handbrake is on the driver's right, and has a guard over the press button, while the sun visors are properly crushable and the headlining perforated for sound absorption.

VOLVO P1800 S

SPECIFICATIONS

ENGINE:

Cylinders	four, in line
Bore and stroke	73.07 mm by 70.01 mm
Cubic capacity	1780 cc
Compression ratio	10 to 1
Valves	pushrod, overhead
Power at rpm	115 bhp at 5800 rpm
Maximum torque	NA

TRANSMISSION:

Gearing (O/D Top)	21.7 mph per 1000 rpm
Ratios, overall.	
First	14.25
Second	9.08
Third	6.20
Top	4.65 (O/D top . . . 3.45)
Final drive	4.56 to 1

SUSPENSION:

Front	coils, wishbones, anti-roll bar

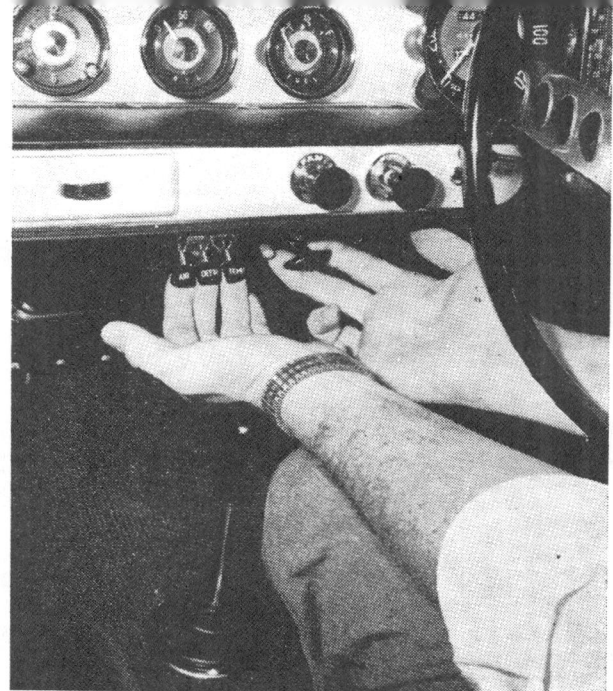

The controls — at hand.

Styling — clean-cut, stimulating.

Few changes have been made to the facia. The top level carries the clock, oil and fuel gauges, then the tachometer and the speedometer, with the tacho lined from 6000 to 6500 in stripes and from 6500 to 7000 in solid red. The lower level has the lighter, ashtray, heater fan switch and ignition switch. The wiper/washer control and the overdrive warning light are on the right of the wheel.

At each end of the dash are controls for fresh air vents and three-position interior light switches. The three sliding controls for the fantastically good heater/demister system are under the dash in the centre and are illuminated. Next to them is the choke control, which is one of those twist-to-lock ideas which we have always disliked on the principle that it is easy to forget the choke is in action.

We complained about the earlier car that the instruments were not easy to read. The same still applies. The gauges have light blue background with chromed centres and a white needle. It looks a bit jazzy, and does not help clear identification particularly as the fuel and speedometer needles on the test car oscillated badly. However, the facia itself is done in patterned and embossed alloy, and there are no reflections at all into the windscreen, so why complain?

Why complain indeed? Despite our objections, which are really only minor, we fell completely in love with this car. It stands as an object lesson to every other manufacturer in terms of quality, safety and sensible design. If all Volvos are like the beautifully-prepared test car from Sydney's Truck Sales and Service Pty Ltd, you can put three in the mail for us, please.   #

Rear	coils, trailing radius
Dampers	arms, Panhard rod telescopic

STEERING:

Type	cam and roller
Turns, 1 to 1	3⅔
Circle	31 ft 6 in.

BRAKES:

Type	disc front, drum rear
Swept or Rubbed area	350 sq in.

DIMENSIONS:

Wheelbase	8 ft 0½ in.
Track, front	4 ft 3¾ in.
Track, rear	4 ft 3¾ in.
Length	14 ft 5 in.
Width	5 ft 7 in.
Height	4 ft 2½ in.
Fuel Tank capacity	12 gallons

TYRES:

Size	5.90 by 15

Weight:

Kerb (with fuel and water)	2444 lb

GROUND CLEARANCE:

Unladen	6.5 in.

PERFORMANCE

Top speed average	100 mph
Fastest run	100 mph
Maximum, first	36 mph (6500 rpm limit)
Maximum, second	51 mph (6500 rpm limit)
Maximum, third	74 mph (6500 rpm limit)
Maximum, fourth	100 mph (5000 rpm limit)
Standing quarter mile average	18.6 seconds
Fastest run	18.3 seconds
0 to 30 mph	3.8 seconds
0 to 40 mph	6.6 seconds
0 to 50 mph	9.4 seconds
0 to 60 mph	13.2 seconds
0 to 70 mph	17.3 seconds
0 to 80 mph	23.5 seconds
0 to 90 mph	32.3 seconds
0 to 60 mph to 0	15.6 seconds

	Top	Third
40 to 60 mph	8.6 secs	6.1 secs
50 to 70 mph	8.3 secs	7.0 secs
60 to 80 mph	9.2 secs	— secs
Fuel Consumption, overall		25.2 mpg
Fuel Consumption, cruising		30-32 mpg

Volvo 1800S 1,778 c.c.

AT A GLANCE: Swedish GT sports car with occasional back seats. More powerful engine gives extra performance without heavier fuel consumption. Standard overdrive provides economical cruising. Light brakes not entirely fade free, but powerful and progressive. Very safe roadholding; light, positive steering with too much feed-back. Seats mounted too low and instruments vague. Good solid car, rather expensive in the U.K.

MANUFACTURER

A.B. Volvo, Gothenburg, Sweden.

U.K. CONCESSIONAIRES

Volvo Concessionaires Ltd., Tower Ramparts, Ipswich, Suffolk.

PRICES

Basic	..	.. £1,500	0s	0d
Purchase Tax	..	.. £314	1s	3d
Total (in G.B.)	..	.. £1,814	1s	3d

PERFORMANCE SUMMARY

Mean maximum speed	..	107 m.p.h.
Standing start ¼-mile	..	18·6 sec
0-60 m.p.h.	.. ..	11·9 sec
30-70 m.p.h. (through gears)		11·4 sec
Overall fuel consumption		24·0 m.p.g.
Miles per tankful ..	..	240

SWEDISH engineering has a reputation for being sound and reliable. It is not inspired, perhaps, but it does go on and on giving unfailing service. The Volvo 1800S is a good example of the Scandinavian way of looking at sports cars, even though this particular model has strong roots and associations in England. Since the right-hand-drive versions first became available in the spring of 1962 this Volvo has not changed its appearance, yet under the skin there have been several important alterations.

Earlier this year the engine and braking system were improved, following some detail revisions to the trim and embellishments in the latter part of 1965. Production is now centred on the main Volvo plant at Gothenburg, with bare metal body pressings being shipped from the Pressed Steel Company. A lot of the transfer plant and control machinery at the factory is British, and such components as carburettors, clutch, brakes and instruments are imported from the U.K. Originally, Jensen assembled the complete car in Birmingham, but production was transferred to Sweden about three years ago.

The engine is basically the same as that used in the saloon Volvos, only in this more sporting version the peak power is boosted to 103 b.h.p. net at 5,600 r.p.m. However, this is far from just a hotted-up derivative, for it runs more quietly and more smoothly than any of the saloons we have tried recently, with no temperament and lots of low-speed flexibility. There are no difficulties in pulling away from 10 m.p.h. in third gear, and the engine really has two distinctly different characters. For gentle pottering around town and relaxed driving with no urgency, one tends to keep the rev counter needle below 3,000 r.p.m. and enjoy a kind of executive GT without sacrificing too much performance. But with the bit between one's teeth, an extra 3,000 r.p.m. up to the peak gives real bite to the acceleration and enables one to hustle along to the accompaniment of a deep throbbing intake roar and some tappety sewing-machine noises from the pushrod valve gear.

Compared with the last Volvo 1800 we tested on 20 July 1962, performance has been increased quite substantially. For example, acceleration through the gears from rest is 1·3sec quicker to 60 m.p.h., and 6·6sec quicker to 90 m.p.h. Maximum speed in overdrive top, a standard ratio installed as a usable fifth gear, has increased from 102 to 107 m.p.h. with a new best of 111 m.p.h. in the favourable direction.

According to the handbook and the markings on the rev counter, maxi-

MAKE: **VOLVO**

TYPE: **1800S**

WEIGHT

Kerb weight (with oil, water and half-full fuel tank): 21·3 cwt (2,383lb-1,085kg)
Front-rear distribution, per cent   F, 54;   R, 46
Laden as tested   ..   24·3 cwt (2,719lb-1,237kg)

TURNING CIRCLES

Between kerbs   ..   L, 31ft 8in.;   R, 30ft. 11in.
Between walls   ..   L, 33ft. 11in.;   R, 33ft 3in.
Steering wheel turns lock to lock   ..   3·3

PERFORMANCE DATA

Overdrive top gear m.p.h. per 1,000 r.p.m.   21·1
Top gear m.p.h. per 1,000 r.p.m...   ..   15·9
Mean piston speed at max. power   2,935 ft/min
Engine revs. at mean max. speed..   5,070 r.p.m.
B.h.p. per ton laden   85

OIL CONSUMPTION

Miles per pint (SAE 20)   500

FUEL CONSUMPTION

At constant speeds

	OD Top	Top
30 m.p.h.	45·0 m.p.g.	39·2 m.p.g.
40 ,,	44·0 ,,	37·0 ,,
50 ,,	39·6 ,,	34·5 ,,
60 ,,	35·8 ,,	31·3 ,,
70 ,,	32·0 ,,	28·4 ,,
80 ,,	27·6 ,,	23·5 ,,
90 ,,	23·8 ,,	20·2 ,,
100 ,,	19·8 ,,	—

Overall   m.p.g.....24·0   (11·8   litres/100km)
Normal range m.p.g. 20-28 (14·1-10·1 litres/100km)
Test distance   ..   ..   ..   1,136 miles
Estimated (DIN) m.p.g.   25·8 (10·9 litres/100km)
Grade   ..   Super Premium (99·4-101·7 RM)

TEST CONDITIONS

Weather   ..   Showering with 10-15 m.p.h. wind
Temperature   ..   ..   12 deg.C (53 deg.F)
Barometer ..   ..   29·5 in. Hg.
Surfaces   Dry concrete and tarmac with damp patches

Speed range, gear ratio and time in seconds

m.p.h.	O.D. Top (3·45)	Top (4·56)	Third (6·21)	Second (9·08)	First (14·27)
10—30	—	—	6·5	4·5	3·6
20—40	12·1	8·7	5·7	3·6	—
30—50	12·8	8·3	5·6	4·5	—
40—60	13·2	8·0	5·8	—	—
50—70	13·7	8·9	6·8	—	—
60—80	16·3	9·9	—	—	—
70—90	21·4	12·8	—	—	—

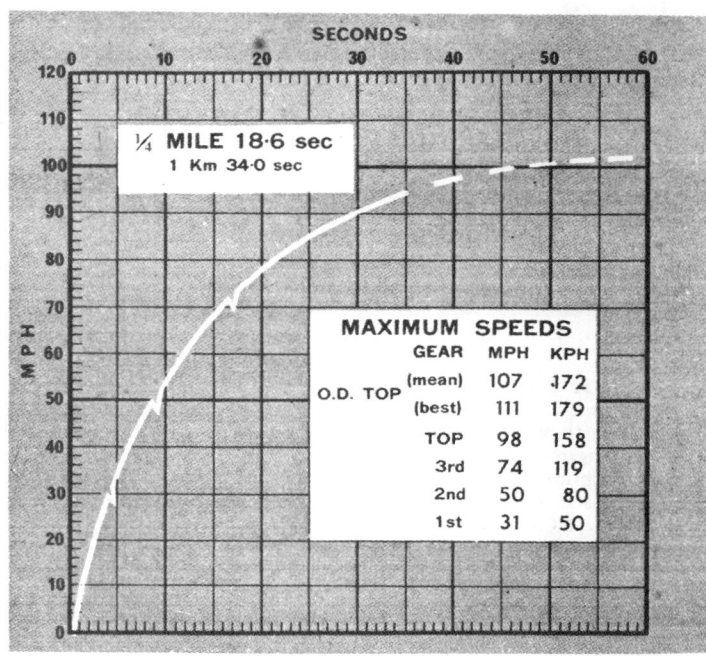

¼ MILE 18·6 sec
1 Km 34·0 sec

MAXIMUM SPEEDS			
	GEAR	MPH	KPH
O.D. TOP	(mean)	107	172
	(best)	111	179
	TOP	98	158
	3rd	74	119
	2nd	50	80
	1st	31	50

TIME IN SECONDS	4·2	6·2	8·7	11·9	15·6	21·2	28·6				
TRUE SPEED MPH	30	40	50	60	70	80	90	100	110	120	
CAR SPEEDOMETER	30	41	51	61	71	82	92	103			

BRAKES	Pedal load	Retardation	Equiv. distance
(from 30 m.p.h.	25lb	0·30g	100ft
in neutral)	50lb	0·60g	50ft
	75lb	0·90g	33·4ft
Handbrake		0·30g	100ft

CLUTCH Pedal load and travel—40lb and 5in.

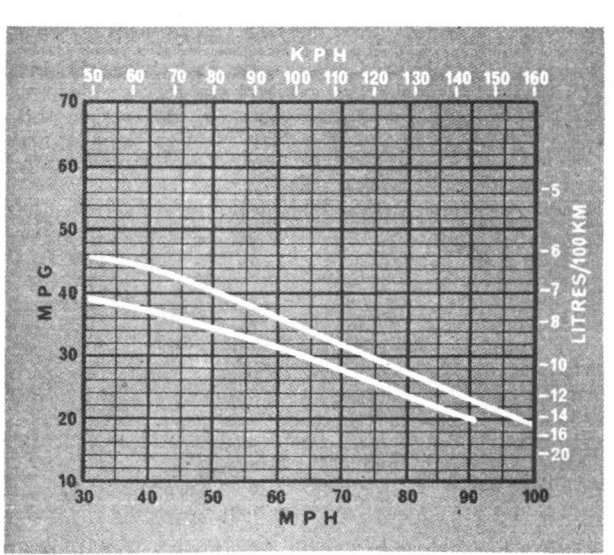

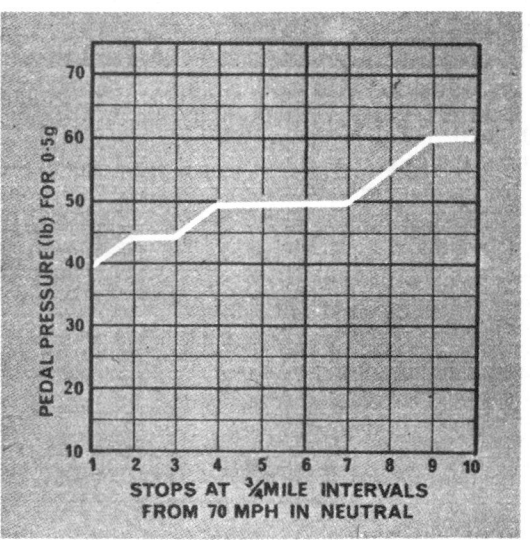

STOPS AT ¼MILE INTERVALS
FROM 70 MPH IN NEUTRAL

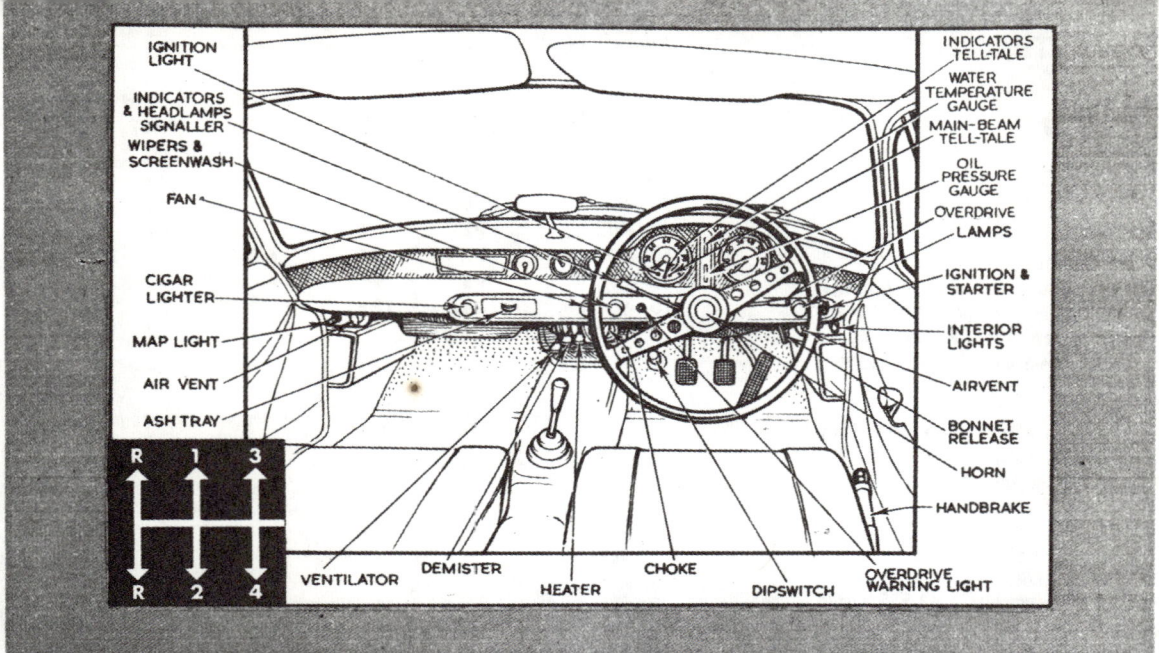

IGNITION LIGHT
INDICATORS & HEADLAMPS SIGNALLER
WIPERS & SCREENWASH
FAN
CIGAR LIGHTER
MAP LIGHT
AIR VENT
ASH TRAY

INDICATORS TELL-TALE
WATER TEMPERATURE GAUGE
MAIN-BEAM TELL-TALE
OIL PRESSURE GAUGE
OVERDRIVE LAMPS
IGNITION & STARTER
INTERIOR LIGHTS
AIRVENT
BONNET RELEASE
HORN
HANDBRAKE

VENTILATOR   DEMISTER   HEATER   CHOKE   DIPSWITCH   OVERDRIVE WARNING LIGHT

mum revs should be 6,500. Using this as a limit gave times about 1sec slower than going on to 7,000 which the engine seemed very content to do without getting harsh or sounding distressed. For normal road use, of course, 6,000 is plenty and, in fact, during our testing we found that by keeping to this lower limit only 2sec were added to the times right through to 90 m.p.h.

Overdrive Included

Gearbox ratios are well spaced out up to almost 100 m.p.h. in direct top, and overdrive can only be engaged with this ratio. A stalk on the right-hand side of the steering column just under the wheel rim operates the solenoid when moved in any direction, on the repeater principle. A purple warning lamp on the facia lights when overdrive is selected and it is possible to set the control before engaging top if one wants. On our test car this touch-switch did not always contact immediately, and as the warning lamp was mostly masked by a steering wheel spoke, there were times when we were not sure whether we were in overdrive.

Upward changes into overdrive were smooth with the throttle open for acceleration, but changing down, either on the over-run or with power on, proved so jerky that we usually stabbed the clutch at the appropriate moment to cushion the change.

The gearbox itself is operated by a very positive and stubby little lever in a nice position on the tunnel and close to the wheel rim. There is strong spring loading towards the top and third gear plane which helps fast upwards changes when accelerating. The synchromesh (on all ratios, incidentally) could never be beaten, and the shiny black plastic knob is thoughtfully shaped to fit the palm of one's hand.

The steering of the 1800 is very quick and precise, but there is a lot of feed-back to the driver's hands. We took the car abroad to measure maximum speed, and on French roads the driver finds the rim continually sawing through quite large arcs as the front wheels follow the bumps and gulleys on the road surface. The steering column is mounted almost horizontally, which puts the wheel within comfortable reach at an easy angle to wind on.

This quick steering response and its associated effects could be ultra-sensitive if the suspension of the Volvo were not set up very carefully.

Within normal bounds the handling is neutral, with a balanced and taut feel that encourages one to toss it through bends with confidence. On a wet test track we were surprised at how stable the car remained towards the limit of adhesion, with no tail swing at all even when applying power to the rear wheels suddenly in the middle of a turn. More extensive examination from outside on a steering pad showed the car to be under-steering predominantly under these extreme conditions to the extent of practically dragging the tyres side-ways off the rims of the front wheels. With the excellent grip of the Pirelli

Accessibility is good with all fillers easy to reach. The bonnet has a self-supporting strut and positive locks

Left: Seats are comfortably padded, but lack lateral support. Floor covering is stout woven carpet. Doors are wide for easy entry and exit.
Right: The rear seat backrest folds down to provide a carpeted platform for luggage which can be secured with the leather straps provided

Volvo 1800S . . .

Cinturatos this characteristic never reached the stage where we found ourselves running out of road, and the Volvo is the kind of car that helps you out of trouble should an emergency arise, or over exuberance get the better of the driver.

Spring rates are rather soft, too soft for a GT car in the opinion of some of our testers. The ride, on the other hand, is comfortable and quite firmly damped although there is quite a lot of body roll on corners. The radial tyres rumbled on certain types of road surface, but otherwise suited the suspension characteristics very well indeed.

The Girling braking system is the conventional mixture of discs at the front with rear drums and it works with the aid of a powerful vacuum servo. Pedal pressure is therefore light and it took only 75lb load to lock the wheels on a damp surface for an ultimate stop of 0·9g. On a dry road we could undoubtedly have bettered this figure and probably achieved 1g or more. The fade tests showed some loss of efficiency as the temperatures rose, but this was a gradual and progressive process with an increase in load from 40 to 60lb over 10 stops. Recovery was very quick.

With a big, pull-up lever on the right of the driving seat, the handbrake held securely facing either way on a 1-in-3 test hill and stopped the car with 0·3g when used on its own from 30 m.p.h. Moving off again on the test hill was easy.

Fuel economy does not seem to have been affected at all by the extra engine power and our overall consumption for 1,136 miles in this country and abroad worked out at exactly 24 m.p.g. In our test four years ago the corresponding figure was 24·9, and even the steady-speed consumption graph has not changed significantly. The economy of having an overdrive for cruising is well illustrated by this graph, the saving at 70 m.p.h. being 3·6 m.p.g. or nearly 13 per cent.

A lot of the original P.1800 was the work of stylists rather than designers and the instruments are an example of their misguided efforts. These have not changed on the latest model and are still a confusing collection of colourful gauges, difficult to read and even harder to interpret.

For a sports car the boot is large. The lid is counterbalanced, and the fuel filler has a separate locking flap

Latest cars have rear bumpers without wrap-round corners to protect the wings, and a rubber insert across the full width

HOW THE VOLVO 1800S COMPARES:

	TOTAL PRICE		
Volvo 1800S	£1,814		
M.G. MGB GT	£998		
Sunbeam Alpine	£878		
Lancia Flavia Coupé	£2,498		
Porsche 912	£2,387		

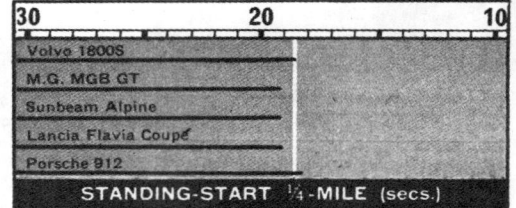

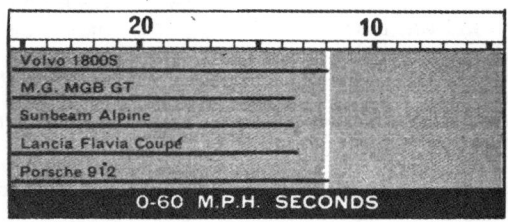

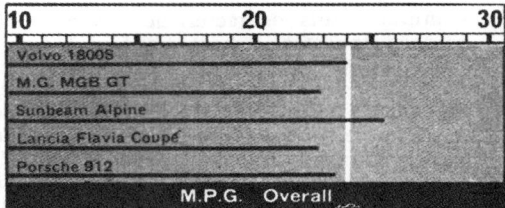

Minor Controls

In front of the driver are a large speedometer and matching rev counter with two manometer-type temperature gauges for oil and water in between. Over to the left are three more circular dials for fuel tank, oil pressure and a clock. These all have sunken faces and vague calibrations that are practically impossible to read without bending down and peering into them. Even then the fuel gauge appears to have two different and conflicting scales, so one can never rely on it.

Minor Controls

The switches are scattered across the facia below the instruments and work on combined push, pull and twist principles rather than those of the more modern flick toggles. There are two-speed wipers which we timed at 77 and 43 sweeps per min, and pushing this knob works the electric screenwash, with very powerful jets. There is a three-speed heater fan and a really high-output hot

matrix designed to cope with sub-zero winters. Little T-handles under the dashboard each side are supposed to open cold air vents to the footwells, but we never succeeded in getting more than a dribble of ram air through.

By far the loudest and most universal complaint from all our staff concerned the seating position, which is much, much too low. An average 5ft 9in. man getting in and settling back finds his eyes on a level with the instruments, so he must sit up and crane over the scuttle to see the nearside wing in traffic. Even our tallest six-footer would have liked to be higher and although there is a small vertical adjustment provided, we could all have been sitting at least 2in. up without coming near the limit of headroom. We did in fact drive a similar car with blocks under the runners last year, and found it transformed. Even the passenger has trouble seeing out, and the scuttle is lower that side.

The seats themselves have been

reshaped recently and they give good support in the small of the back, but have little sideways location. This is not so important if the standard seat belts are worn, although one gets stiff on a long fast journey when bracing against cornering forces all the time. The backrests can be adjusted over a small angular range, but as mentioned earlier, we mostly set them upright to see out.

With difficult access and thin padding only, the back seats are of the plus-2 variety intended mainly for children or occasional short runs for adults bending over to clear the roof. The backrest can now be dropped down to form a large carpeted luggage shelf in addition to the very roomy boot.

Although we had yellow bulbs fitted for our Continental trip, the headlamps were extremely impressive in their powerful throw on main beams and their good spread when dipped. The foot dipswitch, however, is rather a stretch to reach and not nearly as convenient as a finger-tip lever when there is gear changing to be done. Pulling up on the indicator arm, by the way, flashes main beams any time.

During our fortnight with the car, and especially when making trips, we found the lack of stowage space inside the car an annoyance. The two big boxes on the sides of the footwells have shrunk to tiny elastic-topped pockets on the latest models, and that is the total extent of locker space.

There is no cubby-hole in front of the passenger, no hollow armrest between the seats, no door pockets and no under-facia shelf.

This latest Volvo 1800 is still much the same car as it has always been, but now are several worthwhile improvements to keep its performance well up with the competitors in its class, as our charts show so well. The price in the U.K. is now almost the same as four years ago, largely be-cause purchase tax has decreased by as much as the basic price has been forced up. At over £1,800 it is not a cheap car, and although well equipped it somehow seems lacking in the luxury touches one would expect for the money. Nevertheless the quality of engineering can be taken for granted, and this Volvo can still offer the performance and reliability which are so important to many motorists. ■

SPECIFICATION : VOLVO 1800S, FRONT ENGINE, REAR-WHEEL DRIVE

ENGINE
Cylinders	4, in line
Cooling system	Water; pump, fan and thermostat
Bore	84·1mm (3·31in.)
Stroke	80mm (3·15in.)
Displacement	1,780 c.c. (109 cu. in.)
Valve gear	Overhead, pushrods and rockers
Compression ratio	10-to-1
Carburettors	2SU HS6
Fuel pump	AC mechanical
Oil filter	Full-flow, Wix or Mann
Max. power	103 b.h.p. (net) at 5,600 r.p.m.
Max. torque	108·5 lb. ft. (net) at 3,800 r.p.m.

TRANSMISSION
Clutch	Borg and Beck, diaphragm spring 8·5in. dia.
Gearbox	4-speed, all-synchromesh
Gear ratios	OD Top 0·756; Top 1·0 Third, 1·36; Second, 1·99; First, 3·13; Reverse 3·25
Final drive	Hypoid bevel, 4·56 to 1

CHASSIS AND BODY
Construction	Integral steel body

SUSPENSION
Front	Independent, coil springs and wishbones, telescopic dampers
Rear	Live axle, coil springs, trailing arms, Panhard rod, telescopic dampers

STEERING
	Gemmer, cam and roller wheel dia. 16in.

BRAKES
Type	Girling disc front, drum rear
Servo	Girling vacuum
Dimensions	F, 10·88in .dia.; R, 9in. dia; 2in. wide shoes
Swept area	F, 226 sq. in.; R, 113 sq. in. Total 339 sq. in. (279 sq. in. per ton laden)

WHEELS
Type	Pressed steel disc, 5 studs, 4·5in. wide rim
Tyres	Pirelli Cinturato tubed 165-15in.

EQUIPMENT
Battery	12-volt 60-amp. hr.
Generator	Bosch 240 watt d.c.
Headlamps	Bosch sealed 45/40 watt
Reversing lamp	Standard
Electric fuses	3
Screen wipers	2-speed, self parking
Screen washer	Standard, electric
Interior heater	Standard, fresh air
Safety belts	Standard
Interior trim	Leather seats, pvc headlining
Floor covering	Carpet
Starting handle	No provision
Jack	Screw pillar
Jacking points	4 next to wheel arches
Other bodies	None

MAINTENANCE
Fuel tank	10 Imp. gallons (no reserve) (45 litres)
Cooling system	15 pints (including heater) (8·5 litres)
Engine sump	6·5 pints (3·75 litres) SAE 20 or 10W/30. Change oil every 3,000 miles; change filter element every 6,000 miles.
Gearbox and overdrive	2·9 pints SAE 30. Change oil every 25,000 miles
Final drive	2·25 pints SAE 90. Change oil every 25,000 miles
Grease	No points
Tyre pressures	F, 26; R, 28 p.s.i. (normal driving). F, 28; R, 30 p.s.i. (fast driving). F, 28; R, 30 p.s.i. (full load)

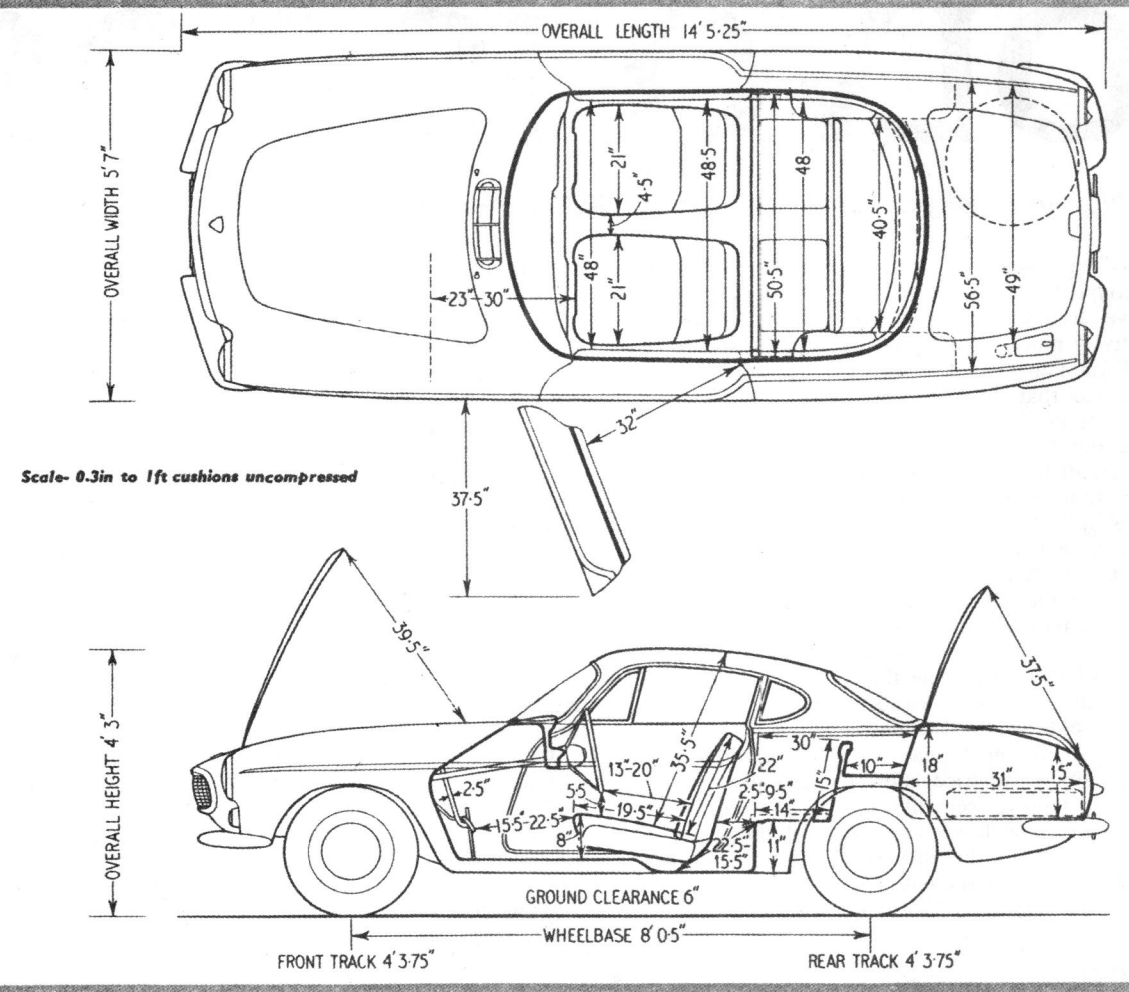

Scale- 0.3in to 1ft cushions uncompressed

VOLVO 1800S

And if 115 bhp isn't enough, there's a hop-up kit that offers more

HAVING BEEN WITH us since early 1961, the Volvo 1800 coupe has attained Old Friend status. A conservative design when it first appeared, it has become comparatively more so over the years, but it still holds a lot of appeal for many people and it's still a soundly constructed, rugged car that offers decent value for the money.

Over its years of production the 1800S has remained very much the same but has been refined in small details, such as a change to small hub caps from the original, over-styled wheel covers; a simpler, more pleasant front bumper; some interior changes including new seats; and two power increases with the latest (as of 1966) bringing the output of the coupe's engine to 115 bhp at 6000 rpm. Another significant change to appear in the 1966 car is a front/rear brake proportioning valve to reduce the chance of rear brake lock-up in hard braking—a laudable improvement that is also applied to the rest of the Volvo line this year.

Getting behind the wheel of the 1800S, one is immediately aware of a rather old-fashioned atmosphere about the seating position. You sit low in the car, the steering wheel is as nearly vertical as any we've tried lately; headroom is a little restricted and the windows seem like narrow slits compared with those in some of the low-waisted cars of today.

This classical feeling in the driving position is visually counterbalanced by an instrument panel that smacks of American Contemporary circa 1955. It's a handsome enough layout but a bit more stylized than many sports car drivers would care for, with heavy chrome bezels for each instrument and a speedometer that has only 10-mph increments marked out. All the information is there, though—tachometer, speedometer, trip odometer, oil temperature gauge along with the water temp, clock—and in addition to the expected warning lights, a bright red telltale reminds you when overdrive is engaged.

Seats are sufficiently adjustable for fore-and-aft position and rake, and in addition have the novelty of a variable lumbar support. A small hole in the outboard side of the back rest gives access to the large Phillips-head screw that turns a pivoted lateral frame from which are stretched india rubber straps: turning the frame tightens or relaxes the straps to make the seat back stiffer or softer. These seats are covered with real leather and are comfortably soft, vertically and laterally. The lateral softness does not make for sidewise security, but the seats seem comfortable for all, and lateral location of the driver and passenger has been left to the excellent seat belt-body harness arrangement.

Behind the two main seats is a generous luggage area, with leather straps for holding the cargo in place, that doubles as minimal extra seating space. The trunk itself is generous for the size of the car.

Sweden is a country of severe climate, and hence the design of Volvos is influenced by the need for rugged, all-weather cars that will perform reliably and keep the occupants happy in all kinds of weather. Because America is

also a land of extremes in weather, the Volvo is better suited to American use than are many imports. There has been more than token attention to rustproofing of the body, for instance, and Volvo heaters are in a class with their American counterparts, as evidenced by a recent test conducted by a Finnish magazine which showed a Volvo 122 to be capable of raising interior temperature from 9°F to over 80°F in 40 min. Too, Volvos have a reputation for living a long time, and their claimed 11-year car life may not be far off.

Sweden also has bad roads in abundance, as do so many European countries. Again the local influence shows to advantage: the 1800S is very much at home on the worst kind of roads with the staunch body structure and fairly soft springing making the road surface a [relatively] negligible factor in determining driving speed. The live rear axle can be made to hop, but the provocation must be severe. On smooth roads where the cornering properties can be evaluated separately, we found moderate understeer, moderate body roll, good directional stability and light, positive steering. Volvo engineers consider radial-ply tires essential to the design and install Pirelli Cinturatos as standard equipment; these combined with tight shock control give the low-speed firmness one expects in this kind of car, but with increasing speed the ride improves. In fact, there are few sports cars with a more satisfactory ride for the long haul. Along with the radial tires, however, comes the slight vibration problem inherent in such tires: our car had a slight resonance coming through the steering wheel at around 70 mph, and careful re-balancing didn't eliminate it completely.

Along with all the rock-solidity comes high weight and modest performance: an 1800-cc engine pulling 2410 lb of curb weight is somewhat restricted by Newtonian physics. The latest power increase shows in the performance figures, but the acceleration of the 1800S is still on the leisurely side. The engine is a most impressive unit, of itself, for a four: vibration periods and power throb are at a minimum and it starts easily, idles smoothly, and runs quietly. To answer

the demand for a little extra, Volvo has worked out a hop-up kit for the B-18 engine and after completing our road test of the standard version we returned it to the distributor's technical center for installation of the kit.

Not a factory-installed option yet, the kit is part No. 419350 and it can be applied to all B-18 engines. For the latest 1800S engine, no changes are required before installing the kit, and it consists of the following pieces:
- Cylinder head, compression ratio 11.1:1 with 1.65-in. intake valves and 1.38-in. exhaust valves (standard 10:1, 1.97 and 1.65-in. respectively)
- Camshaft with 0.406-in. lift
- Lighter flywheel (17.6 lb with ring gear)
- Oil pump and timing gear covers
- Pulley hub
- Carburetor needles, richer than standard
- Lighter springs for carburetor damper pistons
- Bosch W280 T 13 S spark plugs
- Bosch TK 12 A10 ignition coil
- Sheet metal exhaust header (tuned for extraction)

VOLVO 1800S
AT A GLANCE...

Price as tested	$4280
Engine	4 cyl in line, ohv, 1780 cc, 115 bhp
Curb weight, lb	2410
Top speed, mph	109
Acceleration, 0-60 mph, sec	13.9
50-70 mph (3rd gear)	8.0
Average fuel consumption, mpg	24.5

VOLVO 1800S

In order to install the kit on earlier 1800S cars and B18D engines (122S) certain other preparatory modifications are called for, such as installing correct pistons and/or the oil cooler. The hopped-up engine output is 135 bhp at 6000 rpm, and there is a modest and noticeable increase in performance through the gears without a serious loss in flexibility. Idling speed went up from 700 rpm to 1000 with the kit, but overall noise level didn't increase. The kit will be available through Volvo dealers and will cost $299; installation should run about $100 on current 1800S models.

Staff opinions on the 1800S styling were generally unenthusiastic, with low marks going to the chromium sweepspear and the semi-finned rear fenders, both cliches of a bygone American era. The formerly expensive-looking eggcrate grille has been superseded by a stamped affair that doesn't affect the basic styling but does look less elegant.

Good marks go to the shift linkage on this car for precision, easy reaches and low shift efforts. In addition to the good shift linkage, we also liked the method of engaging the overdrive, a handy directional-like lever on the right side of the steering column that's pushed toward the dash to either engage or disengage the overdrive. The unit does not cancel itself when the shift lever is taken out of 4th (the only gear to which the od is applied). Personal taste decrees whether this is an advantage or not, but it didn't seem a bad thing to just leave it on for leisurely driving, going directly from 3rd to 4th od. The overdrive is standard on the 1800S. All indirect gears are quiet and the ratios seem appropriate for the car. Brake, clutch and acclerator efforts are all light and their action smooth, and the whole drive train was tight and slack-free after being attended to by the technical center.

We understand that pops and clunks from the rear suspension and/or axle have been a common occurrence with the model, and our car was delivered to us with a rather severe pop. However, we were pleased to know that the trouble could be (and was) corrected. A small gripe was an oily film deposited on the windshield by the defroster.

To summarize, the 1800S is for the man who wants a solid, conservative and durable car with a little verve and good road manners. Set up properly it gives a feeling of pleasant precision in its responses to driver demands; servicing should be inexpensive, fuel economy is good (24 mpg in all-round driving) and 100,000 miles should be the rule rather than the exception.

ROAD TEST
VOLVO 1800 S

SCALE: 10" DIVISIONS

PRICE

Basic list	$4200
As tested	$4280

ENGINE

No. cyl & type	4 in line, ohv
Bore x stroke, mm	84 x 80
In	3.31 x 3.15
Displacement, cc/cu in	1780/109
Compression ratio	10.0:1
Bhp @ rpm	115 @ 6000
Equivalent mph	135
Torque @ rpm, lb-ft	112 @ 4000
Equivalent mph	83
Carburetors	2 SU
No. barrels, dia	1 x 1.75
Type fuel required	premium

DRIVE TRAIN

Clutch type	sdp diaphragm
Diameter, in	8.5
Gear ratios: od (0.756)	3.45:1
4th (1.00)	4.56:1
3rd (1.36)	6.19:1
2nd (1.99)	9.07:1
1st (3.13)	14.24:1
Synchromesh	on all 4
Differential type	hypoid
Ratio	4.56:1
Optional ratios	none

CHASSIS & SUSPENSION

Frame type	unit with body
Brake type	disc/drum
Swept area, sq in	339
Tire size	165 x 15
Make	Pirelli Cinturato
Steering type	cam & roller
Turns, lock-to-lock	3.2
Turning circle, ft	31.2

Front suspension: independent with unequal A-arms, coil springs, tube shocks, anti-roll bar.

Rear suspension: live axle on trailing arms with Panhard rod, coil springs, tube shocks.

ACCOMMODATION

Normal capacity, persons	2
Occasional capacity	3
Seat width, front, in	2 x 18.5
Rear	39.5
Head room, front/rear	38.0/28.0
Seat back adjustment, deg	10
Entrance height, in	46.6
Step-over height	13.7
Door width	38.0

Driver comfort rating:

Driver 69 in. tall	90
Driver 72 in. tall	85
Driver 75 in. tall	65

(85–100, good; 70–85, fair; under 70, poor)

GENERAL

Curb weight, lb	2410
Test weight	2770
Weight distribution (with driver), front/rear, %	52/48
Wheelbase, in	96.5
Track, front/rear	51.8/51.8
Overall length	173.2
Width	67.0
Height	50.5
Frontal area, sq ft	18.8
Ground clearance, in	6.0
Overhang, front/rear	31.2/45.5
Departure angle, deg	14
Usable trunk space, cu ft	8.1
Fuel tank capacity, gal	12

INSTRUMENTATION

Instruments: 120-mph speedometer, trip ocometer, 7000-rpm tachometer, water & oil temperature, oil pressure, fuel level, clock.

Warning lights: generator, high beam, directional signals, overdrive on.

MISCELLANEOUS

Body styles available: coupe only
Warranty period: 6 mo/unlimited mileage

CALCULATED DATA

Lb/hp (test wt)	24.1
Mph/1000 rpm (overdrive)	19.7
Engine revs/mi (60 mph)	3040
Piston travel, ft/mi	1595
Rpm @ 2500 ft/min	4760
Equivalent mph	102
Cu ft/ton mi	69.0
R&T wear index	48.5

EXTRA COST OPTIONS

Radio, limited-slip differential.

MAINTENANCE

Crankcase capacity, qt	4.0
Change interval, mi	3000
Oil filter type	full flow
Change interval, mi	6000
Chassis lube interval, mi	3000

BRAKES

Panic stop from 80 mph:

Deceleration, % G	68
Control	good
Parking: hold 30% grade	yes
Overall brake rating	good

ROAD TEST RESULTS

ACCELERATION

Time to speed, sec:	standard	with kit
0–30 mph	4.1	3.8
0–40 mph	6.8	6.3
0–50 mph	10.3	9.4
0–60 mph	13.9	12.7
0–70 mph	18.5	17.4
0–80 mph	24.5	23.2
0–100 mph	51.5	49.0
50–70 mph (3rd gear)	8.0	7.8

Time to distance, sec:		
0–100 ft	3.6	3.6
0–500 ft	10.2	9.8
¼-mile	19.0	18.4
Speed at end, mph	71.0	72.0

Passing exposure time, sec:
Car ahead going 50 mph ... 6.4 ... 6.8

SPEEDS IN GEARS

	normal	with kit
Overdrive mph	109	114
4th (6000)	100	100
3rd (6000)	66	66
2nd (6000)	44	44
1st (6000)	29	29

SPEEDOMETER ERROR

30 mph indicated	actual 30.0
40 mph	40.0
60 mph	58.6
80 mph	76.9
90 mph	86.0
Odometer correction factor	1.006

FUEL CONSUMPTION

	standard	with kit
Normal driving, mpg	24.5	23.5
Cruising range, mi	294	281

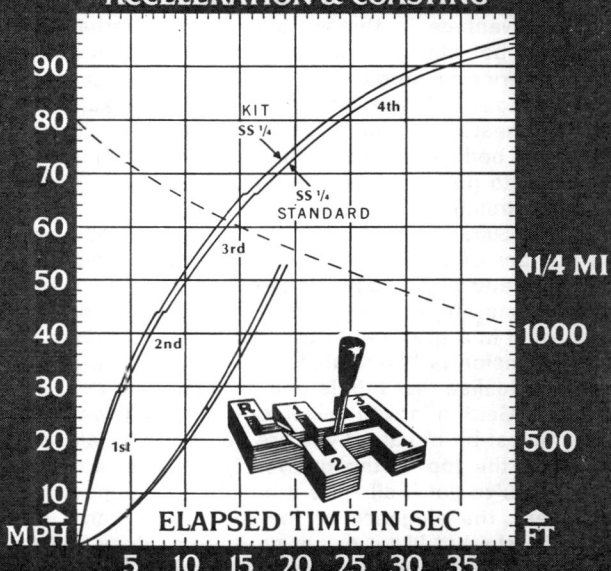

ACCELERATION & COASTING

ELAPSED TIME IN SEC

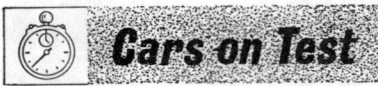

VOLVO 1800S

Engine: Four cylinders, 84·14 mm x 80 mm 1,778 c.c.; compression ratio 10·1 to 1; twin S.U. HS6 carburettors; push-rod overhead valves; 115 b.h.p. at 6,000 r.p.m.

Transmission: Four-speed and reverse gearbox with synchromesh on all forward gears. Overdrive on top gear.

Suspension: Front, independent with wishbones, coil springs and anti-roll bar. Rear, live axle with coil springs, located by panhard rod and radius arms with torque arms. Pirelli Cinturato tyres as standard.

Brakes: Front, disc; rear, drums. Vacuum servo assistance, and limiting valve to balance front and rear brakes.

Dimensions: Overall length, 14 ft. 5¼ ins; overall width, 5 ft. 7 in. overall height, 4 ft. 2½ ins; ground clearance (unladen) 6 in.; weight, 2,625 lb.

PERFORMANCE

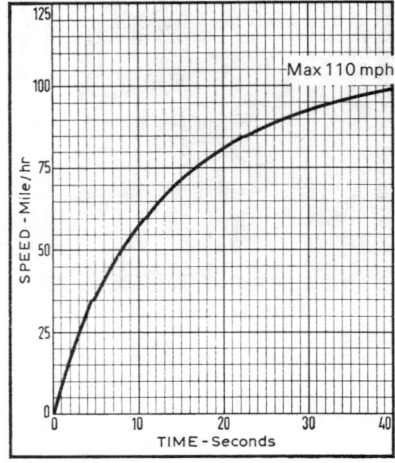

	m.p.h.			secs.
MAXIMUM SPEED	110	ACCELERATION	0–30—	3·3
Mean of two ways	110		0–40—	4·3
SPEEDS IN GEARS	First—33		0–50—	7·1
	Second—53		0–60—	10·0
	Third—80		0–70—	15·5
	Direct 4th—98		0–80—	21·2

Manufacturer: Volvo AB., Gothenburg, Sweden
Price in U.K.: £1,845 including purchase tax

SPORTS CAR ROAD TEST ▶ VOLVO 1800S

IT CAN'T *ALL* be due to the Saint and that sort of thing— the Volvo 1800S obviously has charm of its own. We must admit that during our test we didn't manage to pack the car with half as many gorgeous females as Simon Templar regularly seems to on the telly, but we didn't hold that against it.

Volvos have always appealed to us, and the 1800S, for obvious reasons, more so than the others. Whether or not you think it is good-looking depends, presumably, on your taste: speaking for ourselves, we reckon that the styling is by current standards a bit long in the tooth, and while this may or may not matter all that much it does carry with it a slight disadvantage in that visibility is not, perhaps, all that it might be. Mind you, the inside of the thing is well up to date in terms of roominess and comfort, you can pack a lot of luggage into it and although it is only really supposed to be a two-seater you can pack four adults into it, although so far as the bodies in the back seat are concerned it might be kind not to go too far in one hop without giving 'em a chance to stretch the old legs.

The latest 1800S is still largely the same as it has been for a number of years now, but the current version has more power and a revised braking system: from the garage-on-Sunday-mornings aspect, there are fewer points you have to plug in a grease-gun and among other things the front suspension is "lubricated for life". As soon as you hop in you realise that this is one of those cars designed by a driver. Getting in with the window wound down needs just the tiniest bit of care if you are not going to take your eye out on the top of the quarter-light frame, but once you're in you've got it all—it is a beautifully-equipped car. Once again, the elegance of the instrument panel is a matter of taste, but like it or not no-one can deny that the instruments are all there and are easily read at that. There's even an oil-temperature gauge.

Well it's ugly or just plain beautiful, all depending on your point of view.

The engine is the B18 B type power unit, which means that it is the four-cylinder o.h.v. job, with a five-bearing crank, which you find all over the Volvo range. In 1800S form, this unit has a 10·1 to 1 compression ratio and its 1,778 c.c.s push out a total power output of 115 b.h.p. at 6,000 r.p.m. Five bearings on the crank and oversquare proportions (bore and stroke are 84·14 mm x 80 mm) give a hand in letting it run up to this speed with unusual smoothness for a "big four." Maximum torque of 112 lb. ft. arrives at 4,000 r.p.m. and on the overdrive model, direct top gives you 15 m.p.h. per 1,000 r.p.m. and overdrive top (fourth, by the way, is the only gear it works on) puts this up to 20 m.p.h. per 1,000 r.p.m., which means that 80 m.p.h. cruising in overdrive works out at exactly the maximum torque figure, and you can stay there with complete effortlessness all day long. Or you can abroad, we hasten to add before we offend Our Babs.

Twin S.U. HS6 carbs are fitted on the inlet manifold, and the exhaust system ends in a twin outlet. Everything is nice and easy to get at; a full-flow oil filter and an oil cooler as standard equipment help to keep you out of trouble in that department, too.

The transmission starts off with an 8½ in. single-dry-plate clutch which links up with a four-speed, all-synchromesh gearbox with, in the case of the test car, the optional overdrive on top only. This in fact provides you effectively with five well-spaced ratios which give over thirty in bottom, fifty in second, eighty in third and just under the ton in direct top, overdrive allowing the car to go on to 110 m.p.h. (which is a bit slower than Volvo claim, but to balance that we got better acceleration figures than they talk about!) Fifty in second is obviously a bit low in comparison with eighty in third, but while this a mathematical fact it doesn't seem to worry you when you are actually driving. The gear-lever works beautifully, with absolute precision, and there is no doubt that this is one of the nicest gearboxes in current production. Mated to the Volvo engine, they form together an unbeatable partnership, and there's no question of one being let down by the other as is the case with one or two other motors in a similar capacity class and of similar type that come to mind.

Another good thing about the Volvo is that it has the road-holding to match. Mind you, this is essentially a touring car and in no sense a racer, and so perhaps the cornering power isn't as high as it could be made to be. But there's no point in all this because the car is too heavy for success in that direction anyway, so why bother altering it all and probably spoiling it? There is independent front suspension with wishbones and coil springs in the usual way, and at the back the live axle is also coil sprung and is satisfactorily located, so that you don't get fussed about with axle tramp and all that nonsense. It gives a smooth ride, comfortable without being sick-making, and on rough surfaces the radius arms and panhard rod keep it in one place, while torque arms stop it from winding up just as they do in acceleration. The handling is damn near neutral: if you press the car to the limit it is the back which goes first, but you get plenty of warning and it is easily controlled. Corner it at a more gentlemanly pace — you must be really pressing on if you lose it—and it simply goes round the corner, with no fuss and no drama.

Stoppers are self-adjusting discs on the front and drums at the back, with a balancing valve linking them to stop the drums locking up first. There is a fairly powerful servo, and in exchange for light pedal pressure the car comes to a halt. Stamp hard on the pedal and you'll really stop it! They also work well in the wet, and it isn't easy to lock them even under these conditions.

So much for the bits that are out of sight. Inside the car, as we said before, it is all there. There is plenty of room: the upholstered back seat provides more than sufficient room for children or one adult (except that headroom under the rear window can be a bit dodgy) and you can get two adults in if they're willing and easy-going. When no behinds are placed upon it, the back seat folds down to provide additional luggage space in estate car or Hillman Imp style. The front seat's adjustable in all sorts of ways—fore and aft in the usual way, up and down by means of nuts and bolts, and they have adjustable back-rests. The centre of the back rest—what we apparently call the "lumbar support"

in the trade—is separately adjustable if you use a screw-driver and follow the directions in the Book. Front seat safety belts are standard equipment. So is a heater which supplies warmth to front and rear of the car, two-speed wipers, screen washers, fresh-air ventilation and a full-set range of instruments—rev-counter, red-lined at six-five, speedometer, oil temperature and pressure gauges, and water temperature gauge. There is an electric clock, and warning lights for dynamo charge, headlamp-main beams and flashing direction indicators: the indicator lever also flashes the headlights. There is an automatic reverse light, variable instrument lighting and so on.

The steering wheel is pretty large by modern standards, but it provides a light precise control with plenty of feel, and wants just over three turns from lock to lock. Everything is exactly where you want it on the Volvo, which bears out what we said at the start that this is one of those cars designed by a driver.

It isn't the easiest car in the world to get the best out of, we thought. You can go fast with no trouble at all, but to go *very* fast needs a little experience of this particular model. The thing is that it is a better car than you expect it to be, somehow, and you fight a little shy of taking liberties until you begin to realise that they aren't liberties at all. Once you've got this idea in your head the Volvo will cover the ground all right. Pirelli Cinturatos are standard equipment, and the whole thing sticks down in a leech-like manner: when it is going fast it doesn't seem to be, either inside or outside the car. A lot of thought has gone into it, which shows up in the little things, such as the provision of stout leather straps to secure luggage carried inside the car.

So far as performance is concerned you have to bear in mind, as we have already emphasised, that the 1800S is a touring car. And when you bear that in mind add the fact that it is a touring car, moreover, which weighs about 25 cwt, and that this considerable hunk of metal and people has to be shoved around by an engine of under two litres' capacity. Do all this, and you'll very likely be surprised by the fact that it wants only ten seconds to get to sixty, and not much over twenty to reach eighty. This, plus a top whack of 110, adds up to a pretty lively car, and what's more it isn't hard work to make it so. From rest to the legal limit takes fifteen-and-a-half seconds, and this isn't done by being snappy on one occasion, because you can make it do this time after time after time. It's just the way the 1800S likes to get around.

The gearing in overdrive top makes it long-legged, to say the least: at a steady ton you still have a thousand revs to go before the needle gets anywhere near the red, and by making the step between direct and overdrive fourth gears a wider one than is usual the result is not only this long easy stride, but a direct top which is really a bit low. So that the direct top gear acceleration is as sharp as that of some cars in third, and if you need a bit of extra go while you are cruising in overdrive, all you have to do is to wag the tip of a finger at the overdrive switch and brother, you're in business! Naturally, you have to pay a bit for all this. The price of the Volvo 1800S is £1,814 by the time you have added on a good bit over three hundred quid for the tax man. On the credit side, you get the 25 m.p.g. you might expect from less than two litres, and it is possible (though much less fun) to push this up something like 28 m.p.g. The tank holds 10 gallons. We used no oil at all during the test, and so far as reliability is concerned—well, the thing is obviously built to last, it has been in production long enough to have ironed out all the bugs, and anyway they have a wonderful reputation in this respect. A man we know has done over seventy thousand miles of hard driving in a Volvo, and all he's had to replace so far are plugs and tyres!

PRICES

Car for sale at Nottingham at £1,025

Typical trade advertised price for same age and model in average condition £1,050

Total cost of car when new including tax £1,652

Depreciation over 2½ years £627

DATA

Date first registered	9 October 1964
Number of owners	1
Tax expires	30 September 1967
Fuel consumption	23-26 m.p.g.
Oil consumption	600 m.p. pint
Mileometer reading	22,208

1964 Volvo 1800S

Left:
From the extent of rust and chipping around edges of wheels and bodywork it may be presumed that the car has stood out quite a lot in its short life. The rear quarter windows are fixed

Below left:
Although with evidence of reasonable wear, the interior is very clean. This is a particularly comfortable car for long journeys

Below:
A true enthusiast would want to start at once on thorough cleaning of the under-bonnet compartment. A new battery filler cap is needed—a detail, but still a fault especially for an expensive quality car

IN last week's "Choice" article dealing with the question of whether to buy new or secondhand, some parallels were drawn of typical used cars against the sort of new car which the same money would buy. As a further and particularly interesting example one could quote the Volvo 1800S, subject of this test; only 2½ years old, it is priced just over the £1,000 mark, and is in the same category as a new MGB GT or the Ford Corsair 2000E. The Volvo is a very fully equipped car, and the vendors, N.C.V. of Nottingham, provided a written assurance that any faults revealed in the test would be rectified.

Comments under the bodywork section suggest that this car may have had a fairly hard life, and is not one which has been "kept in mothballs" and had care lavished on it; yet it is very fit mechanically. The only slight need for

attention is for a general tune-up of the engine, as response to the throttle is rather hesitant below 3,000 r.p.m. In spite of this, the performance is fairly impressive, with acceleration from rest to 60 m.p.h. in 14·7 sec, and a 0 to 90 m.p.h. time of 34·6 sec. Top speed is above 100 m.p.h. in overdrive. The acceleration figures do not compare too well with the Road Test published last year, but the latest car had more power which accounts for much of the difference. The performance is slightly better than that of the original P1800, which we tested in July 1962.

The engine is a 4-cylinder unit of 1,778 c.c. It always starts promptly, with ample rich mixture when cold, and is quiet even when taken up to high revs; oil consumption is low although there are signs of leakage. This engine is renowned for long life.

An almost embarrassingly loud crackle and rort from the exhaust was found to be caused by a fracture of the pipe just after the first silencer box, putting the second one out of action altogether.

Good synchromesh on all gears, and a crisp change—with very small travel of a short lever mounted at the end of the transmission hump—match the sporting character of the car. Overdrive engages very smoothly, works on top gear only, and allows 90 m.p.h. cruising at 4,250 r.p.m. Provided the throttle is opened at the right moment, a tendency to snatch on cutting out overdrive can be avoided, and there is a tiny purple tell-tale ahead of the driver to show when overdrive is engaged. The clutch takes up smoothly, and although the travel is rather long it is not too heavy in traffic.

PERFORMANCE CHECK

(Figures in brackets are those of the slightly more powerful model—103 b.h.p. (net)—introduced in 1965; Road Test published 15 July 1966)

0 to 30 m.p.h.	4·2 sec (4·2)
0 to 40 m.p.h.	7·0 sec (6·2)
0 to 50 m.p.h.	9·9 sec (8·7)
0 to 60 m.p.h.	14·7 sec (11·9)
0 to 70 m.p.h.	19·6 sec (15·6)
0 to 80 m.p.h.	26·5 sec (21·2)
0 to 90 m.p.h.	34·6 sec (28·6)

In direct top:

20 to 40 m.p.h.	10·2 sec (8·7)
30 to 50 m.p.h.	10·1 sec (8·3)
40 to 60 m.p.h.	10·2 sec (8·0)
50 to 70 m.p.h.	10·2 sec (8·9)
60 to 80 m.p.h.	11·0 sec (9·9)
70 to 90 m.p.h.	13·3 sec (12·8)

Standing quarter-mile 19·7 sec (18·6)

TYRES
Size: 165-15in. Pirelli Cinturato on all wheels. Approx. cost per replacement cover £8 6s 6d. Depth of original tread 9 mm; remaining tread depth: 8·5 mm (front); 7 mm (rear, right and spare); 4 mm on irregularly worn left rear.

TOOLS
Original tool kit complete, and handbook with car.

CAR FOR SALE AT:
N.C.V. of Nottingham, Ltd., Bulwell Forest Works, Bulwell, Nottingham. Telephone: Nottingham 271272-3.

CONDITION SUMMARY

Bodywork

The white paintwork is original, but in relation to a life of only 2½ years, its condition is a little disappointing. There are a few small blemishes, and more rust than would be expected, particularly along the sills and around the inside edges of the wings. The chromium also has not lasted too well, and speckles of corrosion are noticed, particularly on the side trim strips. The interior is finished in maroon, and the seats are upholstered in leather; they are fairly well creased, but sound. The carpets, and most of the trim show little wear, except for a few marks on the p.v.c. roof lining, and the driver's heel mark on the carpet at one point. There is also an ugly hole on the arm rest of the driver's door where the p.v.c. covering has broken up and the foam padding is showing through. There is little underbody corrosion.

Equipment

Everything including the clock is in working order, but the fuel gauge occasionally sticks at E. Original equipment included a heater which is highly effective, but difficult to adjust for mild warmth. The windscreen washer is electrically operated, and there are two-speed windscreen wipers. A good area of the screen is cleared but—a common used car fault—new blades or rubber inserts are needed. The instruments are all somewhat difficult to read, with calibrations vaguely embossed on the background. An oil temperature gauge is included, mounted between the speedometer and rev counter. ROBO headlamps fitted as standard give extremely good range and spread for fast, confident night driving.

Accessories

A Lucas FT6 fog lamp on the left and LR6 spot lamp on the right have been added and there is also a fine Motorola push-button radio with the car. Safety belts, fastening to a common anchorage between the seats, are standard with every Volvo.

ABOUT THE 1800 SPORTS

Though the exciting Volvo sports car was first shown to the public at the Brussels Show in January 1960, it did not actually go into production until May 1961. Under a unique manufacturing agreement, the bodies were built by Pressed Steel (Linwood), and the cars were assembled with Volvo mechanical parts and many British accessories at the Jensen factory in West Bromwich.

The early cars, chassis numbers 1 to 8,000, had a 100 b.h.p. (gross) engine of 1,778 c.c. For the British market a Laycock overdrive was standard, with a rear axle ratio of 4·56 to 1. After the first 6,000 P1800s had been assembled at Jensen, there was a short hiatus as production was transferred to the Volvo factories at Gothenburg, and the 8,000th car was built in August 1963.

From chassis number 8,001, the car's power output was increased to 108 b.h.p. (gross) and the car was renamed the 1800S. Production continued unchanged until the end of 1965, when a further power increase was made—to 115 b.h.p. (gross)—and minor styling changes made. The front bumper is now straight (whereas earlier cars had swept up bumpers near the grille) and there have been some instrument panel styling changes. The overdrive switch on the current cars is now a self-centring prong; on earlier cars this was a small switch, hidden among other minor controls.

The 1800S is still in full production at Gothenburg. Many components are British made; bodies are still made at Linwood, now owned by Rootes (Pressings) Ltd.

Steering, ride and roadholding are still up to the high standard remembered from our comparatively recent Road Test of the 1800S, but although extremely comfortable over all surfaces the car suffers from a tiresome vibration period caused by out-of-balance wheels. It begins to be noticed above 60 m.p.h. and one has to go right up to 80 m.p.h. before it is completely smooth again.

The ride is well-damped and extremely comfortable over all surfaces, and the car retains the splendid feeling of rigidity and strength which characterizes all Volvos. The handling is well-balanced with only slight understeer, and the car can be cornered hard with confidence, but the steering transmits too much reaction. All the time the wheel seems to be trying to turn one way or the other against the driver's hands, calling for a lot of correction; however, it provides excellent response to small movements, and the car can be held to a dead straight course at speed. Side winds have little effect.

Slight sag of the driver's seat makes even more noticeable the excessively low seating position criticized in all tests of the 1800 so far, and we had to resort to using a cushion to obtain high enough eye level for good visability. Even then, the exact position of the front of the car is difficult to judge when parking, and the severely restricted headroom does not allow one to sit much higher. In other respects the seats are comfortable; they have reclining backrests. The rear seat squab can be dropped as a tray for extra luggage, or with the seat in use there is room for two children, or for one adult to sit in a rather cramped sideways position.

Very effective servo assistance on the brakes gives good response to light pedal pressures (disc at the front only), and the handbrake is unusually effective. The tiny guard has been broken, but still surrounds the button to prevent accidental release when the driver is getting out of the car.

Volvo engineering has the reputation of quality and long life which leads one to expect to find everything in peak condition, and although it has admittedly seen little service, the test car's mechanical condition lives up to expectations, and there are no faults in any of the mechanical components or electrical equipment, other than the need for engine tuning and exhaust repair mentioned. The quality of construction, and the high initial cost, need to be borne in mind when considering the value now offered on the used car market. ■

VOLVO 1800 S

HIGH ROADABILITY, OPTIMUM COMFORT, PEAK PERFORMANCE, BEAUTIFUL EXTERIOR & NO ADS ABOUT "GT"! VOLVO, WE LIKE THAT APPROACH!

BY THE EDITOR

■ In this day of high speed touring automobiles with sports car capabilities, the Volvo 1800 S is just coming into its own. It offers all the features that one could ask of (and that can only be had in) a truly expensive automobile, with few compromises. Full seats for more than two persons would force you to shop elsewhere, of course, but if you are at all impressed by the current talk of GT cars these days you'll find that many of these automobiles have pretty chromed "GT" medallions on the side or back but no more seating space than the 1800 S. Many of them have more powerful

The basic 1800 Volvo is about six years old now and, like the 122 S, has proven itself in terms of ruggedness and durability. Horsepower in the 18 B engine has gone from 100 to 115 and the performance has improved to the point where it can no longer be considered just respectable. Volvo seats are among the most comfortable in the world today and the 1800 S is no exception. This car rates more notice here in the States.

engines, too, yet we found that they just would not handle as well as our test car.

Back in 1960 the company called the car the P 1800 and while we liked it immensely there was always the feeling that, enginewise, it was really no stormer. There were a number of good 100-horsepower cars around that didn't cost nearly as much and had lighter bodies which made them go faster. They broke faster than the P 1800, however, but one realizes this only in retrospect.

Volvo "engineered" what they call their B 18 B engine until today it develops 115 horsepower at 6000 rpm. It has a 10:1 compression ratio with a capacity of 109 cubic inches. This is the engine, incidentally, that went into the Volvo 144 S about which we wrote in our last issue. It is fitted with twin side draft Skinner Union carburetors which, we state once again, we have found to be most

reliable. Our experience with them has extended over a period of ten years and three personally owned automobiles. One well known import came into this country about eighteen months ago fitted with another dual carb setup, having made a switch from SU's. The car developed all sorts of carburetor trouble until recently the company changed back to the SU's. They stay synchronized longer than any other dual setup we've tested.

The 1800 S is also equipped with overdrive on fourth gear. This is a device we've become more familiar with in recent years because so very much of our driving has been relatively "short haul." It is actuated from a stem just under the right side of the wheel and, surprisingly, this position encourages the use of the overdrive much more than if there were a toggle switch on the dash. All of this overdrive talk, of course, is in terms of

VOLVO 1800 S

high speed driving. The dual carbs work for you on the low end, too—getting away from a traffic light, for example.

This brings to mind the exhilerating "sound of music" that goes with taking the 1800 S up through the gears. The exhaust doesn't scream nor does it rumble. It sounds off with a gutty rap, particularly from first to second gear, which is delightful. We got out and looked under one time to see what kind of tailpipe there was back there. Two fairly big bore pipes under the right side tune that sound especially for the ears of pretty girls!

We did not make any zero to sixty runs with our test car but we understand the 1800 S time is down around ten seconds. We

cornered it hard, though, and let it do a legal sixty mph plus five. At these speeds it just made us think of those long roads out West where we could have added another ten miles or so to the top speed. The safety built into this car would almost have demanded it! We bypassed some vital home work one weekend to wring this car out and although it meant burning the midnight oil for a couple of nights the next week, the mere reporting about the car makes us want to take it out again.

One thing kept cropping up all during this test that became annoying. The cranks for raising and lowering the windows are positioned badly. One almost has to squeeze his elbow between the seatback and the door to wind the window at all. We even tried it with our right hand but we don't recommend this.

Getting into the driver's seat can't be compared with entrance into a Checker cab, either, but once you're behind the wheel the seating seems to have been designed especially for you. The wheel slants very slightly and you can drive with your arms practically straight out which we find less tiring than any other position. You could drive all day with just your left hand on the wheel and your right on the stubby shift lever if you wanted to be that reckless. The steering is that good.

The brakes, big discs up front with drums in back, are better than average. The car comes to a decided halt in a nice, straight line and we got absolutely no brake fade.

Visibility is good all around and the interior is really luxurious. Our test car had **all** that tan leather reaching way up under the dashboard to the firewall and back on the occasional rear seat. Quite like the 144 S, adjustments abound for backward or forward movement of the seats and the seat back, itself, can not only be cranked toward the front or back, but it can be tightened on the lower portion for additional support.

In summing up, we would like to mention that, in addition to watching for brake fade, we checked constantly for overheating when we were held up in heavy traffic. The temperature gauge rose to a certain point when the engine warmed up fully and never moved again until we turned off the ignition.

The price on the Volvo 1800 S is about $4100 East Coast POE. Figuring the longevity built into the car, the excellent fittings, the sturdy, high performance engine and the overall styling, we think it is a good buy for this type of automobile. We think, too, that the designation should be changed to 1800 SS (style with speed). All-in-all 'twas a good, good ride!

VOLVO P1800S $4,285
West Coast P.O.E.

Four cylinder engine, five main bearing crank. 118 HP at 5800 rpm. 1998 c.c. Compression 9.5:1. Overdrive standard. Engine longevity legendary. Good resale value. Manufactured by A. B. Volvo, Gothenburg, Sweden.

Volvo's 1800 S for 1969 is no longer just 1800cc, but bored out to 1986cc. It is a stretch of the existing 4 cylinder engine that has been around for years. Bigger, freely rotating valves, stronger pistons and rods, and various other minor detail changes have gone into the engine. The extra displacement has not been used so much for extra power but to give the torque a bit more boost in the lower to middle speed ranges. Power is increased from 115 bhp at 6000 to 118 bhp at 5800. The peak torque is now 123 lb-ft at 3500 rpm, much more usable than the older 112 lb-ft

at 4000 rpm. The compression ratio is 9.5:1.

Alternators are at last now fitted on all Volvos. This item has been standard on domestic cars for years but is just being introduced in Europe.

The sealed cooling system is retained but the oil cooler has been dropped. Electrics are still Bosch but the British S.U. carburetors have been replaced by the Stromberg-Zeniths, part of the efficient smog system that is standard on all Volvos, regardless of where they are sold.

The independent front suspension

is by coil springs with telescopic shock absorbers. Rubber mounted control arms and an anti-sway bar make up the package. No lubrication of the front suspension or the drive shaft components is required for the life of the car.

The rear suspension is a simple solid rear axle carried by longitudinal rubber mounted control arms and torque rods. The transverse location is done by rubber mounted track rod. Coil springs with telescopic shock absorbers make up the assembly.

The four speed transmission is the same as before with a full synchro-

Despite its low roofline and high, slab sides, the Volvo still contrives to be one of the sleekest sports coupes on the market today.

Fully equipped. The Volvo has it all — air conditioning, tachometer, oil pressure and temperature gauges included.

mesh on all gears. Reverse is hidden on this one and to engage it, the lever must be lifted up and moved over the first slot. The box is rubber mounted and will jiggle noticeably when in use.

Overdrive is available on fourth gear and is engaged by the stalk on the right hand side of the steering column. It is easily operated just by tapping the lever and care must be taken when cornering not to accidentally engage it.

The seating in the 1800 is 7-way adjustable and the seats are the orthopedic type. The lumbar adjustment is excellent and relieves the

fatigue effect on a long trip. The seat travel is 9″ which allows the tallest driver ample room. The controls are still well grouped but the same complaint can still be found with the foot rest beside the clutch. It is possible to catch the side of a large shoe on it and thereby be unable to fully depress the clutch. Most drivers would prefer to have it removed because of this.

Instrumentation is good and fully comprehensive and all the instruments are well recessed. The full shoulder harness has had the attachment point in the floor modified and each belt can be released by the flick

of a small red lever. A much easier operation than the previous 'cheese-cutter' unit. The rear jump-seat is usable only by small children and should be looked upon as bonus luggage stowage. The back of the seat folds down and there are two leather straps for securing luggage in place.

The brake system has gone over to the full safety system that was introduced on the 144 sedan series. The car uses discs on the front and drums on the rear. No matter how the brake line may be cut, the driver will always have two front wheels and one rear wheel brake in operation. The system

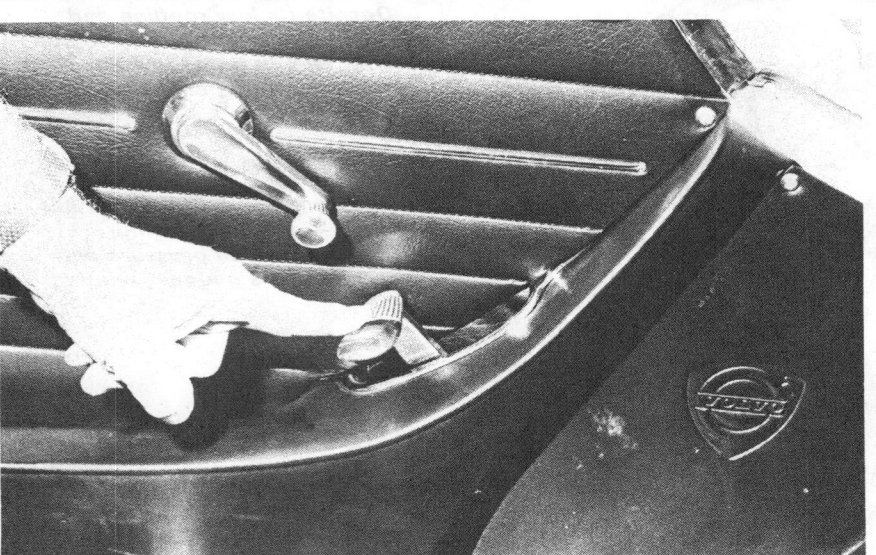

That tail-end design is one of the smoothest yet. Clean, simple and uncluttered by excessive trim.

Volvo has long been big in the field of safety, especially in interior design. This recessed door catch is typical of their thinking.

also has the relief valves that prevent the rear wheels locking up before the front under emergency braking. As this unit is probably the most advanced of its kind in the industry, it is worth a closer look. The front disc pads are operated by separate dual actuating cylinders and the rear discs have the normal single cylinder. The system is designed so that the primary cylinder will operate the lower cylinders on the front wheels together with the right rear wheel; and the secondary system, the upper fronts and the left rear wheel. This will still give 80% of normal braking

efficiency, although, when on the secondary system, the pedal has to be depressed almost its full travel before the brakes will work. This gives the feeling that there is no brake there at all but the car does stop to all intents and purposes as normal. There is a warning light on the dash to indicate that the car is on the emergency system. This is a simple pressure/ micro-switch combination which is actuated whenever hydraulic pressure between the two separate systems is unequal, indicating a leak in one of the lines. If the secondary system has failed, the light is essential

as the braking from the primary system gives the feeling that all is normal. Also included in the system is a pressure relief valve which prevents the rear wheels from locking up before the fronts. To top it off, the car has a mechanical linkage hand-brake to a drum on the left rear wheel. This simplifies the normal difficulty in utilizing the disc system for parking use.

The Volvo 1800 S has never really hit it off strongly with the younger set and unaccountably tends to be likened to the Mercedes 280 SL, big and heavy and alright for older folks.

It is unfortunate that salesmen don't rectify this situation as this car is more than capable of mixing it with Porsche 912 and the Alfa GTV coupes. The car can be really thrown around corners with the radial Pirellis hanging on well and it always comes as a pleasant surprise to glance at the speedometer; the car just doesn't feel that it is going that fast.

As a touring car, the 1800 S really comes into its own and with the judicious use of overdrive, is capable of turning in some pretty impressive gas mileage figures, well up in the high twenties. The orthopedic seats go a long way towards driver comfort and with the new powerplant and overdrive engaged, the previous engine roar has to all intents been eliminated; all tending to reduce driver fatigue.

Availability of 1800 S models has stiffened the retail price of the car and 'deals' are almost unheard of. The car does have a high resale value but the difficulty is in finding a late model car. The only ones around are usually 62/63 vintage thereby indicating a high satisfaction rating by the owners. For someone desirous of Volvo's lasting qualities, the 1800 S deserves a close look and more than a run 'round the block. ♠

Volvo
Data in Brief

DIMENSIONS

Overall length (in.)	182.7
Width (in.)	68.1
Height (in.)	56.7
Wheelbase (in.)	102.5
Turning diameter (ft.)	16.4

WEIGHT, TIRES, BRAKES

Weight (lbs.)	2340
Tires	165 x 15
Brakes, front	disc

ENGINE

Type	4 cylinder
Displacement (cu. in.)	116
Horsepower	118

SUSPENSION

Front	independent coil springs
Rear	coil springs and torque arms

THE ELEVEN YEAR CAR

The new Volvo 1800E doesn't look new... yet, maybe there's more to it than meets the eye/by Paul Van Valkenburgh

THIS IS A RE-TEST. As you may recall, we first tested the Volvo 1800 in November 1961 — or so we thought. 1961! That's over nine years ago, when names like Moss, Phil Hill, Von Trips, Scarab and Sadler were "box office," Roger Penske was winning races driving his Birdcage Maserati, and Jerry Titus was merely an SCG test driver.

At that time it was called the P-1800. Today, we thought the 1800E was the same car — and except for different bumpers and chrome trim and wheels, there *is* no apparent difference. To be sure, we expected detail improvements and a horsepower increase, but otherwise...well, it *is* an old design. Volvo just announced a new fuel-injected engine, however, to meet anti-smog regulations, and we thought we'd see how it worked. Actually, we use every excuse to get our hands on *every* Volvo product as frequently and for as long as possible just because they are predictably enjoyable and reliable. That's not just PR, either — that's fact.

Well, to leave as much time as possible for driving, the thought occurred: Why not just copy the text from the '61 test, and from the P-1800S test in '63, and change the performance and specification numbers where applicable. Who would notice? Who has been with us that long — or been with Volvo that long, for that matter? So out came the musty dusty old issues, and we started to self-plagiarize.

Hell, man, things *do* change in nine years. In the first place, we thought we knew how to evaluate a car then, before the advent of electronics and precision instrumentation and controlled variables. But now, if we are a little wiser, Volvo is a *lot* wiser, after all these years of single-minded devotion to improving what was originally a very fine car.

Back in those days the 1800 styling was quite advanced, so much so that today, our "automotive virgin" was really impressed by the styling — since she wasn't aware that it was a decade-old design and, therefore, "outdated." Perhaps professional testers get a little jaded, and a little *too* wise. After all, Volvo didn't *need* a styling change, and their design time was better spent cleaning up details. If that sounds like the philosophy of other famous car builders, it's intentional — and fortunate — for those who want or need a truly trouble-free form of transport and are above Volkswagen and below Rolls-Royce. Volvo uses the slogan "The eleven-year car," which supposedly is the average age of all Volvos still running in Sweden, though it could be misconstrued as the length of the styling change cycle.

References to "tank" are frequently made in print or conversation about Volvo products, and in their case it is hardly derogatory. It's hard to find a line of cars that feel and sound as solid, and yet have adequate agility for the typical *Sports Car Graphic* reader. For the price, that is. In its range a Volvo has to be one of the best buys from the quality standpoint.

The feeling of security comes not only from the body and chassis, but from intimate contact with the interior. Someone at Volvo really cares for your body, and knows how to treat it right (where you sit). We have been trying to get them to adapt' their lounge buckets to castered pedestals so that we could use them for office chairs, but some of our staff are sedentary enough *without* the influence of truly great seats. As in our test of the Volvo 164, we found the radical adjustability of their lush buckets to be the most outstanding feature over the long trip, and second only to reliability over the long range.

The rest of the interior takes a back seat, with a jump seat—or "squat seat" as the case may be—that is hardly habitable for adult humans, but then they don't even claim the car to be a "plus 2," so instead we'll give them credit for all the luggage space when the backrest is folded down. The windows were a little drawbackish compared to most European quality cars we've driven, because for all the friction and awkwardness in the winders, they weren't all that tight and we couldn't avoid a wind hiss. Uncommon for them. The facia was neat in '61 and is neat today, as they have done no more than change two gauges and add a couple of switches. The shifter has been relocated farther away, to where you can crunch your knuckles on the ashtray when you get active on the stick, but the rest of the interior is just excellent. Part of the aura of security must come from the cockpit layout, since with a low top and high window sills, you sit low in the greenhouse, well protected from side impact, sight, snowballs, bullets and what have you. Irregardless, there is no difficulty in seeing all four fenders (though only two at a time) when maneuvering in close parking quarters.

Handling was excellent—back in '61—but only "good" by today's standards of a GT car in any price category. The steering is still heavy up to the point of front-end breakaway, where you don't spend a lot of time, and there is a lot of understeer. The 6-cylinder sedan felt as good if not better than our 4 cylinder in handling, but it wasn't able to reach as high a lateral acceleration—0.72 g in either direction. Even at that, the limiting factor was inside-rear wheelspin, and with a

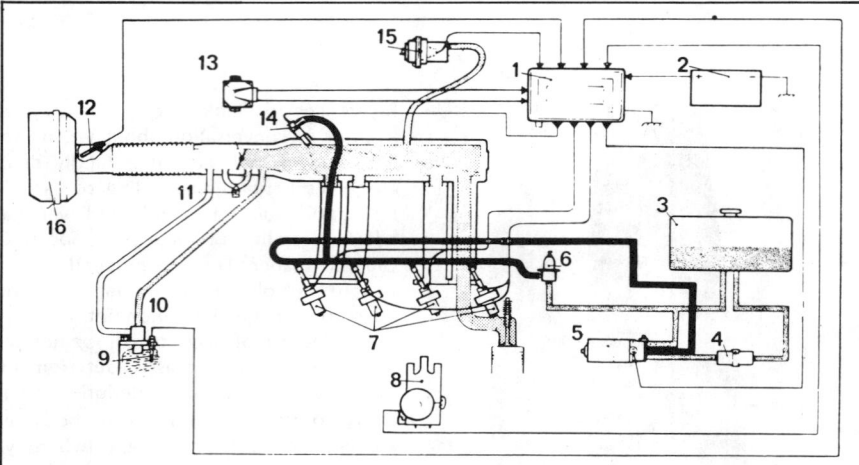

Diagram showing fuel system, B 20 E

1 Control unit (electronic)
2 Battery
3 Fuel tank
4 Fuel filter
5 Electric fuel pump
6 Pressure regulator
7 Injection valves
8 Impulse contacts in distributor
9 Temperature sender for cooling water
10 Supplementary air control
11 Adjuster screw for idling
12 Temperature sender for inlet air
13 Throttle flap contact
14 Cold starting valve
15 Pressure sender
16 Air cleaner

 Partial vacuum in inlet manifold
Fuel at atmospheric pressure
Fuel at pressure of 30 lb./sq.in.
(2 kg/cm²)

THE ELEVEN YEAR CAR

good limited-slip differential, you might find enough power available for "throttle steer." A good independent rear suspension might even the car up some, as Volvo is about the last holdout in the GT class to stick with a live rear axle — though it is well controlled with adequate locating linkage. Front suspension is very conventional also, with unequal A-arms and concentric coil shocks. For a GT it seemed to have a little more roll than usual, so perhaps a rear anti-roll bar would reduce both roll and understeer.

Brakes are unequivocally excellent. Four-wheel discs and a good front/rear balance stop you short and hard with excellent stability. In all, the handling and

braking are very good, but aren't the Volvo's long suit. Volvos have a tendency to undistinguish themselves in the performance department by having neither the best nor the worst in any particular category. Until now there hasn't been any significance in the engine room either. The 2-liter, iron 4-cylinder was originally derived from half of a V-8 they make for trucks, and is accordingly strong. But the American low-emission requirements goaded them into developing a fuel-injection system for it, which is the *real* justification for our test. In principle, the system is typical of most electronically controlled injectors. A number of sensors are attached to the engine to measure the variables that have an effect on fuel mixture: i.e., throttle opening, inlet air temperature, engine cooling water temperature, inlet

manifold vacuum and engine rpm. The signals from all these sources are integrated in the electronic control unit (or "brain"), and the calculated optimum fuel ratio is injected into each port. The nozzles are solenoid-actuated plungers and the amount of fuel is controlled by the duration of opening. Fuel pressure is supplied by an electric fuel pump, and the undistributed fuel is returned to the tank through a pressure relief valve. With this type of system a more accurate control of fuel ratio is possible under varying conditions, which results in better combustion and reduced exhaust emissions. To aid in satisfying the California fuel evaporation limits, a device is also fitted to eliminate gas tank "breathing."

That's how it works — but how *well* does it work? That's an awkward question to answer. Volvo claims it gives 10-percent more horsepower (to 130) and it's obviously more efficient, but, well... dammit, the computer just doesn't seem to cooperate with how we feel an engine ought to run sometimes. In the beginning we thought it was all confused, because on a cold start we just couldn't seem to keep the engine running — it wouldn't respond to throttle blipping (aha, vee zee der probolem — no exzellerator bumps!). Push on the throttle — nothing, harder — nothing, harder... suddenly — WAOW! It runs up to redline. But when we gave up and decided to let it stall — it wouldn't do *that* either. It seems that the electrickery has it's own ideas on how to run a cold shop — just leave it alone.

After it warms up, however, there is no difference from carburetors, or if anything, the injection is smoother. The backoff and get-on response between gears, combined with a very easy clutch, make for silky shifts and nearly automatic acceleration.

On the other hand, when we tried to flog it at the drag strip, we ran into obstinate independence again. A combination of apparent delay in the injection during quick shifting, and a missed shift or two, made us very wary of too much experimentation. Still, the car turned the quarter in 16.8 secs. compared to the 20.8 secs. that Titus got out of his 1800S back in '63, so it looks like the electrons are doing whatever they're supposed to.

If you are now confused as to how we rate the car, don't be put off by our critical comments — it's just that we expect so much for so little so often from Volvo, that *any* bad news *is* news. A good average box score from a wide sample of experienced drivers categorizes the 1800E as follows. Earning the "Extraordinary" award: seating comfort, strength and security, value-per-dollar, longevity. In the "Excellent" department: braking, fuel economy, smoothness, quality. And finally, in the merely "Very Good" group: acceleration, handling, styling, and silence. As for the criticisms... well... ah... hmm... wasn't there *something*?

VOLVO 1800E

PRICE
Base $4595
As tested $4595

ENGINE
Type .... 4 cylinder, water-cooled, iron block, iron head
Displacement .... 121 cu. in. (1990 cc)
Horsepower .... 130 hp @ 6000 rpm
Torque .... 130 lbs.-ft. @ 3500 rpm
Bore & stroke .... 3.50 in. x 3.15 in. (88.9 mm x 80.0 mm)
Compression ratio .... 10.5 to 1
Valve actuation .... Ohv, rocker arms
Induction system ... Electronically controlled .... fuel injection
Exhaust system ...... Iron headers, 3 into 2
Electrical system .... 12-volt alternator, point distributor
Fuel .... Premium
Recommended redline 6500

DRIVE TRAIN
Clutch .... Dry disc, hydraulic

Transmission   Gear Ratio   Overall Ratio
	Gear Ratio	Overall Ratio
1st Synchro	3.14	13.50
2nd Synchro	1.97	8.47
3rd Synchro	1.34	5.76
4th Synchro	1.00	4.30
Overdrive	0.797	3.43

Differential ... Limited slip, hypoid, 4.30 ratio

CHASSIS
Frame .... Steel unit construction, front engine, rear drive
Front suspension ... Double A-frame, anti-roll bar, coil springs with telescopic shocks
Rear suspension .... Live axle, traction bars, Panhard rod, coil springs with telescopic shocks
Steering .... Cam and roller, 3¼ turns, turning circle 29.8 feet
Brakes .... Four-wheel power disc, dual circuits, 10.6-in. dia. front, 11.6-in. dia. rear
Wheels .... 15-in. dia.; 5-in. wide
Tires .... Michelin 165 HR 15, pressures F/R: 26/29 (rec.), 30/32 (test)

BODY
Type .... Unit steel, 2-door, 2-passenger
Seats .... Front bucket, rear shelf
Windows .... 2 manual, 2 vents
Luggage space .... Rear trunk, 6 cu. ft.
Instruments .. 120 mph speedo, 7000 rpm tach
Gauges: .. fuel, water, oil temp & pressure
Lights: .... alternator, overdrive

WEIGHTS AND MEASURES
Weight ... 2595 lbs. (curb), 2750 lbs. (test)
Weight distribution F/R 52%/48%
Wheelbase .... 96.5 in.
Track F/R .... 51.7 in./51.7 in.
Height .... 50.5 in.
Width .... 67.0 in.
Length .... 173.3 in.
Ground clearance .... 6 in.
Oil capacity .... 8 qt.
Fuel capacity .... 12 gal.
Coolant capacity .... 9 qt.

MISCELLANEOUS
Weight/power ratio (curb/advertised) .... 20.0 lbs. per hp
Advertised hp/cu. in. 1.07
Speed per 1000 rpm (top gear) ..... 21.6 mph
Warranty ..... 12 months/no mileage limit

AERODYNAMIC FORCES AT 100 MPH

CORNERING CONDITIONS

PERFORMANCE
Acceleration .... 0-30 (3.3 sec.), 0-60 (9.6 sec.), 0-100 (29.5 sec.)
0-quarter mile (16.8 sec.), 82.4 mph)

Top speed .... 122 mph (est.) at 5700 rpm (power limited)

Braking .... Distance from 60 mph: 143 ft. (0.88 g av.)
Number of stops to fade: Not attainable
Stability: Excellent
Maximum pitch angle: 2.3°

Handling .... Maximum lateral: 0.72 g right, 0.72 g left
Skidpad understeer: 6.3° right, 9.7° left
Maximum roll angle: 5.2°
Reaction to throttle, full: Wheelspin; off: Less understeer

Speedometer	30.0	40.0	50.0	60.0	70.0	80.0	90.0	100.0
Actual mph	27.0	36.5	45.5	54.0	63.0	73.5	81.5	89.5

Mileage .... Average: 25 mpg
Miles on car: 900 to 1200

Aerodynamic forces at 100 mph:
Drag .... 270 lbs. (includes tire drag)
Lift F/R .... 190 lbs./0 lbs.

TEST EXPLANATIONS
Fade test is successive maximum g stops from 60 mph each minute until wheels cannot be locked. Understeer is front minus rear tire slip angle at maximum lateral on 200-ft. dia. Digitek skidpad. Autoscan chassis dynamometer supplied by Humble Oil.

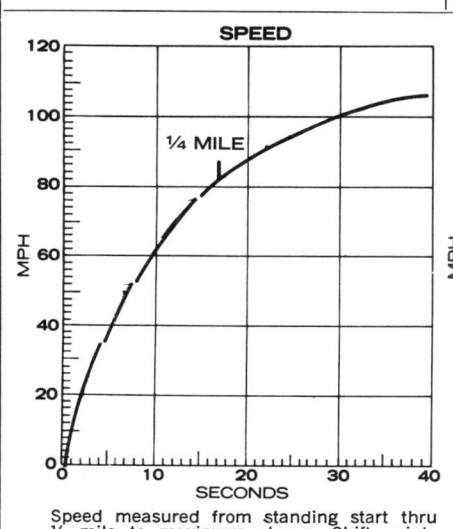

SPEED

Speed measured from standing start thru ¼ mile to maximum shown. Shift points indicated by line breaks.

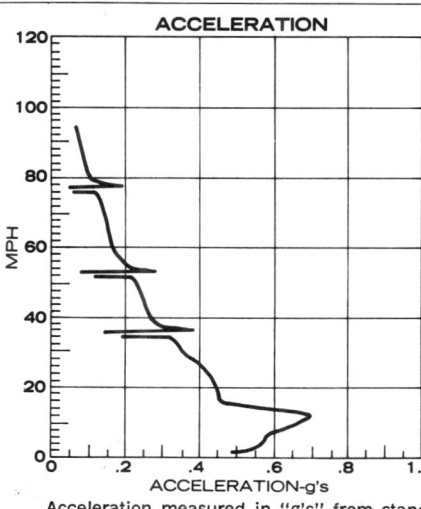

ACCELERATION

Acceleration measured in "g's" from standing start to speed shown. Shift points indicated by "spikes" on graph.

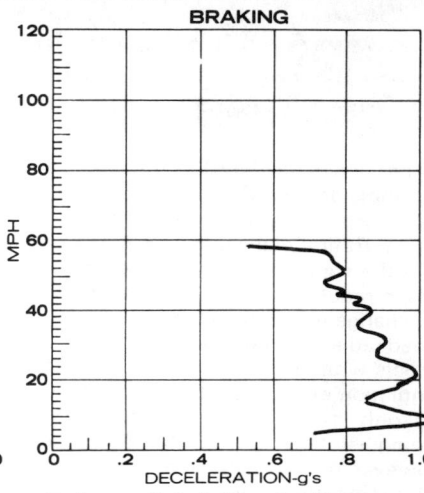

BRAKING

Brakes applied at 60 mph with maximum force, but using pedal "feathering" technique to prevent wheel lockup.

VOLVO 1800 E $4535 WEST COAST P.O.E.

Four cylinder, fuel injected B20 engine. Disc brakes all around. Revised electric overdrive. New dashboard layout. New lockable glove box. Compression ratio 10.5:1. Same basic durable engineering. Excellent resale value. Manufactured by A. B. Volvo, Gothenburg, Sweden.

The Volvo for 1970 is another example of the European philosophy of steady improvement of an original theme. At first glance, the 1800 is basically the same shape as it was when it was introduced in 1962. The most striking change in the car's looks is the high speed radial tires on new aluminum alloy wheels with steel rims. The flo-through ventilation exhaust vents at the rear are the only other external features that distinguish this car from the '69 model. However, under the hood and inside the cabin it is quite a different story.

The Volvo B20 engine is retained but now has a Bosch derivative fuel injection system. This is similar to the VW computer controlled unit but without, Volvo claims, the flat spot that occurs in the VW unit under acceleration. Bore and stroke are 3.50 in. and 3.15 in. Displacement is 121 cu. in. Maximum output is quoted at 130 bhp, SAE at 6000 rpm. Maximum torque is 130 lb./ft. at 3500 rpm. Compression ratio is 10.5:1.

The car comes standard with a sealed cooling system with anti-freeze already included.

Power from the engine is taken through a diaphragm spring clutch. The Volvo transmission has been replaced with the ZF box as used in the six cylinder sedan. This is an extremely positive unit with an unbeatable synchromesh. The throw with this lever is so short that it allows incredibly fast shifts.

The overdrive on fourth gear is operated by finger touch on the control to the right of the steering column. The ratio is 0.797:1.

With a 10% increase in power and torque over last year's model, the 1800E should show a better time for the quarter mile. As the first car won't be available for driving until after the first of January, we have no acceleration figures to quote at this time.

Based on previous figures, the car

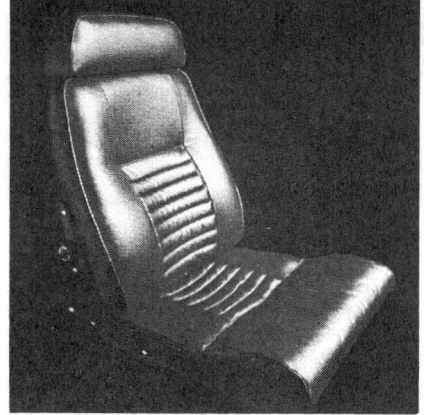

Volvo's excellent seating is carried over into the 1800E. The backs adjust for lumbar support. Center cubby is lockable. Overdrive is standard.

Volvo 1800E has more than average space in trunk, additional luggage space behind seats.

1800E Volvo has several important new features for '70. Styling innovation is the wider mag type wheels with standard radial ply tires. There are now disc brakes on all four wheels.

should be in the same bracket as the Alfa GTV and that is good company to say the least.

The suspension for 1970 is the same as before except that no lubrication of front suspension and drive shaft components is required for the life of the car.

The front suspension is independent with rubber-mounted control arms and ball joints. Rear suspension still has a solid rear axle carried by longitudinal rubber-mounted control arms and torque rods. Transverse location is by rubber mounted track rod. Coil springs with telescopic shocks complete the assembly.

This well located axle assembly allows the car to be thrown around on corners. Added to this is the good adhesion from the radial tires which makes for a very fine handling car with no vices.

Steering is by cam and roller with 3 ¼ turns lock to lock. This gives it a turning circle of 32 ft. 10 in.

The 1800 models have always been good on braking but this year they have improved their performance even further. The '70 model now has disc brakes all around. This is the same safe 'three wheel' system that Volvo sedans offer. No matter what happens to one line, under these emergency conditions there are always two front wheels and one rear wheel in operation. Added to this is the handbrake operating two drum brakes with a lining area of 27 sq. in. The net effect of the disc brakes under emergency amounts to a safe usable 80 % of normal efficiency.

The discs are 10.6 in. front and 11.6 in. rear.

Volvo cars abound in safety features that were designed in long before safety became fashionable. The 1800 continues in this tradition with the addition of one item over last year's cars. The rear window is now electrically defrosted, thereby ensuring that it is possible to see out under any conditions.

All federal safety requirements are exceeded in all Volvos by a large margin, making this one of the safest cars on the road.

For 1970, the interior of the 1800E has undergone a major facelift. The whole instrument panel has changed and the tachometer and speedometer are now redesigned. The tach shows the thousand of rpms in four number digits, making it an impressive display. Between these two instruments there are

Six cylinder 1970 engine has Bosch type electronic fuel injection, develops 10 per cent more horsepower. Unit has five main bearings, should be long lasting.

two separate gauges for oil and water temperature. These were originally combined and not too readable in the older model. A gas gauge and oil pressure gauge complete the facia. There is also an electric clock in the center of the panel, easily seen by both occupants.

All switches are of the rubber variety, clearly marked and well recessed. The heater controls are below the dash in the center and are also easily identified. It has all the power of a Bessemer blast furnace.

The three spoke steering wheel is well padded with horn buttons at each end of the spokes.

A flow through ventilation system has been added and this will go a long way to making the car quieter. Quarter windows for ventilation do have their penalties with increased wind noise. The flow through systems allow a fresh interior without a howling gale ruffling your lady's expensive hair-do.

A lockable glove compartment behind the floor shift is a new item that will be appreciated by owners who have always wanted a small place to put loose items.

Both of Volvo's leather bucket seats are fully reclining and feature their famous lumbar adjustment control. Securely strapped in with the full shoulder harness, they give the passengers a good sense of security. They are extremely comfortable for long distance touring, which is really the role for this GT machine.

Another new feature is the warning buzzer for a door being left open, part of the new safety package.

The rear seat is purely usable only by *small* children. It is much more likely to be used for luggage stowage when folded down. This makes the carrying capacity of this car quite large for its size, there being a useful sized trunk in the rear.

A heavy underseal coating is applied at the factory and must rate as the best offered by any manufacturer. The quality of the paint has long been used as the yardstick by which to compare others and the 1800E is from the same mold.

The gas tank has a capacity of 11 ¾ gallons and now has the required evaporation control.

The new features of the 1800E bring it into hot competition with the Alfa GTV.

The new look to the outside with the sporty wheels will probably make the younger swinging set take a closer look at what has usually been regarded as more of a sporty car for older folks. How

this situation ever came about is not known but certainly this new car is going to go a long way to rectifying that image.

Couple this to Volvo's record for longevity and the 1800E must rate as one of the sharpest buys for the money on the road today. As always with a hot item like this, cars are scarce but the product is one that is well worth waiting for. ♠

Volvo 1800E
Data in Brief

DIMENSIONS

Length (in.)	173.3
Width (in.)	67.0
Height (in.)	50.5
Wheelbase (in.)	96.5
Track, front and rear (in.)	51.7

ENGINE

Type	four, in-line, water cooled, five main bearing crankshaft, fuel injection
Displacement (cu. in.)	121
Horsepower at 6000 rpm	130
Torque at 3500 rpm (lb./ft.)	130
Compression ratio	10.5:1

WEIGHT, TIRES, BRAKES

Weight (lbs.)	2490
Tires	165HR 15 radials
Brakes, front and rear	discs

SUSPENSION

Front	independent with rubber mounted control arms and ball joints, anti-sway bar, coil springs and shocks
Rear	solid axle, longitudinal arms and torque rods, coil springs and shocks

THE ELEVEN YEAR PLAN

Volvo has always prided themselves on manufacturing an eleven-year automobile. With the 1800 they may be a little short.

If it had been left to Reid Chesworth, nobody would have known what an XKE was. For him, only one sports car made sense, the Volvo P-1800. Of course Reid Chesworth had never driven one because in 1961 the P-1800 had just come out, and there weren't many around. But he knew about the Volvo 444s, bolt-upright three-quarter scale '48 Ford sedans that were tighter, faster, and more reliable than anything Dearborn had ever made. And then there were those Volvo ads that put a P-1800 shoulder-to-shoulder with a Jag and Ferrari and a Maserati, and you could hardly tell which was which except when you went to pay for it. And that was Chesworth's telling argument: at $3,900 everything else seemed like investing in livery stable futures.

That was 9 years ago. And it isn't significant except the style and the engineering of the 1800 is now precisely a decade old, 10 years in which the world itself seems to have turned inside out. The obvious question, then, is the 1800's relevancy in the '70s; does it still score a high percentile on the Reid Chesworth sliding index of value? Has it, like the other machines in that long-ago comparison advertisement, retained its elusive magic of desirability? Or, does a Datsun 240Z render it into the elephants' graveyard of the Morgan Owners Club.

A lot of sheet metal has gone by the boards since the days of the New Frontier, whole schools of style have been born and lost, and yet the 1800's lines work as well as they ever did. Put on a set of thin, horizontal bumpers, instead of the jobs that swept up in the center with the same dihedral as the wings of an F4UF Corsair, a blacked-out grille, semi-spoke mags, and the boulevard curb cruiser in his 396 Chevelle knows not that it isn't just off the boat. Somewhere the 'P' was dropped but suffix or no the 1800 has the good old long-hood-short-deck-close-coupled look and that's all you've ever really needed. Besides, Volvo's total 1800 production since birth has been something in the magnitude of 31,000 units, 51 percent of which came here, not a lot in America's 104-million-place parking lot.

Inside the promise is the same. A bank of precisely-lettered Smiths instruments set into an up-to-the-second imitation wood-grain panel transmits information back to the driver in sufficient quantities to satiate any contemporary sports car nut. It is all so right, somehow: the big round tach and speedometer looking back at you through the top of the large-diameter three-spoke steering wheel; the genuine red-leather seats with so much travel they need an interstate permit; and the low-roofed kind of intimate compartment feeling. As you sit with your arms straight out in the classic driving position, caring that the machine wasn't designed yesterday doesn't seem to matter anymore than it does in a Ferrari.

Einspritzung, that's the mark of Volvo's progress, the E in 1800 E. Fuel injection, as the Germans spell it. Electronic, as Bosch builds it. It is the same device first seen on the 1600 VWs 2 years ago and which every thoughtful person knew would appear on any European four- or six-cylinder engine that wanted to inhale the U.S. atmosphere. Like all good things, it is computer-controlled. Monitors gather data, the engine's temperature, breathing, beat,

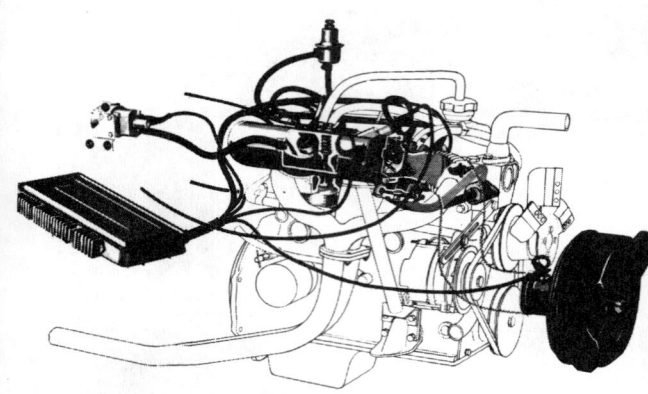

This is the plan (above), for a Volvo med elektronisk styrd bransleinsprutning, electronic fuel-injection to you. Note long manifold runners (below), and cold air intake. Little black spot on right rear fender is exhaust outlet for cockpit.

SPECIFICATIONS

Engine .... B 20 E
Bore & Stroke ..... 3.50 ins. x 3.15 ins.
Displacement .... 121 c.i. cu. in.
Max. horsepower .. 130 SAE @ 6000 rpm
Max. torque .... 130 SAE @ 3500 rpm
Compression ratio 10.5:1
Carburetion .... electronic fuel injection
Transmission .... 4 speed manual
Final drive ratio 4.3:1
Steering type .... cam & roller
Turning diameter .... 30 ft.
Tires .... 165 HR 15
                radial ply with inner tube
Brakes .... 4-wheel discs
Front suspension .... independent with
    coil springs and telescopic shocks,
    anti-roll bar, double A Frame
Rear suspension .... rigid axle, support
    arms and torque rods, traction bars,
    coils and telescopic shocks
Body/frame construction .... steel
                unit construction
Dimensions, Weights, Capacities
Overall length .... 171¼ ins.
Overall width .... 67 ins.
Overall height .... 50½ ins.
Wheelbase .... 96½ ins.
Front track .... 51¾ ins.
Rear track .... 51¾ ins.
Curb weight .... 2710 lbs.
Fuel capacity .... 12 gals.
Oil capacity .... 7 pints

PERFORMANCE

Acceleration (2 Aboard)

0-30 mph	3.3 secs.
0-45 mph	5.85 secs.
0-60 mph	9.55 secs.
0-75 mph	14.6 secs.
Standing start ¼ mile	83.33 mph, 16.61 secs.

Passing speeds (3rd gear)

40-60 mph	4.25 secs.
50-70 mph	6.1 secs.

Speeds in gears at rpm

1st	33 mph @ 6000
2nd	53 mph @ 6000
3rd	78 mph @ 6000
4th	93 mph @ 5500
MPH per 1000 RPM	16.9 mph

Stopping Distances

from 30 mph	26 ft. 5 in.
from 60 mph	136 ft. 4 in.

Volvo continued

and send it in an uninterrupted stream to the little black box that deals out milli-second judgments on what it is to be fed under any circumstance. The bottom of Death Valley or the top of Mt. Rushmore, it makes no difference, the computer knows what's best.

And the computer is right. The Volvo B 20 E, 121 cubic inch engine at 130 hp (at 6000 rpm) sustains 10 percent more horsepower than before, passes its parts-per-million bogey, and is smooth through the power range, with two minor qualifications. Cold-starting an 1800 E is funny sometimes. You press the accelerator to the floor once and release it. The engine catches immediately and then dies – almost – before it slowly picks up shakily to life. But, it doesn't always happen. That's one thing. The other is on trailing throttle at idle speed where the engine seems to fade out but never quite does. The reason for this is not so much that the unit is calibrated on the lean side but the principle of operation depends on some kind of air velocity to smooth the injection cycle and the manifold runners are plenty long.

Someone once said that 1800 series Volvos are like the old Porsche Supers – very deceiving. They really don't feel too fast but suddenly everybody is behind you. To a certain degree this is true in the 1800 E, mainly because of the injected engine's silky character and that rear axle movement, even on hard acceleration, is very well controlled. Volvo's long suit has never been drag racing; still, making consistent 16.60-70 elapsed times allowed the 1800 E to blow the doors off a 318 Plymouth Belvedere and a 350 Buick Special. Therefore, Porsches and even BMWs won't be a problem. You really have no right to do this with a 2-liter 2700-pound car but somehow Volvo does it anyway.

The one thing you don't want to do with an 1800 E is baby it. For reasons known only to Volvo engineering, the further you get on your trip into the car's potential, the better you'll like it. Piddling along over uneven road surfaces offers a medium-hard ride no doubt due in part to the 165 HR 15 radial-ply tires. Flog the same pieces of pavement 20 mph faster and the car is

the greatest thing on wheels. Clearly, the 1800 was designed to easily negotiate rough, narrow European roads flat out, a characteristic the company has put in all of its vehicles.

Suspending the 1800 is the very unexotic mix of unequal length front wish bones and a coil-sprung live rear axle. In these times of McPherson struts and I.R.S., the Volvo is dated, though dated in a solid, secure, run-forever mode. The 3½ turns lock-to-lock worm and roller steering tends to be heavy at low speeds and the Swedes might be well advised to try something like a ZF power unit that would have the compound benefit of allowing a reduction in the size of the rather big steering wheel which occasionally hampers your braking leg because of a close relation to the seat. Of course, the car understeers, no doubt to keep the predictability factor in your favor. The 1800 just doesn't do anything unexpected, so you can have a grand time running it through corners with all the confidence you'll come out in one piece. Occasionally, the inside rear wheel will spin in which case you just slow down a bit.

On twisty, undulating mountain roads the car is in its own realm – threading a path with probably a trace too much lean but with an easy gait bonded to the pavement. To permit this, the 1800 has one peach of a brake setup, four-wheel power assisted discs. From 60 mph, the machine will stop in 130 feet and although the pedal goes down a little, they do not fade away, ever. A proportioning valve in the system all but completely prevents rear wheel lockups on hard deceleration for plumb-line stops. Volvo's idea of a dual braking system is not the cut-and-dried, front/rear alternative of almost all other manufacturers. No, by incorporating three wheels in each circuit, a full 80-percent of four-wheel braking efficiency is available. It costs more this way but then you only live once.

Volvo also has a pretty good idea about seating, too. The great leather lounge chairs of the 164 started us off on the road of high expectations and the 1800 E has not defaulted it. You seem

continued on page 134

Motorway Express

Dated but rejuvenated by fuel-injected engine;
effortless high-speed cruising;
poor visibility; very heavy steering; good ride;
superbly finished but expensive

To many the Volvo 1800 is the ultimate grand tourer. Perhaps frequent appearances on television in *The Saint* series as Simon Templar's personal transport have irretrievably linked the Volvo's distinctive shape with excitement. In this context it is surprising to reflect that the basic design is 10 years old.

Volvos have been available here since 1959, the P1800, as the car was originally known, appearing late the following year. Initially the bodies were built by Jensen Motors but in 1963 Volvo took over, gave the car a more powerful version of the 1780 cc B18 engine and renamed it the 1800S. With only detail improvements, which included a further increase in power

output, the 1800S continued in production until 1968. That year the whole Volvo range received an engine increase to 1985cc, exhaust emission control equipment was fitted as standard and the engine given the designation B20. The announcement of the 1800E in Sweden last year brings history up to date.

It's basically the same car as its predecessor. Alloy wheels, 'E' badges on the rear panel, and a slightly different grille identify the new model externally; internally the facia has been improved and the seats now have built-in headrests. Under the skin there are now split-circuit brake lines operating all-round discs and of course fuel injection replaces carburetters.

We haven't road tested an 1800 since 1962; even then we thought the driving position rather vintage and the scuttle high. The past decade has seen a dramatic increase in glass area, a

PRICE: £1,725 plus £529 7s. 6d. tax equals £2,254 7s. 6d. Extras fitted to test car: wing mirrors £5 (pair). Total as tested £2,259 7s. 6d.

general lowering of waist lines and considerable progress in the field of ergonomics. These factors combine to make the substantially unchanged Volvo seem positively old fashioned though the adoption of Bosch electronic fuel injection has certainly give the car a lot more zest.

The increased power, up from 105 to 120 bhp DIN, is reflected by the performance figures—a maximum speed of 108 mph and a 0–50 mph time of 7.1 sec. Even so, the 1800E is still more of a marathon runner than a sprinter. The standard overdrive makes it a very relaxed high-speed tourer and reasonably economical. But its performance on secondary roads is less satisfactory and it doesn't compare well with some of its more modern rivals in the £2300 bracket.

As Sweden is a fellow EFTA country the price is not inflated by import duty. What you pay for is the car's superb finish and general quality feel. Volvo AB are the largest foreign buyers of British-made automobile equipment (about £21 million annually) so patriotic buyers need have few qualms about not buying British. Imports began a couple of months ago but Volvo intend to sell the 1800E in limited numbers only, so if you are prepared to pay Elan or E-type money for Volvo engineering in a sporting tourer then the 1800E is worth short-listing.

Performance and economy

The Bosch electronic fuel-injection equipment used on the 1800E (the E refers to fuel injection) includes an electronic control unit. This picks up signals from various senders in the engine and then regulates the opening time of the injection valves and hence the amount of fuel supplied. The senders transmit information to the control unit on engine rpm, cooling water temperature, inlet air temperature, manifold vacuum and the position of the throttle butterfly which is located at the forward end of the cast alloy inlet manifold. An electric fuel pump, aided by a pressure regulator, maintains a steady pressure of 30 psi to the injection nozzles, themselves located just upstream of the inlet valves.

The cold start procedure is to leave the throttle alone and to keep the starter turning for up to 15 seconds until the engine fires. At each new attempt a starting valve functions and squirts fuel into the inlet manifold. Nevertheless as cold starting is not immediate and the engine hesitates before it runs evenly, it's best to remain stationary until the control unit sorts things out. Then the car will pull away without hesitation. The warm-up period is very brief. For subsequent hot starts, you depress the accelerator half way and let the slow pre-engaged starter turn the engine until it fires.

The additional capacity of the B20 engine was obtained by increasing the bore of the B18 from 84.14 to 89.9 mm, keeping the stroke constant at 80 mm. So in its current 2-litre form the unit is still oversquare. The crankshaft runs in five main bearings, and the engine is normally remarkably smooth, though very rough and tappety at idle. The rev counter has a striped red

PERFORMANCE

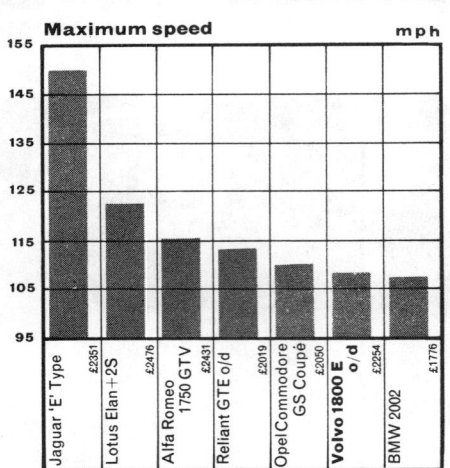

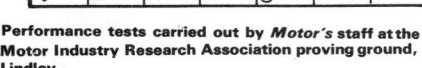

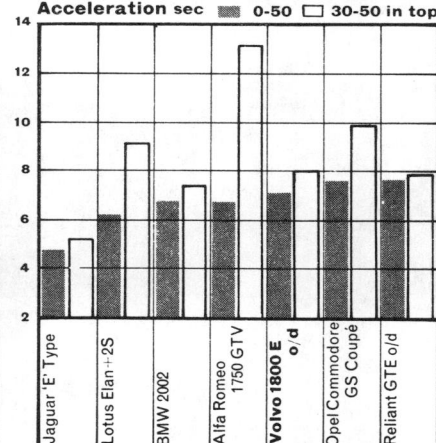

Performance tests carried out by Motor's staff at the Motor Industry Research Association proving ground, Lindley.

Test Data: World copyright reserved; no unauthorized reproduction in whole or in part.

Conditions

Weather: Dry, sunny wind, 0-15 mph
Temperature: 78-92°F
Barometer 29.51-29.46 in. hg.
Surface: Dry tarmacadam
Fuel: Premium 98 octane (RM), 4 Star rating

Maximum Speeds

	mph	kph
Mean lap banked circuit	108.0	173.8
Best one-way ¼-mile	112.5	181.0
3rd gear	76	122
2nd gear } at 6000 rpm	52	83
1st gear	32	52
"Maximile" speed: (Timed quarter mile after 1 mile accelerating from rest)		
Mean	109.8	—
Best	112.5	—

Acceleration Times

mph	sec
0-30	3.3
0-40	5.2
0-50	7.1
0-60	9.6
0-70	13.0
0-80	16.7
0-90	22.9
0-100	31.4
Standing quarter mile	17.4
Standing kilometre	32.1

mph	O/d Top sec	Top sec	3rd sec
10-30	—	—	6.5
20-40	12.0	8.4	6.0
30-50	11.0	8.0	5.6
40-60	11.5	8.0	5.6
50-70	12.2	8.4	6.1
60-80	13.6	9.1	6.7
70-90	16.0	10.7	—
80-100	—	13.9	—

Fuel Consumption

Overall	21.75 mpg
	(= 13.0 litres/100km)
Total test distance	1532 miles

Brakes

Pedal pressure, deceleration and equivalent stopping distance from 30 mph

lb.	g.	ft.
25	0.27	111
50	0.57	53
75	1.00	30
Handbrake	0.37	81

Fade Test

20 stops at ½g deceleration at 1 min. intervals from a speed midway between 40 mph and maximum speed (=74 mph)

	lb.
Pedal force at beginning	50
Pedal force at 10th stop	65
Pedal force at 20th stop	50

Steering

Turning circle between kerbs:	ft.
Left	26⅔
Right	28
Turns of steering wheel from lock to lock	3.6
Steering wheel deflection for 50 ft. diameter circle 1.0 turns	

Clutch

Free pedal movement	= 2 in.
Additional movement to disengage clutch completely	= 4 in.
Maximum pedal load	=40 lb.

Speedometer

Indicated	10	20	30	40	50	60	70
True	9	18	27.5	36	45	55	63.5
Indicated	80	90	100				
True	72.5	81	90				
Distance recorder 5% fast							

Weight

Kerb weight (unladen with fuel for approximately 50 miles)	
	22.25 cwt.
Front/rear distribution	54/46
Weight laden as tested	26.0 cwt.

Parkability

Gap needed to clear 6 ft. wide obstruction in front

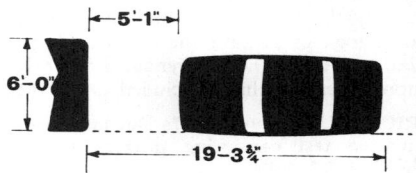

line running from 6000–6500 rpm and beyond that solid red defines the prohibited area.

Maximum power of 120 bhp DIN is given at 6000 rpm, but the engine feels delightfully unstrained at 6500 rpm and we used this for the performance tests to accelerate to 50 mph in 7.1 sec. and to the quarter mile post in 17.4 sec.—impressive figures for a 22¼ cwt. car. Over a lap of the banked MIRA track we recorded 108 mph and a best quarter mile of 112.5 mph. On the slowing-down lap the car emitted clouds of oil smoke from the exhaust; presumably oil was being drawn into the combustion chambers through the valve guides. Although alarming it didn't seem to have any detrimental effect on the car's performance and only one pint of oil was needed during our 1500-mile test.

Unfortunately the engine's smoothness at the top end is not matched by low speed flexibility. At low rpm it is snatchy and there are loud unpleasant vibrations from under the dash panel up to 25 mph in top and up to 20 mph in third. The engine is not happy pulling below 2000 rpm in the higher gears, which is reflected in the acceleration times; beyond 2000 rpm it pulls strongly. This high gearing pays off in fuel economy—we achieved nearly 22 mpg overall and an intermediate check showed over 23 mpg; on a long run at a steady 70 mph we recorded 26 mpg. The B20E engine has a higher compression ratio than the B20 as well as larger inlet valves and a different camshaft. But even at 10.5:1 the makers recommend only 97 octane fuel; we used 4-star 98 octane petrol and could detect no pinking.

Transmission

The 1800E excels on long straight-road journeys. This is in no small measure due to the high gearing, which some of our testers thought too high for the car's power output. Nevertheless it just managed to start on the 1-in-3 test hill, though a previous attempt immediately after the acceleration runs had failed. The clutch pedal pressure (40 lbs) is too high and pedal travel excessive—a total movement of 6 in. is required fully to disengage the drive; we suspect the cable needed adjustment.

The ratios are quite well spaced with 70 mph easily attained in third; it is geared to do 76 mph at 6000 rpm. The overdrive operates on top gear only and is controlled by a stalk mounted on the left of the steering column shroud. It engages with a perceptible thump to reveal a really unstrained high-speed cruise capability. Top gear at 1:1 gives a fairly average 16.9 mph per 1000 rpm but overdrive top at 0.797:1 give a really long-legged 21.2 mph. A red light on the facia, which can be distracting at night, shines when overdrive is engaged. The Laycock unit slurs out of engagement with no jarring.

There's an enormous circular knob mounted atop a stout gearlever which is pleasant to grasp, unlike many modern spindly devices, and controls a smooth though rather heavy change. This is particularly noticeable when the gearbox oil is cold—the change from first to second needs a firm hand. It is spring loaded towards third and top and works in a semi-horizontal plane, so you tend to place your hand either on the forward or the under

An imposing front; the B20 badge refers to the 2 litre engine

The rear compartment is best considered as additional luggage space rather than a passengers' seat. Straps are provided to hold luggage in situ. Our 5 ft. 10 in. tester has his head firmly pinned on the roof and little room for his legs

Flat seats set too low do not help to improve basically poor visibility. They don't provide much lateral support either. The circular knob on the side of the seat adjusts a lumbar support pad. The steering is very heavy

side of the knob when preparing to change. The movement from second to third is particularly slick—just a forward prod and it's home—and even a really fierce change won't beat the synchromesh. Both the gearbox and final drive are quiet.

Handling and brakes

One thing that did not endear the 1800E to us was its heavy cam and gear steering. When parking it requires a lot of effort to get any movement at the road wheels; when the car is stationary it is not possible to turn the wheel with one arm. But once it's moving the gearing (3.6 turns lock-to-lock) is good and only one turn is required to scribe a 50 ft. circle—a typical right-angled turn. The turning circle is reasonable for a largish car, which it needs to be as three-point turns soon bring the driver out in a sweat. Out of town the steering is acceptable but ponderous. It's fairly accurate and readily transmits information on front-end breakaway to the driver.

Basically the Volvo understeers and displays quite a lot of body roll. Wishbones and coil springs are used at the front (mounted on a sub-frame) with a substantial anti-roll bar to increase front-end weight transfer and thus promote understeer; but towards the cornering limit controllable roll oversteer predominates. The live rear axle is also coil-sprung and located fore and aft by trailing arms with a Panhard rod to control lateral movements. We think the rather imprecise behaviour of the rear end during high speed cornering may be due to the very large rubber bushes in which the trailing links are located at their forward end.

Our test car was shod with Irish-made Michelin XAS tyres which provided good squeal-free grip in the dry but were prone to rather sudden breakaway in the wet. They are mounted on large handsome five-stud "mag" wheels which have a steel rim and alloy centre; they are made by Cromodora Fergat.

There are servo-assisted discs all round, and dual-circuit hydraulics with three wheels in each circuit so that if one circuit is damaged 80 per cent braking efficiency is maintained. The handbrake operates on separate drums and achieved a 0.37 g stop, but would not hold the car on the 1-in-3 hill. With 25 lb brake pedal pressure we recorded a 0.27 g stop; trebling the pressure to 75 lb gave a creditable 1 g. The car stopping all square.

The brakes are very reassuring during normal driving so we were surprised to find their performance was affected by our fade test. Initially 50 lb pressure was required to give a 0.5 g stop, but after only seven applications (when the brakes began to smell) this rose to 75 lb. They recovered towards the end of the test. The watersplash had no effect on their performance.

Comfort and controls

One of the outstanding features of the 1800E is undoubtedly the ride, which belies its live axle specification. Small ridges and bumps are soaked up without murmur, and no joggling is transmitted to the body. Yet the suspension, though evidently fairly soft (witness the body roll), feels taught and is in no way

The spare wheel occupies much of the boot which only took 5.3 cu. ft. of our test boxes. The pile on the left fits on the ledge behind the front seats giving a total luggage capacity (assuming only two occupants) of 10 cu. ft.

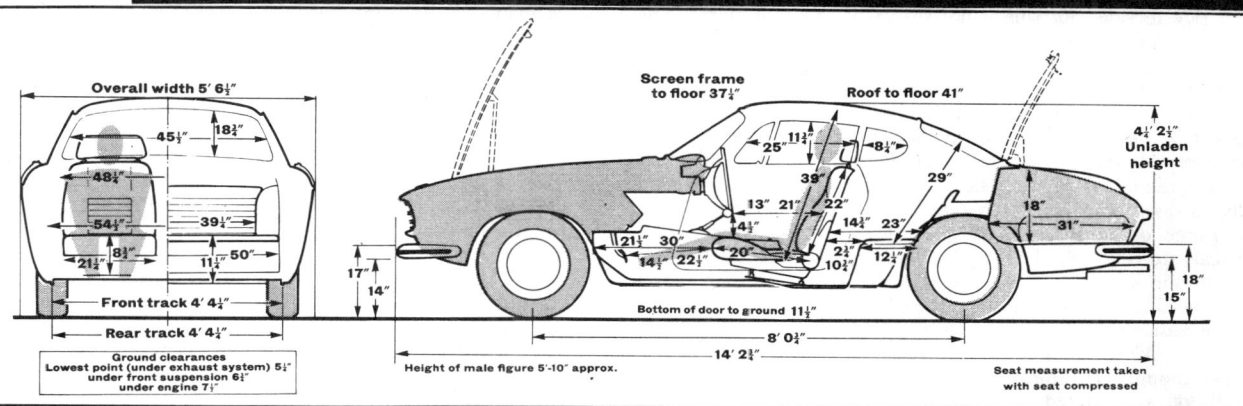

1985 cc four-cylinder engine with fuel injection; live rear axle; all-round disc brakes

Engine

Block material	Cast iron
Head material	Cast iron
Cylinders	Four in line
Cooling system	Water, pump, thermostat and viscous coupling fan; sealed
Bore and stroke	88.9 mm (3.50 in.) x 80 mm (3.15 in.)
Cubic capacity	1985 cc (121 cu. in.)
Main bearings	Five
Valves	Pushrod operated ohv
Compression ratio	10.5:1
Induction	Bosch electronically controlled fuel injection
Fuel pump	Electric
Oil filter	Full flow
Max. power (net)	120 bhp at 6000 rpm
Max. power (gross)	130 bhp at 6000 rpm
Max. torque (net)	123 lb. ft. at 3500 rpm
Max. torque (gross)	130 lb. ft at 3500 rpm

Transmission

Clutch	8½ in. dia. sdp, diaphragm spring

Internal gearbox ratios

Overdrive top	0.797
Top gear	1.00
3rd gear	1.34
2nd gear	1.97
1st gear	3.14
Reverse	3.54
Synchromesh	On all forward gears
Overdrive type	Laycock J-type
Final drive (type and ratio)	Hypoid bevel, 4.30:1

Mph at 1000 rpm in:

O/d top gear	21.2
Top gear	16.9
3rd gear	12.61
2nd gear	8.6
1st gear	5.4

Chassis and body

Construction Unitary

Brakes

Type	Split circuit servo-assisted discs all-round. Drum for handbrake
Dimensions	Front 10.59 in. dia. disc, rear 11.6 in. dia. disc

Friction areas:

Front:	Effective area 27 sq. in.
Rear:	Effective area 15.5 sq. in.

Suspension and steering

Front	Coil springs, wishbones with anti-roll bar.
Rear	Coil springs, live axle located by trailing arms and a Panhard rod

Shock absorbers:

Front and rear	Double acting telescopic
Steering type	Gemmer cam and roller
Tyres	165 HR 15 Michelin XAS
Wheels	Pressed steel rims with cast-aluminium hubs
Rim size	5J

Coachwork and equipment

Starting handle	No
Tool kit contents	Box spanner for plugs and wheel nuts; tommy bar; adjustable spanner; pliers; plain blade and crosshead screwdrivers
Jack	Scissor type
Jacking points	Four
Battery	12 volt, negative earth, 60 amp hrs. capacity
Number of electrical fuses	12
Headlamps	45/40W
Indicators	Self-cancelling flashers
Reversing lamp	Yes, operated automatically by gear lever
Screen wipers	Two-speed electric
Screen washers	Electric
Sun visors	Two

Locks:

With ignition key	Steering lock
With other keys	a. doors and boot; b. central lidded console
Interior heater	Fresh air type with booster fan
Upholstery	Leather
Floor covering	Carpet
Alternative body styles	None
Maximum load	484 lb. without driver

Maintenance

Fuel tank capacity	10 galls
Sump	6.6 pints SAE 20W-50 (incl. filter)
Gearbox	2.46 pints SAE 20W-50 (incl. overdrive)
Rear axle	2.28 pints SAE 90 EP
Steering gear	0.44 pints SAE 90 EP
Coolant	1.87 galls (1 drain tap)
Chassis lubrication	None
Minimum service interval	6000 miles

Ignition timing	10 deg. btdc at 700-800 rpm vacuum pipe disconnected
Contact breaker gap	0.016-0.020 in.
Sparking plug gap	0.028-0.032 in.
Sparking plug type	Bosch W225T35
Tappet clearance (warm or cold)	Inlet 0.016 in. Exhaust 0.016 in.

Valve timing:

inlet opens	29° btdc
inlet closes	71° abdc
exhaust opens	71° bbdc
exhaust closes	29° atdc
Rear wheel toe-in	0—.16 in.
Camber angle	0—+½°
Castor angle	0—+1°
King pin inclination	8° with no camber

Tyre pressures:

Front	26 psi
Rear	28 psi

Safety check list

Steering Assembly

Steering box position	Mounted on o/s front inner wing
Steering column collapsible	Yes
Steering wheel boss padded	Yes
Steering wheel dished	No

Instrument panel

Projecting switches	Yes, but of collapsible type
Sharp cowls	None
Padding	Yes, top and bottom

Windscreen and Visibility

Screen type	Laminated
Pillars padded	No
Standard driving mirrors	Day/night interior mirror
Interior mirror framed	Yes
Interior mirror collapsible	Yes
Sun visors	Two

Seats and Harness

Attachments to floor	On slides
Do they tip forward?	Yes
Headrest attachment points	Headrests standard
Safety harness	Static lap and diagonal

Doors

Projecting handles	Window winders
Anti-burst locks	Yes

1 clock. 2 oil pressure gauge. 3 fuel gauge. 4 overdrive tell-tale. 5, 14 and 25 horn. 6 tachometer. 7 oil temperature gauge. 8 battery charge warning light. 9 odometer. 10 speedometer. 11 mileometer. 12 main beam tell-tale. 13 handbrake and brake system warning light. 15 cigar lighter. 16 ashtray. 17 and 18 heater distribution controls. 19 heater temperature control. 20 wipers and washers. 21 heater booster fan. 22 indicator/headlamp flasher stalk. 23 hazard warning lights. 24 water temperature gauge. 26 indicator tell-tale. 27 instrument panel lighting rheostat. 28 overdrive stalk. 29 steering lock/ignition/starter. 30 side and headlights. 31 heated rear window

soggy. Over long-wavelength irregularities the car displays a certain rear wheel steering tendency, with the back end waddling from side to side, but this is not sufficient to cause alarm. The body remains fairly pinch free over such surfaces.

Seats can spoil a comfortable ride if not properly tuned to the suspension. Volvo got their sums right. Although we think the seats are set too low and too flat, lumbar support is good. Lateral support is poor and is not helped by the slippery leather upholstery. There is plenty of fore and aft adjustment of the seat for even the tallest person, but he will have to sit so far forward fully to disengage the clutch that it is unlikely he will use the full range of adjustment. So you sit rather too close to the vertical steering wheel and the backrest doesn't recline far enough for you to get a straight arm driving position. (You would need strong biceps to turn the wheel with straight arms.)

The pedals are reasonably well placed for heel and toe changes but the brake could be closer to the accelerator, and one of our testers thought the former awkwardly offset to the left. The handbrake is mounted to the right of the driver's seat with the release button surrounded by a circular ring to prevent accidental operation when climbing in or out—a clever idea.

Minor controls are operated by push-pull switches spread across the facia. Only the indicators and headlamp flashers are controlled by a stalk which is too short and too far from the wheel rim. Wipers and washers are on the left of the wheel, one click for slow, the second fast, and the third for fast and washers. So you merely have to pull the switch right out to get wash and wipe. On the other side of the wheel, which has a horn button mounted in each of its three spokes, a switch operates powerful lights on main beam; the dip is a self-centring micro-switch on the indicator stalk.

The car falls down badly on visibility. Sitting very low down in a car with high sides is not a good starting point; added to this is a very limited glass area (some described the windows as portholes). With high headrests on the front seats you can't see much to the rear either (though the pronounced tail fins are useful parking aids), so the optional wing-mounted mirrors are essential. And the lack of three-quarter rear vision becomes almost dangerous when joining a main road from an oblique junction, such corners must be approached at right angles van-style for a safe exit.

Symmetrical wipers sweep a reasonable arc, but there is a blind spot on the right of the screen. For rear seat passengers the accommodation is claustrophobic—they really can't see anything with the headrests blocking the view forwards and only tiny slots to the side. But the rear seats are not really meant for passengers,

though they're fairly accessible through the wide doors. But once in the back your head is pinned to the roof and if the occupants of the front seats are selfish there's no rear leg room. It's not much better with just one person in the back.

Cars with a price tag of £2300 should have a proper through-flow ventilation system. Ford manage to fit one of the best there is on their bread-and-butter Cortina. Volvo apparently don't like facia-level fresh air vents as they think there is a possibility of, for example, cigarette ash being blown into the driver's eyes. So the 1800E has vents under the dash, which are not really adequate, and they don't cope with radiated heat from the transmission tunnel. To keep cool you have to open a window, itself an art as the winders are stiff to operate and very close to the door panels. Moreover, they cause a lot of wind roar. The heater, as to be expected in a Swedish car, is very efficient.

Induction roar is well muted while the exhaust note is pleasantly 'fruity'. A single exhaust splits into two tailpipes at the rear of the car.

The viscous-coupled fan helps to subdue engine noise, which at 70 mph in overdrive top (3300 rpm) is very low, but the sealing of the frameless windows is not good particularly in side winds. Road noise is low and radial thump almost imperceptible.

Fittings and furniture

An imposing array of instruments, including an oil temperature gauge, faces the driver. Volvo warned us that the speedometer was inaccurate and because no spare was available we had to make allowances for a 10 per cent error. It is matched by a rev counter and the two are separated by oil and water temperature gauges. The oil gauge needle rarely moved but that for the water temperature often approached the red sector; the handbook said this was acceptable for short periods. The facia is attractively laid out and the instruments mounted on a simulated matt wood background with black leathercloth top and bottom. Standard equipment includes a heated rear window (there is an alternator to cope with supply) which has a two-position switch, one for clearing the window and the other for keeping it clear. There are courtesy switches for two rear-mounted interior lights on both doors—the lights can also be operated by a flick switch above the driver's knees or by pulling out the trailing edge of the lights themselves. There is a map-reading light on the passenger's side.

There is plenty of oddment storage space inside the car. Between the seats a carpeted console within easy reach of the driver takes oddments and behind it there is a lidded lockable box. In each footwell there is a map pocket and behind the rear seat a deep full-width shelf for more bulky articles.

We think most prospective buyers will regard the rear compartment as an extension of the luggage capacity rather than potential occupant space. Volvo evidently planned it this way, too, so the accommodation in proportion to total vehicle size is small. The backrest of the rear ledge folds flat and under the squab there are straps for retaining luggage. We got our biggest test box in here though it only just went through the door. Without restricting rear visibility we got a total of 4.7 cu. ft. inside the car and an additional 5.3 cu. ft. in the boot. Much of the boot space is taken by the spare which is concealed in a neat cover. The unlit boot has a rubber mat on the floor.

Volvo's own brand of seat belts are fitted; they are easy to use and adjust.

Servicing and accessibility

The self-propping bonnet (it uses a stay like that on a BLMC 1800) is released by a substantial lever under the dashboard. Most items are readily accessible, though the distributor is rather hidden by the brake servo unit. The labelled fuse box is in the cockpit mounted on the nearside bulkhead above the passenger's legs.

There are now about 300 Volvo dealers and distributors in Britain. After the first 3000 miles the 1800E needs attention at 6000-mile intervals when the oil is changed. There are no greasing points, and there is a towing bracket welded to the front subframe should your Volvo ever break down.

1 oil filler cap. 2 clutch cable. 3 coolant expansion tank with filler cap. 4 brake fluid reservoir. 5 brake servo unit. 6 coil. 7 dipstick (hidden). 8 windscreen washer reservoir

MAKE: Volvo. **MODEL:** 1800E. **MAKERS:** Aktiebolaget Volvo Goteborg, Sweden. **CONCESSIONAIRES:** Volvo Concessionaires Ltd, Raeburn Road, Ipswich, Suffolk

— the maximum, in fourth, had it showing about 6 600.

Accelerating from rest, it took 5·1 seconds to reach 60 km/h, 80 came up in 7·7 seconds, and 100 in 11·1. This was after fairly gentle take-offs, as the clutch showed a tendency to slip if asked to take too high a load. In third and fourth gears it took 4·0 and 5·5 seconds respectively to accelerate from 60 to 80 km/h, and 3·8 and 5·4 seconds from 80 to 100.

Braking from 100 km/h, six times in rapid succession, produced a minimum stopping time of 3·4 seconds, a maximum of 4·0, and an average of 3·6 seconds. The

VOLVO 1800E COUPE

Report: **LEICESTER SYMONS**
Pictures: **GEORGE ELS**

ROAD IMPRESSIONS

MR. Matthew Lawson's Volvo 1800E is an interesting car for at least two reasons — firstly because the Volvo coupé has always been rare in South Africa, and secondly because this latest version is fitted with Bosch electronic fuel injection as standard.

As a bonus, putting it through its considerable paces turned out to be great fun.

The brain and nerves of the injection system are a control unit and five sensor units. The sensors inform the control unit of the temperature of the air in the intake, cylinder head temperature, atmospheric and intake manifold pressure, throttle opening, and engine speed and load. The control unit correlates this information and signals the injectors when to inject fuel and for how long.

A high-pressure electrical pump maintains fuel pressure at about two bars (28-30 lb./sq. in.), and a by-pass system passes surplus fuel back to the tank.

COLD STARTING

An idiosyncrasy of the system is that the accelerator pedal must not be touched when starting from cold. This is because switching on the ignition operates a cold-starting device, sensitive to engine temperature, which sends a squirt of fuel into the manifold as required. It was noticeable that the engine started immediately, and at once idled and pulled smoothly and without hesitation, on a winter morning on the Highveld.

The main reason for fitting the injection

The inlet manifold of the injection system, with its sensor units and connections, is the most prominent feature under the bonnet. The injectors themselves are the cylindrical units mounted directly above the inlet ports, where the manifold is bolted to the cylinder head.

system is exhaust emission control. This is achieved through keeping the air-fuel ratio virtually constant — in this case at 14 : 1 — and doing it far better than carburettors can.

At the same time it provides considerable gains in economy, power and torque — particularly torque at low and medium revs. The way the car pulled from low revs in fourth testified to the amount of torque available and the flatness of the torque curve.

A further advantage of the injection, in South Africa, is that it practically eliminates the problem of getting satisfactory performance from a high-compression engine on our so-called premium fuel.

The two-litre B20E engine of the coupé has a compression ratio of 10·5 : 1 and develops 120 bhp DIN (130 SAE) at 6 000 rpm and 123 lb/ft of torque, DIN (130 SAE) at 3 500. The similar B20B engine, with twin carbs and 9·3 : 1 compression ratio, puts out 100 bhp DIN at 5 500 rpm (118 SAE at 5 800) and 112 lb/ft. of torque, DIN (123 SAE) at 3 500.

Bosch electronic injection is unfortunately an expensive way of complying with the emission control regulations which Los Angeles, with its peculiar climatic conditions, has succeeded in selling to the rest of the United States, and which are spreading from there. According to Matthew Lawson it adds about R400 to the cost of the engine at source, which means far more by the time the car reaches the buyer.

ROAD PERFORMANCE

Timed runs showed the performance of the coupé with its two-litre engine to be similar to that of the three-litre Volvo 164 saloon with manual transmission — as was to be expected.

Mean maximum speed, near Johannesburg, was 176·6 km/h (109·7 mph), with the car reaching this figure in both directions, in fourth gear. In overdrive, which operates only on this gear, it reached the same speed in one direction but was slightly slower in the other, for a mean of 174·5 km/h (108·4 mph).

In the three lower gears 6 000 rpm on the tachometer, which is where the red sector starts, represented 53, 82 and 120 km/h (about 33·3, 51 and 74·5 mph). The tachometer needle would go well over 6 000 without the engine showing any signs of stress

There is a full range of instruments, including oil and water temperature gauges — the former partly and the latter completely obscured by a steering wheel spoke in this shot. Controls are well arranged.

times varied by only 0·2 of a second in the first five stops, and then increased markedly, indicating that harder pads might be a good idea to combat fade.

The brakes, incidentally, are discs all round, with the Volvo dual hydraulic system which ensures that both front brakes and one rear brake will operate if one system fails. The servo provides only about half the assistance provided on the 164, but I did not find the pedal pressure required to be high.

The ride, on Michelin XAS tyres, was firm and the fairly direct steering, though a little heavy at low speeds, was positive and accurate. The car understeered, but there was enough power available to counteract this with the throttle, producing overall handling characteristics which I enjoyed.

The overall "feel" was typical of Volvo — good performance, engineering, finish and equipment all contributing to make the 1800E a first-class car.

I found myself wishing that the excellent seat belts could be produced here and fitted in the locally-manufactured Volvos, but did not like the built-in head restraints. It struck me that these requirements of the U.S. safety regulations, designed to prevent whip-lash neck injuries in rear-end collisions, could help cause accidents of this type by the blind spots they create. ●

VOLVO 1800E

CAR AT A GLANCE: Sporting ride and handling, sufficiently fast with zero to 60 mph in 9.9 seconds. Remarkable fuel economy with "Einsprutning" ranging from least (during performance testing) of 20.0 mpg to best Overdrive cruising at 26.5 mpg. Average of 24.3 mpg for 1,412 total miles on all kinds of roads.

This 2-litre, fuel injected sports model of "the eleven year car" should be a credit to the marque. The 1800E is tough, fast (extended it should top 115 mph although the speedometer is less than accurate), and it handles exceptionally well.

Volvo got off to a bad start with their initial effort to produce a sports car. The author drove one of the open-mouthed grille jobs back in 1956. The firm was interested in fiberglass bodies at that time and a few dozen soft top examples were built through 1958. These were based upon mechanical components of the type 122 Amazon sedan. That initial effort was not an outright failure but neither was it a howling success.

In 1959 the P-1800 all-steel sports coupe was introduced. Until 1963, chassis were shipped from Gothenburg, Sweden to the United Kingdom where the coachwork was built and installed in the Jensen works in West Bromwich. When factory space became available, the P-1800 was built from start to finish in Sweden. The new 1800E is clothed in the same sheet metal styling that graced the "P" model but new grille, bumpers and trim have been added. Underneath and inside, however, the changes have been extensive. Not apparent, the weight has increased by approximately 160 pounds.

Torsional rigidity is a Volvo hallmark as is the customary submersion of the integral body-frame unit in an enormous tank containing rust-proofing primer. Next comes three coats of paint, inside and outside. The color exterior is sprayed on three times, each coat building up on the previous wet layer. The rigors of Sweden's famous winters necessitates heavy salting of all roads. Consequently, as is the case with Volvo sedans and wagons, the entire underside of the 1800E is sprayed with a unique sealing wax after which rubber-based undercoating is applied. With such finishing given to the basic structure, which is built around box-section pillars, the Volvo is one of the World's sturdiest cars. The manufacturer's claims are as true as any and more so than many.

Obtaining a well run-in example for road testing is always a pleasure—and a rather rare one at that. Collecting the 1800E from the West Coast distributorship in Los Angeles was facilitated by the need to return the Datsun 240Z to Nissan Motor's USA headquarters in neighboring Gardena. The famous six-digit odometer read 008186 miles.

As rapid an escape as possible was made from Smogsville up over US-99 where continuous maximum legal speed cruising in Overdrive produced 26.5 miles per gallon of premium grade fuel. The hot and humid central valley of California proved the effectiveness of the flow-through ventilation system, particularly with the blower control button pulled out to high speed. Opening vent windows helped fresh air flow and fast cruising was pleasant and relatively comfortable.

A fairly long run—more than 450 miles immediately after signing for the Volvo for example—quickly acquaints one with a car. These observations were recorded, a mixture of

positives and negatives. The seating is very comfortable for a person of the writer's height (a bit over 70 inches), and the nearly vertical plane of the three-spoke steering wheel with three and three-quarters turns lock-to-lock permits nearly straight arm driving with the seat positioned well toward the rear. Because most of this initial run was at night, I found the combined turn signal and headlight dipper lever to be rather short. Several times when signalling a turn for overtaking other cars, the quick stabbing finger overshot the turn signal lever and hit the headlight switch which is directly beneath the latter on the dash. The result was a momentary blackout.

The dashboard buttons are very close to the steering wheel and require some familiarization. On the other hand, another lever on the right of the steering column actuates the electrically operated overdrive when pushed downward. Operative only in 4th gear, the overdrive is recommended for use at speeds over 45 mph. At a true speed of 60 mph (indicated 65.6 mph) the tachometer showed 3,200 rpm in 4th gear, but switching to overdrive while maintaining speed brought the engine speed down to 2,600. Even more impressive—and useful in enlightened Nevada for example—is the decrease from 4,800 rpm at 90 mph in 4th gear to 3,800 in overdrive. At a true 90 mph, incidentally, the speedometer was wild and said 99.

Signalling with one's headlight high beams is an accepted custom in Europe when overtaking for passing. Volvo permits this; lifting the turn signal lever toward the steering wheel lights the lamps temporarily when they are otherwise turned off.

In my opinion, the accelerator pedal should be relocated an inch or more to the right. As it is, the gas pedal is a scant inch to the right of the brake pedal while to the gas pedal's right there is a gap of some two inches between it and the transmission bulge. The throttle foot, therefore, gets weary during long hours at the wheel while a sudden emergency jab at the brake pedal can result in simultaneous (and unneeded) acceleration. Long hours make it desirable to shift one's position too; at such times I found my knees bumping against the steering wheel. The seats could be a bit lower. Fortunately there is a dead pedal footrest for the left foot.

Raising or lowering the side windows can be a clumsy proposition for either driver or passenger because the crank, at high point during turning, comes within one-half inch of the inward extending window sill. Winding the window up can result in a split finger nail. Short people will find, with

the seat positioned well forward, that there is little space for cranking the window because the crank is also located too far toward the center of the door. Happily the 1800E retains vent windows. A mere two and one-half turns raises or lowers a main window.

Full instumentation merits acclaim. None of of the dials reflect, but it would seem that the oil temperature and oil pressure instruments should be adjacent rather than separated because these two conditions are more or less dependent upon each other. Like the optimistic speedometer, the Smith's clock was quite inaccurate but the push-button radio was excellent once I became accustomed to the sound coming forth from the rear of the interior. Essentially a two seater in the grand touring tradition, the 1800E does give the appearance of being a two-plus-two until one tries to cram persons larger than toddlers into the rear occasional seat. The space behind the front seat is best used for extra luggage to supplement the normal luggage boot.

Well padded, the dashboard contains a hand grip for the passenger but lacks a glovecase. The function of the latter missing receptacle, however, is provided by a deep box on the console between the seats which is wide enough to accommodate a 120 mm. twin lense reflex camera or a compact tape recorder with space to spare for other small items. The forward portion of the central console is an open box for other paraphernalia like sun glasses. The gear shift lever grows out of the console and falls nicely to hand; the knob is pleasantly large but the entire lever has the unpleasant habit of turning in its socket which is slightly annoying. Whether AB Volvo is embarked upon a campaign to stamp out smoking is not known but shifting into third gear can produce skinned knuckles if the ash tray is open—a scant inch separates the lever from the ash receptacle.

A twisting road course is as efficiently negotiated in the 1800E as is a super highway at high speed. The worm and roller steering is heavy at low speeds but above 15 mph becomes progressively lighter. The front suspension incorporates a long kingpin which is inclined at 8-degrees and good castoring action makes the steering almost neutral but

(Continued on next page)

BELOW:
Coolant expansion container (at left of radiator), large heater blower shroud (on firewall center), dual brake master cylinder reservoir and Bosch electronic computer monitored fuel injection system fill the compartment housing the otherwise compact 1,986 cc engine. Bonnet is unlatched by lever beneath dashboard.

Locking fuel tank access on left rear quarter panel is shared with stylized vent for flow through air; matching vent is on right side. Attractively styled alloy wheels require no bothersome covers.

LEFT:
Leather upholstery on fully adjustable seats, side-swivelling sun visors, opening vent windows, efficient heating and flow-through ventilation system, full instrumentation and easy access to fuse block (on left scuttle side panel beyond gear change lever) evidence Nordic thoroughness.

with a slight amount of understéér, a characteristic the writer finds most efficient for rapid mountain driving. The fairly firm suspension keeps lean on tight corners to a minimum. The ride is controlled, moderately sporting and comfortably firm. The car is difficult to bottom, will track straight for at least a tenth of a mile, hands off, as long as the road is level. This is good control and makes driving a relaxing operation.

The Bosch computerized electronic fuel injection never faltered from sea level on hot days to 5,000 foot elevations. The electronic brain eliminates any need to fiddle and adjust for altitude or atmosphere. Response to the throttle is instantly smooth as is the fully synchronized four-speed gearbox. Quietness is another 1800E virture; it goes and rapidly without noisy showing off. The three bottom gear speeds are 32, 54 and 79 mph.

As mentioned, we were able to clock 111 mph in overdrive at which point the speedometer needle was hard on the peg at the maximum 120 mph indication. No doubt the car will exceed the 115 mph mark relatively easy but a higher figure speedometer is needed. Through the gears acceleration is exhilarating and takes one from zero to a corrected 60 mph. in 9.9 seconds. For the boulevard stop light grand prix, 45 mph from scratch comes in just 6.5 seconds.

A tune up would have bettered these times fractionally in my opinion. Passing speeds are equally good. Cruising at 50 mph in fourth gear and dropping to third gets the car to 70 mph in 6.4 seconds while the 40 to 60 mph mark comes in 5.6 seconds. Maximum use of gears was made for these acceleration times and two aboard at all times.

Strangely the type 1800E Volvo's styling still takes many motorists by surprise. We found a small crowd gathered after parking for a while in most instances. The impression we gathered is that sales of the 1800E will be limited only by the numbers produced.

by Joseph H. Wherry

My RIB reports:

"A nice looking car of quality; fast, and good handling. However, it is not built for a short person to drive with comfort. To sit close enough to be able to use the clutch pedal efficiently, one is touching the steering wheel and one's head is too close to the windshield."—Betty C. Wherry

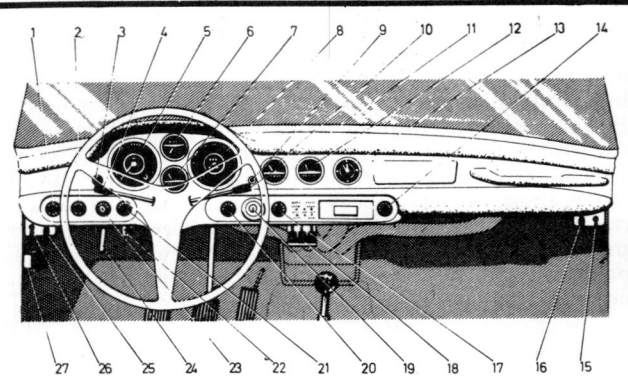

Dashboard

1 Control for windshield wipers and washers	16 Control for direct ventilation
2 Fan control	17 Switch for electrically heated rear window
3 Warning lamp, handbrake and brake systems	18 Controls for heating and ventilation
4 Control for turn indicators, lighting switch and headlight full beam flasher	19 Ignition switch and steering wheel lock
5 Revolution counter	20 Control for instrument lighting
6 Oil temperature gauge	21 Switch for for all-round emergency flashers
7 Cooling water temperature gauge	22 Tripmeter reset control
8 Speedometer (combined instruments)	23 Lighting switch
9 Warning lamp for overdrive	24 Control for hood catch
10 Fuel gauge	25 Control for direct ventilation
11 Control for overdrive	26 Switch for interior lighting
12 Oil pressure gauge	27 Fuses
13 Clock	
14 Cigarette lighter	
15 Switch for map-reading	

Ancestor of all Volvo cars was this 1.5 litre, 4-cylinder, 1927 open touring model called "Jacob." (AB Volvo)

VOLVO 1800E SPECIFICATIONS

ENGINE: front-mounted 4-cyl., in-line, pushrod-operated OHV. Bore and stroke 3.50 x 3.15 in. (88.9 x 80.0 mm). Displacement 121 cu. in. (1986 cc). 5 main bearing crankshaft. Cast iron cyl. block and head. Compression ratio 10.5 to 1. Fuel intake by injection. BHP 130 @ 6,000 rpm. Torque 130 lb. ft. @ 3,500 rpm. Premium grade fuel.

TRANSMISSION: 4-speed manual on floor, fully synchronized, with overdrive (4th gear only). Ratios: 1st-14.50, 2nd-8.47, 3rd-5.76, 4th-4.30, Overdrive-3.44. Rear axle ratio-4.30 hypoid.

SUSPENSION: Front independent unequal length wishbones, anti-sway bar. Rear axle solid on longitudinal control arms and torque rod, track rod. Coil springs at each wheel.

STEERING: Cam and roller with 3-¼ turns lock-to-lock. Turning circle 30 ft. Ratio 15.5 to 1.

WHEELS AND TIRES: 15 inch diam. aluminum alloy, steel rims, 5 lug bolts; 165R15 radial ply.

BRAKES: Power-assisted 4-wheel discs; front 10.6 in., rear 11.6 in.; dual circuit.

CAPACITIES: Fuel 12 US gallons. Crankcase 4 US qts. incl. filter. Transmission 3 US pints. Rear Axle 2-¾ US pints. Cooling system 9 US qts.

BODY AND FRAME: All-steel, integral.

DIMENSIONS: Wheelbase 96.5 in. Length 171.3 in. Width 67.0 in. Height 50.5 in. Ground clearance 6.1 in. Curb weight 2580 lbs.

PRICE: $4,560 basic, POE East Coast; $4,655 Basic West Coast.

Volvo

Styled wheels were added and the grille changed slightly in 1970. The rear quarter windows are fixed and vent windows retained although the car has forced-flow ventilation.

Body styling, with its high waist and narrow glass is a carryover from the first 1800 of 1960. This is a homemarket model in '71 configuration but without U.S. side lights.

There is something distinctly vintage about Volvo's sports coupe with its high sides and scuttle, the big 15-inch wheels and small glass areas. The low driving position with an upright steering wheel close to the driver's chest and controls that take some masculine strength to operate convey the same impression.

Although outmoded bodywise—the lines have hardly changed since the car was introduced back in 1960—there is nothing old-fashioned about the mechanics. The ''E'' stands for both *electronic* and *einspritz*, the car using the now popular Bosch electronically controlled fuel injection that not only meets the American emission laws but gives the engine a useful performance boost. Compared to the old carbureted 1800 S, it gives 130 horsepower instead of 118 and a worthwhile increase in low-speed torque.

The chassis is basically that of the 140-series with wishbone front suspension and a well located, coil sprung, live rear axle. A lower center of gravity and stiffer springs and damper settings, however, give the coupe a sportier road behavior with less roll in corners and a harsher, but by sports car standards quite comfortable, ride.

Since last year the brakes are all discs like those on the Volvo sedans. The splitting of circuits is of the proper kind with both front brakes operating should any of the circuits fail, thereby giving at least 80% efficiency and no danger of rear wheel lock up.

The big changes to the Volvo 1800 were made last year. The only signifi-

cant news for 1971 is that the car now can be had with an optional automatic transmission. It is basically the same Borg-Warner 35 that is used in the sedans but the charge-up points are higher and it has higher torque multiplication for quicker getaways. We have not tried it yet but Volvo says that it only loses 0.5 secs from zero to 60 mph compared to the manual transmission. With the hefty clutch and gear lever movement of the manual 1800 E, this could be a useful option even for those who normally would not have an automatic sports car.

It is hard to find a good driving position in the 1800 E. Even a fairly tall driver finds problems in seeing over the high scuttle and if the seat is raised, his head will very likely touch the low roof. The new (for 1970) instrument panel is a great

improvement with legible and handsome instruments.

Handling is predictable on smooth roads and high speed comfort excellent for a sports car. The steering, like all the controls, takes some strength but it is reasonably direct and has plenty of road feel. On bumpy surfaces the steering is badly affected and needs constant correction. The brakes fade a bit more than expected for an all-disc system but this hardly has any consequence even in hard normal driving. They are well graded and always stop the car in a straight line. The 1800 E is strictly a two-seater, the rear compartment only being suitable for small children. As a complement to the rather cramped luggage compartment, however, it is useful.

Volvo's reputation is based more on solid engineering and longevity than on styling frills and high performance. The 1800 E no doubt falls into this mode but it also has personal looks that a surprising number of people still find attractive and performance that, if not outstanding, is quite respectable for a two-liter standard sports car. Volvos are distributed in this country by Volvo, Inc., Rockleigh, N.J. 07647.

Data in Brief
VOLVO 1800 E

ENGINE: 4-cylinder ohv, 121 cu. ins., 1986cc, 130 hp at 6000 rpm, 130.0 lb.-ft. of torque at 3500 rpm, Bosch electronic fuel injection.
DRIVELINE: 4-speed manual transmission plus overdrive, rear drive, 3-speed automatic optional.
SUSPENSION: Independent A-arms, coil springs in front, live rear axle with coil springs and Panhard rod.
BRAKES: Power operated discs front and rear.
STEERING: Worm and roller, manual.
DIMENSIONS: Wheelbase 96.5 ins., overall length 171.3 ins., width 66.9 ins., height 50.4 ins., weight 2300 lbs.

"IT'S THE first car I've driven since I was fourteen that has felt too big for me."

Thus commented the Motor Manual staff member as he raised himself from the sumptuous depths of the latest version of Volvo's long-lived thoroughbred, the 1800E coupe.

And he wasn't that far wrong.

Although the svelte Swedish body of the car occupies only a relatively meagre portion of the roadway, internally it seems positively gargantuan.

From the tops of its deeply padded, high backed individual seats to the untapped depths of the footwells on either side of the towering central console the car feels huge and all-enveloping.

Large, prominently marked instruments spread across the width of the dash panel and the steering wheel is a real man-sized unit which the average driver finds himself craning to look over the top of.

Further increasing the impression of hugeness is the firm, solid feel of all the controls — a chunky gearshift which moves heavily through the ratios, weighty, but accurate steering and floor pedals which require a hefty push to operate.

But before we start giving the Volvo a truck-like image, we'd better explain that this is far from being the case.

Like the evergreen E-type Jaguar (tested elsewhere in this issue), the Volvo coupe's body design has been around for some time — almost nine years in Australia — but it is still one of the best-looking shapes around.

Basic powerplant and driveline mechanicals have seen little change in all this time, which is testimony to how good the car must have been in the first place, and the usual long-lived qualities for which Volvo has become renowned have been largely responsible for its peculiarly stable position on the second hand market.

And unlike the Jaguar, which is due to be replaced (we believe) in the near future, the Volvo 1800E shows all the signs of being around for some time to come.

How does a formula seemingly so unexciting as that used by Volvo gain recognition in a field where mechanical sophistication would seem to be a prerequisite to acceptance?

Electronically controlled fuel injection aside, there is little about the latest 1800E to create any great excitement in terms of mechanical design.

The powerplant is a sturdy, but Plain Jane unit, lifted fairly recently in cubic capacity to 1990 ccs. The four cylinder unit is slightly oversquare with bore/stroke dimensions of 88.9mm x 80mm, runs on five main crankshaft bearings and uses a conventional pushrod overhead valve layout.

Driveline layout is equally as conventional and the rear axle is a live unit using coil springs and is located by trailing links and Panhard rod.

This sort of specification is common in lower-priced fields, but decidedly unusual in the $7000 plus bracket where the Volvo resides, so it would seem the 1800E would be at an immediate disadvantage in comparison to its more sophisticated competition.

But it is the philosophies of the Goteburg, Sweden based Volvo company that save the day.

Here, possibly more than in any other automotive manufacturing concern in the world, the accent is on two things — safety and durability.

The Volvo people have spent vast amounts of money in accident research and have made good use of the lessons learned, producing sheafs of statistical information as to how and why accidents occur and how best to prevent them, or minimize their effects. A good example is the extensive survey carried out recently in Sweden to determine the advantages of wearing seat belts — which brought to light the staggering fact that of all accidents studied there was not one death in cases where people were travelling under 62 mph and wearing safety belts!

All the acquired knowledge of years of research is applied to make Volvo cars as safe as is practicably possible.

Volvo was one of, if not the first to introduce safety belts as standard equipment on its cars and even now leads most manufacturers with its simplified plug-in system which enables the passenger to "buckle up" with a minimum of inconvenience.

Volvo seats are almost legendary for their comfort, support and safety features and such things as whiplash rear-impact injuries, which are only just being recognised as a hazard on the local scene, have been seen as such by the Swedish firm for some time and head restraints on the front seats are now standard equipment on all models.

Secondary safety features like a universally jointed steering column which reduces the risk of having the wheel pushed back into the passenger compartment on frontal impact, laminated windscreen, and breakaway rear vision

Nine years later Volvo's sleek 1800 coupe is still one of the best status machines around — despite a price tag of $7125.

VOLVO'S THINK-MACHINE

mirror are backed up by primary safety features like the "twin triangle" braking system which substantially reduces the risk of total failure, the use of disc brakes on all four wheels and stable, predictable handling.

On top of all this, Volvos are engineered to last — although the only clue to any exceptional abilities in this respect is confined to an odometer which is confidently graduated to read to 999,999 miles.

So to justify its position in the upper segment of the market, the 1800E relies simply on the fact that it is a Volvo.

Forget briefly about this fact during the first moments behind the wheel, and you are likely to be a little disappointed.

The "swallowed up" feel as you first sink into the depths of the driver's seat, the slightly intrusive clatter from the engine compartment, coupled to the heavy, notchy feel of the gearshift all add up to make the car one which requires more than the usual amount of acquaintance.

But as you gain a feeling of mastery over the car it becomes decidedly pleasant and easy to drive, superbly comfortable and an easy relaxed cruiser on the open highway.

The fuel-injected four has enough torque to allow it to handle the tallish intermediate ratios without any signs of low-rpm protest, yet it will run easily and willingly — albeit noisily — to the 6500 rpm redline.

An electrically operated 0.797 : 1 overdrive operates on top gear through a steering column mounted lever and when engaged, drops engine noise to the point where it is drowned by transmitted road noise.

Quick gear changes through the four-speed box show no signs of weakness in the synchros, but our test car tended to "baulk" at really ham-fisted changes from first to second.

Ratios are well spaced for the two litre engine, first giving 34 mph, second 54 mph and third 82 mph.

At speed, the 1800E is rock-steady and the big discs bite evenly and readily when required, the anti-lock valve for the rear brakes doing its job efficiently in all types of conditions.

Despite its accuracy, the steering is rather too slow for a car of the Volvo's sporting nature, although the 3¾ turns from lock to lock are mostly used up by

Below: Man-sized steering wheel, speedo and tacho fill driver's line of vision. Comprehensive instrumentation even runs to oil temp. gauge (obscured by steering wheel rim).

putting on the last few inches of wheel lock to achieve the conveniently tight 31'2" turning circle.

The fuel injection system, which is similar to the one currently being used by Volkswagen, uses a compact electronic "brain" to feed exactly the right amount of fuel needed to the cylinders. Sensors placed strategically around the engine read air temperature, engine temperature, engine rpm, etc., and relay information to the "brain" which, through an electric injector pump, meters out the fuel. The result is cleaner, more efficient engine operation and, in theory, fewer trips to the workshop for peak-performance tuneups.

In practice, it made the Volvo an unfussy, but reasonably potent performer with a petrol thirst averaging out at a very moderate 24 miles per gallon.

Just the thing for an up-and-coming Simon Templar . . .

data sheet

SPECIFICATIONS

CAR FROM:
Volvo Australia, Market St., South Melbourne

PRICE AS TESTED:
$7125 (plus radio)

OPTIONS FITTED:
Blaupunkt radio

ENGINE:
Type ....4 cyl. ohv
Bore and Stroke ....88.9mm x 80mm
Capacity..................................1990 cc
Compression ratio ....10.5 : 1
Power ....130 bhp at 6000 rpm
Torque............130 ft/lbs at 3500 rpm

TRANSMISSION:
Type: Four speed manual plus .797 :1 overdrive
Ratios:
1st..3.13 : 1
2nd...1.99 : 1
3rd..1.36 : 1
4th..1.00 : 1
Final drive ....4.30 : 1

CHASSIS:
Wheelbase ....96.4 inches
Length ....171.2 inches
Track F ....51.8 inches
Track R ....51.8 inches
Width ....67.0 inches
Height ....50.5 inches
Clearance (Minimum).......................NA
Test weight ....2541 lbs
Fuel capacity ....10 gallons

SUSPENSION:
Front: Independent, coil springs, telescopic shock absorbers
Rear: Live axle, coil springs, telescopic shock absorbers, trailing links, Panhard rod

BRAKES:
Power assisted, divided system
Front: Disc
Rear: Disc

STEERING:
Type: Cam and roller
Turns lock to lock: 3¾
Turning circle: 31'2"

WHEELS/TYRES:
Alloy centre steel wheels with 165 x 15 Michelin XAS tyres

PERFORMANCE

Zero to
30 mph............................3.8 seconds
40 mph............................5.5 seconds
50 mph............................7.2 seconds
60 mph............................9.5 seconds
70 mph..........................12.3 seconds
80 mph..........................15.6 seconds
90 mph...NA
100 mph.......................................NA
Standing quarter mile: 17.0 seconds
Fuel consumption on test: 24 mpg on S fuel
Fuel consumption (expected) 22-26 mpg
Cruising range: 240 miles

Speedometer error:
Indicated   30 40 50 60 70 80 90 100
Actual   27 36 45 54 64 73 82 91

MAXIMUM SPEEDS IN GEARS:
1st. ....34 mph
2nd ....54 mph
3rd ....82 mph
4th ....117 mph

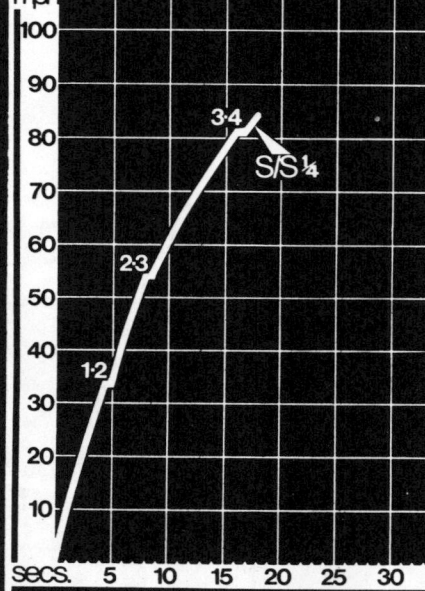

COMMENTS

ENGINE:
Response ....Good
Vibration ....Low
Noise...Moderate

DRIVE TRAIN:
Shift linkage...............................Heavy
Synchro action...............................Good

STEERING:
Effort ....Moderate
Road feel.......................................Good
Kickback ....Low

SUSPENSION:
Ride comfort ....Good
Roll resistance ....Good
Pitch control ....Good

HANDLING:
Directional control ....Very good
Predictability.........................Very good

BRAKES:
Pedal pressure........................Moderate
Response....................................Very good
Fade resistance ....Very good
Directional stability ....Very good

CONTROLS:
Wheel position...............................Good
Pedal position ....Good
Gearshift position..........................Good

INTERIOR:
Front seat comfort ....Very good
Front leg room........................Very good
Front head room.....................Very good
Rear seat comfort ....Fair
Rear leg room.................................Poor
Rear head room.............................Poor
Instrument legibility ....Very good

VISION:
Forward...Good
Front quarter.................................Good
Rear ....Good

CONSTRUCTION QUALITY:
Paint..Very good
Chrome ....Good
Trim ....Good

GENERAL:
Headlights — highbeam ....Good
Headlights — lowbeam................Good
Parking/signal lights ....Good
Wiper coverage ....Good
Wipers at speed............................Good
Maintenance accessibility ....Good

VOLVO P1800E

DIAL 999 999

NO, SCOTLAND YARD does not have a Volvo dealership! The familiar digits symbolise Volvo's latest piece of sports car one-upmanship — an odometer that reads to a million miles!

About the closest Volvo has got to the legendary criminal hounds of Great Britain is the equally legendary Saint television series in which dapper Roger Moore private eyes-off crims with great success while punting a Volvo Coupe with true skill and daring.

Despite its idiot-box image, the Volvo Coupe is equally a car for retired businessmen, still-posing managing directors and even wives of the affluent. And it has the

The shadow of a near Melbourne haystack could be the ideal place for a Volvo driver to rest with bird and bottle. Volvo's Coupe puts across ultimate classic luxury image despite ageing body.

wheels ROAD TEST

durability to go a million miles.

It's not all brawn and brute power but it is a gentle boulevardier in any sensitive driver's hands.

So what else is new? Isn't that the format of the Volvo Coupe that has been around for many years, even on the local market.

Basically it is — but for the 1971 silly season, Volvo has gone the full performance/dress-up package route for the vehicle that has inevitably

been pushed into the high echelon price market by import taxation.

Dare I say, that Volvo Aktiebolaget, Goteborg, Sweden has *injected* the long-lasting coupe with new power from a sohpisticated induction system developed specially for its well-proven four-cylinder engine?

Despite a facial high-rise, the engine boost is the main news. Bosch-developed four-port fuel injection lifts power on the well-developed B20 engine to 130 (SAE) bhp at 6000 rpm and puts torque at an identical figure (130 lb/ft) at 3500 rpm. It adds up to great performance with flexibility and smoothness.

Your 1971 Volvo Coupe will trot out standing quarters in the low 16-second bracket if you can get the rear skins to break traction, and 120 mph in overdrive top is a pretty casual affair if you have the right road.

The engineers didn't neglect other aspects of the vital torque and

Pleasant place to live/work. Volvo wraps up its front seat passengers in ultimate seating, with high-sill cockpit and that aircraft-style wrap-around feeling. Instrumentation is complete.

E is for Einspritzen — or fuel injection — and the B20E engine pumps 130 bhp through four speed with O/D for impressive performance and remarkable fuel economy. Engine compartment is ultra-tight but most vitals are accessible.

Perfect profile blends into stubby, finned tail that European-style advocates find appealing. The 1971 style changes include full magnesium road wheels, black air-extractor/fuel filler vents

power curves and built-in a flat-graph characteristic that gives top gear lugging figures close to V8 times — 20-40 mph in 7.4 seconds, 50-70 mph in 6.4 seconds.

That means the little-old-lady-from-Pasadena can drop it into top and carve up the outbound traffic without having bad moments from the opposite direction. If she does get in a squeeze, four-wheel power-assisted discs will slot her back in a conveniently located space or she can do the full production and stop dead in a straight line with a sickening stomach from the G-loadings. From 60 mph it takes only 3.3 seconds, from 30 mph the car will be stationary in 1.4 seconds — not bad for 2700 lb-plus (unladen).

At first I didn't believe my Breitling. The wrist chronometer may not read to split-tenths but 0-60 mph times in close 9 seconds and standing quarters under the mid-16s looked pretty exaggerated. The next step was a battery of recently-corrected stopwatches and a dead-serious run against the sweep second hand on Calder's main dragway. There is something clinically convincing about figures recorded on a drag strip.

The figures were confirmed — in fact they kept getting better and better. Calder is quite an accommodating place to test a really hot bit of gear — so I ran out another important test time. From a standstill to maximum rpm in top gear (fourth — not O/D fourth) took just 31.6 seconds. That's virtually standstill to 110 mph in just over 30 seconds — a very impressive time for a social boulevardier.

Still on the Calder scene, I put down three laps from a flying start on a surface smattered with the scars of the previous day's rallycross meeting.

VOLVO P1800 E

That meant plenty of slippery dirt and mud in all the tweaky bits, but road pressures and little familiarisation time still brought times crashing to 62.5 seconds on the Michelin XAS tyres which naturally rolled and distorted without pressure to reduce the sidewall loadings. For a stock sporty — any stock sporty — that's a competitive time.

To achieve fast laps, the Volvo has to be punted hard — right to its maximum performance level. But it reaches and holds that level with the greatest safety of any sports car I've driven. The steering was also the best in any road car - light, sensitive, precise with adequate feel, no feedback, and a perfectly balanced castor section that spins the wheel back to neutral without over-handling.

Performance is punched out in short, sharp stabs of power through a beautifully swift gearbox that is controlled in the cockpit by a big-diameter lever with a massive four-ball shifter on top. The overdrive fifth (which you won't use on the circuit) is on a special steering stalk.

The ratios are not close and are definitely not circuit or ultra-performance-oriented — they're meant to provide practical all-round use of an engine built for general purpose motoring. The clutch is disappointingly heavy — for the traffic light grand prix you have to pop it on the yellow, drop it quickly on the green and use as little as possible on the shifts. It seems lighter as you get to know the car. The promised automatic transmission for women drivers has been delayed by the fantastic demand from the American market — we won't see it in Australia until the end of 1971.

Overdrive is a great saver. It slashes engine rpm by an average 1000 rpm, effectively kills the thrashy four's engine noise at medium range speeds and knocks the thirst right back — you can save 8 mpg or more with careful and experienced use of the little steering column stalk. But if you want to drive smoothly, you have to help the O/D in and out with the clutch.

The engine's willing torque is so great it pulls strongly all the way to 5600 rpm in O/D top — and gives the impression it will go further. The limiting factors of wind pressure, and available space is unlikely to allow this on a flat road, but the Volve Coupe gained from 5000 O/D to 5500 in a mile and to 5600 in another mile with the engine still swinging — it could grab another 100 rpm or so but it's not really significant. It will get to 120 mph easily.

Up top, the car has a few problems. Its shape ducks crosswinds beautifully — we had a sidewind factor of 20 mph through hedges, forests and windbreaks without shifting the beast off line at better than the ton, but the wind noise above 90 mph is appalling. The test car had no exterior mirror (which it needed badly) so that can't be blamed — it's simply fussy design around the windows. With through-flow ventilation already installed, Volvo should aim for sealed (or eliminated) quarterlights and better soundproofing.

There are two uncharacteristic hang-ups for high speed work. The wipers float frantically above 70 mph and are never really fully effective in any speed in heavy rain. The lights are stretched to show the way at 80-90 mph. Both problems are clearly easily shelved.

But these points apart, Volvo does get your up in the road-bound jet-set faster, smoother and more comfortably than most other cars.

The cockpit is incredibly compact, detailed and well-equipped. Visually it looks good, with a vast wrap-around console blending into high sills that give a comfortable, ensconced feeling, with obvious safety benefits. Instrumentation is comprehensive, beautifully arranged, visually well-coded and perfectly blended to the interior treatment.

The steering wheel is originally located, perfect for most heights/reaches and gives a good view of the instruments with a ready access to the controls. And all the switchgear and controls can be reached from the driver's seat even when fully buckled-in by the centre-located auto-clip-in lap-sash seat belts.

Visible through the tri-spoke wheel are the main instruments — clear and obtrusive. The tacho is good for 7000 (but you'd best cool it at 6000) and a speedometer runs to a humorous 120 mph and contains the legendary one million mile odometer (plus trip meter).

Between the two master dials are smaller gauges for oil and water temperature. I'd like to see the oil temperature gauge swapped for the more important oil pressure gauge — one of the three other ancillary dials out to the left on the console (oil pressure, fuel level and clock). The oil temperature gauge registers only in extremely hot conditions, or when pushed very hard or subjected to track-type conditions. Water temperature stays constantly in its vital green operation area due to sealed cooling system and a slip-coupling fan that works efficiently down to idle

Rear seat is convertible style — folded down there's extra luggage space with locating straps to stop it floating. Lock the rear squab up and you have occasional room for adults, great place for small children.

Boot faces the typical sports car problem — with a low-profile shell, where do you put the spare? Volvo laid it on the floor and covered it, but it's greedy for space and a holiday means bootlid racks or gear stacked behind the front seats.

speed in traffic and never exceeds 3500 rpm — it saves energy, uses the fan's ideal calculated effective blade angle, and reduces noise.

The oil pressure on the test car was a constantly healthy 70 psi at good operating speeds. It never wavered on the track or during performance runs.

Switchgear covers the usual fuctions, plus a few bonus offerings. There's a special panel switch to mute the instruments when you light them with the headlights. A two-speed fan switch works on the Continental principle of fast speed on the first pull-stop. The washer/wiper switch has two speeds with a third to give great electric gushes of water to the screen and there's a hazard warning flasher (not connected to the test car).

The final touch is the knob for the rear window demister — two stages, with a warning light of varying density for each standard of demisting control. On fast speed, the rear wires cut the fog in 60 seconds with a 150 watt putput. Drop the switch to phase two and 40 watts keep the glass constantly clear on a muted warning light glow. Or you can switch off and call in the demister as you need it. All knobs are soft, pliable crash-proof plastic.

Under the dash, controls in simple slides vary temperature and distribute warm/cool air to face and feet. Supplementary side-panelling booster vents for the through-flow ventilation system combine with this set-up which is great in the cold, but totally inadequate in Australian conditions in a closed Coupe of this type. An engine/transmission tunnel that runs down the centre of the cockpit along the occupants' legs doesn't help and black upholstery as on the test car is the final killer. The answer is air conditioning — and if you can pay seven grand for a Volvo Coupe you can take the jump to full "air" if the heat hurts.

Otherwise, cockpit comfort is plush. The leather/vinyl seats are great — providing three obvious and instantly adjustable positions, plus several others. Basically, rails let the seat slide horizontally, a rake gives you a variety of squab angles (without layback) and a strategically located knurl on the squab will adjust to the individual spine curvature of drivers.

If you want to get highly technical there are special sleeves for extra seat length, slots in the seat locating bolts for even further adjustment, extra slots in the seat for more vertical travel, plus extra height adjustment in the main rail bolts. And the integrated headrests are infinitely adjustable.

Carpeting is comfortable — but a little tatty in appearance. Odd item storage runs to two document bins — the centre console, plus the glovebox. Rear seat room is in the occasional quick-across-town-to-a-party two-plus-two category. A fold-down backrest with adequate padding does a good job and supplies great additional luggage stowage space when laid flat — aided by special straps to stop it floating round the cockpit.

Detail touches include a dippable interior mirror, interior light that has a remote master switch but also acts by tipping the glass itself, and easy-to-reach fuses under the dash.

For the safety bugs, a well-padded impact-absorbing steering column is built on the split-universal principle, but window wipers which virtually have to be operated with the opposite hand reaching across the body need transferring to a sensible location down near the front lower-corner of the door. However they open windows that provide breeze and buffet-free motoring at speed.

The boot is above average for a compact sports coupe — it carries reasonable gear, has a big (covered) spare on the floor and contains jack and adequate tool kit.

The handbook carries a terse warning to owners on driving with the boot lid partially open — and this serves as good advice for owners of many cars with through-flow ventilation. Since extraction of cockpit air is through the boot, induction of CO emission is easy in reverse via the same route — if you have an overloaded and slightly open boot drive with all windows closed, and the through-flow on full-blast (including fan).

The mechanicals are not vastly reworked. The engine is the B20 development of the B18 four cylinder water-cooled four. It has no fancy tricks like overhead camshafts or hemi-heads, and in standard form is not capable of pushing a sports coupe to today's market demands. Built of solid cast iron with liners machined in the block, it is a tough, durable motor, easily capable of carrying the demands imposed by a sophisticated four-port computerised fuel-injection system developed by Bosch (B20E engine).

For those who understand, the electronic injection has triggering contacts or sensors in the distributor timing (spark), coolant (actual engine temperature), induced air temperature (to cylinders), and engine pressure (actual engine load). By computing the information from these areas and controlling the data by impulses through a throttle switch, precise fuel delivery is guaranteed — four solenoids control the injectors. It is dramatically efficient — with a hefty boot, the car can be persuaded to optimum performance without dragging excess reserves from the tank, and gentle use pushes the fuel economy way up. Over 28 mpg is possible with gentle running, and full-bore work shouldn't ever push the car below 20 mpg. Added to that, efficient burning means reduced emissions. And the overdrive helps.

The transmission is not new — and Volvo has mated it to the overdrive unit proved over many years. Getting it all to ground is a live rear axle locating by coils, support arms, torque rods and a lateral track rod. It's so efficient the car won't spin it's back wheels if you drop the clutch at 6000 rpm — unless you get a well-worn surface such as the start-line on Calder's dragway.

There is no tramp with power-on in the dirt and hard cornering doesn't introduce snarky rear wheel angles that give changeable handling characteristics.

The front end is pretty conventional — wishbones and coils with an anti-roll bar, but it is well engineered to keep the loaded wheel upright under cornering, and positive location in a strong boxframe gives isolation from road shock and great durability.

Steering is cam and roller, the shock absorbers are telescopic and the differential is optioned for limited slip — not yet available here. A two-piece prop-shaft cuts transmission vibration and mechanical noise — apart from the engine which isn't adequately soundproofed from the interior.

Brakes are comforting discs, built on dual circuit to Volvo's unusual triangle system — in case of failure the two front discs and one rear brake always work, and though the distributed effort is normally 50 percent each system, this can rise to 80 percent for a single system in an emergency. There is a pressure limiting valve for normal braking.

The whole product is exceptionally durable and can take the worst punishment our roads can hand out — unlike most imported sports cars. Volvo still offers a completely free first (1500 mile) comprehensive service, and other services at about 6000 mile intervals are reasonable for a luxury car.

The Volvo's compromises are few. Most of the observations of this road test are ultra-critical — they wouldn't be noticed by the average Volvo owner. And the line-up of potential owners is great. There's already a queue at your friendly Volvo dealer.

Millionaires in Volvo terminology are owners who've wound the numbers right off the clock. The odometer — not the speedometer.—END.

wheels ROAD TEST

TECHNICAL DETAILS

MAKE	Volvo
MODEL	P1800E Coupe
BODY TYPE	2-door Coupe
PRICE	$7125
OPTIONS	Radio
COLOR	Red
MILEAGE START	.2271
MILEAGE FINISH	.2590
WEIGHT	(1230 kg) 2706 lb

FUEL CONSUMPTION:

Overall	22 mpg
Cruising	26 mpg

TEST CONDITIONS:

Weather	hot, dry
Surface	hot mix
Load	2 persons
Fuel	pump premium

SPEEDOMETER ERROR (mph):

Indicated	30	40	50	60	70	80	90
Actual	27.8	37.5	46	55	65	75	84

PERFORMANCE

Piston speed at max bhp	(960 m/min) 3150 ft/min
Top gear mph per 1000 rpm	(5th) 21.6 (4th) 17.2
Engine rpm at max speed	.5600
Lbs (laden) per gross bhp,(power-to-weight)	(9.8 kg) 22 lb

MAXIMUM SPEEDS:

Fastest run	124 mph
Average of all runs	122 mph
Speedometer indication, fastest run	See text — approx 135 mph

IN GEARS:

1st	(51 kph) 32 mph (6000 rpm)
2nd	(78 kph) 53 mph (6000 rpm)
3rd	(126 kph) 78 mph (6000 rpm)
4th	(172 kph) 108 mph (6000 rpm)
5th	(198 kph) 124 mph (5600 rpm)

Graph: 4TH 108 M.P.H. 5TH 124 M.P.H. STANDING ¼ MILE 16·6 3RD 78 M.P.H. 2ND 53 M.P.H. 1ST 32 M.P.H. TOP SPEED 122 M.P.H. ACCELERATION THROUGH GEARS WITH CHANGE POINTS. MPH ▶ELAPSED TIME IN SECONDS

ACCELERATION (through gears):

0-30 mph	.2.7 sec
0-40 mph	.4.9 sec
0-50 mph	.6.9 sec
0-60 mph	.9.1 sec
0-70 mph	.11.8 sec
0-80 mph	.15.8 sec
0-90 mph	.19.2 sec
0-100 mph	.21.8 sec

	2nd gear	3rd gear	4th gear
20-40 mph	3.2 sec	5.3 sec	7.4 sec
30-50 mph	3.2 sec	4.9 sec	7.3 sec
40-60 mph	3.6 sec	4.3 sec	6.6 sec
50-70 mph	—	4.5 sec	6.4 sec

STANDING QUARTER MILE:

Fastest run	16.4 sec
Average all runs	16.6 sec

BRAKING:

From 30 mph to 0	.1.4 sec
From 60 mph to 0	.3.3 sec

SPECIFICATIONS

ENGINE:

Cylinders	Four in line
Bore and stroke	(88.92 mm) 3.5 in. x (80 mm) 3.15 in.
Cubic capacity	(1990 cc) 121 cu in.
Compression ratio	10.5 to 1
Valves	overhead
Induction	four — port fuel injection
Fuel pump	mechanical
Oil filter	full flow
Power at rpm	(19.6 kg/m) 130 (SAE) bhp @ 6000 rpm
Torque	(19.6 kg/m) 130 (SAE) bhp @ 3500 rpm

TRANSMISSION:

Type	four speed all syncro with overdrive
Clutch	mechanical SDP diaphragm
Gear lever location	floor

Ratios:	Direct	Overall
1st	3.1	13.5
2nd	1.9	8.4
3rd	1.3	5.7
4th	1.0	4.3
5th	0.7	3.4
Final drive		4.3

CHASSIS and RUNNING GEAR:

Construction	unitary
Suspension front	wishbones/coils/anti-roll bar
Suspension rear	live by coils/support arms/ torque rods/track bar
Shockabsorbers	telescopic
Steering Type	cam and roller
Turns I to I	3¼
Turning circle	(9.5 m) 31 ft 2 in.
Brakes type	servo assisted four wheel discs

DIMENSIONS:

Wheelbase	(245 cm) 96.5 in.
Track front	(131.5 cm) 51.6 in.
Track rear	(131.5 cm) 51.6 in.
Length	(435 cm) 14 ft 3.25 in.
Height	(128 cm) 4 ft 2.4 in.
Width	(170 cm) 5 ft 7 in.
Fuel tank capacity	(50 litres) 11 galls

TYRES:

Size	(55 x 15) 165 HR-15
Make on test car	Michelin XAS

GROUND CLEARANCE:

Registered	(15 cm) 6 in.

VOLVO 1800 E Sports Coupe

By PAUL WEISSLER

IN SPITE OF BEING FUEL IN-JECTED THIS GT GETS A RATING THAT IS "NOT BAD". IT HAS SOME UNIQUE ASPECTS TO IT.

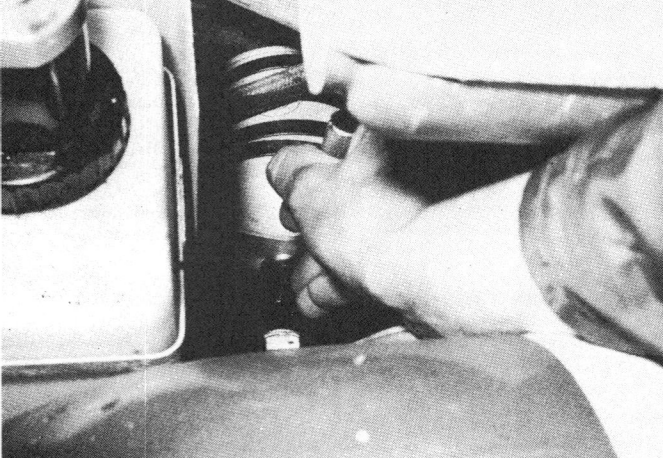

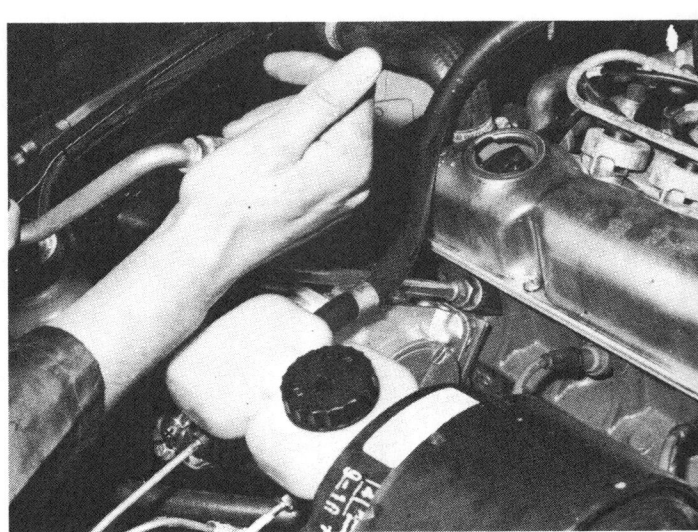

TOP: Would you believe—access to the air filter by removing the grille? Well, in case you didn't, here it is. ABOVE: Oil filter on P-1800E is best removed with a spring-type oil filter wrench turned with a ratchet. Intake manifold is close to firewall making job harder. RIGHT: Air conditioning compressor obstructs access to No. 1 spark plug. RIGHT CENTER: Distributor accessibility is good, including distributor lock as shown. FAR RIGHT: Rocker shaft must be removed before head bolts can be torqued with ordinary sockets.

■ I lifted the hood of the Volvo P-1800E and decided, per the usual procedure for a Service Test, to remove the air cleaner first. On the typical car, the huge air cleaner virtually covers the engine and its removal is the first order of business. A quick look disclosed that something was funny—lots of ducting from the intake manifold of this fuel-injected car, but no air cleaner in sight. I followed the ducting, which went from the engine compartment to the area between the radiator and grille. I then went to the front of the car, looked through the grille and there it was just behind the grille.

Volvo can't expect someone to pull the grille just to change an air cleaner element, I thought, so I went back to the engine compartment, to see if there was some access from there to the air cleaner. No luck. Good grief, the grille has to come out. I then inspected the grille, discovered that it was held by four thoroughly accessible screws. I removed the grille (about a two-minute job) and there was the air cleaner, easy as all get out. Unconventional, yes. Difficult, no. The rating is good and seven points.

The oil filter is best removed with a coil spring-type tool. You'll have to compress the spring to get it between the intake manifold and the cowl, but once you do, you can slip it onto the oil filter. The room is a bit tight, but the job isn't overly difficult. The rating is fair and five points.

The spark plugs should be no problem at all on the typical 1800E. Our test car was equipped with air con-

ditioning, and the air conditioning compressor can prevent fitting a ratchet onto the socket when you're trying to remove No. 1 spark plug. The solution is to use a very long extension or a speed handle. The rating on plugs is good and eight points.

The distributor is right out in the open and the breaker points and distributor lock each get a good rating and eight points.

The generator lower bolt cannot be reached from on top because the intake manifold prevents you from getting your arms down far enough. You've got to get underneath the car to get at it (although the car requires no jacking to do this). The rating for generator removal is fair and five points (the reason for the difference is that we feel fan belt replacement is a more routine item and should be easier).

The cylinder head bolts cannot be tightened without a crowfoot wrench (a special tool not in the typical weekend mechanic's tool chest) or removal of the *Continued on page* 134

Continued on page 134

SERVICE TESTING CHECKLIST
(Max. 8 points each)

1. Spark plugs	7. Cylinder
2. Ignition	head bolts
breaker points	8. Fuel pump
3. Distributor lockbolt	9. Battery cables
or locknut	10. Air filter
4. Generator	11. Oil filter
5. Carburetor	12. Brake master
6. Fan belt	cylinder

13. Heavy repairs

Bonus Points
(Max. 2 points each)

1. Speedometer cable connection at speedometer
2. Dashboard bulbs.

VOLVO

First Impressions of new Sports Estate

The most expensive Volvo is a 2+2 coupé with an unusual estate car type of back end. It costs £2,623 in the UK and is based on the 1800 first introduced 11 years ago.

IT was in October 1960 that the Volvo two-seater coupé was first announced in the UK, with the body built by Jensen and the final assembly taking place at West Bromwich. Two and a half years later production was transferred to Sweden and the original P.1800 name changed to 1800S. In October 1965 the power output was raised from 108 to 155 bhp and three years later the capacity increased to 2 litres. The last carburettor 1800S was made in August 1969, after which the model became the 1800E with electronic fuel injection and cast alloy wheels.

During the summer of this year, pictures began to filter through in the Continental press of an estate car conversion of the 1800E with long side windows and a deep all-glass tailgate. The close resemblance to the Reliant Scimitar GTE was more than coincidental and it seems pretty obvious that Volvo did exactly the same kind of skin restyling to their rather dated sports car that was first initiated by Ogle for the Scimitar.

In terms of mechanical specification there is little change compared with the 1970 1800E and from the driver's point of view the car looks the same ahead of the front seats. In the back, though, the hard occasional bench has been improved and its backrest now lifts up and drops down to give a long, but shallow load space with a flat floor all the way from the back window.

Prior to carrying out a full test on this unusual sports estate, we tried a new demonstrator for a few days. It was a very low mileage car, not yet fully run in with a much stiffer than normal gearshift linkage. Performance felt brisk, but the level of mechanical refinement was low and a lot of harshness and roar was transmitted through to the cockpit.

For a car from a country with such cold winters as Sweden, the 1800Es has a very poor heater arrangement with only an insensitive water-valve temperature control and slow warming up characteristics. The blast of scorching hot air which eventually comes through is tremendous on a cold morning, but there seems to be no intermediate position on the regulator between very hot and stone cold.

The driving position is cramped by modern standards, tall drivers touching the roof with their heads and shorter ones having trouble seeing over the high scuttle. The steering wheel feels large and too close to one's chest. It now has a padded three-spoke boss with horn buttons at the outer end of each spoke.

Instruments have been considerably up-dated since the peculiar stylist's dream of the original P.1800, and they now have black circular dials with clear white lettering. There is a rev counter, speedometer, oil pressure and temperature gauges, water temperature gauge and fuel gauge. Switches are mainly of the push-pull type, with soft rubber knobs and clear labels. Overdrive is standard, on top gear only, and there is a hot-line heater in the tailgate.

Under the floor in the back is a deep well for the spare wheel and tools. There is plenty of extra room here for other bits and pieces. With the back seats folded, valuables like cameras and handbags can be hidden out of sight under the horizontal backrest.

Sitting in the back is rather claustrophobic as the high-backed front seats completely mask out the forward view. Padding is noticeably thin and there is only enough legroom for an adult if the front seat occupants are prepared to move forward.

Air extractors are built into the rear quarters and the front quarterlights swivel. Window winders in the front doors are impossible to operate with the adjacent hand, and a cross-hands technique is the only way that works.

There is no glove locker in the facia but a usefully deep box just behind the gearlever has a locking lid and there are map pockets in each front door.

Despite some of the anatomical shortcomings of the 1800ES, we were impressed with the high standard of body finish inside and out and there was no doubt that the car attracted a lot of attention wherever it went. The total price with tax is £2,623.12. □

Above: Revised instruments and switches with soft rubber tops; three horn pushes on steering wheel. Right: Rear seat arrangements; leg room is only adequate with the front seats moved forward. Below: All-glass unframed tailgate and (right) complicated-looking plumbing

1800 ES

PHOTOGRAPHY: GENE BUTERA

VOLVO 1800ES SPORTWAGON

People have tried to make sports cars out of station wagons but it took Volvo to successfully reverse the concept.

● Talk about fast response. The George Meaney Generation is little more than a half-dried promise on an old man's lips and Volvo announces a car for it. Understand that life really is going to be worth living in the GMG. . . . A mere four days at the mill will get you a fat paycheck. Vacations will come in increments of months. Everything right down to clean socks will be included in the benefit package. Only ingrates could ask for more.

Of course, when all of this happens, not everyone will be driving Volvo Sportwagons. Mr. and Mrs. MiddleAmerica, with their three kids and two Airedales and a place in the country will still need a three-quarter-ton-truck-size estate wagon—probably with plastic wood on the sides, just like they have now. Because affluence with a union label isn't going to negate the fact that some people have to haul a lot of stuff every time they get into a car—even if it's just to go to the nearest Jack-in-the-Box. And you're going to need a saw to fit a sheet of four-by-eight plywood into the Volvo. An overstuffed chair will have to be tied on the roof. It's going to require three trips to assemble a sandlot baseball team. In fact, there isn't even enough room in the back of the Sportwagon for two consenting adults. And, with possible exception of the latter, that is the Sportwagon's beauty: *It's not a station wagon.*

In the strict sense of the word it's not a sports car either, which in that wonderful Generation-to-come is perfect. All those fast moving, dues-paying studs are going to find that a real sports car is too single purpose, too, ah, confining. It's great for driving, but that's all; it's just not compatible

with other toys that will fill out the new Everyman's life. Corvettes and E-type Jaguars, with their luggage compartments that snuggly enclose two slices of whole wheat toast, are not going to make it. What the car enthusiast of the GMG will need for those long weekends is a machine that comes as close as possible to sports car handling and response—a car that won't bore him to sleep or scare him wide-eyed—but still has enough cargo area for the *equipment.* Which is exactly the idea behind Volvo's Sportwagon. Two golf bags can be tossed in; no fussy arranging is necessary to get the door shut. There is enough space for a 30-hp outboard plus a can or two of gas . . . enough picks, pitons and rope to climb Mt. McKinley . . . a couple of those small trail Hondas with the folding handle bars . . . or a tent and enough beer to rough-it painlessly at Watkins Glen. Whatever it is, the Sportwagon won't put a lid on your lifestyle.

The Sportwagon has taken a little pressure off of Volvo too. The fin-tailed 1800E coupe and the weight of all of its years were pressing heavily on the company's planners. After all, nothing lives forever, not even a Volvo, and the coupe has racked up ten years since its introduction in the U.S. Clearly, its appearance can't be very fashionable any more. That little hump of a greenhouse may have been just the berries on a Lincoln Zephyr, or even on a 1948 Chrysler, but it doesn't make it in the days of formal roofs and hulking fast-backs. And the tail fins, well, Virgil Exner wouldn't touch those with Rapidograph now.

But instead of just giving up and swal-

VOLVO 1800ES

lowing the tooling like any right-minded car company would have done, those crafty Swedes peeled back the top of the coupe and made a station wagon out of it. Which turns out to be what the coupe needed all along. The low roofline and ample tumblehome of the sideglass just happen to hit the cyclical note of high fashion in station wagons. Of course, you can still buy the coupe if you prefer.

To keep the record straight, Volvo doesn't deserve exclusive credit for the sportwagon concept. We still get an occasional phone call about our October 1966 cover car, an emerald green Mustang wagon that Intermeccanica, an Italian car building concern, hammered out for Bob Cumberford and Barney Clark, and certainly British Leyland is close to the pin with the MGB/GT. Even in the high dollar range, you can see that evidence of this type of thinking. The Maserati Indy and the Lamborghini Espada are right in there . . . but with a slight change of emphasis. In fact, the sportwagon concept could be the savior of the American sporty car. How about a sleek little Z-28 wagon? Or one based on the road-grabbing Firebird Trans-Am? Maybe what GM needs is an intravenous injection of Volvo courage.

Certainly technology is not the problem. The whole idea of the sportwagon, apart from the styling considerations, is to retain the accurate handling and driving pleasure of a sporting car and at the same time gain some cargo space. Not a lot. If you try to make it a 3-suiter it gets too big . . . you end up with a regular station wagon. The

point is just to make a sports car more useful without killing it. GM already has a fair example of this in the Vega Kammback. It takes a very perceptive driver (unless he looks in the rear view mirror) to know that he's not driving a Vega coupe. The Kammback is only a dozen or so pounds heavier than a coupe so it has the same spring rates, the weight distribution is the same and the center of gravity is only fractionally higher. So naturally it feels like a coupe to the driver. It pulls the same G loads on the skid pad, it locks in on mountain roads with the same tenacity and it has none of the usual station wagon bad habits, like tailwag, to put your once-a-day deodorant to the test.

The same principles apply to Volvo's 1800ES Sportwagon. At 2610 pounds it's only 65 pounds heavier than the coupe and its two inches of extra length are purely because the new rear bumper sticks out farther behind to protect the all-glass tailgate. The 4-wheel disc brakes are the same, the all-coil spring suspension is essentially unchanged and the drivetrain is identical. So the wagon drives like a coupe, which is a recommendation of the highest order.

The engine, however, has been changed somewhat for the new model year so that it can comply with emission control laws. It's still the same basic electronic fuel-injected 2-liter pushrod Four but the ignition timing has been altered and, most significantly, the compression ratio has been dropped to 8.7-to-one (from 10.5). A subsistence diet of 91 octane lead-free gasoline is perfectly in order now. Such alterations

have been costly in the horsepower column. Like most American makes, Volvo has switched to SAE "net" power ratings. On that basis the 1800ES produces 112 hp at 6000 rpm, five real horsepower less than last year, when it was rated at 130 SAE *gross*. That difference is noticeable in acceleration. The Sportwagon still has reasonable performance—it covers the standing-quarter in 17.1 seconds at 79.4 mph—but it is 0.4 seconds and 3.2 mph slower than the Coupe of a year ago. Which, to the driver, is perhaps the most conspicuous difference between the new and the old. Certainly you fit in the cockpit in the same old way. The connotation that goes along with "cockpit" is appropriate to the Volvo too. Like a fighter plane or a Formula One car, you can't just fold up and fall in like you can an Oldsmobile and there is a certain warm feeling of exclusivity in that . . . unless you have rheumatism. That feeling comes from the door. It's short and it is positioned squarely beside the seat, which seems reasonable enough at first, except you soon realize that very little of the opening extends in front of the seat cushion. You can do a reverse squat and get your butt in but how your feet make it inside is strictly a freeform exercise. When you've finally dealt with that inconvenience and are latched in, the war machine feeling is stronger than ever. The car's beltline comes up to your chin. You are surrounded by steel, upholstered of course, and the black dashboard confronts you with as many complex-looking dials as you will ever find in a land-bound machine. At first things are a little clumsy. The parking brake lever is on the floor between the driver's seat and the door, and the door itself is so far rearward that the window crank is right by your shoulder. It's so out of place you can't ever turn it with your left hand. But those are only the initial observations. They count for little after a few moments in the supple embrace of the seats. There is not a single bad thing you can say about the 1800's new bucket seats. They have that same functional, sculptured-in-leather look that makes Scandinavian furniture so expensive and if you don't agree with the way they conform to the contours of your backside, you just keep adjusting them until you do. Back . . . forth . . . tilt . . . crank in a little more lumbar support . . . whatever it takes. They are the most hospitable in the business. And Volvo hasn't forgotten the driver's extremities either. The driving position is good, the pedals are large and easy to find in the dark, and when you aren't using your left foot there is a solid block to

CONTINUED ON PAGE 134

ACCELERATION standing ¼ mile, seconds

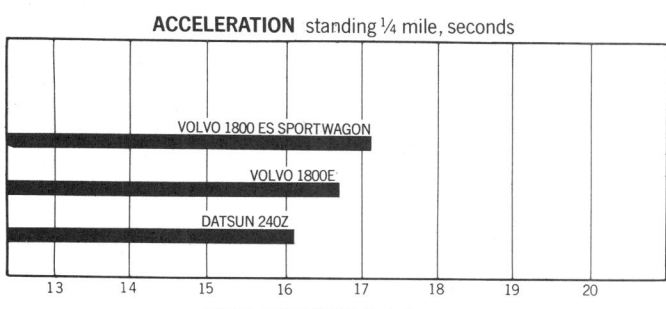

VOLVO 1800 ES SPORTWAGON
VOLVO 1800E
DATSUN 240Z

13 14 15 16 17 18 19 20

BRAKING 80-0 mph panic stop, feet

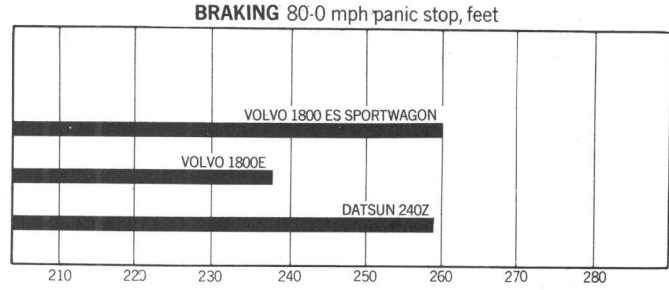

VOLVO 1800 ES SPORTWAGON
VOLVO 1800E
DATSUN 240Z

210 220 230 240 250 260 270 280

FUEL ECONOMY RANGE mpg

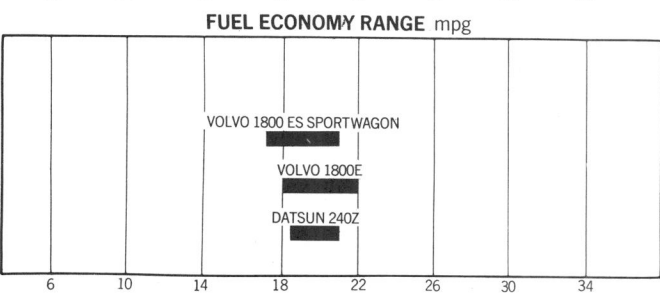

VOLVO 1800 ES SPORTWAGON
VOLVO 1800E
DATSUN 240Z

6 10 14 18 22 26 30 34

PRICE AS TESTED dollars x 1000

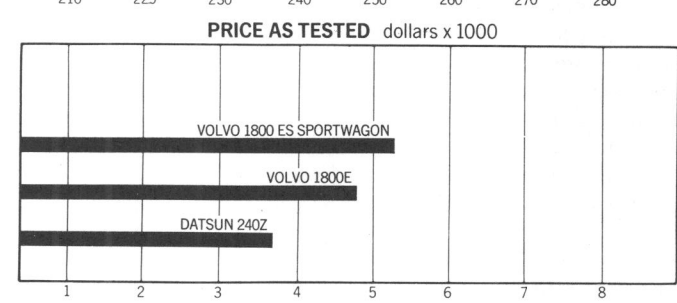

VOLVO 1800 ES SPORTWAGON
VOLVO 1800E
DATSUN 240Z

1 2 3 4 5 6 7 8

VOLVO 1800ES SPORTWAGON

Importer: Volvo Incorporated
Rockleigh, New Jersey

Vehicle type: Front engine, rear-wheel-drive, 2 + 2-passenger station wagon

Price as tested: $5218.23
(Manufacturer's suggested retail price, including all options listed below, Federal excise tax, dealer preparation and delivery charges, does not include state and local taxes, license or freight charges)

Options on test car: No options.

ENGINE
Type: 4-in-line, water-cooled, cast iron block and head, 5 main bearings
Bore x stroke .... 3.50 x 3.15 in, 88.9 x 80.0 mm
Displacement .... 121 cu in, 1987cc
Compression ratio .... 8.7 to one
Carburetion .... Bosch electronic fuel injection
Valve gear .... Pushrod operated overhead valves
Power (SAE net) .... 112 bhp @ 6000 rpm
Torque (SAE net) .... 115 lb-ft @ 3500 rpm
Specific power output .... 0.92 bhp/cu in, 56.5 bhp/liter
Max recommended engine speed .... 6500 rpm

DRIVE TRAIN
Transmission .... 4-speed, all-synchro with overdrive
Final drive ratio .... 4.30 to one

Gear	Ratio	Mph/1000 rpm	Max. test speed
I	3.14	5.6	36 mph (6500 rpm)
II	1.97	9.0	58 mph (6500 rpm)
III	1.34	13.2	86 mph (6500 rpm)
IV	1.00	17.7	106 mph (6000 rpm)
OD	0.80	22.1	110 mph (5000 rpm)

DIMENSIONS AND CAPACITIES
Wheelbase .... 96.5 in
Track, F/R .... 51.7/51.7 in
Length .... 172.6 in
Width .... 67.0 in
Height .... 50.4 in
Ground clearance .... 6.0 in
Curb weight.................................. 2610 lbs
Weight distribution, F/R .... 50.3/49.7 %
Battery capacity .... 12 volts, 60 amp-hr
Alternator capacity .... 420 watts
Fuel capacity .... 11.8 gal
Oil capacity .... 4.1 qts
Water capacity .... 10.0 qts

SUSPENSION
F: Ind., unequal length control arms, coil springs, anti-sway bar
R: Rigid axle, 4 trailing links, Panhard rod, coil springs

STEERING
Type .... Recirculating ball
Turns lock-to-lock 3.5
Turning circle curb-to-curb .... 30.9 ft

BRAKES
F: .... 10.6-in solid disc, power assist
R: .... 11.6-in solid disc, power assist

WHEELS AND TIRES
Wheel size .... 15 x 5.5-in
Wheel type .... Stamped, styled steel, 5-bolt
Tire make and size .... Goodyear, 185/70 HR 15
Tire type .... Tubeless, radial ply
Test inflation pressures, F/R .... 25/27 psi
Tire load rating .... 1210 lbs per tire @ 32 psi

PERFORMANCE
Zero to	Seconds
30 mph	2.8
40 mph	4.4
50 mph	6.4
60 mph	9.2
70 mph	12.5
80 mph	17.2
90 mph	24.1

Standing ¼-mile .... 17.1 sec @ 79.4 mph
Top speed (observed) .... 110 mph
80-0 mph .... 260 ft (0.82 G)
Fuel mileage .... 17-21 mpg on 91 octane fuel
Cruising range .... 200-250 mi

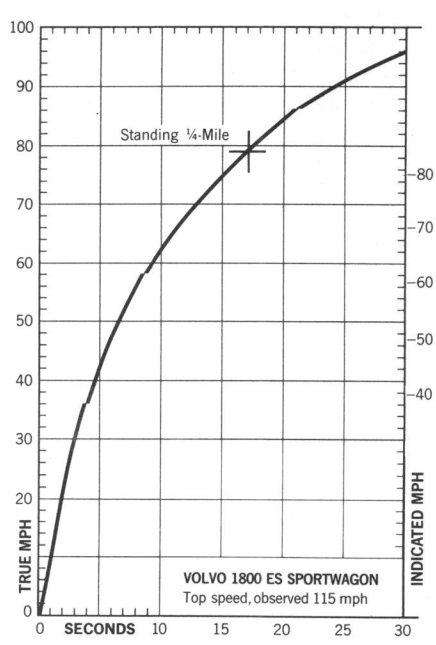

VOLVO 1800 ES SPORTWAGON
Top speed, observed 115 mph

Standing ¼-Mile

TRUE MPH / INDICATED MPH

SECONDS

VOLVO 1800ES SPORTWAGON

CONTINUED FROM PAGE 132

rest it against.

Once on the road, the need for a few improvements becomes apparent. The steering has a kind of unwelcome independence about it. Small directional changes are made without the permission of the steering wheel, a behavioral trait which strongly threatens the "sport" part of the Sportwagon. While this is working on your confidence the engine is rattling away in its best imitation of a Deisel—a long standing Volvo trait. Partial relief is on tap from the overdrive lever sticking out of the steering column on the right like an extra turn signal. With just a flick of your finger you can knock back the engine revs in fourth gear by 20%. But it's only partial relief, and it is served up with overdrive-in-use warning light on the dashboard bright enough to give you a sunburn. This, in turn, is compensated for by a miniature dimmer switch tucked away below the dashboard, and so forth.

All the joys and all of the ills of driving apply equally to the Coupe and the Sportwagon. It's the convenience that's one-sided. Neither the Coupe nor the Sportwagon are true four-passenger cars but the Sportwagon comes the closest. It has a replica of a rear seat that can be folded flat to lengthen the cargo floor and that is its most successful position. As a passenger-carrying device it's strictly emergency only.

At the other end of the load floor is the one-piece glass tailgate which is hinged at the roof and swings up, opening the entire rear of the car right down to the floor. Visibility is outstanding—both for you when you're parking and for thieves when they're casing—and resistance heating elements in the glass assure that the view will be clear year round. The inside floor is completely flat, interrupted only by three flush trapdoors at the rear. The huge center one covers the spare tire compartment and flanking it are two smaller compartments which give access to certain necessities below . . . like taillight bulbs. It's all very simple and very cleverly assembled in the rock-solid Volvo manner, and it looks like it should cost a lot of money.

And this is one time looks aren't deceiving. Leather seats, overdrive and the rear window defogger are standard attractions and the whole show runs you a cool $5218.23. If your taste runs to such extras as an AM/FM radio, automatic transmission and air conditioning you won't get much change back from a $6000 bill. Alas, the weakness of the dollar. That is one of the fringe benefits that George Meaney didn't mention. ●

ELEVEN YEAR PLAN
CONTINUED FROM PAGE 106

to sit well down into the bucket and it sort of molds to your shape – a circumstance expanded by a lumbar adjustment on the edge of the back rest. Elevational corrections are the only possibilities not provided, and with the large steering wheel, are hardly required by most drivers.

Almost all the great cars of our time have embodied some great faults, things that you had to live with because they were outweighed by other offsetting brilliances. Perhaps this is why the 1800 has had such a sustained success, existing comfortably 10 years after its creation. Volvo designed out all the hangups. You get in and the door closes with the solid authority of real heavy-gauge Swedish steel. There is no question of being comfortable because of the seats and the good driver position where everything is within reach. Up from the floor and over the dash comes a gentle stream of fresh air as the flow-through ventilation system exchanges a compartment full every 15 seconds. Pull on the heater fan that also works the cold air and it is almost like being in a tiny air-conditioned room. Add heat and it is a sauna if you like.

Like everything else, the transmission is overbuilt, having been originally constructed for the big 164 six-cylinder sedan. Shift action is not the electric solenoid-like push-pull, click-click of a BMW, and nothing will ever hurt the thing. While Detroit has been locked in its toe-to-toe struggle building thousand-inch muscle cats, the status trip in Europe is the 5-speed box. To be without one is only less embarrassing than a bumper without a BP sticker. Volvo sort of backed into the 5-speed gap with ingenuity. Somewhere about the time that engine noise becomes noticeable, you pull a little lever to the right of the steering column, engaging an electric overdrive, and the revs fade away into a quiet 100-mph cruise. Four-on-the-floor and one-on-the-column.

In 1961 the P-1800 cost $3,900 and in 1970 the 1800 E is $4,595 with inflation and P.O.E. charges. You'd have thought by this time someone would have come along to challenge the 1800, but that would mean a competitor with all of its virtues and none of its faults and Volvo has that one pretty well covered.   /MT

"Who's the dummy that owns the electric car?"

VOLVO 1800E

Continued from page 127

rocker shaft. The rocker shaft is held by four bolts and so presents no real problem. The rating for tightening head bolts is fair and five points.

The battery cables are both very accessible at both ends. The rating for their replacement is good and eight

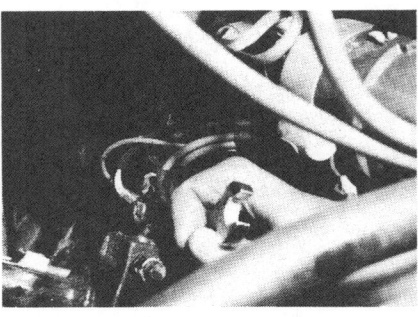

Battery cables are easy to disconnect and reconnect at both ends. Photo shows cable at starter solenoid.

points. The brake master cylinder is wide open, making its replacement an easy job. The rating is good and eight points.

Because the car is equipped with fuel injection, which isn't a weekend mechanic's item, the point total will be adjusted to reflect the fact that carburetor and fuel pump replacement are not applicable.

The P-1800E picks up three out of a possible eight points in the bonus category. The starter and radiator hoses cannot be removed from the top of the engine compartment. However, the speedometer cable connection at the speedometer is easy, and gets the two bonus points. And several of the dashboard bulbs can be reached without difficulty (a few others would skin the knuckles of any but very small hands), and this item gets one of the two points.

The rating for heavy repairs is fair-to-good, and six points. Although a fuel injection system does add to the car's complexity, such items as engine removal and replacement (about three hours), clutch job (less than three and a half hours) and transmission replacement (about three hours) are not excessive at all.

The Volvo P-1800E ends up with 75 points out of a possible 96. Adjusting this score brings it up to 88 out of a possible 112. Not bad for a fuel-injected GT car.   ●

VOLVO 1800ES

*A successful conversion from dated GT
to genuine sportswagon*

WHO'D HAVE THOUGHT the Volvo people would turn the 1800E into a sports wagon? It certainly never occurred to us until the car appeared. The 1800 coupe, now in its 13th year, seemed a candidate for discontinuance but not much else. After all, it was heavy, ugly, cramped, noisy and overpriced. Frank insiders at Volvo didn't equivocate about it: they weren't sure two years ago whether they'd continue the 1800 a while longer, replace it with an up-to-date car, or simply get out of the sporty car business altogether. That business certainly isn't a major part of their activity, although the 1800's design is a good reason it isn't.

But lo and behold, they've had a clever spell, spent a little money on the old coupe and turned it into a sports wagon. And, we must grudgingly admit, the result is amazingly successful. Whoever is responsible for Volvo's station wagon rear sections does nice work indeed, having proved his mettle earlier with the large rear window of the 145 wagon. On the 1800ES he went further with a window that takes up two-thirds of the rear end's height, has hinges and locking handle attached directly to it, and is the entire tailgate. It's futuristic and handsome.

Extension of the roofline straight back put more head-room over what are jokingly called rear seats in the coupe, and in profile view the wagon roof and the well done rear side window give the car such a different profile that many people approached us to ask what the car was, as we toured car-knowing Southern California in it. The whole front end, which was the most acceptable portion of the coupe anyway, is unchanged. The windshield and side glass remain narrow slits, the beltline high and the sides bloated in a most antique way. There's still that corny upsweep in the door that leads to the equally corny chrome-topped fins, but we can't deny that given what they had to work with the designers did a nice job of the transformation.

Sports wagons are by no means a new idea. The MGB, a borderline case because it's so small, has been around since 1966, Chevrolet's first Nomad was based on the Corvette, Reliant builds its Scimitar GTE in England, and there was a handsome Pininfarina one on the Peugeot 504 sports platform last fall. We cannot help being a little parochial, though, and so we note that Volvo's sports wagon, nearly 20 inches longer, roomier, and more wagon-like than the MGB, is the one that's going to put sports wagons on the U.S. map. If the reactions we got from people "on the street" and the fact that Volvo's western U.S. branch is or-

VOLVO 1800ES

dering all its 1800s for 1972 in the wagon body are any indication, it's going to be successful in spite of its dated characteristics and stiff price.

So much for styling critique and market prognostications. What's the car like? Well, as one might have guessed, pretty much like the last 1800 we tested, the first fuel-injection 1800E two years ago. The engine is still two liters, not 1.8—it mystifies us why Volvo doesn't go ahead and rename the car 2000—but it's one of those that suffered a power cut at the hands of no-lead fuel this year. The rating used to be 124 bhp net with 10.5:1 compression ratio; 10.5 is mighty high and Volvo had to lop off 1.8 points to make the engine run on 91-octane blend, so the power is down to 112 bhp. This shows in two ways. First, the performance is off as expected, with this 1800ES taking 1.2 sec longer to reach 60 mph and 0.7 sec longer to cover the standing quarter-mile than the older car which was 100 lb lighter at test weight. Second, the engine is slightly smoother and quieter than before, a natural consequence of a lower compression ratio. It's still a relatively noisy unit, its pushrod-operated valves clicking classically. It sounds just like the vintage engine it is, but vintage or no it's sturdy and produces good power for its size. Another of our many plugs for electronic fuel injection: it helps this engine to start well from cold, warm up gracefully and run cleanly at all times, its only problem being hard starting when hot.

The 1800's gearbox, inherited from the big Volvo 164, reinforces the engine's sturdy character with its big, heavy shift lever and knob and is a most satisfactory unit. Behind it is the old Laycock-de Normanville overdrive, which engages or disengages hydraulically at the flick of a steering-column stalk and works on 4th gear only. A modern 5-speed box would be better because after slowing down and down-shifting the driver has to do two separate operations or skip a gear on the way back up; but at least the OD provides mechanically relaxed, if not quiet, cruising. A lot of wind noise keeps the car from being quiet at speed.

Seating for the 1800 driver is classic too, with a near-vertical steering wheel, tight dimensions for the shoulders and a "buried" feeling resulting from the relatively high window sills and cowl. The seats are very good, offering not only a backrest angle adjustment but Volvo's unique lumbar-support adjustment. One-operation inertia belts are standard

and this was our first test car to have the federally required belt warning: a light on the dash shines until the driver has plugged the belt into its center receptacle between the seats, which is supposed to be lighted but wasn't on the test car. We found no provision for warning the front passenger about his belt.

The rear area encompasses 10.8 cu ft when loaded up to the side window sills; if the jump seats (which are still good only for small kids) are folded down this goes to 14.8 cu ft. And if one is willing to sacrifice rear vision he can stuff nearly 28 cu ft of things into the back end. So the ES is a very capacious 2-seater for long trips, and for local hacking the rear area will be handy too. It always takes a key to get the tailgate open, which is a bother in this sort of use.

Vision outward is far better in the ES than in the coupe because of the large rear glass areas; the super-window at the rear makes it one of the easiest cars imaginable to parallel-park. Up front the slit-like windshield is a problem, however, when the sun visor is needed; it takes up half the windshield's height when it's down! The visor is contoured to conform to the roof shape and its bent-back edge makes it impossible to pivot it down close to the windshield itself— Volvo would do well to adopt a floppy-edged visor.

The ES is a good-riding car over a wide variety of road surfaces and despite having a live rear axle has good suspension travel for large bumps and dips. In fact the car is a little on the soft side and there's a lot of body roll in hard cornering. Combine this with the new and larger Goodyear 70-section tires (same as on the Capri V-6 but in a 15-in. size) and you've got a car that handles well in ordinary-to-brisk driving but gets tippy and squishy at the limit. Thus the benefits of the wider wheels and tires now standard on both the coupe and wagon aren't so significant, at least in comparison with the smaller Michelin tires on our last coupe; the ES has little more cornering power than an average sedan. The steering is precise and reassuring but heavy in parking maneuvers; our test car had a slight steering shimmy at about 50 mph.

The 1800ES is one of those cars that leaves a road-test staff a bit frustrated. Here Volvo has done a nice transformation, produced the first sports wagon big enough to really serve as one that we can buy in America, and done such a nice job with the esthetics that the car is a real head-turner. But they did it on a car that should have been replaced, not reworked. It's a good, solid car but a crude and old-fashioned one; still it's one-of-a-kind and if you must have a sports wagon this is the one you have to choose. We don't think Volvo will have any trouble selling it.

ROAD TEST
VOLVO 1800ES

SCALE: 10" DIVISIONS

PRICE

List price, west coast......$5032
Price as tested, west coast...$5340
Price as tested includes standard equipment (overdrive, radial tires, leather upholstery, rear window defroster), AM-FM stereo radio ($212), dealer prep ($95)

IMPORTER

Volvo, Inc.
Rockleigh, N.J. 07647

ENGINE

Type........... ohv inline 4
Bore x stroke, mm... 89.0 x 80.0
Equivalent in.... 3.50 x 3.15
Displacement, cc/cu in.. 1986/121
Compression ratio..........8.7:1
Bhp @ rpm, net... 112 @ 6000
Equivalent mph.........124
Torque @ rpm, lb-ft..115 @ 3500
Equivalent mph........74
Fuel injection.... Bosch electronic
Fuel requirement... regular, 91-oct
Emissions, gram/mile:
Hydrocarbons.............1.5
Carbon Monoxide..........28
Nitrogen Oxides..........2.3

DRIVE TRAIN

Transmission: 4-speed manual plus overdrive
Gear ratios: OD (0.797)....3.43:1
4th (1.00)............4.30:1
3rd (1.36)............5.85:1
2nd (1.99)............8.56:1
1st (3.13).............13.45:1
Final drive ratio..........4.30:1

CHASSIS & BODY

Layout....front engine/rear drive
Body/frame..........unit/steel
Brake system: 10.6-in. disc front, 11.6-in. disc rear; vacuum assisted
Swept area, sq in.........400
Wheels....styled steel, 15 x 5½ J
Tires.............Goodyear G800 185/70 HR-15
Steering type........cam & roller
Overall ratio............15.5:1
Turns, lock-to-lock.......3.2
Turning circle, ft.........31.5
Front suspension: unequal-length A-arms, coil springs, tube shocks, anti-roll bar

Rear suspension: live axle on upper & lower trailing arms with Panhard rod; coil springs, tube shocks

ACCOMMODATION

Seating capacity, persons.... 2+2
Seat width, front/rear.2 x 19.0/41.0
Head room, front/rear.. 35.5/35.5
Seat back adjustment, degrees..40

INSTRUMENTATION

Instruments: 120-mph speedometer, 7000-rpm tach, 99,999 odometer, 999.9 trip odo. oil press, oil temp, coolant temp, fuel level, clock
Warning lights: ammeter, high beam, directionals, hazard flasher, handbrake, overdrive, seatbelt

MAINTENANCE

Service intervals, mi:
Oil change...............6000
Filter change............6000
Chassis lube............6000
Minor tuneup............6000
Major tuneup..........12,000
Warranty, mo/mi.....6/unlimited

GENERAL

Curb weight, lb...........2570
Test weight..............2935
Weight distribution (with driver), front/rear, %....50/50
Wheelbase, in...........96.5
Track, front/rear......51.6/51.6
Length.................172.6
Width..................66.9
Height.................50.4
Ground clearance..........6.1
Overhang, front/rear...30.2/45.9
Usable trunk space, cu ft.....10.8
Fuel capacity, U.S. gal......11.9

CALCULATED DATA

Lb/bhp (test weight)........26.2
Mph/1000 rpm (o'drive).....21.4
Engine revs/mi (60 mph o'drive).........2800
Piston travel, ft/mi.........1470
R&T steering index..........1.02
Brake swept area, sq in/ton...272

RELIABILITY

From R&T Owner Surveys the average number of trouble areas for all models surveyed is 11. As owners of earlier-model Volvos reported 10 trouble areas, we expect the reliability of the Volvo 1800ES to be average.

ROAD TEST RESULTS

ACCELERATION

Time to distance, sec:
0–100 ft.............4.0
0–500 ft.............9.9
0–1320 ft (¼ mi).....18.2
Speed at end of ¼-mi, mph....74
Time to speed, sec:
0–30 mph.............3.7
0–40 mph.............5.6
0–50 mph.............8.0
0–60 mph............11.3
0–70 mph............15.5
0–80 mph............21.4
0–90 mph............30.1

SPEEDS IN GEARS

O'drive (5600 rpm)........116
4th (6500)...............108
3rd (6500)................80
2nd (6500)................56
1st (6500)................36

SPEEDOMETER ERROR

30 mph indicated is actually..28.5
50 mph.................47.5
60 mph.................57.0
70 mph.................66.5
80 mph.................75.0
Odometer, 10.0 mi.........9.9

BRAKES

Minimum stopping distances, ft:
From 60 mph..........178
From 80 mph..........299
Control in panic stop.......good
Pedal effort for 0.5g stop, lb....20
Fade: percent increase in pedal effort to maintain 0.5g deceleration in 6 stops from 60 mph......50
Parking: hold 30% grade?....yes
Overall brake rating......good

HANDLING

Speed on 100-ft radius, mph. 31.5
Lateral acceleration, g.......0.660

FUEL ECONOMY

Normal driving, mpg.........22.5
Cruising range, mi (1-gal res.).245

INTERIOR NOISE

All noise readings in dbA:
Idle in neutral.............57
Maximum, 1st gear........84
Constant 30 mph..........65
50 mph.................75
70 mph.................77
90 mph.................82

ACCELERATION

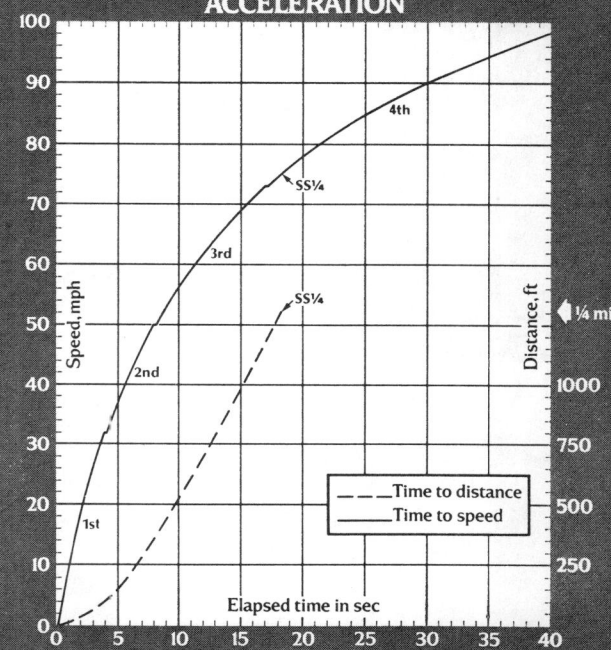

— — — Time to distance
———— Time to speed

Elapsed time in sec

ROAD TEST

VOLVO 1800ES

Twelve years ago, when the P1800 was first shown in public (at the 1960 Brussels Show) Volvo pledged that its dateless styling would allow a very long production run. Well, they kept their pledge even though the high-waisted semi-finned body dated a lot more quickly than Volvo perhaps anticipated. Ultimately one suspects the car sold — albeit in dwindling numbers — despite its appearance rather than, as originally planned, because of it.

Mindful of the astronomical cost of retooling for something quite different, Volvo have remained faithful to the original theme by cleverly grafting on a new tail, Reliant GTE style, to produce the 1800ES. With the new shape — highly distinctive if hardly beautiful — comes a welcome new versatility since the luggage accommodation has been significantly increased and the enormous rimless glass tailgate, the car's most striking visual feature, allows estate car access to it.

But clever though the grafting may be, it doesn't in any way camouflage the car's ancestry: in many respects the 1800ES feels as long in the tooth as it is. For instance, the high scuttle and sills and rather cramped cockpit make the car feel decidedly claustrophobic. The heavy long-travel clutch and gearchange make driving in traffic rather tiresome, while long-distance touring — which is what the 1800ES is really all about — is marred by a very high level of engine and wind noise, an almost uncontrollable heater and virtually non-existent ventilation.

Certain weaknesses in the suspension and chassis departments — like roll oversteer and rather vague steering — perhaps also betray the car's age, though we must hastily add that the ride is good, the cornering powers are high and the handling on the whole very sound, entirely in keeping with the car's sporting pretensions. In fact it is these qualities, together with an excellent performance from the 2-litre fuel-injected engine — better even (on acceleration) than that of the cheaper 3-litre Scimitar GTE — that are the 1800ES's most endearing features.

Volvo owners tend to be fanatically partisan, a loyalty largely induced by the marque's almost legendary reputation for reliability and longevity. We certainly hope that these qualities are strongly evident in the 1800ES for it is a car, we feel, that must rely heavily on such things, not only to justify its very high price but also to compensate for its many dated features.

PERFORMANCE AND ECONOMY

Eight years ago Volvo raised the capacity of their engine from 1780 cc. to 1985 cc. With Bosch electronic injection the unit now

develops a healthy 124 bhp at 6000 rpm and a useful 123 lb. ft. of torque at 3500 rpm. Owing to the design of the injection sensors (which work off engine speed, cooling water temperature, inlet temperature and manifold vacuum) a few seconds' churning is needed when starting from cold. This is followed by a short period of uneven running after which the engine — a bit rough and noisy at low speeds — warms up quickly. It then smooths out up to its rev limit of 6500 rpm, although the sheer noise — a deep roar — is sufficient to deter many owners from making full use of the available performance.

We achieved a maximum speed of 110.5 mph round MIRA's banked circuit — corresponding to maximum revs in direct top gear. Overdrive top gave a more relaxed 107.1 mph at 5050 rpm although this would probably build up to a higher speed on a flat road. For a 2-litre car of some 23 cwt. this is a respectable speed, as is the acceleration with 60 mph coming up in 9.7 sec. and 100 mph in 33.1 sec.

The low speed flexibility of this version of Volvo's B20 unit (not a feature of the 1800E that we tested two years ago) is largely attributable to the vice-free Bosch electronic

injection; the car pulled happily from 20 mph in top gear and took just 8.1 sec. to accelerate from 30—50 mph.

A 10-gallon fuel tank gives the ES a touring range of only 200 miles at our overall consumption of 20.6 mpg, as usual the product of hard driving. Doubtless continued motorway cruising in overdrive would produce considerably better figures. Due to the fuel injection we were unable to measure the steady speed (and hence the touring) consumption accurately. Despite the relatively high compression ratio of 10.5:1 the engine runs happily on 4-star petrol and at no time did we detect any pinking.

TRANSMISSION

In an age of featherlight clutches and finger-tip gearchanges, the rather agricultural feel of the Volvo's transmission is a bit of a shock; fast changes are possible although they certainly demand a fair amount of effort. Some of our testers disliked the fat gear knob that literally fills your hand, but it probably facilitates the operation of what is on the whole a rather awkward change with easily beatable synchromesh.

The clutch is in keeping with the gearbox; it not only has a very long travel (every bit of which was required to make a gearchange) but it is also very heavy to push. The clutch of our 1800E suffered from much the same maladies, which at the time we put down to lack of suitable adjustment on the operating cable. Now we're not so sure. The ratios, however, are well chosen and there are certainly no awkward gaps. 35 mph is available in first gear — which coped easily with the 1-in-3 test hill; 55 mph is on tap in second and a useful 81 mph in third for overtaking.

The ES has a J-type Laycock overdrive, operating on top gear only, controlled by a stalk on the steering column. It is particularly smooth in engagement on both up and down changes and a warning light on the dash indicates when the unit is engaged.

There was no detectable noise from either gearbox or the live axle.

HANDLING AND BRAKES

Perhaps because the 1800ES has a steering box rather than the more common rack and pinion set-up, the steering has a rather slack feel in the straight ahead position; but it is good on lock, inspiring confidence at high speed with a ratio of $3\frac{1}{2}$ turns from lock to lock, the steering is reasonably direct. Parking requires rather more effort, as the steering becomes heavy at low speed. However, the car is very manoeuvrable with a turning circle of under 30 ft. A certain amount of bump steering causes the car to wander over undulating surfaces. Although this can be a little disconcerting it requires little correction.

The handling of the ES is good and quite fun to exploit, and the car can certainly be thrown about with confidence. The initial understeer is followed by a controllable amount of roll oversteer, whereupon the car tends to dig in at the rear. Thus hard cornering is sometimes terminated with the inside front wheel off the ground. Despite this and fairly prominent body roll the ES remains quite controllable, even though there is not a tremendous amount of feel, either through the steering or the seat of your pants.

The front suspension is by double wishbones and coil springs, together with a substantial anti-roll bar. At the rear, the live axle is located by trailing arms, lateral positioning being taken care of by a Panhard rod. The roadholding on the fat Goodyear

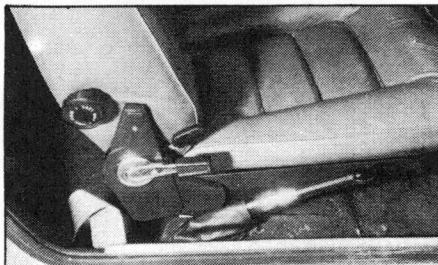

Above: The famed Volvo lumbar support is wound in and out by this knurled knob. Left: We found the leather seats, with built in head restraints to be lacking in lateral support. Below: Strictly a +2

Grand Prix radials is pretty good even on a wet surface, and the car made short work of long journeys, taking both long and tight corners in its stride. Our test car was affected by side-winds, but not to any alarming degree.

The servo-assisted all-disc brakes certainly passed our tests without any trouble: 1g maximum retardation, no fade and virtual immunity to a soaking in the watersplash. Yet despite this good performance — not to mention the hidden asset of diagonally split circuits which, should one fail, still leaves braking on two front wheels and one back one — we did not like the feel of the brakes at all. As the figures show, a panic stop requires a very hard push: worse still, the brakes did not release as progressively as they came on so that it was difficult to "feather" them smoothly when coming to rest. The handbrake, a particularly powerful device, easily locked the wheels at 30 mph to give a good deceleration figure of 0.43g. It certainly had no trouble in holding the car on the 1-in-3 test hill.

COMFORT AND CONTROLS

The ride of the ES is unexpectedly good and the car soaks up bumps without fuss, thumping or undue jarring. Since our test of the 1800E, though, Volvo appear to have changed the seats — most of our test staff found the new ones a bit hard and lacking in lateral support. For a few, the fully adjustable lumbar support — a unique feature — proved ideal and they were able to obtain a really restful position; for most of us, however, the backrest was too hard even with the lumbar support fully retracted. There's plenty of fore and aft adjustment and the squabs almost fully recline (almost, because they come to rest against the rear seat arms before reaching the horizontal).

The rear seats are very much of the occasional variety, with a particularly hard backrest and very little leg or elbow room. A reasonably comfortable compromise can be obtained for one person by sitting side-saddle. Headroom in the back is tolerable for people of average height.

The driving position feels rather old fashioned and restricted, with the high scuttle and window sills and thick pillars pressing in. Your hands rest on a large, relatively upright steering wheel and your feet on large, heavy pedals. In this respect the 1800ES compares more with sports cars of the 'fifties than with saloons of today.

The range of push/pull switches on the leading edge of the dash includes an effective wiper/wash control and the light switch. Two column stalks control the overdrive, indicators, headlamp dip and flash. Other controls include the heater boost and the hazard warning light switch.

Visibility is not a strong point: the side windows mist up very easily as well as suffering from a build-up of dirt on the outside. Add to this thick pillars and a low driving position and you'll understand why vision is rather poor on a wet night. The heated rear tailgate keeps surprisingly clean, but there is no wiper (as on the Volvo estate). The lights are not outstanding, being only 45/40 watt filament units, but the two-speed wipers and electric washers are particularly effective.

Noise is the worst fault in the ES; it seems

Motor Road Test No 12/72 Volvo 1800 ES

Maximum speed mph (chart): Datsun 240Z £2389; Lotus Elan + 2S 130 £2659; Triumph Stag £2176; Reliant Scimitar GTE £2379; Volvo ES £2651; BMW 2000 Touring £2248

Acceleration sec (chart): Lotus Elan + 2S 130 (0-50, 30-50 in top); Datsun 240Z; Volvo ES; BMW 2000 Touring; Triumph Stag; Reliant Scimitar GTE

Fuel consumption mpg (chart): Datsun 240Z (Overall, Touring); BMW 2000 Touring; Lotus Elan + 2S 130; Triumph Stag; Volvo ES; Reliant Scimitar GTE

Make: Volvo
Model: 1800 ES
Makers: Aktiebolaget Volvo, Goteborg, Sweden
Concessionaires: Volvo Concessionaires Ltd, Raeburn Road, Ipswich, Suffolk
Price: £2119.00 plus £531.62 purchase tax equals £2651

Performance tests carried out by *Motor's* staff at the Motor Industry Research Association proving ground, Lindley.
Test Data: World copyright reserved; no unauthorised reproduction in whole or in part.

Conditions
Weather: Dry and sunny; Wind S.W. changing to S.E., 0-10 mph.
Temperature: 40-43°F.
Barometer: 29 in. Hg.
Surface: Damp initially.
Fuel: 98 octane (RM) 4 Star rating.

Maximum Speeds
	mph	kph
Mean lap banked circuit	110.5	177.8
Best one-way ¼-mile	112.4	180.8
3rd gear at	81	130
2nd gear } 6500	55	88
1st gear } rpm	35	56
"Maximile" speed: (Timed quarter mile after 1 mile accelerating from rest)		
Mean	105.9	
Best	107.2	

Acceleration Times
mph		sec
0- 30		3.3
0- 40		4.8
0- 50		7.0
0- 60		9.7

			sec
0- 70			13.0
0- 80			16.7
0- 90			23.8
0-100			33.1
Standing quarter-mile			17.1
Standing Kilometre			32.0

| | | O/d | |
| | Top | Top | 3rd |
mph	sec	sec	sec
10- 30	—	—	6.3
20- 40	12.4	8.0	5.7
30- 50	12.0	8.1	5.6
40- 60	12.5	8.1	5.6
50- 70	12.8	8.7	5.9
60- 80	14.7	9.7	7.1
70- 90	19.0	11.3	—
80-100	—	15.8	—

Fuel Consumption
Overall 20.6 mpg (=13.7 litres/100km)
Fuel tank capacity . . . 10 gals
Total test distance . . . 1330 miles

Brakes
Pedal pressure, deceleration and equivalent stopping distance from 30 mph
lb	g	ft
25	0.27	111
50	0.50	60
75	0.73	41
100	0.88	34
150	1.00	30
Handbrake	0.43	70

Fade test
20 stops at ½g deceleration at 1 min intervals from a speed midway between 40 mph and maximum speed (= 75 mph)
	lb
Pedal force at beginning	37
Pedal force at 10th stop	33
Pedal force at 20th stop	32

Steering
Turning circle between kerbs:	ft.
Left	30
Right	28¾
Turns of steering wheel from lock to lock . . . 3.6
Steering wheel deflection for 50 ft. diameter circle 1.0 turns

Clutch
Free pedal movement . . . . 2 in.
Additional movement to disengage clutch completely 3¾ in.
Maximum pedal load . . . . 47 lb.

Speedometer
Indicated	20	30	40	50	60	70
True	21	31	41	50	58	69
Indicated	80	90	100			
True	77	86.5	97			
Distance recorder 3% fast

Weight
Kerb weight (unladen with fuel for approximately 50 miles) . 23.1 cwt.
Front/rear distribution . . . 51/49
Weight laden as tested . . 26.8 cwt.

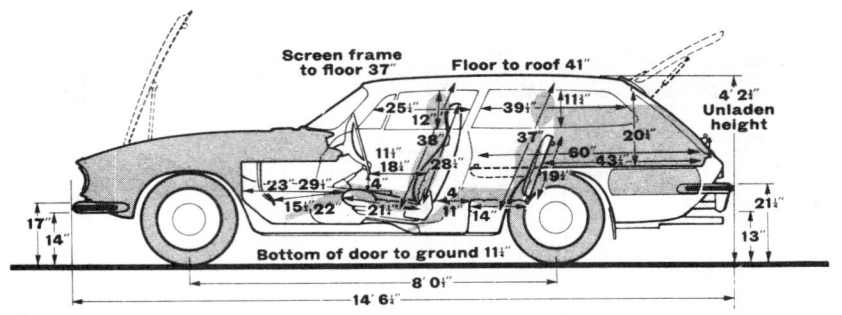

Engine

Block material	Cast iron
Head material	Cast iron
Cylinders	4 in line
Cooling system	Water; sealed
Bore and stroke	88.9mm (3.50 in.)
	80mm (3.15 in.)
Cubic capacity	1985cc. (121 cu. in.)
Main bearings	5
Valves	ohv
Compression ratio	10.5:1
Induction	Bosch electronic fuel injection
Fuel pump	Electric
Oil Filter	Full flow
Max. power (net)	124 bhp at 6000 rpm
Max. torque (net)	123 lb.ft. at 3500 rpm

Transmission

Clutch	8½ in. dia., sdp, diaphragm
Internal gear box ratios	
Top gear	1.0
3rd gear	1.36
2nd gear	1.99
1st gear	3.13
Reverse	3.13
Overdrive top	0.797
Synchromesh	On all forward gears
Overdrive type	Laycock J type
Final drive Hypoid bevel	4.30:1
Mph at 1000 rpm in:—	
o/d top gear	21.3
top gear	17.0
third gear	12.5
second gear	8.5
first gear	5.4

Chassis and body

Construction	Unitary, all steel

Brakes

Type	Split circuit servo assisted discs all round. Drums for handbrake
Dimensions	Front 10.59 in. dia. rear 11.6 in. dia.

Suspension and steering

Front	Coil springs, wishbones with anti-roll bar

Overall width 5' 6¼"

63"

20¼"
40"
38¼"
48"
25¼"

Front track 4' 4"

Rear track 4' 4"

Ground clearances
Lowest point:—
(under exhaust system) 5"
under front suspension 6¼"
under engine 7"

Rear	Coil springs, live axle located by four radius arms and a Panhard rod.
Shock absorbers	
Front and rear	Double acting telescopic
Steering type	Cam and roller
Tyres	Goodyear G800 Grand Prix 185/70 HR-15
Wheels	Pressed steel with cast aluminium hub caps
Rim size	5½ J

Coachwork and equipment

Starting handle	No
Tool kit contents	Box spanner for plugs and wheel nuts; tommy bar; adjustable spanner; pliers; plain blade and crosshead screwdrivers
Jack	Scissor type
Jacking points	4
Battery	12 volt negative earth 60 amp hrs capacity
Number of electrical fuses	12

Headlamps	45/40W
Indicators	self cancelling flashers
Reversing lamp	yes; operated automatically by gear lever
Screen wipers	Two-speed electric
Screen washers	Electric
Sun visors	Two
Locks:	
With ignition key	steering lock
With other keys	a. doors and boot
	b. central lidded console
Interior heater	Fresh air type with booster fan
Upholstery	Leather
Floor covering	Carpet
Alternative body styles	None
Maximum load	484 lb.
Major extras available	Automatic transmission

Maintenance

Fuel tank capacity	10 galls
Sump	6.6 pints SAE 20/50
Gearbox	2.46 pints SAE 20/50
Rear axle	2.3 pints SAE 90 EP
Steering gear	0.44 pints SAE 90 EP
Coolant	1.87 gals (1 drain tap)
Chassis lubrication	None
Maximum service interval	6000 miles
Ignition timing	10 deg btdc at 700-800 rpm, vacuum pipe disconnected
Contact breaker gap	0.016-0.020 in.
Sparking plug gap	0.028-0.032 in.
Sparking plug type	Bosch W225T35
Tappet clearance	Inlet 0.016 in.
(hot or cold)	Exhaust 0.016 in.
Valve timing:	
inlet opens	29°btdc
inlet closes	71°abdc
exhaust opens	71°bbdc
exhaust closes	29°atdc
Rear wheel toe-in	0-.16in.
Front wheel toe-in	0-.16in.
Camber angle	0-+½°
Castor angle	0-+1°
King pin inclination	8° with no camber
Tyre pressures:	
Front	25 psi
Rear	27 psi

to come from everywhere. To start with the engine has a loud induction roar, which is joined at various times by harsh tappet noise and other mechanical mutterings. There are no particular vibration periods and the transmission is inaudible, the chief source of noise other than the engine is the leading edge of the doors, the windscreen pillars and quarter-lights which promote tremendous wind noise. Talking becomes strained at 70 mph, and the particularly good radio fitted to our test car was inaudible at 100 mph, even in overdrive.

There is no proper through-flow ventilation on the ES, just some fresh air vents, operated by ram pressure, below the dashboard and some extraction vents in the rear wings. There is no face-level ventilation. The heating is controlled by means of three sliding knobs — two for distribution, one for temperature — which are not very clearly marked. Moreover, the latter is so sensitive that it's difficult to maintain the desired temperature in the car without continuously altering the lever. The two-speed heater blower is very powerful when full on, although very noisy in operation. The car was leakproof, but there were some draughts around the leading edge of the doors which may account for some of the wind noise.

FITTINGS AND FURNITURE

Instrumentation on the ES is comprehensive. Through the steering wheel, the driver views the water and oil temperature gauges together with the symmetrically mounted speedometer and rev-counter. The oil pressure gauge, fuel gauge and clock are laid out in a line to his left. We found them to be well positioned and easy to read, although there seems little point in having all the noughts on the rev-counter calibrations. The rather bright overdrive and main beam warning lights can be dimmed by means of a switch under the driver's side of the dash. The corresponding switch on the passenger side operates a map light; automatic courtesy lights are fitted in the passenger compartment and inside the tailgate. Safety has obviously featured high on the list in the design of this car and some of the standard fittings include head restraints, laminated windscreen, heated rear screen, mud flaps all round, and an anti-glare mirror.

The facia is quite tastefully laid out, although the simulated wood instrument background could never be confused with the genuine article. The seats are trimmed in quality leather and the main floor and rear compartment are neatly tailored with carpet. There are plenty of cubby holes, with map pockets in the doors, an oddments tray and locker on the end of the console — neatly built into the rear floor — a couple of deep wells for extra tools and other more bulky oddments. The safety belts, which are factory fitted, are of the inertia reel lap-and-diagonal type. Fixed clips are mounted on the transmission tunnel, and the seat belt warning light is only extinguished when the driver's belt is locked into place. Automatic reversing lights are standard.

SERVICE AND ACCESSIBILITY

The lockable bonnet is self-supporting, and is released and secured by means of an

1 cigar lighter; 2 clock; 3 oil pressure gauge; 4 wiper/washer switch; 5 fuel gauge; 6 overdrive tell-tale; 7 seat-belt warning light; 8 tachometer; 9 oil temperature gauge; 10 water temperature gauge; 11 speedometer; 12 tripmeter; 13 odometer; 14 handbrake and brake system warning light; 15 ashtray; 16 and 17 heater distribution controls; 18 heater temperature control; 19 heater boost switch; 20 indicator/headlamp dip and flash stalk; 21 hazard warning lights; 22 trip zero; 23 horn press; 24 panel light rheostat; 25 bonnet catch; 26 steering/lock/ignition/starter; 27 overdrive stalk; 28 light switch; 29 rear window heater switch

over-centre catch under the facia. Most items are fairly accessible except for the dipstick, which has a tiny handle and no extension tube. Reaching for it usually means an oily sleeve. There is a labelled fusebox mounted on the nearside bulkhead of the cockpit, above the passenger's legs.

There are now over 300 Volvo dealers and distributors in the country and the ES needs their attention every 6000 miles after the first 3000. There are no greasing points. Tow hooks are built into the front and rear. The spare wheel, jack and tools are under the rear floor, concealed by a trap door. ∎

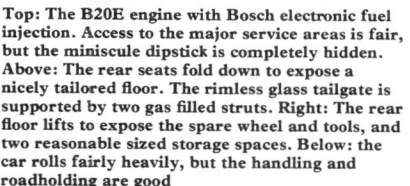

Top: The B20E engine with Bosch electronic fuel injection. Access to the major service areas is fair, but the miniscule dipstick is completely hidden. Above: The rear seats fold down to expose a nicely tailored floor. The rimless glass tailgate is supported by two gas filled struts. Right: The rear floor lifts to expose the spare wheel and tools, and two reasonable sized storage spaces. Below: the car rolls fairly heavily, but the handling and roadholding are good

The Ultimate Sportwagon

Volvo's 1800 ES combines sports car performance with station wagon practicality.

From time to time a new and innovative automotive concept comes along to capture the public's fancy. The heyday of the Muscle Car has subsided, having been superseded by the era of the Super Coupe which has yet to approach its zenith. A new phenomenon has now marched upon the scene and stands bravely in the wings waiting to claim its place in the limelight of public acclaim. We refer to the sportwagon concept — of which there could not be a more fitting example than the Volvo 1800 ES. The sportwagon is created by extending the roof line of the coupe straight back to meet a nearly vertical rear door. This idea was first expressed in volume by the MGB-GT, and more recently by the Vega Kamm-back wagon. Of course, the one-off builders fill exposition halls every year with cars based on this concept, but it is the Volvo which will make heads swivel everywhere.

While the expression "making a silk purse out of a sow's ear" might be a harsh oversimplification, the fact remains that the styling concept of the bubble-topped 1800 E coupe, whose greenhouse and tail fins were very much *de rigeur* when they were introduced ten years ago, have now gotten very long in the tooth. A major styling change was clearly in order at Goteborg. The engineers and stylists at Volvo have put it all together, coming up with the most visually exciting package to get off the boat from Sweden since the arrival of Anita Ekberg. The canny Swedes lucked out in another category, too. The ES, which looks fresh and new in 1972, is achieved essentially by sheet metal changes to the coupe, allowing the development costs normally associated with the introduction of a new model to be transferred directly to the profit account, much to the delight of the stockholders. Volvo's timing is right on also.

Low roof line and single chrome strip on side add to illusion of length although sportwagon is only 1.5 inches longer than coupe. Pressed steel wheels have chromed acorn nuts, need no other adornment.

The impression is of a $10,000 interior in a $6,000 car. Complete instrumentation sweeps across dash. Recess around base of gear selector serves to store loose articles, as does glove box immediately rearward.

Addition of straightback roof line makes a new car out of venerable Volvo 1800 styling. Liberally sized rear window provides unexcelled vision rearward. Louvers ahead of filler cap opening extract air from interior.

The considerable tumblehome of both side and rear glass coupled with the low roofline are the focal points of contemporary station wagon styling.

This is complemented by a new grille for the '72 models. The outstanding visual impression is further enhanced by the excellent overall finish and paint quality, a handsome dark green in the case of our test car.

What the sportwagon concept accomplishes is to retain sporting car driving pleasure and performance, especially handling, while providing enough cargo space for the couple whose recreational interests involve carrying more than the spare jump suit and mini-skirt which tax the luggage capacity of the average sports or GT car. We say couple, but there are rear seats in the sportwagon, and they actually provide more room than the rear seats in the coupe. But with the front seats back far enough to provide comfortable leg room for the front seat passengers there's only about six inches of rear seat knee room and we'd like to meet the adult who could ride comfortably in the back of the sportwagon for more than a hundred yards.

With the rear seat back folded down, though, there is 35 cubic feet of cargo space available — plus room under the rear seat back for such things as attache cases. There's room, for example, for a pair of golf bags with carts as well as enough luggage to contain clothes for a weekend at anyone's country club. Or, an outboard motor, gas cans, tackle box, and rod cases. Or a couple of the small trail bikes whose handles fold down. Or a couple of air tanks, wet suits, and the rest of the scuba gear. Very much the thing for types who carry their toys to the playground.

Access to the rear is gained through an amply fixed all-glass swing-up rear door. Only the horizontal defroster wires obstruct potential thieves' view of the contents. To counter this Volvo has provided auxiliary covered storage compartments on either side of the spare tire compartment which can be used to store the things "which normally collect in the back of a station wagon." It

makes for a very satisfactory arrangement.

In addition to cargo space the interior of the sportwagon provides a level of comfort, quality, and luxury well beyond the standards of its peer group. First of all there are the unmatched Volvo seats, upholstered in real leather and capable of enough adjustments to boggle the mind. In addition to front and back and up and down (this requires tools) the back rake is infinitely adjustable and there is a handwheel on the inboard side of the seat back which can be rotated to vary the degree of lumbar support. Add to this the superb countouring, particularly in the area of leg support and you have a combination virtually unmatched in the industry.

Along with this the Volvo seat belt concept is worthy of mention. The lap and shoulder belts are one continuous piece on which the moveable latch slides freely. An inertia reel mounted at shoulder height retracts the whole belt when out of use and pulls it up tight. However the driver's belt won't often be

out of use, for a switch mounted on the fixed latch which is between the seats keeps a bright red light on the dash illuminated until the driver's belt is fastened. There's no reason not to use the belt either — the lap belt tension can be readily adjusted with one hand when it is fastened, and the inertia device will allow the shoulder belt to extend so that the wearer can lean forward freely but will lock tight if tension is applied abruptly.

Volvo has also considered the driver's extremities. Steering wheel and gear shift are easily reached from a comfortable driving position. Stalk controls for the wipers, headlight dimmer and overdrive can be operated without removing hands from the wheel. Pedals are easily reached although we would like to see a little less clutch travel or a little higher clutch pedal. We do like the rest for the left foot, but when the seat is far enough back to have the right foot comfortable on the throttle and the left foot comfortable on its rest it becomes difficult to reach far enough to depress

Directional control on hard braking is excellent as four wheel discs bring Sportwagon to a stop from 60 mph in 146 feet.

the clutch all the way.

Once nestled into the driving position — and nestled is the word, since the deep seating position puts the bottom of the windows just below eye level, the driver is confronted with a comprehensive and attractive array of white letter on black dial instruments. The tach, redlined at 6000 rpm, and the 120 mph speedometer are separated by a pair of vertical temperature gauges — one for oil and one for water. An ammeter, fuel gauge and clock are centered on the dash, with a lower row of switches for headlights, wipers, rear window demister and instrument light rheostat.

Although it's pleasant to sit and admire the luxury, driving is still what it's all about, and the driving experience of the sportwagon is indeed enjoyable. In spite of certain detoxing changes re-

intermediate gears.

Mid-range speeds in the intermediate gears are accompanied by an easily noticeable engine noise which is amplified by a rattling vibration emanating from the shift lever. Engine noise reaches a peak as the red line is approached, but this can be readily alleviated in fourth gear by a flick of the overdrive switch which drops the revs 20 percent — and helps the gas mileage by an equal amount as the effective final drive ratio is reduced from 3.24 to 2.6 to one.

The use of the overdrive, which operates only when the top gear is engaged, allows a closer spacing in the four speed gearbox. The effect is quite noticeable in town driving, where there is enough overlap between gears that the engine never wants to lug.

Possibly the greatest virtue of the

Terminal understeer would be result of pressing much harder than this. Test driver considered this a very flat cornering car, was amazed at amount of roll shown in photo.

quired to conform to '72 emission standards, performance is still brisk, although a bit buzzy in the mid-range. Power comes from the inline pushrod four B20F engine on which a sophisticated fuel injection was introduced in 1970.

The Bosch fuel injection has an electronic computer which monitors and controls the flow of the air/fuel mixture to the cylinders. Information on air temperature, air pressure, water temperature, throttle position and engine speed is received and integrated by the computer where it is transformed into a set of operating signals for the electric fuel pump, the separate fuel injectors for each cylinder, and the air intake system. At the same time, automatic compensation is provided for changes in altitude, air temperature, and coolant temperature.

Changes required to meet emission requirements include revised ignition timing and a reduced compression ratio (from 10.5 down to 8.7 to one) which will allow the engine to subsist on 91 octane lead-free fuel. These changes have resulted in a drop of five horsepower to a net SAE value of 112, compared to last year when the figure was quoted at 130 SAE gross. The drop in power is accompanied by a commensurate drop in performance — with 65 more pounds of weight to haul than the coupe, the sportwagon gets through

Live rear axle does a good job of keeping rear wheels on the ground in this situation, but look at negative camber assumed by front wheel.

the quarter mile in 17.2 seconds at 80 mph. While certainly nothing to sneeze at, these values are about half a second and three mph slower than those obtained with the coupe in 1971. In spite of being a little slower through the quarter, there is a solid feeling of power from about 3000 rpm on up to the 6000 rpm red line, and the torque curve allows the engine to pull well through the

sportwagon, and a confirmation that the name is honestly applied, is the fact that although it looks like a station wagon, it still handles like a sports car. The sportwagon carries the same suspension as the coupe — A-arms with coil springs, hydraulic shocks, and stabilizer bar in front and a live rear axle with coil springs and tube shocks. Another plus toward good handling is contributed by the nice fat 185/70 HR 15 tires mounted on 5½ in. wheels. The elevated roof line has raised the vertical center of gravity only incrementally, and the longitudinal center of gravity and spring rates are unchanged from the

From the front it's a very familiar looking Volvo with exception of grille insert which is restyled for 1972. Low center of gravity and wide track suggest a good handling car.

Spare tire storage below rear deck also provides anti-collision buffer behind gas tank. Extra wells on either side of spare are used to store loose articles.

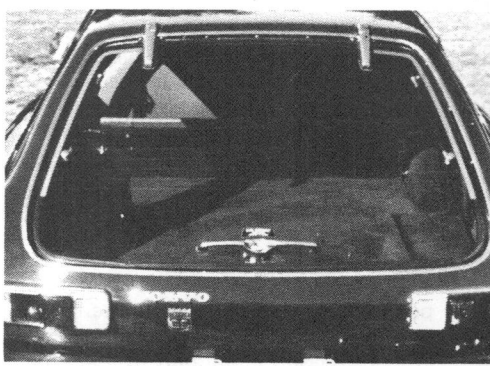

Rear window is single glass without metal rim, with handle and hinges set into solid glass. Piston dampers at each side hold window open. Horizontal lines are defroster wires.

coupe. Consequently the sportwagon will generate the same G-forces as the coupe — both on the skid pad and when squirted up a twisting canyon road, as we demonstrated to our satisfaction on several occasions while we were living with the car.

Having been designed for eleven years of service in a country where the paving ends at the city limits, all Volvos have a superlative ride, and the sportwagon is no exception to this tradition. The driver is subjected to very little feeling of any rough surface, and minor irregularities — such as expansion strips on concrete highways — go equally unnoticed. Pitch control is particularly good, and the sportwagon will waltz at speed through dips which find domestic cars slowing to a crawl.

Steering is by a cam and roller type with a nice tight 3 ¼ turns lock to lock. While control and effort are precise and modest when inputs are desired, there is a tendency toward unannounced directional changes when proceeding in a straight line which at least will tend to keep a driver's attention riveted to the road ahead.

Volvo was one of the first companies to offer dual circuit brakes, and their system is still an industry leader in the safety aspect. Each brake circuit operates on both front wheels and one rear wheel, with the result that either circuit alone will provide 80 percent of the total braking effectiveness in the event of failure of the other circuit. A power assist multiplies the input to the pedal by a factor of 2.7 for application to the four discs. With this degree of retarding force applied to the fat Goodyear radial tires stops are made from 60 mph in 146 feet at a deceleration rate of .82 G. Even with solid discs the sportwagon readily passes our fade test consisting of a series of 'panic' stops from high speeds.

Proper attention has been given to driver and passenger comfort as well as to driving performance. The interior finish materials provide a sense of luxury, which was complemented in our test car by a superlative AM-FM stereo radio which filled the car with music from the two rear speakers.

Since the southernmost part of Sweden is further north than the northernmost part of Maine, a Volvo's heating system has to be extremely powerful. To cope with American summers adequate provision must be made for proper ventilation and removal of stale air. The thermostatically controlled system is operated by three levers below the dash which regulate the temperature and distributes air between defrosting and the floor level. Stale air is automatically exhausted through vents below the rear windows, and the system is normally so effective that the two speed blower is

not normally required to be used.

We feel that the 1800 ES sportwagon will appeal to three market groups — most importantly to those who want sports car driving and handling characteristics but also need the extra storage space, secondly to those who are seeking Volvo quality and are attracted to the fresh contemporary styling and finally to those wanting that difference in styling and quality at less than a luxury car price.

Unfortunately, however, the price

does border on luxurious. The POE West Coast price with radio and dealer prep runs over $5400. Add automatic transmission, air conditioning, tax and license and there goes most, if not all, of a $6000 bill. Of course it will last for eleven years, and $500 per year with $500 residual salvage value doesn't sound quite as bad. At least it's a financial problem not too many shoppers will have an opportunity to worry about. Volvo says that only 1657 sportwagons will be imported into the United States in 1972. (How they established this figure we couldn't begin to guess.) At that rate they will all be sold by the middle of May. ●

If you think this looks busy wait till they put in the air conditioning! Nevertheless major engine components are accessible. Materials and finish inside engine compartment are unusually sanitary.

VOLVO 1800ES SPORTWAGON

SPECIFICATIONS AS TESTED

Engine. . . . . 121 cu in, ohv in-line 4
Bore & stroke . . . . 3.50 x 3.15 ins.
Compression ratio . . . . 8.7 to one
Horsepower . . . . 112 (SAE net) at 6000 rpm
Torque . . . . 115 lbs-ft at 3500 rpm
Transmission . . . . 4-speed, manual
Steering. . . . . 3.25 turns, lock to lock
                            31.5 ft, curb to curb
Brakes* . . . . disc front, disc rear
Suspension . . . . coil front, coil rear
Tires . . . . 185 x 70, HR15
Dimensions (ins.):

Wheelbase	96.5	Rear track	51.6
Length	172.6	Ground clearance	6.0
Width	66.9	Height	50.4
Front track	51.6	Weight	2610 lbs

Capacities:

Fuel	11.8 gals	Oil	4.1 qts
Coolant	10.0 qts	Trunk	35.0 cu ft

*Power assisted as tested

BASE PRICE OF CAR

(Excludes state and local taxes, license, dealer preparation and domestic transportation): $5150 at P.O.E. West Coast
Plus desirable options:
$ 213 AM-FM Stereo radio
$5363 TOTAL

ANTICIPATED DEPRECIATION

(Based on current Kelley Blue Book, previous equivalent model): N/A 1st yr. + N/A 2nd yr.

N/A—Not applicable

PERFORMANCE AND MAINTENANCE

Accleration: Gears:
   0-30 mph . . . . 2.9 secs. 1st
   0-45 mph . . . . 6.0 secs. 1st, 2nd
   0-60 mph . . . . 9.3 secs. 1-2-3
   0-75 mph . . . . 15.1 secs. 1-2-3
   0-¼ mile . . . . 17.2 secs. at 80 mph
Ideal cruise . . . . 80 mph
Top speed (est) . . . . 112 mph
Stop from 60 mph . . . . 146 ft
Average economy (city) . . . . 16.4 mpg
Average economy (country) . . . . 21.2 mpg
Fuel required . . . . Regular
Oil change (mos/miles) 6/6000
Lubrication (mos/miles) 6/6000
Warranty (mos/miles) . . . . 12/unlim.
Type tools required . . . . Metric
U.S. dealers . . . . 386 total

RATING

RATING	Excellent (91-100)	Good (81-90)	Fair (71-80)	Poor (60-70)
Brakes		86		
Comfort	94			
Cornering		86		
Details	89			
Finish	92			
Instruments	94			
Luggage	96			
Performance		85		
Quietness			80	
Ride		88		
Room		88		
Steering		85		
Visibility		90		
Overall		89		

A bold expression of the sportswagon theme

photos by John Plow

VOLVO 1800/ES

THIS month, we're combining two Volvos of distinctly different pretensions. Recently, the venerable 1800 series was updated with an astute bit of coachwork magic. The Swedes took this twelve-year-old design and gave it a totally new personality by stretching out the roofline, adding a huge window-hatch at the rear and named it the 1800ES (actually that 1800 is now largely erroneous . . . the engine displacement has long since been bumped up to two liters). As a basic concept, the sports-wagon idea as applied to the 1800ES is clever. You'll never be able to carry the same kind of loads as a "normal" station wagon, but the available space is still impressive. We were able to carry a fully

assembled bicycle with room to spare. If you're a golfer, two full-sized bags and their carts will fit in the rear with no trouble, too. As far as baggage is concerned, the space will take two passengers' luggage with ease. There is a rear seat of sorts in the ES, but it's best suited to the use of small children or medium-sized dogs. It's just too small for an adult, and we found that most times we left it folded down, allowing for full use of the 60-inch-long load bed. The feature that received most comment was the generously-sized rear window. It's so large that the handle has been installed right in the glass, and an added safety feature is that you cannot open this without the key. From the driver's spot you

can literally see the road right behind the car . . . in fact, the road less than *six feet* behind. This may not be wholly useful, but it inspires a lot of confidence. Of course, 70% of the window area is covered with electric defroster wires, assuring a clear view at all times.

The 1800 series first hit the road in 1960, and since that time the car has not been changed in any radical way. The engine has been enlarged, and a couple of years ago, fuel injection was added, along with minor body changes and some trim alterations. But the basic car is still very much as it was then: rather weighty with narrow windows and fairly limited visibility. In fact, the car has needed a new body design for the last three years. There are reasons

Up front the Volvo 1800 retains the basic appearance of the P1800 introduced in 1960

why Volvo hasn't seen fit to make any startling changes over the years, and this latest modification is the biggest since the car was introduced. The coupe version is still being offered alongside the ES at about $400 less, by the way, but given a choice, we'd opt for the ES . . . it just makes more sense from an appearance and practicality standpoint.

Our test ES was equipped with the optional Borg-Warner three-speed automatic transmission, and while we had preferred the manual version with overdrive, it was difficult for Volvo Canada to find one for us. The automatic works well, but soaks up some of the car's potential performance through the speed ranges. On a long drive, we noticed a few vagaries that were not annoying, just there, and in need of attention. At cruising speeds in the area of 60 to 70 mph, the ES tended to show a little "wander," particularly

in the side winds. Overall noise level was high for a car in the ES's $6,000 price bracket. This could be traced to the old, reliable B20 engine, working away at around 4,000 rpm, and a goodly part of this noise emanated from the overhead valves. The heating system was, as with all Volvos up to the task, but the ventilation left a little to be desired. Once the weather warmed up we found that the cockpit area became very hot, and the ventilation system couldn't keep up to the heat wave from the engine room.

Volvo is known for spending engineering time on good seats, and the buckets in the ES were no exception to this rule. They feel just right (though we found the black leather a trifle hot, preferring cloth-covered seats for all-year use) and for added comfort, you can set a lumbar control for lower back support. The ES can't be faulted

for the way it's put together. The interior has the "bank-vault" feeling, and the instrumentation is laid out so that you can see everything at a glance. In addition to the speedometer (120 mph) and matching tachometer (7000 rpm), there are neat white-on-black gauges for oil temperature, water temperature, fuel and clock. Warning lamps are included to tell you about alternator charge, handbrake, high beams, flashers and seatbelts. The steering wheel, as in other Volvos, seems over-large, with an outside diameter of over 16 inches. If a smaller, leather-rimmed wheel were substituted, we're sure the steering effort wouldn't be measurably increased.

Many manufacturers should study Volvo's inertia reel seat belts. They're easy to adjust, simple to snap on, and allow lots of movement. If all belts were as well designed as these, you'd

151

Simple, but amazingly successful

Huge steering wheel dominates

see many more people harnessed up while driving.

We didn't expect to set up any shattering times with the ES at Cayuga's Dragway Park because of a lag in the fuel metering system. Several times, the car would bog on the line, losing about 5/10 of a second. After much practice, we were almost able to cure this, and some of the times reflect the problem. Our best 0–60 time was 12.7 seconds with the worst 14.3. Through the quarter mile, we averaged 18.9 seconds, or 73 mph. Braking was the ES's long suit. We managed 171 feet from 75 mph and an impressive 124 from 60, and at no time did we feel any loss of pedal pressure or braking force. As tested, the ES weighed in at 2800

pounds (1410 pounds front, 1390 rear) which all adds up to almost neutral distribution, about 51/49%. We're certain that the ES automatic could easily make the 60 mark in under 12 seconds, given a fuel metering system in top-notch operating order.

The ES exhibits a tendency to lean heavily in tight bends, but the light positive steering, 185/70 radial ply tires, and almost 50/50 weight distribution go a long way to assisting enthusiastic driving.

There is another problem with noise level in the ES (we also noted it in the 145E, but to lesser extent). The fuel pump, mounted at the rear near the fuel tank, gives off a middle-pitched

hum that you cannot ignore at idle and low speeds. It does tend to vanish at higher speeds, wiped out, so to speak, by other operating sounds.

Price of the 1800ES is set at a base of $5800, so if you do buy one you'll see little change from $6000, and if you order a radio, automatic box and special styled wheels, the tag will be considerably over six grand. The ES falls into a category all its own, really, but looking at the car objectively, it's frankly a little dated. Judging by the attention we received from the general public while driving it, this will make little difference to potential buyers. In most every case, questioners thought it was an all-new car. Score another one for the Swedes.

Considerable understeer is evident

Bosch fuel injection helps engine pump out 125 hp.

technical data

VOLVO 1800 ES

SPECIFICATIONS

ENGINE
Location	front
No. of cylinders	four in line
Valve operation	pushrod operated overhead
Compression ratio	8.7:1
Carburetion	electronic fuel injection, computer under dash
Bore/Stroke	3.50 ins./3.15 ins.
Displacement	121 cu. ins. (1986 ccs)
Power	125 hp @ 6000 rpm

TRANSMISSION
No. of forward speeds	three, BW automatic
Gear ratios	1st—2.39; 2nd—1.45; 3rd—1.00; Rev.—2.09
Final drive	3.91:1

BRAKES
Front	discs 10.7 in. dia. power
Rear	discs 11.6 in. dia. power
Lining area, swept	38.8 sq. ins.

DIMENSIONS
Wheelbase	96.5 ins.
Track	front — 51.6 ins.
	rear — 51.6 ins.
Width	66.9 ins.
Height	50.4 ins.
Weight, as tested	2800 lbs. (51% front, 49% rear)
Fuel capacity	10 gals.
Tires	185/70 HR radial ply Goodyear

STEERING
Type	Cam and roller
Turning circle	31 ft. — 6 ins.

SUSPENSION
Front	Independent, wishbones, ball joints, rubber mounted control arms, Anti-sway bar, coil springs, telescopic shocks.
Rear	Solid axle, longitudinal rubber mounted arms, torque rods. Rubber mounted transverse track rod.

CALCULATED DATA

Braking distances in feet: average of 3 stops

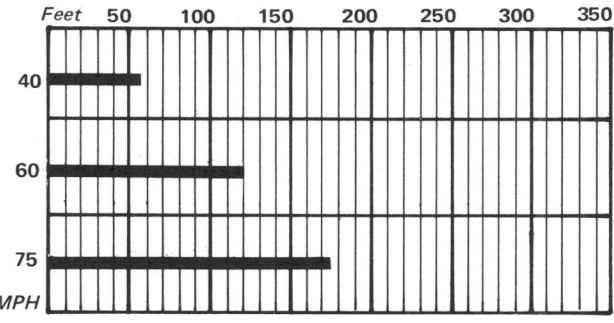

Acceleration in seconds

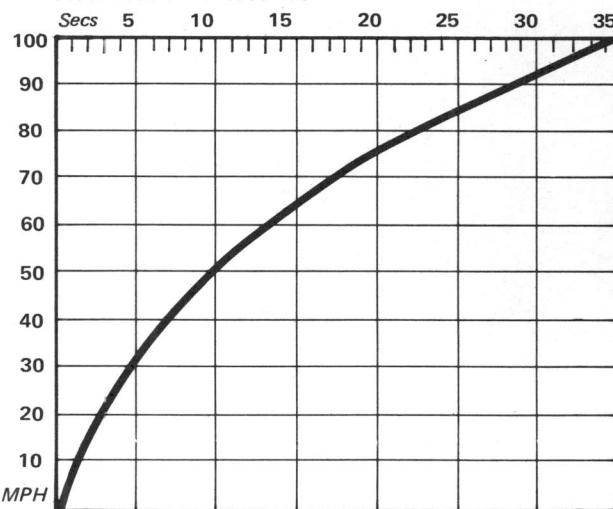

BRAKING
75-0	176 feet
60-0	120 feet
40-0	57 feet
Fuel consumption	22.3 mpg
Quarter mile	18.0 secs./74 mph.

ACCELERATION
0-40	7.0 secs.
0-60	13.5 secs.
0-80	22.8 secs.

SUGGESTED RETAIL PRICE

$6,185.00*
(manual trans. version $6,125.00)*

*Standard equipment includes inertia reel seat belts, rear window demister, lockable console, map light.

SAINT's Alive

It was Roger Moore alias *The Saint*'s favourite car in the 1960s, but what's a Volvo P1800 like for today's classic car-buying heroes? Chris Horton investigates. Pictures: Julian Mackie

The Swedish-built P1800S, showing the car's inspired styling and ingenious details

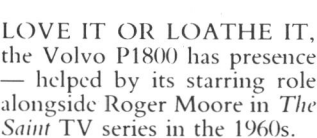

Right: Tony Whitton and his two P1800 Volvos, an 1800S is the background and an 1800ES in front

LOVE IT OR LOATHE IT, the Volvo P1800 has presence — helped by its starring role alongside Roger Moore in *The Saint* TV series in the 1960s.

And despite the fact that Volvo now claims to have thrown the rule book out of the window, there probably won't be anything quite like it again.

For all its wonderfully over-the-top *Buck Rogers* looks, though, the P1800 makes a remarkably practical classic sports car. A simple, four-cylinder pushrod engine drives through a four-speed-plus-overdrive gearbox to a conventional, coil-sprung rear axle — there's little a half-competent DIY mechanic couldn't fix.

But nothing in this world is perfect, of course, and the

YOUR GUIDE . . .

In this month's *Fact File* we tell you all you need to know about buying a Volvo P1800. Beginning on this page we tell you exactly what faults to look for, with a visual checklist on page 28, plus advice on prices, and an interview with an expert on the cars on page 29. And, on page 32, read what *The Motor* had to say about the Volvo P1800 when it was new in 1962 . . .

P1800 *does* suffer dramatically from body rust. In theory it's no worse than most of its contemporaries, and a lot better than many other now-desirable classics, but then with only some 30,000 built it doesn't have the same replacement-panel back-up as, say, an MGB or a Jaguar Mark II. Few pattern panels are available and, although you can still get certain body panels from Volvo itself, prices are discouragingly high.

So . . . examine a potential purchase very carefully for corrosion.

Don't worry too much about mechanical condition — just about anything is repairable there — but keep firmly in mind that body repairs could be expensive even if technically easy.

Starting at the sharp end, you should look carefully at both front wings. Expect rust around and above the headlights, and also in a vertical line from top to bottom just behind the front wheels. There should be a splash panel inside each wing here but if it's disintegrated (sometimes if it hasn't) it will encourage rust to burst through from inside.

There's also a box-section running along the top of each inner front wing and this can corrode badly. You can only assess its true condition by taking off the outer panels, but you can get some idea by crouching down and peering up into the wheelarch with a torch.

EIGHT FASCINATING FACTS ABOUT THE VOLVO P1800

1 The first cars were assembled in Britain by Jensen in West Bromwich, using bodies built by Pressed Steel at Linwood, Scotland; quality-control was so awful, though, that production was transferred to Sweden in 1964.

2 The car cost about the same in the 1960s as an E-type Jaguar, and was shrewdly marketed at the time to suggest it represented far better value for money. That might appear optimistic now, in view of current E-type values, but imagine how much the Jag will cost to restore . . .

3 Tyres are an unusual size — 165 section on 15in wheels (with different stud patterns on the later E and ES models) — and are becoming more difficult to find and correspondingly expensive. Wider-section tyres like those used on Jaguars won't fit inside the wheelarches.

4 Despite its enduring popularity in the UK, the P1800 was never as fashionable in Sweden, where one car in three was a Volvo (albeit a saloon of some sort). There, it was

always more chic to be seen in something like an 'exotic' MGB . . .

5 There was a glassfibre-bodied P1900 sports car built in the mid-1950s, but Volvo management dropped it because it was afraid its poor quality would damage Volvo's reputation. Only 63 were built — most were destroyed.

6 Although Volvo never offered a convertible P1800, just two were built in the early 1960s by British coachbuilder Harold Radford for a Hull Volvo dealer. Where are they now?

7 The P1800 uses almost exactly the same running gear as the Volvo 120 'Amazon' saloon, so mechanical restoration is no problem. Relatively few body panels are available, however, and most of those are very expensive, so you should avoid very seriously corroded cars.

8 If your car needs a pair of headlamp rims don't bother with the genuine Volvo items at £90 a pair; Vanden Plas 1300 rims are much cheaper — and fit perfectly!

VOLVO P1800 CHRONOLOGY

The P1800 was introduced in 1961 with a 1.8-litre, twin SU carburettor engine. When production of the P1800 was transferred to Sweden the car was renamed P1800S, 'S' standing for Sweden. These early cars have chassis numbers up to 6000, plus red-only rear lights, opening rear quarter-lights and little Jensen badges on rear window pillars — and, of course, those distinctive, split 'cow-horn' front bumpers which everyone now wants . . .

In 1968 the mechanically similar 2-litre engine became standard equipment. The last 2-litre P1800S was built in 1969 and, at the end of that year, the 1800E arrived, now with a 2-litre Bosch fuel-injected engine.

The 1800ES came in 1971 with the same 2-litre fuel-injected engine, but with its two-door coupé body reworked as a stylish three-door sporty hatchback in the Reliant Scimitar idiom. This model had a Hella electrical system instead of the Lucas circuit used on all earlier cars. All P1800 production ceased in 1973.

Left: Early, silver painted dash. Right: Rugged and dependable four-cylinder engine

Wings *are* available, but they'll set you back about £240 each and they are difficult to fit properly — ideally the windscreen has to come out and you have to make an invisible join on a highly conspicuous flat panel. It's also quite tricky to align the wings correctly round the headlamp openings.

The nose of the car is inevitably susceptible to knocks and bumps, of course, although corrosion shouldn't be a problem. Bonnets last well too, although sometimes the hinges seize and tear out of the metal. Secondhand replacements are available.

The doors rust at their bottoms like most others, but the really bad news is that you can't get replacement skins, only complete panels at a huge £315 each! Below the doors, the sills suffer rust too. If it's just the outer panel there's no great problem, but more often than not you must replace the complete inner section.

This takes a lot more fixing and, needless to say, costs more, so lift the carpets and check where the floorpan meets the inner sills. Incidentally, there should be two

VOLVO P1800 — WHOSE MASTERPIECE

The Volvo P1800's styling has an intriguing story: Volvo asked Ghia, an Italian design and coachbuilding company, to tender a design for a new Volvo sports car to replace the unsuccessful P1900 roadster, in April 1957. The job was given to its chief designer, Pietro Frua, an accomplished stylist who had designed the first Vespa scooter and several Maseratis.

However, he was also an impetuous man and, while working on the car, parted company with Ghia to set up his own studio. He then tendered his *own* design proposal, to the fury of his old Ghia boss Luigi Segre.

In the end *neither* was chosen, the Volvo board instead opting for a design by one Pelle Petterson, the son of a Swedish engineering consultant.

Three prototypes were built in Frua's Italian workshop, Petterson junior supervising the shape while his father developed the internal structure.

The later ES estate was the work of another Italian design consultant, Sergio Coggiola, who continues to build prototypes for Volvo today . . .

Immaculate P1800S — these Swedish-made cars are, some say, better made

Above: Fuel injection replaced carbs on last cars

Left: later cars, like P1800ES, had black plastic, fake wood dash finish

THE P1800 OWNER

Gillian and Tony Whitton, who own the cars featured here, found their concours-winning 1800S in a Nissen hut! Advertised in a local paper, the Volvo was sound but one headlamp was hanging out and the carburettor was flooded with water!

Two hundred and fifty pounds changed hands, but that was only the start of an 18-month rebuild and finished with a 20-coat respray. Gillian estimates the cost at £5000.

Most expensive was the rechroming, involving many parts, and new items like window rubbers. One part which proved incredibly elusive was an armrest in tan. By a stroke of luck the Whittons had bought one before they ever saw the car from a Volvo dealer's sale.

Earlier this year the blue 1800ES joined the Whitton's double-figure collection of Volvos; with its 1986cc fuel-injected engine it makes an interesting comparison to the older car. Gillian finds it less economical than the coupé, which can average 36mpg.

With an active part in the Volvo Owners' Club the Whittons have a very full diary and many friends, but even they can't explain why they have so many cars.

"A lot of people think we're totally bananas", says Gillian.

vertical seams visible on each outer sill, and their absence points to varying quantities of filler. Check the sills from underneath, too, and make sure that the outriggers which carry the jacking points are sound.

Moving back, expect to find rust where the inner and outer rear wheelarches meet, then have a good look at the boot area. Rust here stems from collected water in the channel round the boot-lid aperture.

There should be two drain holes with rubber tubes to lead the water safely back on to the road, but these become blocked and/or dislodged, and water finds its way into the boot to wreak havoc in some dark and forgotten corner. Rust in the aperture channel should be fairly obvious, but look carefully at the floor and the vertical stay for the lock mechanism — this often breaks away completely.

The boot lid itself often rots through at its folded-over rear edge for much the same reason, and the petrol filler

flap is a big problem. Once again there's a drain hole — often blocked — but usually you'll find the lid has rusted off around the hinge. This is a very difficult area to tidy up properly, of course, and the problem is compounded if a poorly sealing flap has allowed water into the fuel tank. New flaps have been unavailable for many years, and good secondhand ones are hard to find, so check it carefully.

If that's all the bad news, the good news is that, mechanically, the car is almost indestructible. Engines are the same from the start to the finish of production, and although the capacity was increased in 1968 from 1800cc to 2-litre (coinciding with the fitting of Bosch fuel injection) there are many common parts.

These engines can cover enormous mileages and, even then, simply wear out rather than breaking suddenly. It's usually the valve guides which wear first, but if the unit is not noisy or smoky the chances are it's fit for duty. Early cars had

a pair of SU carburettors, but the Bosch L-Jetronic fuel injection system on later examples shouldn't present any problems either.

Gearboxes are either four-speed manual units with Laycock overdrive or three-speed Borg Warner automatics (the latter rare in the UK). Both are largely trouble-free but it obviously pays to ensure that they work.

Check manual boxes for jumping out of gear and bearing noise (both of which will have been caused by abuse rather than any inherent fault); check that the overdrive engages and disengages, or that an automatic changes gear as it should.

Back axles are robust too, but it'll pay to listen for grumbling bearings that might be the result of running with little or no oil — in which case you'll possibly find rear brake drums full of oil too.

Which brings us to one of the few mechanical snags of the P1800. As with many classic cars, the brakes suffer from lack of use. Because the

P1800ES has a very useful, opening glass hatchback

Below: Publicity material showed P1800S as a roomy car for luggage, but ES, with useful load area straps, is better for cargo

Check for rust around front lamp surrounds

Rust can also build up on the seams of inner panels

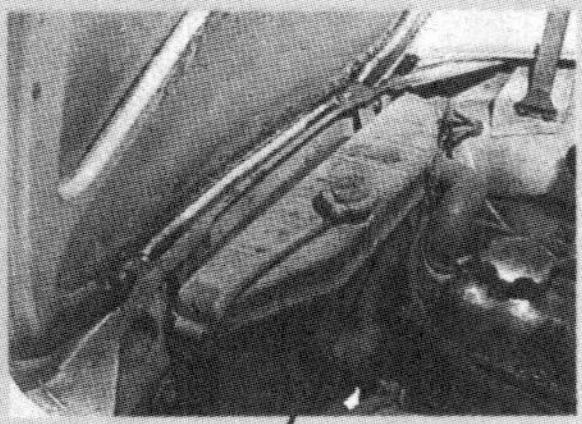

Split and cracked seats can be costly to repair

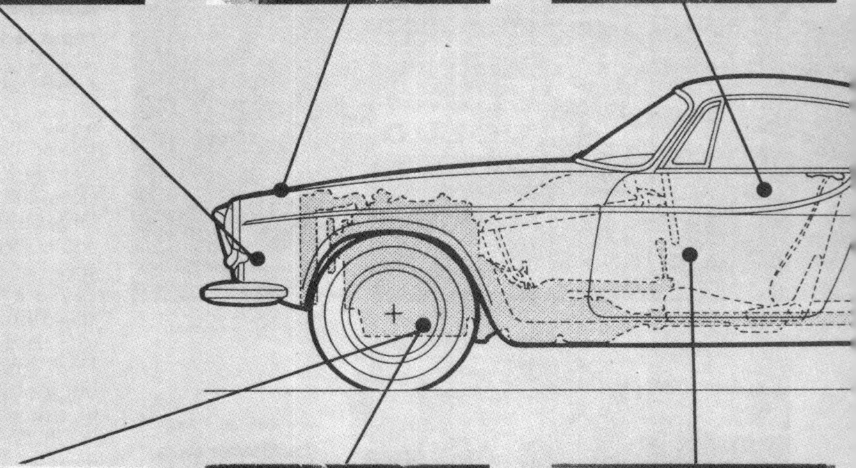

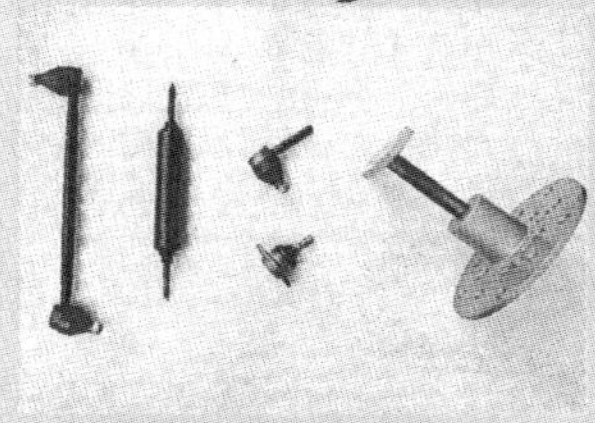

Specialists offer repair kits for the steering

Chassis leg rusts, where steering box is fixed

Split door-pulls/armrests are a common problem

VOLVO P1800 PRICES

Expect to pay quite a lot for even a tatty P1800 — *any* car today is in high demand. They can change hands for as little as £600, but that sort of car will need lots of tender loving care to get it safely back on the road and won't have an MoT — not a legal one, anyway . . .

£1000 should buy you a legit MoT but plenty of rust; double that and you'll get a car that's tatty in places but with a long MoT and maybe some road tax — generally sound for, say, a 24-year-old car.

You'll pay £5500 for a *really good* car, albeit one that probably still won't win a *concours d'elegance* competition, and from there upwards they are worth what you're prepared to pay. Only 30,000 were built so it's a seller's market, but supply keeps pace with demand and cars are always available if you're prepared to wait and look around. Just remember that the mileage on the clock is about as relevant as the colour it's painted, and that condition — particularly of the body — is what *really* matters. Don't buy the first one you see because you're scared it's the *only* one you'll see!

front discs and pads are so big (they are virtually identical to those on the big Volvo 240 estate) and because the 1800 is a relatively light car, the pads wear very slowly. This lack of movement between pad, piston and caliper causes every-

Below: P1800S is no racing car, but has reasonable 'go'

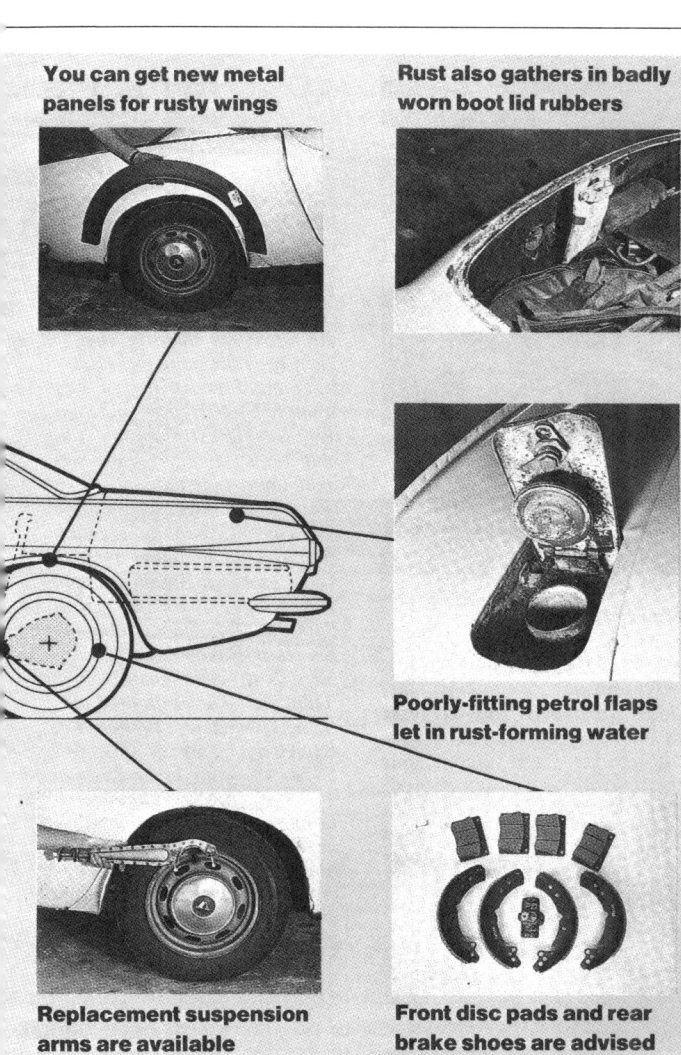

You can get new metal panels for rusty wings

Rust also gathers in badly worn boot lid rubbers

Poorly-fitting petrol flaps let in rust-forming water

Replacement suspension arms are available

Front disc pads and rear brake shoes are advised

A rare Radford convertible — where is it today?

WHICH P1800 TO CHOOSE?

The P1800's rarity means you can't afford to be too choosy. It's more important to get a good body shell than worry about which model it is or what colour it's painted.

None of the cars has a specific weakness. Often the later examples of a classic are better than earlier ones; the early 1970s 1800ES hatchback is undoubtedly more practical but that's no reason to worry if you can only find an early car.

It's said the Swedes were never happy with the quality of the early Pressed Steel/Jensen-built cars but, a quarter of a century on, there's no appreciable difference between UK and Swedish models. Plus, of course, there's more cachet with those early cars' distinctive 'cow-horn' front bumpers.

THE P1800 MAN

Tony Barrett has a thing about Volvos. His daily transport, a battered left-hand-drive 140 estate with a raised rear roof, once saw service with the Swedish post office — it has more than 560,000km on the clock . . . What else would the proprietor of a respected Volvo specialist drive?

South Service, Tony's company, has operated from a railway arch under Stamford Brook tube station in West London for a decade and, although dealing mostly with Amazons and 240s, he clearly has a great knowledge of and affection for the P1800.

"They are wonderful cars," he says. "Dead easy to work on, and it's only really the bodywork that presents any real problems . . . and even then it usually looks worse than it is.

"They are straightforward to 'MoT' once the rust is sorted out, and provided people take the trouble to look for a good one, I think they make excellent first classics.

"Spares are expensive, I'll admit, but at least the stuff *is* available, and there aren't many classics going back to the early 1960s about which you can say that.

"And if it's any consolation," he continues with a laugh, "you'd have to pay the same for spares in Sweden".

Tony concedes, though, that spares are inevitably increasingly hard to find, and it seems the wise long-term P1800 owner will be buying now with an eye to the future.

I still stock 1200 different lines for the P1800 so I can get hold of most people's requirements."

And Tony has one VITAL piece of advice for anyone searching for a P1800. "Don't be taken in simply by the looks of the thing and ignore rust. I know it's easier said than done, especially if it's been tarted up a bit for sale, but look for rot in all the places we've talked about and do a sort of running cost analysis as you go along.

"The state of the running gear doesn't really matter — that's as cheap and easy as you'll find anywhere, but make sure you don't buy a pile of rust. And watch out for that steering box!"

thing to seize, and then the disc finishes up with an uneven wear pattern, covered in rust or with big 'tramlines' all over it.

All the parts you need for a full overhaul are available, so it's an irritation rather than a

major problem, but it'll add to the cost of getting a neglected car back on the road.

It also pays you to make sure the brake servo works properly. If you're a stickler for originality the *bad* news is that the early-type Girling servo is unobtainable; but the good news is that there's a perfectly adequate alternative. And if you plan to do your own servicing, budget for a special puller for the combined rear hubs/brake drums. You can get them off without one, but they are easily damaged and expensive to renew.

The suspension is one of the best for the DIY mechanic. The steering system is good too and, even if the box itself is worn, you can easily replace it with a good secondhand unit (a new one could cost you well over £300!). One thing you must watch for, though, is

THE VOLVO & THE SAINT

The Volvo P1800 owes its TV fame, curiously enough, to Jaguar.

When planning to bring Leslie Charteris's vigilante do-gooder to the small screen, producer Robert Baker and backer Lew Grade wanted to give the hero the very latest, most exciting, sports car to go buccaneering in. That was in 1961, and the Jaguar E-type had just been launched; what better than the latest British sports car for an exciting new British TV series?

But Jaguar wasn't interested, saying it didn't need the publicity and that it could sell every car it could make anyway. So the producers turned to the *second* most exciting-looking new sports car of the year, the Volvo P1800. Seizing the chance, Volvo sent a sparkling white car over within the week. And that's why the most British of heroes drove a Swedish car in over 100 TV episodes.

Jaguar had learnt its lesson by 1977 — it was eager to supply a white XJS for *The Return of the Saint*, starring Ian Ogilvy.

Above: Intricate rear lights and badge are clever touches

the carpets may have seen better days, but it's a robust, hard-wearing passenger cabin.

Headlinings last well, but you'll probably find at least one of the combined door-pull/armrest assemblies is split and possibly a similar problem with the top of the facia just below the windscreen: if so you'll have to look for good secondhand items.

corrosion of the chassis leg to which the steering box is mounted. This will, of course, be less of a problem on cars with leaky engines and steering boxes, but can easily make an otherwise sound-looking car an absolute deathtrap.

On cars built before 1966 there's also a risk that the pressed-steel axle-locating links will have rusted through, but this is not so terminal as that steering box problem. Replacement arms *are* available, and later cars have a more robust, troublefree rod arrangement.

The leather seats split and wear on all but the best-preserved cars (you can repair them, of course, at a price) and

THE *ONLY* CLUB TO JOIN!

There's only one club catering for *all* Volvos. For more details write to Mrs Suzanne Groves at 90 Down Road, Merrow, Guildford, Surrey GU1 2PX, enclosing a stamped, addressed, envelope.

Perhaps it's time some enterprising souls got together and formed a club specifically for the P1800. YOUR CLASSIC will be happy to publicise the club if anybody wants to give it a try.

SPECIALISTS

Don't expect to find P1800 specialists under every railway arch, but you can take heart from the fact that, if it's available from Volvo in Sweden, you can go into your local Volvo dealer and order it.

That said, you'll be doing the classic car industry (not to mention your bank balance) a lot more favours if you buy from Tony Barrett — and your Volvo dealer certainly won't be able to sell you the good secondhand alternatives that Tony can supply.

Tony's company, South Service, can be found at Arch 162, Stamford Brook, London W6, telephone 01-741 3300/ 5500; and he also has a base in Somerset from which he supplies mostly secondhand items. That address is Unit 48, Fox's Mill, Tonedale, Wellington, Somerset, telephone 082 347 6858.

An alternative supplier in London is Chris Hart in Putney (01-788 2406); and if you live in Essex, Kent or Sussex, give Amazon UK a try; they are on Rochester (0634) 290789.

Window winders are tough, but don't expect great things of the door locks (some form of extra security is a very good idea on a car as stealable as this). Make sure that the windscreen wipers work smoothly; the mechanism can seize, and it's the devil's own job to get at.

Cast an eye over the instrument panel too. All the gauges should be repairable, but just make sure that they're all there and that the whole panel hasn't been hacked about to fit a radio. And yes, the tachometer is probably wildly inaccurate!

Either of the P1800 models is supremely stylish, but they are *both* practical and easy to maintain

The Ultimate Volvo

The proud owner. This view shows just how narrow the windscreen actually is.

When Brandon Smith of East Dulwich bought his Volvo 1800ES for £2500 in February 1983 he saw the new acquisition as, for him, the ultimate Volvo. He was already the proud owner of a two-door Amazon, which itself had replaced an Amazon estate, so was definitely no stranger to the strong Swedish marque.

Although not by any means perfect, the car was certainly very presentable (provided one didn't look too closely at the black sills) and four years of largely trouble-free motoring then followed during which the car visited Germany, Cornwall and Wales. In fact it was while returning from Wales that the car suffered it's only major breakdown, when late on a Bank Holiday Monday the fuel pump failed. The AA couldn't locate a replacement so that journey ended on the back of a Relay transporter. Various running repairs were required including a new stainless steel exhaust, brake caliper overhaul, a rear suspension rebuild (the need for which was discovered when the low rear end made it difficult to load the car on to the AA transporter) and, of course, the usual oil and air filters.

The decision to restore the car was taken for two reasons. It was mainly because, while looking underneath one day, Brandon spotted severe rot in the front crossmember. Probably because the member is 'buried' behind a selection of steering rods, idlers and the like the rot hadn't been spotted during the previous MoT test but Brandon reckoned, quite rightly, that the car was structurally unsafe. Additionally, his two now-teenage children were beginning to find the ES's very 2+2 accommodation less than satisfactory. So the car was taken off the road and work began . . . .

The Rebuild

Like most restorations, this one started with Brandon, unaware of quite how much work was going to be involved, stripping out all the interior trim, seats, carpets and so on. The glass also came out at this stage. Particular care was taken with the rear screen/tailgate which is unobtainable. This lot was stored in the loft at home. When it was time to refit, Brandon regretted that he hadn't taken the trouble to label parts or even sort them according to where they'd come from.

Brandon knew that the sills were getting very ragged but was relieved to find, when the outers were cut away (which also involved removing the bottom rear corners of the front wings), that the quite complex inner sill structure was still sound. This area is difficult to repair and complete sills cost around £140 each. Surface rust was cleaned off and the whole lot painted in red oxide. Off came the rear wings, too, but not until the new ones had been bought, so that Brandon knew exactly where to cut.

Volvo parts availability is superb and everything Brandon needed was readily available but, as we've just seen, some parts, particularly body panels and some other '1800 only' items, are very expensive. Having been involved with Volvos for some years Brandon knew this, so wasn't that surprised when he learnt that the rear wings were £318 each, the rear panel £239 and even the outer sill panels were £35 each. Most of the parts needed came from Tony Barrett who specialises in new and secondhand parts for older Volvos; contact him on 081-741 7500 or 0823 666858.

While he was in a spending mood, Brandon also invested £120 in a small Clarke MIG welder. He'd no experience of welding but was sure that, with practice and patience, he'd be able to tackle much of the panelwork himself. Many sheets of steel and

Rear view. The once-piece glass tailgate is certainly distinctive!

Under the bonnet everything is as it should be. The fuel-injection gear takes up a lot of space. Unlike the Lucas PI, Bosch injection is generally reliable although it's beyond the scope of DIY repair.

bottles of gas later he felt confident enough to start putting pieces on to the car, although as we'll see, he started with the easy bits.

Rubber-based undersealant covered the entire underbody and, as usual, it had flaked off in places which, of course, promotes corrosion (water gets trapped behind it) rather than prevents it. There were numerous small and some not so small holes, both rear inner wheelarches needed repair and the outrigger ends all needed replacing. Brandon spent many dirty hours scraping off all the old undersealant using the time-honoured 'scraper and hot air gun' method. Once this was done and using his new-found welding skill, Brandon was able to carry out all the repairs needed to the floor and fit new outriggers. These again came from Tony Barrett. The new outer sills were also fitted at this stage.

Next it was time to look at fitting the rear wings and rear panel. This had deliberately been left till now because he reckoned it would be the hardest part of the whole job. Before welding in new panels, however, Brandon stripped the paintwork off and took the car back to bare metal. It was while doing this that he found something he wished he hadn't; the offside front wing, which he thought was perfectly sound, was a replacement which had been fitted badly. 'Modifications' had been carried out to the rest of that side and, with the rear wing and sill positioned correctly, the door wouldn't fit! It appeared that the car had been accident-damaged at some time. Although sturdy in most respects, the 1800 shell can distort if given a nasty front-end shunt and rectification is often tricky.

Brandon recognised that curing this was really beyond the capabilities of a beginner like himself so called in professional help. The car was transported down to sunny Rochester where Volvo restoration specialists Amazon UK are located (Tel: 0634 290789). Before the car left, Brandon posi-

With its square-backed GTE bodywork Brandon Smith's Volvo 1800ES is an example of the 1800 family's last variant. The first, the P1800, was launched in May 1961 in Sweden, British supplies starting in October. This used mainly Volvo Amazon saloon mechanical components clothed in the familiar coupe bodyshell which was soon to become world-famous as 'The Saint's Car'. The shell was made in Britain by the Pressed Steel Co at Linwood. Not only this but the P1800 was originally assembled in Britain, too, by Jensen at their West Bromwich factory. Many Amazon components (around 50% total content at first), including brakes, carburettors, overdrive units and some electrics, were already sourced from the UK, so the decision to buy British bodyshells and assemble them into complete cars here perhaps isn't that surprising. The major components were shipped to the UK alongside complete Amazons.

Volvo became dissatisfied with the quality of what was coming out of Britain, however, and production was switched to Sweden in March/April 1963 where, initially, the 1800S, as the Swedish-built cars were known, were built at the same factory as the last of the PV544 range. However, Linwood continued supplying bodyshells until 1968/9 shortly after the plant was sold by BL (who by then owned Pressed Steel) to the Rootes/Chrysler UK operation.

The first Swedish-built cars were virtually identical to the Jensen assembled ones but changes were made as years went by. For 1964 the badging and wheeltrims were changed and the following year the distinctive 'cowhorn' front bumper was replaced by a straight bar and new seats fitted. These 'medically idealised' seats, like those fitted to the contemporary Amazon, are good even by modern-day standards. External appearance was changed in late 1966 by a new type of grille and straight side mouldings.

By autumn 1968 the 1780cc B18 engine

Volvo 1800 history

was obsolescent in the 120 and 140 type saloons and the 1800 was given the l986cc B20 engine. Almost identical externally, the B20s increased capacity was achieved by increasing the cylinder bore size. Although this engine is undoubtedly the more desirable (although at first it had just 3bhp advantage over the B18) it's thought by some to be slightly less durable, although by non-Volvo standards even the B20 is as strong and long-lasting as the pyramids; 200,000 miles between overhauls isn't unusual!

The B20-engined 1800S (the name remained, despite the capacity increase!) lasted just one year and in late 1969, Bosch fuel injection appeared. The model designation was then changed to 1800E. Borg-Warner automatic transmission was offered as a option from 1971.

The 'sporting estate' 1800ES was introduced to Britain in late 1971. Design work on this had started as far back as 1967. The modified body, with its potential 5ft loading platform and trendy but glass tailgate, was certainly striking and Volvo's accountants were undoubtedly pleased that the existing floorplan needed very little modification and most outer panels, including the rear wings, were retained. Various safety improvements and updates were incorporated, along with larger tyres on wider rims and 5bhp more was squeezed out of the engine.

Coupe production continued alongside the ES until June 1972. The ES carried on for another year; this was available as an automatic in the UK from September 1972. Production finally ended in June 1973. Like so many good cars the 1800 fell foul of tightening American safety regulations; had they wanted to continue 1800 exports to the USA, Volvo would have to fit 5mph impact bumpers from 1974 onwards. Total production was 47,585 cars, of which 8,078 were square-backed estates.

Early stages in the restoration. The sill has been cut away. The rear wing was actually much worse than it looks here.

In Amazon UK's workshop, awaiting painting.

Here the rear wings are off but the new sill has been fitted. Notice how the sill runs underneath the wing. The joints between the sill and wing are lead-loaded.

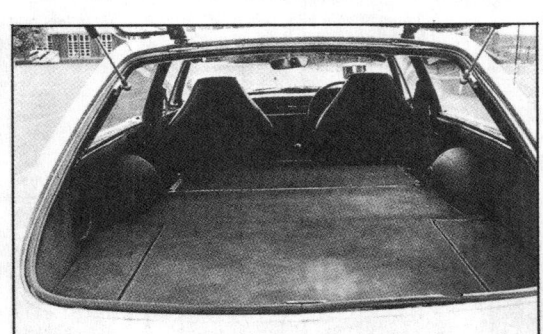

Long but low loadspace!

The Ultimate Volvo

Specifications

Engine cc: 1986
Bore/Stroke: 88.9 X 80mm
Compression Ratio: 10.5 : 1
Fuel System: Bosch electronic injection.
Transmission: Four-speed manual with overdrive on top gear only.
Brakes: Servo-assisted disc brakes all round. Handbrake operating via shoes inside brake disc.
Performance: 0-60 in 9.9 seconds, max speed 112mph, average fuel consumption 20-24mpg.

tioned the rear wings and gave the bare shell a light coat of primer from an aerosol can to stop it rusting. Amazon UK sorted out the offside front problem (the original wing was re-used), fitted the new panels to the rear half, leaded up all the panel joints that should be (virtually all of them) and primed and painted the shell. They advised Brandon to invest in a new air intake panel which he did; it cost £159. Expensive but nothing compared to the new windscreen which was also required; that cost £320! The paintwork is now superb and Brandon says that once the car was home he "tried hard but couldn't find even the slightest defect anywhere."

As the car was running well and had a recorded mileage of 52,000 (just about enough to run-in a Volvo!) which Brandon thought was probably correct, he decided against carrying out any mechanical work. He also refitted the trim largely 'as it was', something he now regrets as, although it looked presentable enough in an average car, it appears a little sad compared to the new shiny paintwork. A new set of carpets and some attention to the leather seats would improve matters enormously, however, and Brandon plans to do this very soon.

Final fitting-up took some time (this, like all the work Brandon did himself, was carried either in his domestic garage with about 9in space each side of the car or on the driveway in front) but eventually all was back in one piece. A new fuel pump was needed

The car as it now is. It took £1900 worth of parts and £5000 of paid-for labour to reach this point.

and, for the MoT, the car needed a new steering idler bush and steering column flexible joint; very common jobs on both Amazons and 1800s. The idler bush is dead-easy to do; you don't even have to remove the idler from the chassis, only the drop-arm has to come off. The flexible joint is rather more tricky, however.

The car was finished in spring 1990. Shortly afterwards, however, a nasty grinding sound started which was diagnosed as a gearbox bearing. The car went back to Amazon UK who rebuilt the box and it's now perfect.

On the road

I've driven several Volvo 1800s before so knew roughly what to expect from Brandon's. The car is far from spacious inside, in fact, let's be honest about it, a Volvo 1800 is pretty cramped! The rear seat is only for small children or dwarfs (headroom is even worse on the coupe!). On the other hand, the seats are extremely comfortable; plenty of support in all the right places and once you've shoehorned yourself into the car it's all quite cosy. Some people may not like the high window line which does impair vision to an extent but it does give one a feeling of security. Or perhaps it was just that I knew I was in a Volvo ... Looking around the cab I spotted lots of switches and trim parts that were identical to those on my own 1974 Volvo 144DL.

The engine started easily enough and, once on the move, it revved freely but, as I expected, seemed to lack 'go' somewhat compared with other sporting vehicles of the size and type that I've driven. I also found

the steering extremely heavy, something that Brandon had warned me about. As a London taxi driver he should know all about that! There was a fair amount of top-end noise too; again this is a characteristic of the B18/20 engine.

On the positive side, however, the ride was extremely comfortable, handling safe if a little predictable and the car felt very sturdy and strong without being cumbersome; there seemed to be none of the body flexing one so often finds on two-seaters. The controls, too, were precise; switches go on and off with a reassuring 'click' and the gearchange is very definite. As with the 120 and 140 saloons, the 1800 handbrake is mounted on the right-hand side, something one doesn't expect on a two-seater. It is extremely effective, however, and unlike the parking brake on many cars, once set up it remains effective for a very long time. Overdrive, engaged by a stalk on the steering column, operates on fourth gear only and gives relaxed high-speed cruising. The cabin is very well-insulated from road and transmission noise. Volvo really intended the 1800 as a long-distance touring vehicle rather than an out-and-out sports car and, as something capable of conveying two people in comfort at a reasonable pace, the 1800 has a lot to recommend it.

FIRST

Four classic owners whose first old car is a Volvo — this selection of sports P1800s all have very different stories and specifications, says Chris Rees

Andy Davey, a 28-year-old designer, was attracted to the **Volvo P1800** because, he says, "It's one of the last true statements of car design." But the 1968 example he purchased as his introduction to classic car motoring turned out to be something of a handful.

He was aware that the car was rusty and didn't drive well, but when he discovered that the chassis was actually dangerously bent he resigned himself to the fact that it was only good as a 'donor'. Purchasing another 1965 P1800 as a wreck, he had one car built from the two.

"I felt that the Volvo was sluggish and rather agricultural as it stood," says Andy, "so I decided to uprate the '65 car to post-1970 spec with a 2-litre engine, uprated camshaft and larger carburettors. The suspension, brakes and chassis were all upgraded and the whole thing thoroughly rust-proofed, so the car should last another 25 years.

Andy uses the car every day and drives it mostly in London as his only car. "It's certainly not the most practical car, with terrible visibility, a lack of space and general sluggishness — it just shows how far modern cars have advanced. But I don't think I'd ever buy a new car now. If the Volvo has one thing, it's character. You put up with its deficiencies — you have an affinity with it which is almost masochistic — and it *is* genuinely enjoyable."

All the restoration and modifications to the car have taken 18 months to finish and have swallowed an incredible

Alexandra and Pavel Büchler with their unusual and long-lived round-light P1800

£12,000; but Andy feels he now has a car which dates from 1965 but is like new — it certainly looks it.

The **P1800 coupé** owned by 38-year-old artist **Pavel Büchler** has an unusual history and must be one of the most durable cars of its type anywhere in the world.

"I wanted a car that looks and lasts like nothing else," says Pavel, "and the P1800 has been an ideal choice. I've covered 6000 miles in the last six months and the car hasn't even needed topping up with oil or water."

This example was an 'interim' model, one of the first cars made in Sweden from UK parts after Volvo suspended Jensen's initial production involvement. The car was shipped to an expatriot Briton in Singapore where it stayed until 1980. Back in the UK, it was hardly used until Pavel bought the car in 1988.

"It had covered 219,000 miles at that time," he says.

Incredible restoration job for Andy Davey's '65 Volvo

"I've since discovered that the rear lights, which are round, differ from every other P1800 I've seen. They seem to be original and I think they come from an Australian Falcon.

"Apart from a previous owner's fitment of sports wheels and a tiny steering wheel, the car appears to be original. Cosmetically, it's not 100 per cent but it *is* reliable transport — it's regularly taken me from Cambridge to Glasgow on business.

"The steering is heavy, the acceleration non-existent and it doesn't start happily in cold weather, but overall I'm very happy with the car."

Ever since **Andrew Murray** leant his pushbike against the showroom window as a schoolboy and had a sit in a new **Volvo P1800ES**, it has been the car of his dreams. Four years ago, he fulfilled it by acquiring a 1972 example which he set about restoring over the following two years.

Andrew is a 36-year-old teacher living in the highlands of Scotland. His round trip to and from work every day is 74 miles but this doesn't bother him: "I drive the Volvo to work every day in all weathers, covering about 20,000 miles a year. As the car has been 100 per cent reliable so far, I'm confident about getting home each day.

"The 1800ES naturally has its faults — the design is 30 years old after all. It's hard work to drive and you have to be pretty enthusiastic to go above 60mph because of the noise level. But these are easily outweighed by its strengths. The shape is lovely, it's practical, and economical too, at about 30mpg.

Andrew Murray's P1800ES is driven 74 miles every day

"I sometimes think I'll sell it, and my local Chinese takeaway owner keeps asking if I'd like to part with it. But then I think again and realise I can't do it. With proper maintenance, this car should last indefinitely."

As a **Volvo P1800** enthusiast of 20 years standing, **John Culham**, a 40-year-old welding engineer from Plympton, Devon, may not qualify as a classic starter with his **P1800S**, but since he's not owned any other classics, well . . .

John discovered HTX 777D sitting in a nearby garden and persuaded the owner to part with it for £450.

Getting it out proved troublesome, though. All the tyres were flat, the handbrake had seized and the car was sitting on gravel.

Remarkably, since the car had rolled over about six years ago, John took the brave decision to have a go at making his own convertible, as so many people have done in California. Making his own new inner sills to strengthen the car up, he also replaced two wings, the doors, front lower panel, boot lid and gutter and two chassis sections.

Having taken the Volvo down to its bare bodyshell, John tackled the hood. The result is superb: a hood which duplicates the line of the original coupé's roof and which folds down into the line of the car.

A bare metal respray and 14 coats of paint have brought the car to its current resplendent condition — after an incredible 850 hours work.

"There's surprisingly little wind noise," says John, "and in the 1000 miles I've covered since completion, I'm nothing but delighted with it. I've also won first prize overall at the local Volvo club concours."

CHOICE

John Culham's unique home-converted P1800 has superbly elegant folding hood

CLASSIC

PROFILE

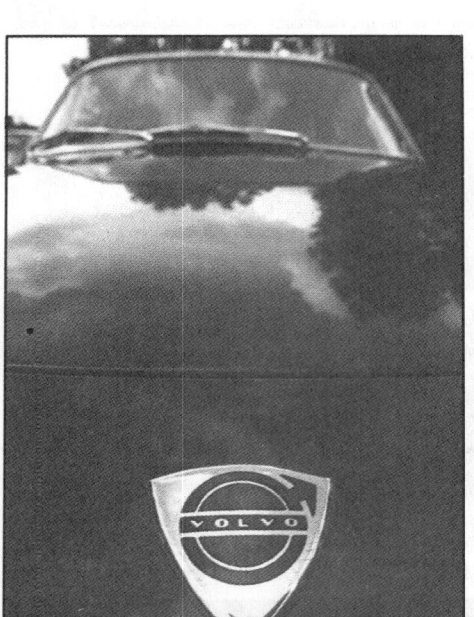

VOLVO

P1800 & ES

To the professional eye, Volvo's P1800 and ES sportswagon were outmoded before they even went into production. To the public, they represented a sophisticated image in a reliable, long-lasting package, recalls Martin Buckley. Pictures by James Mann

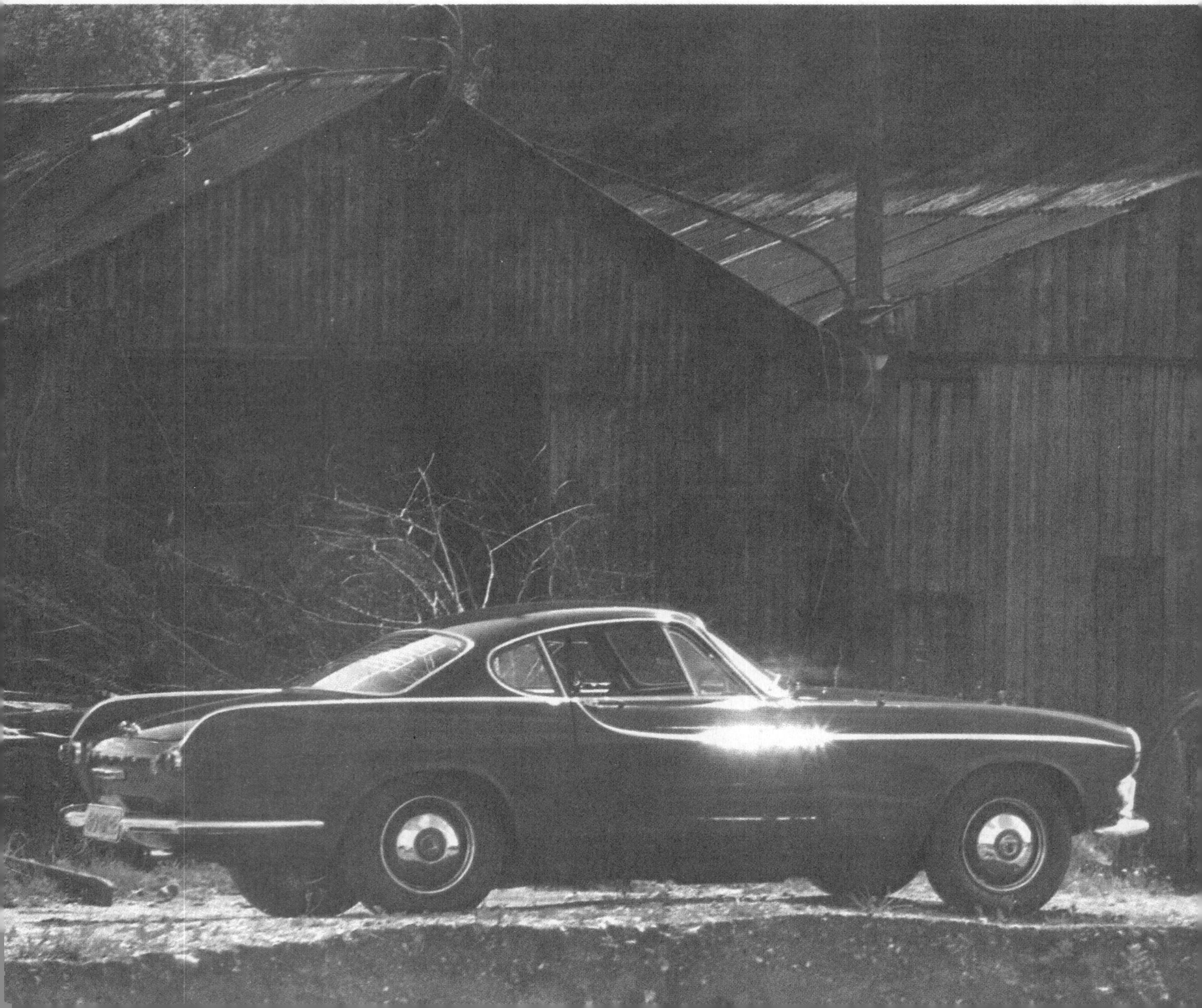

The Volvo P1800 had no business being so successful. It was dated when it first appeared in the early sixties, and by the time the last of the ES sportswagons were being built in 1973 it was an antique in GT car terms. The design was positively creaking with age, and Volvo knew it.

Yet, year after year the buyers kept coming back for a second helping, undeterred by the corny styling and stone-age engineering – not to mention a price tag that encroached on E-type territory.

The car succeeded because it filled a gap: a sophisticated European coupé look and image, without sophisticated European coupé complication. So what if dynamically the car never really got past first base? And who cared if the styling looked like a reject from the mid-fifties? It was fast enough for most buyers, looked great as far as most non-car buffs were concerned and was as simple and tough as the workhorse family saloon on which it was based.

The P1800 is a practical Gran Turismo, in other words. Long-legged, comfortable – a marathon runner rather than a sprinter – and liable to keep on going long after most of its faster, highbrow rivals have expired with engine trouble or rust – or both.

The P1800 wasn't quite Volvo's first sportscar. The P1900, based on the PV444 and bodied in glass-fibre, showed promise for a while in the mid-fifties but in the end only 67 production cars were built. It was killed by Volvo's then-new boss, Gunnar Engel-

FOR

Affordability, reliability, styling, longevity.

AGAINST

Utilitarian engine, heavy steering, some spares prices.

US and Britain were top export markets for the P1800, which sold 25,000 a year during the sixties. The Scimitar GTE-style ES, introduced in 1971, won the range new friends just as sales were waning. P1800's glamorous body houses B18B in-line 'four', developing 90bhp

lau, who couldn't see a future for a car that was expensive to put together and didn't match the quality standards of Volvo's popular saloons.

But Volvo was not against the idea of a sporting model in its range, and in 1957 it was decided that a new 2-plus-2 sports coupé would be built on a shortened 120 series platform. Ghia were approached to style the car, and the job was given to the company's chief designer, Pietro Frua. Apparently, Frua walked out on his job at Ghia while designing the P1800, to set up his own studio, and then had the cheek to tender his own proposal, much to the consternation of his old boss at Ghia, Luigi Segre.

It is at this point that the Pettersons, father and son, come into the picture. Helmer, engineering consultant and long time Volvo associate, had a son – Pelle – who was working at Ghia as a trainee stylist at the time. Helmer used his influence to have his son's sketches slipped in when Segre and Frua presented their four proposals to the Volvo management in August 1957. Engellau unwittingly opted for the Petterson design, but was none too pleased when he learned of their origin.

So quite to whom the P1800 is officially attributable is uncertain, although the official Volvo version is that the car was styled by Frua. Certainly Frua built the three prototypes in 1957/58, under the stylistic guidance of young Petterson – while his father attended to the engineering side. In early 1958 Gunnar Engellau approved the design, asking only that one or two details, such as the twin tail pipes that emerged from the body of the car between the split bumpers, should be changed.

Most universal complaints concerned low seating and vintage-style steering

Now the only problem was finding somewhere to build the P1800, which by the spring of 1958 had become public knowledge. Volvo's own Olofstrom factory was at full capacity and the new Torslanda plant was years away from completion, so Volvo had to look outside Sweden for a company willing to build the bodies.

Nobody in Italy was interested, but there were a couple of possibilities in Germany, namely Drauz – then building Porsche Cabriolet bodies – and Karmann. Unfortunately the latter were just about to be taken over by NSU, and VW – by far Karmann's biggest clients – put their corporate foot down when they learnt of a possible co-operation between the Osnabruck coachbuilder and Volvo.

Volvo found salvation in England, where the Pressed Steel Company undertook to build and assemble the P1800's body at their Linwood plant near Paisley in Scotland. Nor were only the bodies to be British-built, either: a contract was signed with Jensen for the assembly of 10,000 cars in their West Bromwich Factory, so all Volvo had to do was supply the engine and front and rear suspensions. In fact, about 50 per cent of the car was of British origin: everything from the GKN Sankey wheels to the SU carbs and Lucas electrical system.

It was a far from ideal set-up, as Volvo discovered when the initial 250 cars were delivered to Gothenberg in 1961 for checks, before delivery to the first Swedish customers.

Quality of paintwork and sealing just was not up to Volvo's usual high standards and the bodies Jensen were receiving from Linwood needed a great deal of extra finishing in terms of welds, panel alignment and rectification of dents. On top of all this the cars were getting damaged in transit to Sweden, and needed further repairs on arrival.

By 1963, after 6000 P1800s had been built at Jensen, Volvo had suffered enough, and they transferred the final assembly of the car to their now partly-opened Torslanda plant in March of that year. Pressed Steel still supplied the bodies for some years to come and Jensen, who had originally signed up to build 10,000 P1800s, received a considerable sum in compensation from Volvo, because of a break clause in the contract, and even continued to supply certain bits and pieces.

The Swedish-built cars were called 1800S ('S' for Sweden) and had Amazon-style wheels, hide seats, redesigned door panels, and – best of all – a more gutsy 108bhp version of the B18B engine, with a higher compression ratio and hotter cam.

The 1800 was quickly gaining a following, despite a frightening £1800-plus price and performance about which the press were never anything more than polite. Tipping the scales at 22cwt, the 1800 was a heavy car (0.6cwt heavier than the saloon) so the gears needed to be used if something resembling brisk acceleration was going to be achieved. But with the standard (in the UK) Laycock overdrive engaged, the Volvo was a tireless motorway cruiser, with the ton coming up fairly easily if you had a straight long enough on which to achieve it.

Avant garde glass hatchback looked terrific, was easy to build but not so practical in everyday use

Soft spring rates gave a comfortable ride, if rather extravagant roll angles for a GT car, though the actual handling was deemed good strong understeer. Fairly precise steering was allied to excellent road-holding.

Most universal complaints – even in the early-to-mid-sixties – concerned the low, low seating position, vintage style upright steering wheel, and severe lack of headroom.

Throughout the sixties the 1800 sailed on, selling a healthy 25,000 cars by 1966 with 50 per cent of production going to the US, and Britain as the car's second-most popular export market; in Sweden the car had fewer friends, the Scandinavians preferring the rugged, cheaper, and equally quick Amazon.

It was constantly fiddled with, the 1800. Nothing radical – just slow, careful development and refinement. Volvo obviously thought better of some of the 1800's more ornate styling touches, dropping the cowhorn bumpers in 1964 and discarding that odd piece of bent chrome trim on the side in 1966.

Performance became better as time went on, especially when the new 2-litre B20 engine was dropped in during 1968, although the main improvements were in refinement and those in the know still put the 1800 very much in the pipe-and-slippers GT car department. Volvo did not take the opportunity to re-badge the car '2000', though there was a discreet 'B20' badge on the grille.

Fuel injection was added to the package for the 1969 1800E, using a modern Bosch electronic system which meant 120bhp on tap and dramatically improved acceleration, with 0-60mph now in the sub-10-second bracket, and the top speed now well over 110mph. Still, there was no hiding the basic age of the design, despite Volvo's half-hearted attempts at giving the 1800E a groovy seventies look, with its matt black grille and hip alloy wheels.

The driving position and all-round vision were what probably aged the car most, though the dash on these injected cars was given a fashionable dull fake-wood finish and the anatomically-designed seats now had built-in headrests.

At least the handling and ride were still up to scratch, though the ZF steering box on these cars made town work heavy going and open road driving ponderous. The dual-circuit disc brakes were no bad thing, though they were the least you could have expected on a £2300 2-litre coupé in the early seventies, especially when a new E-type could be had for only a couple of hundred quid extra.

In the summer of 1971, just as everybody thought the 1800 was about to be given the last rites, Volvo introduced the ES. It was a sporting estate or 'sportswagon' in the Scimitar GTE mould, though it wasn't in anyway a copy-cat exercise, as Volvo stylist Jan Wilsgard had been working on the idea of an estate version of the 1800 since the mid-sixties. He came up with two ideas: the 'Rocket' was a way-out confection with a sloping roof and a rear wing/side window line that swooped up dramatically to meet it. The concept was appealing, but the design suffered from severe blind spots and would have required too many basic changes to the existing body shell.

An alternative design kept the familiar coupé rear wing line, but had a higher, flatter roof, with a frameless glass rear-hatch window which had the hinges and handle directly attached to it. Sergio Coggiola built the prototypes and it was the latter which won out, probably because it was much easier to build and wasn't such a shock to Volvo's traditional buyers as the 'Rocket' would have been.

Suddenly the decade-old Volvo was an 'in' car again, and although its moment of glory was brief – production ended in 1973 – those final years were the car's most successful. In fact in the final 1972-73 season, 1800 annual sales broke the 5000 mark for the first time, and that figure did not include the coupés, as the 1800E had been axed in June 1972.

For a time the ES was the required transport for any antique dealer, though there wasn't much room for more than a Queen Anne chair in the restricted,

neatly carpeted load-space, while rear-seat passengers didn't get a much better deal than in the coupé. But there was no disguising how old and tired the 1800 had become. It was noisy, crude and cramped, and the end of production in June 1973 didn't come a moment too soon.

TECHNICAL DESCRIPTION

You could be forgiven for stifling a yawn when glancing at the P1800's specification, because that glamorous body hides engineering which is largely familiar territory for an Amazon owner. There are no subtleties to delight the engineer. The car began life with the B18B unit, an in-line 'four' that at least differs from the PV544 in its use of surface-hardened journals and lead-bronze bearings, while the cylinder head has individual inlet ports. The valves are pushrod operated, but the use of five main bearings is pretty good going for a humble 'four' of that period, especially as they have 54mm journals: Volvo took pains to point out that even the 350bhp Ferrari V12's journals were of only 47mm. Use of aluminium for the lightly-stressed castings keeps the weight down (it is within 4-5lbs of the weight of the older unit) though as before the block and head are cast in iron.

Twin SU 1¾in HS6 carbs are used and Volvo claimed 100bhp at 5500rpm on the bench – which translates into 90bhp net, with a healthy 108lb/ft of torque at 4000rpm. In conjunction with a full-flow oil filter, the standard equipment oil cooler was said to keep oil temperatures down by 20-30° on a fast run, and heats the oil up more quickly from cold too.

When final assembly moved from Jensen to Volvo in 1963 (and the designation changed to 1800S) power went up to 103bhp, achieved by fitting a hotter camshaft, harder valve springs and raising the compression ratio to 10:1.

F-Series cars of 1965 have 115bhp, attributable to a sportier exhaust manifold with separate branches for cylinders one and four, and two and three, and also twin outlets on the rear exhaust box. Closed crankcase ventilation is another improvement.

1968 saw the introduction of the 1986cc B20 engine. This unit has a lower 9.5:1 compression ratio and in North America (and certain other markets) Zenith-Stromberg carbs, though Britons kept the SUs. A bigger oil pump renders the oil cooler superfluous and the fan is equipped with a clutch that cuts out at 3000rpm.

The 1800E unit of 1969 has Bosch Jetronic Electronic fuel injection, producing 120bhp at 3500rpm with 123lb/ft of torque at 3500rpm. 'E' engines have larger inlet valves and yet another variation of camshaft, while the compression ratio takes a hike back up to 10:1. For 1971 cars, the oil cooler reappears and power goes up 124bhp. US market models have lower-power B20F engine, which with all the emissions equipment can only

Prototypes: 'Rocket' (above) and Fissore's

claim to produce 112bhp.

Moving down the drivetrain, the gearbox is Volvo's all-synchromesh installation with optional Laycock overdrive on top only: overdrive cars have a lower rear axle ratio. For a year or so the 'E' cars were given a ZF box but from August 1970 there was a strengthened version of the M41 Volvo transmission and the option of Borg-Warner's Model 35 three-speed automatic.

The suspension remained essentially unchanged for much of the car's life and is totally conventional, being borrowed from the Amazon range. There are unequal length wishbones, with coil springs, telescopic dampers and an anti-roll bar at the front, and at the back a live axle with twin rubber-cushioned radius arms to give fore and aft location, with a further set of arms below them to take the torque reaction through the rubber buffers. The coil springs are kept under control by telescopic dampers.

Girling disc brakes are used at the front with drums at the rear, in conjunction with a vacuum servo. There is a pressure relief valve in the rear brake line from 1965 cars onwards and from cars with the B20 engine onwards there is dual-circuit braking. The 'E' of 1969 brought the fitment of discs back and front.

DRIVING IMPRESSIONS

As stylish commuter transport the 1800 works well. As a driver's car it has less to recommend it.

Smooth and urbane low down, the engine serves up good flexibility, pulling away easily in second without snatch or judder from the well-isolated drive train. No bone-jarring ride either: The simple suspension takes pot-holes and ridges with an unexpected aplomb. It's comfortable inside, though you might not get along with the low seating position

and the up-right angle of the steering if you are short. Small drivers find themselves peering through the wheel rather than over it.

Turn up the heat out of town and the car gets clumsy and untidy, revealing its saloon car heritage. Heavy at town speeds the steering doesn't really lighten up with speed, if anything stiffening the more lock you turn on, with inches of vague slop around the middle.

The P1800 becomes hysterical when you give it the gun – tappety, gruff and generally rather unpleasant. It's happier to cruise.

A willing revver the B18 engine lacks punch in carbs' form, hampered by the 1800's weight. It gets a bit hysterical when you give it the gun too, tappety, gruff and generally unpleasant. It's happier to cruise, settling into a lazy 80mph gallop on motorways and 'A' roads with overdrive engaged.

Thrown into a corner, keen drivers are put off the 1800 right away by the lofty roll angles, the steering's sleepy response and the head-turning squeal from the skinny, hard-pressed tyres. It understeers strongly most of the time, but given enough encouragement it will lurch into its own untidy brand of oversteer. It's a safe but uninspiring handler, much more saloon than sportscar in the way it feels.

From the driver's point of view the best thing about the 1800 is the gearbox. The stubby lever with its perfectly shaped knob has short, positive movements and unbeatable synchromesh.

BUYER'S SPOT CHECK

Engine and gearbox: The engines – both the B18 and B20 – are very long-lived, 150,000 miles being a possibility if the oil has been changed regularly. If the engine burns oil then you can bet there's valve-guide wear, which is not the end of the world. Oil filters ❶ without the non-return valve, and thus not the genuine Volvo item, can finish off bearings, as the lubricant is allowed to drain out back into the sump, starving the bearings of oil when the engine is started from cold.

On later cars, with injection, camshaft wear is a problem. A worn cam gives a thump almost like big-end bearings that are on the way out, but at half engine speed. The latest replacement camshafts do not seem to suffer from the same problems.

Injection systems either work or they don't, and are generally very reliable, though later systems are preferable as a rule. If the thermostat stops working then the engine runs cold, increasing the already heavy fuel consumption. Injection pumps can whine. 140 and 140E saloons, which thrive in breakers'

yards, are a good source of spares for 2-litre models.

There are very few gearbox problems. A transmission that has been run low on oil could jump out of gear or have bearing noise. Clutch slave cylinders leak and the gearbox mountings may be cracked. Check the overdrive engages and disengages: if not it may be low on oil (normal engine oil, which it shares with the gearbox), have a faulty electrical connection somewhere, or possibly a duff solenoid.

Suspension, steering and brakes: On the front suspension, look at all the normal MoT check points, such as wear in the bushes for the upper wishbones, or in the ball joints for the lower wishbone, the latter being freely available from Quinton Hazell. On Jensen-built cars the rubber lower wishbone bushes need replacing every couple of years. Rear springs tend to sag, a possible cure (apart from new springs, of course) being Aeon rubber assisters, as used by caravanners.

Steering boxes are adjustable, and you should be able to check the swivel joint in the lower wishbone by jacking the car up and pulling up and down on the wheel, and pulling it in and out to see if there is any wear in the upper swivel joint. Steering on all versions is pretty heavy, but especially on the 'E' and 'ES', which use a ZF box. Watch out if this is worn, as new ZF boxes are not available and are difficult to find secondhand. While looking at the steering, look very carefully for corrosion on the chassis leg on which the box is mounted as this is a known and potentially lethal problem.

Rear axle: This is very robust, and won't whine so long as the oil level is kept up; it's unknown for halfshafts to break. You need a special puller to remove the hubs.

Brakes: These suffer most from lack of use causing everything to seize up and resulting in scoring of the disc and an uneven wear pattern. Again, to get at the rear brakes you need that special hub puller. The early Girling-type servo and discs ❷ used on the Jensen-built cars are no longer available, although it is possible to modify an early car to take later brakes.

Bodywork: Beginning with the front wings, check first for rust around and above the headlights ❸ Moving on, a vertical line of corrosion often forms from top to bottom just behind the front wheels, especially if the splash panel inside has begun to crumble, letting in the elements. Inner wings, the box sections running along the top above the wheels, go badly and they are not available. At a pinch you might be able to replace them using 120 series sections, which are very much the same.

Wings are difficult to fit, as the windscreen really has to come out to do the job properly, and you have to be able to make an invisible join on a very obvious flat panel. They are difficult to line up around the headlamps, too.

At the front, you can get a little corrosion in the front valance, and corrosion can get into the member beneath the radiator. Bonnets are normally OK, though the hinges can seize and rip out of the panel.

The sills are perhaps the biggest bodywork headache. Water runs down the front edge of the

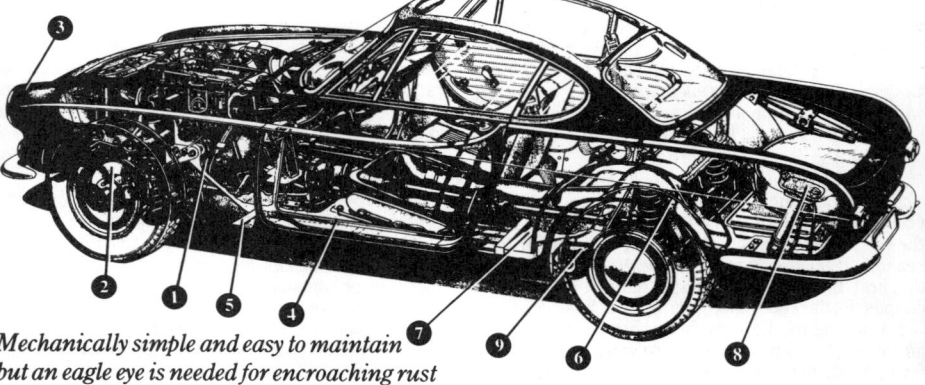

Mechanically simple and easy to maintain but an eagle eye is needed for encroaching rust

Ten things you didn't know about the Volvo P1800

1. The 'P' in the P1800's designation stands for *personvagn*. The car became the 1800S in 1963 when production transferred to Sweden. 'S' stood for Sweden – or, some say, for 'sports coupé'.

2. In 1961 the P1800 was awarded a gold medal at the Californian State Fair, for outstanding design, and it was the official car at the Sebring 24-Hour race in 1963 and 1964. It was awarded the title of 'Most Beautiful Sportscar' at a concours held at Baden-Baden in West Germany.

3. In 1965 Fissore came up with a fastback version of the car, and this was presented at that year's Turin show. Volvo denied any involvement, but the car found its way to Gothenburg.

4. Harold Radford built two 1800 convertibles for a Hull Volvo dealer in 1964. The cars are said to have suffered from structural design weaknesses.

5. The Volvo 1800 has little competition pedigree,

although an 1800S finished second in its class at the 24-Hour Sportscar race at Daytona, in 1967. The car was also rallied briefly in 1961: Ewy Rosqvist took one on the RAC Rally but a holed petrol tank on a Scottish special stage ruined her chances of a good placing – but she did finish.

6. On the North American market Volvo offered a performance kit for the 1800S engine, comprising higher compression ratio, a bigger-valve head, high-lift cam, lighter flywheel, and so on. Power went up to 135bhp, and the cost of the kit was $299, with installation costing $100.

7. When it first appeared, about 50 per cent of the car was of British construction: Pressed Steel body, Lucas electrics, Girling brakes, Vandervell engine bearings, GKN Sankey wheels, and Laycock overdrive. Other British firms were: Clifford Covering Co, Dunlop, ICI, Joseph Fray, Pianoforte Supplies, SU Carburettor Co, Smiths, Wilmot Breeden, Worcester Windshields, Triplex, and Silent Channel Co. Ltd.

8. At the 1971 Paris show Sergio Coggiola presented a one-off based on the 1800ES (also his work) called 1800ESC, or the Volvo Viking. Mechanically the car was totally standard, but slightly longer and wider than the standard car.

9. When the P1800 was being built at Jensen's factory in West Bromwich, quality control was so bad Volvo had to appoint a full-time representative at the factory to keep an eye on things...

10. It is estimated that only 12 Volvo-built P1800s have survived in roadworthy condition in Britain.

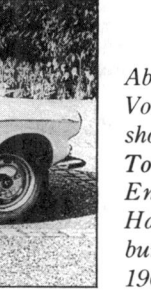

Above: Prototype Volvo 'sportscar' shown in May 1959. To be assembled in England. Left: Harold Radford-built convertible, 1964

doors and is supposed to be channelled down to a hole between the front wing and the sill; what actually happens is that the sills just fill up with water and rot out.

It could be just the outer sills that go (no great problem) but it's more likely to be the inner sill too, so don't forget to lift the carpets and check the inner sections ❹ where they meet the floorpan. It's worth remembering that to do the sills properly the front wings and the front end of the rear wing bottoms have to be removed. While under the car, check the floorpan and the outriggers ❺ which carry the jacking points.

> ## The car does tend to rust under the back seats, water entering through the wheelarch, so it is a must to remove them to check

On the back wings the wheelarches rot quite badly where the inner and outer panels meet ❻, as water collects in the channel around the boot lid aperature. Volvo 120 two-door arches are nearly the same, although the bottom section is slightly different.

The cars also tend to rot under the back seats, water entering the box section from the wheelarch ❼, so try to remove the back seats to have a look. The rear valance is vulnerable, too, as well as the channel around the boot-lid, while the lid itself corrodes on its folded-over rear edge.

As for the boot floor, the drain tubes can be blocked or missing, allowing water to collect. One of the few panels you can't obtain is the petrol filler flap ❽ which rots around the hinge, again due to a blocked drain hole.

On early cars the back axle is located by pressed steel arms ❾ which rot out eventually, but these are available as pattern parts and from Volvo themselves.

Trim: Early Jensen interior trim is difficult to find, as much of it is unique to the British built cars. Leather seats split, as do the armrest and door-pull assemblies and the dashboard top below the windscreen.

SPECIFICATION	VOLVO P1800	VOLVO 1800ES
Engine	In-line four	In-line four
Construction	Cast iron block/head	Cast iron block/head
Bore/stroke	84.1 × 80mm	88.9 × 80mm
Valves	Pushrod	Pushrod
Compression ratios	9.5:1	10.5:1
Power	90bhp at 5500rpm	124bhp at 6000rpm
Torque	108lb/ft at 4000rpm	123lb/ft at 3500rpm
Fuel system	Twin SU HS6	Bosch electronic injection
Transmission	4-speed with o/d	4-speed with o/d or 3-speed auto
Final drive	4.56:1	4.30:1
Brakes	Front disc, rear drum	Discs all round
Suspension front	Coil springs, wishbones, anti-roll bar	Coil springs, wishbones, anti-roll bar
Suspension rear	Rigid axle, coil springs, Panhard rod	Rigid axle, coil springs, Panhard rod
Steering	Cam-and-roller	Cam-and-roller
Wheels/Tyres	Pressed-steel wheels, 165/15 tyres	Pressed-steel wheels, 185/70 HR14 tyres
Body	Integral steel body	Integral steel body

DIMENSIONS		
Length	14ft 5¼in	14ft 6½in
Width	5ft 7in	5ft 7in
Wheelbase	8ft 0½in	8ft 0½in

PERFORMANCE		
Max speed	102mph	112mph
0-60mph	13.2sec	9.7sec
Standing ¼-mile	19.1sec	17.1sec
Fuel consumption	24mpg	20mpg

PERFORMANCE COMPARISON

	Volvo 1800S	Sunbeam Alpine	MGB GT	Porsche 912
Max speed (mph)	107	100mph	103mph	118mph
0-60mph (sec)	12	13	13	12
Fuel cons.(mph)	24	25	23	22
Price (1966)	£1814	£878	£998	£2387

	Volvo 1800ES	Scimitar GTE	BMW Touring	Datsun 240Z
Max speed (mph)	112mph	113mph	107mph	125mph
0-60mph (sec)	9.7	9.5	12	8.5
Fuel cons.(mph)	20	19	24	26
Price (1972)	£2651	£2379	£2248	£2389

Fuel-injection 1800E: note black plastic grille

CONTEMPORARY ROAD TESTS

Road & Track, February 1962 (P1800). 'Acceleration is nothing to get thrilled about. A great many cars less imposing in appearance and less expensive to buy will give the P1800 a terrible drubbing in a contest of speed.'

Autocar, July 20, 1962 (P1800). 'This car is out of the ordinary in being completely free from vice. Whilst it is difficult to pick on any one outstanding virtue, the formula seems ideal and even at £1850 the coupé is very well equipped. Volvo may very well have difficulty meeting the demand.'

Motor Sport, September 1962 (P1800). 'The Volvo is a smooth travelling, quiet car for long journeys, ideal for those who want a coupé smacking of a Ferrari... I cannot help feeling ashamed, however, of the faults in the British workmanship which it is improbable the meticulous engineers at Gothenberg would have permitted.'

Car and Driver, June 1966 (1800S). 'Those first 1800s (called P1800s originally) were a trifle overweight, a bit under-powered and suffered from a drastic lack of headroom. By contrast, the new version is sumptuously comfortable and can hold its own with any GT car made in that crucial (to Grand Touring) 60-90mph range. What it lacks in acceleration it makes up in controllability; what it doesn't have in brute horsepower it more than makes up for in rugged strength and longevity. The latest Volvo 1800S is a marvellous combination of well-tried ideas which have been lovingly executed.'

Road & Track, February 1970 (1800E). 'To summarise, Volvo has kept the performance, handling and braking of the 1800 up to date. But in style, accommodation, refinement of running and the use of available body space it has fallen way behind the times, and though it costs over £4500 it doesn't even have outstanding assembly quality to offset these drawbacks.'

Motor, March 4, 1972 (1800ES). '...But clever though the grating may be, it doesn't in any way camouflage the car's ancestry: in many respects the 1800ES feels as long in the tooth as it is... Volvo owners tend to be fanatically partisan, a loyalty largely induced by the marque's almost legendary reputation for reliability and longevity. We certainly hope these qualities are strongly evident in the 1800ES for it is a car, we feel, that must rely heavily on such things not only to justify its high price but also to compensate for its many dated features.'

Road & Track, March 1972 (1800ES). 'The 1800ES is one of those cars that leaves a road test staff a bit frustrated. Here Volvo has done a nice transformation, produced the first sports wagon big enough to really serve as one that we can buy in America, and done such a nice job with the aesthetics that the car is a real head-turner. But they did it on a car that should have been replaced, not reworked.'

PRICES

There are not that many Volvo 1800s on offer at the moment, with a particular dearth of early cars. Expect to pay the most for cowhorn bumper 1800s, particularly if the chassis number suggests it's a Jensen-built car (6000 and under), least for Es, whilst the long time favourite ES together with straight bumper 'S' cars, are worth somewhere inbetween.

£1000-£2000: For £1000 you can rarely find anything worth rebuilding unless you are lucky, whereas only last year you might have bought something with a vague chance of getting an MoT. Two grand should buy something a lot more promising, possibly a car that has had a few new panels fitted but needs finishing to get on the road. Rough cowhorn bumper 1800s come in at the top of this level. You won't find one on the road at this level.

£2500-£3500: For this kind of money you should find a car that's at least a running rebuild – rusty wings, suspect sills and so on. You won't get a running cowhorn car for this money, but possibly a reasonable E or ES at the top end of the scale.

£4000-£5000: This is where tidy cars come in, not perfect cosmetically but at least sound, usable and not needing any major bodywork. You could certainly start thinking about a good, early coupe for £4500-£5000, and certainly an excellent E or ES.

£6000-£8000: This bracket covers really good cars of all types, so set your standards high and don't compromise! Ten thousand plus has been spent for the best cars, but these rarely come up for sale.

PARTS PRICES

Front wing	£240
Front panel	£206
Near side rear wing	£142
Full sill	£136 n/s, £160 o/s
Rear panel	£109
Doors	£329

SPARES

Many items are still available for the 1800. Trim can be a problem, especially for the early cowhorn bumper cars and pre-67 models come to that.

Wing trims seem to be the most in demand and Volvo have just started reproducing all the side trim for post-67 cars. Bumpers – post cowhorn – can still be found new, which is good to know if, as on many cars, the steel has begun to rot around the brackets that hold the rubber mouldings on.

Volvo still make body panels according to demand and can supply most you might require to rebuild a car from the sills up. Apart from Tony Barrett's unofficial outriggers there are no repair panels, not even door skins: a door rotten beyond repair means a complete new door assembly, which is an expensive way of doing things at close on £400. All panels are for late cars, too, so rear wings will have the vent grille opening and different fuel cap arrangement of the E/ES, and front panels have the larger bumper bar holes.

Mechanically virtually everything is available for as the 1800, although owners of early cars might have problems with brake parts – even pads are now unobtainable, a problem the 1800 shares with the 122S. It is possible to fit later type discs on Jensen-built cars while keeping the original callipers.

Thanks to Kevin Price of the Volvo Enthusiasts' Club for his help with Buyer's Spot Check information, and Tony Whitton for supplying the cars for photography.

OWNER'S VIEW

Kevin Price has owned Volvo 1800s for 12 years, and has a special passion for the Jensen-built cars

As far as Kevin Price is concerned the Jensen-built P1800 is the only Volvo 1800 to own. Apart from his current ES and a brief lapse into 1800S ownership (actually the first 1800 he used on the road), all Kevin's ten 1800s have been West Bromwich cars. They were rare to begin with – only 1000 right-hookers were built – and he is one of perhaps only a dozen people who use these rare British-built 1800s regularly in this country.

Kevin's first contact with the breed came back in his coach-driving days. "I spotted it under a sheet on a piece of waste ground we used to turn the coach round on. I couldn't believe it was a Volvo at first – I thought they all looked like tanks." He eventually bought his first car, a '61 left-hooker, from a man in Peterborough and it was then that he first became aware of, and fascinated by, the Jensen connection.

Now, some might think it odd that Kevin should focus his obsession on the worst, if most charismatic, of the series, but he doesn't see it like that: "I fell in love with the idea that they are a little bit of England, our small contribution to Volvo's history. I don't think the quality problem was all Jensen's fault, because I am told that Pressed Steel at Linwood were letting rust get into unprimed bodies before Jensen had had a chance to touch them. My own car was repainted free of charge by Volvo in 1968 because the paint was so bad. And to be fair, I don't think the Volvo-built cars were so much better, if the rust on my 1800S was anything to go by..."

They were difficult cars to put together anyway, maintains Kevin: "There is a lot of lead in them, hidden joins and difficult curves. When you start taking them apart you see what a lot of car you are getting for your money, and where all the weight comes from. It's very over-engineered."

Kevin's preference is for the earlier cars as driving machines, despite the ES's potent fuel-injected engine. "Yes, the ES is faster but it's noiser too, and you pay for it in fuel consumption which works out about 23 to the gallon on a run, compared with 30mph for the coupe. It doesn't make such throaty noises when you put your foot down either."

He doesn't see the early cars lack of outright go as any real problem. "The point is they are superb touring cars," says Kevin, "and fantastic on the motorway. I did a very early morning run from Bridgnorth in the Midlands to Cornwall in four and a half hours and my coupé didn't miss a beat. If the ES has one major advantage over the coupe it is in its accommodation: The coupe is very intimate for more than two people, whereas the estate at least has the benefit of extra headroom."

It was out of his affection for the 1800 that Kevin started the Volvo Enthusiasts' Club last year. "It started off as a club just for the 1800," says Kevin, "but it became obvious that a lot of owners of older Volvo saloons also wanted a classic Volvo club. It's now going from strength to strength.

No great lover of saloon Volvos – though he wouldn't mind an Amazon, Kevin's ambition is to have one of each type of 1800 and to rebuild as early a Jensen-built car as he can find: he is currently negotiating for an RHD chassis number earlier than anybody thought existed.

Another plan is a Charity run to celebrate 30 years of the 1800 in 1992. Starting in West Bromwich, as near as possible to the Jensen factory. Kevin and a friend plan to drive his 1800 overland, via Ostend, to Gothenburg. Any sponsorship offers?